Dick Wilson was born in Epsom in 1928 and took a first in law at Oxford in 1951. He then took a higher degree at Oxford and a master of laws degree at the University of California, Berkeley. On leaving Berkeley he worked as a goldfield driller in Alaska, an inventory clerk at San Francisco, a law lecturer in Pakistan, and a copywriter for a Japanese travel bureau. He returned to England after becoming ill while doing historical research in India.

He began his career in journalism in 1955 by joining the staff of the *Financial Times*, of which he became labour correspondent. In 1958 he was appointed editor of the *Far Eastern Economic Review* in Hongkong, and since then he has been travelling frequently in Asia. He was the Far East correspondent for the *Guardian* and the *Financial Times*. He visited Communist China with his wife in 1964, going to Shanghai, Peking, Shenyang, Anshan, Fushun and Canton.

Since 1965 Dick Wilson has been working as an independent writer on Asian affairs. He contributes to many newspapers and journals and is represented in three symposia on Asia or China: *Economic and Social Problems of the Far East* (1962), *Asia, a Handbook* (1965) and *Contemporary China* (1966). *A Quarter of Mankind* (also available in Pelicans) was received enthusiastically on its publication in 1966, *Asia Awakes* was published in 1970, *East Meets West – Singapore* and *The Long March 1935*, in 1971. He helped to found the new daily *New Nation* in Singapore in 1971.

Dick Wilson is married to Sally Backhouse (authoress of *Nine Dragons*, a travel book) and has a son and daughter. His other interests include music, antiques, rare books, numismatics and gardening.

DICK WILSON

Asia Awakes

A CONTINENT IN TRANSITION

PENGUIN BOOKS

Penguin Books Ltd, Harmondsworth, Middlesex, England
Penguin Books Australia Ltd, Ringwood, Victoria, Australia

—

First published by Weidenfeld & Nicolson, 1970
Published in Pelican Books 1972

—

Copyright © Dick Wilson, 1970

—

Made and printed in Great Britain
by C. Nicholls & Company Ltd
Set in Monotype Times

To
Abdur Razzaq of Dacca
who first made Asia come alive
in my mind

Contents

PART FOUR: THE FUTURE PROGRAMME

Maps

Sources

The maps on pages 84, 93 and 96 of this book are based on Alastair Lamb, *Asian Frontiers*, Pall Mall Press, London, 1968, pages 41, 118 and 30 respectively; that on page 91 on Alastair Lamb, *Crisis in Kashmir*, Routledge & Kegan Paul, London, 1966, pages viii-ix; those on pages 200–201 on a map which first appeared in the *Scotsman*, 26 October 1968.

Author's Acknowledgements

I wish first to acknowledge the generosity of those friends and colleagues who read some of the chapters of this book in typescript: they suggested many improvements and saved me from many infelicities. They include Peter Ayre, Sally Backhouse, Coral Bell, Jerome Ch'en, Ronald Dore, Dennis Duncanson, Michael Freeberne, Hide Ishiguro, Werner Klatt, Alastair Lamb, Michael Leifer, Robert Le Page, Trevor Ling, Abdur Razzaq, Saul Rose, Hugh Tinker, John White and David Wilson.

This book provides the belated occasion to record another kind of debt, less tangible but more longstanding, to friends throughout the world who have helped me to come to know Asia during the past twenty years. Some must not be named because they are in the service of their government or would for other reasons be embarrassed, but those to whose help, stimulation and companionship I am most heavily indebted are Ronnie Abayasekera, Prok and Pimmsai Amranand, Tatsuo Arima, Ungku Aziz, Nelson Chow, Morihisa Emori, Kimiro Fujita, M. P. Gopalan, Parthasarathi Gupta and his family, Han Nae Bok, Han Suyin, Mozharul Huq, Takeo Iguchi, Raghavan Iyer, K. Krishnamoorthy, Michihiko Kunihiro, Lim Chit-soo, the late Lim Tay Boh, Wasuke Miyake, Shiroo Miyamoto, Frank Moraes, Eijiro Noda, Panglaykim, V. V. Paranjpe, Bernardino Ronquillo, Michio Royama, M. Sadli, Sein Win, Peter and Sanda Simms, Soejatmoko, Kayser Sung, Robert Swann, Jayendra Thapalia, Romesh Thapar, Thon That Tien, Robert Tung, Tarzie Vittachi, C. E. L. Wickremesinghe, Kilbyong Yoone and Toshio Yoshimura.

Finally I would thank those who helped in the typing of the book, especially Diana Gibberd and Kay Smith.

D.W.

Introduction

'Asia! Does It Exist?' The headline to a recent article by one of Asia's widest-ranging minds, that of the Indian journalist Romesh Thapar, was intended satirically, provoked by yet another Western book on Asia which questioned the validity of a label increasingly difficult to attach to that half of mankind enclosed in the largest of all the continents. But Thapar conceded the point in the end, concluding:

> Asia exists, but the image is blurred. One is forced to this conclusion. Yet if we act with good sense, it is possible to salvage the best of what is essentially our common heritage.[1]

Asia, in other words, is a matter of hope rather than fact. Its first appearance as a name is in Pindar, the Greek poet of 2,500 years ago. Herodotus was puzzled to explain how the two mythical ladies, Europa and Asia, had become by his time continents, and no one has traced the latter's origins satisfactorily.[2] Scholars agree only that 'Asia' was at first intended to denote what modern atlases call Asia Minor, and that the Asian languages themselves had no name for what every twentieth-century schoolboy knows as 'Asia'. The Chinese *Ashiya* (*Ajiya* in Japanese) is a transliteration of the European name believed to have been introduced by the Italian Jesuit missionary Ricci, and it made its appearance in Chinese literature (as *Ah-chow*, or Ah-continent) only in the seventeenth century. Nor does the Indian tradition yield a comparable name. To a Chinese, India and South-East Asia were on a par with Europe and Africa as other parts of the inhabited world, while Indians thought of China, the Middle East and Europe as broadly equivalent concepts in the pattern of world civilizations.

Only the cartographers of Europe conceived the audacity of parcelling together the homelands of the Arab, Persian, Turkish, Indian, Chinese and South-East Asian civilizations and allotting to them the single label of 'Asia'. Only the European domination of the world during these past few centuries could have made such a label acceptable even to the Asians themselves. But now power is being diffused through Asia and away from Europe, and a more culturally egalitarian attitude towards history, sociology and even geography is beginning to assert itself. The Chinese do not recognize such names as Mount Everest or the McMahon Line, and gradually the world of the European map-makers of former generations is shrinking.

If an unbiased Martian were to be asked to divide the world into regions for purposes, shall we say, of providing permanent seats on the United Nations Security Council or successive venues for World Fairs or for any other practical administrative function, would he not arrive at nine—Europe, Africa, North America, Latin America, Australasia and an Asia sub-divided into East (dominated by the Chinese tradition and the Mongoloid races), South-East (dominated by the Malays and their distinctive amalgam of indigenous, Indian, Chinese and Arab culture), South (dominated by Hindu civilization) and West (the lands of the Arabs, Turks and Iranians)?* The five continents of the Western atlas would seem absurdly artificial and inefficient, reflecting a European ethnocentricism no longer justified.

In fact the wounds of Western imperialism still throb in the minds of Asians, and the idea of an Asian community, an Asian coherence, remains a favourite medicine to stifle the pain. The Burmese nationalist leader Ba Maw confessed to the Japanese-inspired Greater East Asian Conference in 1943, when the European colonial powers were almost on their knees:

> My Asiatic blood has always called to other Asiatics. In my dreams, both sleeping and waking, I have heard the voice of Asia calling to her children.... Today ... I seem to hear ... the same voice of Asia gathering her children together. It is the call of our Asiatic blood. This is not the time to think with our minds; this is the time to think with our blood...[3]

Indians and Chinese have now discovered, to their chagrin, that they understand each other worse, if anything, than either

*West Asia, which nearly overlaps with the Arab and Moslem worlds, is ambiguously poised between Europe and the rest of Asia and is better treated on its own. Following the United Nations classification, this book concerns itself only with South and East Asia, including South-East Asia.

understands Europe or the West – perhaps recalling the old
Javanese saying that to understand everything is to be badly
misinformed. The exceptional diversity of the Asian tradition is
belatedly revealed, as intra-Asian relationships and intercourse,
artificially suspended by Western intervention, begin to proliferate again. The wars of the coming decades, if there are to be
any more, are likely to be between Asians, not between Europeans
or between Europeans and Asians. Hence the need for everyone,
Asian or no, to recognize that diversity more clearly and to be
more ambitious, more exacting, in the conventional wisdom
about Asia on which he bases his attitudes and actions.

The need for this greater knowledge, this wider sympathy, is
perhaps the last platform to be shared by the entire Asian
community. Carlos Romulo, the first Asian to be elected President of the United Nations General Assembly, seems to suggest
this when he writes:

> The Afro-Asian states do not proclaim that the Afro-Asian com-
> munity is the world. But the world before the Second World War did
> not include Asia and Africa; humanity was not presented in its totality;
> history, even, was not universal enough, and the consciousness of man
> was offered a universe ... that did not represent the entire world nor
> the whole of humanity; hence, man's education was incomplete. The
> revolutionary force that animates Asian society today is not an organi-
> sed hostility towards the West. Nor is it an alliance of new nations in
> support of Communist ideology.[4]

In other words, Asia is neglected, is denied its true weight in
world affairs, but is also heterogeneous. How could it be otherwise across five thousand miles encompassing the birthplaces
of Buddha and Confucius; where every important religion is
practised; where brown skins mingle with yellow, black with
white; where the *dhoti* and *kimono* jostle the *sarong*, and the
Bhagavad Gita vies with the little red book of the *Thoughts of
Chairman Mao*?

We nevertheless live in a world in which there exists an Asian
Manpower Plan, an Asian Agricultural Survey, an Asian Parlia-
mentarians' Union, an Asian Games, *The Asia Magazine*
(in English!) and an Asian Dollar (sister to the Eurodollar).
Old mental habits persist, and not only among the non-Asians.
The European still thinks of Asia as 'a problem', as *a* place,

and from his point of view there *are* common features in the
Asian landscape – poverty (save in Japan), social structure and
traditions very different from his own, darker (or yellower) skin
colours than he is used to, and an irritating habit of threatening
international 'stability' and defying the system of world order
which he has donated to mankind.

Never mind that the Chinese or the Indian could stand these
criteria on their heads and mentally bracket various non-homo-
geneous foreign races together as 'non-Chinese or 'non-Indian'.
They too, as we shall see, like sometimes to think that *they*
stand at the world's centre. This book will take the world at its
face value, examine Asia's dissimilarities and affinities, and see
what its common problems are, how its peoples are setting about
them, and where we outsiders should take our stand on them. The
pages that follow will discuss first the themes that emerge from
our contemporary Asian drama, then the several actors who
occupy this colourful and exciting stage, and finally the noisy and
interfering spectators who either misunderstand the playwright's
intentions or think they could have written (or acted) the play
better themselves.

Part One: The Issues

Chapter One

Building New Nations

THE first Han emperor of China was warned by his advisors, two millennia ago, that, 'the State can be conquered on horseback but must be governed from the throne'. During the 1930s and 1940s, the overriding goal of Asian patriots was to throw off the shackles of Western colonial rule and rid their countries of interference from outside. By 1950 this objective was largely attained; if Asian nationalism in its modern sense was identified at first with anti-colonialism it had now to dedicate itself to the quite different task of nation-building. But it is easier to ride than to rule, to rebel than to reconstruct, and the man who is gifted in one is not necessarily proficient in the other.

The more thoughtful of the first generation of nationalist leaders knew that it was not enough merely to substitute for their white rulers what Tarzie Vittachi, the Ceylonese journalist, has sarcastically called 'the Brown Sahib'.[1]

'I was not interested', declared Nehru, 'in making some political arrangement which would enable our people to carry on more or less as before, only a little better. I felt they had vast stores of suppressed energy and ability, and I wanted to release these and make them feel young and vital again.'[2]

The immediate problem of the newly independent governments was to maintain the unity which the fight for freedom had forged. When an Indonesian foreign minister was asked to comment on his country's lack of progress twenty years after it had won independence, he replied: 'You do not know what is the character of a colonial country. We were only united against the Dutch. After that we are island against island, province against province, intellectual against intellectual, religion against religion ...'[3] In one case, that of Pakistan, a nation had to be created which had existed only on paper before its independence day in 1947. Until then, as President Ayub Khan has explained, 'Ideologically we were Muslims, territorially we happened to be Indians and parochially we were a conglomeration of at least eleven smaller provincial loyalties. But when Pakistan emerged as a reality, we ... were faced with the task of transforming all our traditional, territorial and political loyalties into one great loyalty for the new state of Pakistan.'[4] This particular ambition proved in fact too challenging, and there seems to be a limit to the size and heterogeneity of the political units with which human beings are willing to identify themselves, at least during periods of radical social and economic change.

The foreign minister of Singapore, S. Rajaratnam, recently told an international seminar on 'Beyond Nationalism':

Anti-colonial nationalism in the post-independent era has degenerated into a divisive ideology, breeding with a significant consistency all over Asia sub-nationalisms based on race, language, religion, and tribes. Peoples who were once united are going in for political archaeology. They are rummaging among ancient myths, doubtful legends and historical records to find reasons why they are entitled to be distinct and separate from the rest of the national community.[5]

This aspect of Asian nationalism, like some Indian intellectuals' 'preoccupation with securing the maximum antiquity for the Indian civilization',[6] may be thought merely amusing. But the sub-division of political loyalties is a serious phenomenon. The truth is that in most of Asia nation-building has only just begun, and will take many decades to complete. The countries of Asia are, in Rupert Emerson's phrase, 'not yet nations in being but only in hope'.[7] Sun Yat-sen, the father of republican China, used to describe his compatriots in their hundreds of millions as 'a sheet of loose sand', to which nationalism would add the cement, and the late President Sukarno declared that Indonesia used to be in colonial times 'a nation of toads, a beancurd nation'.[8]

Village life in most of Asia only a few decades ago was largely autonomous, with its own order and hierarchy, its own rudimentary system of self-government. The Japanese *buraku*, the Phillippine *barrio*, the Indian *panchayat*, the Chinese *hsien*, had only occasional contact with the court or the central government of the day. They regarded government officials almost as aliens, and were usually quite unaware of the extent and nature of the state to which the cartographers had allocated them. Not only that: the chief goal in an ordinary man's life was unashamedly to promote his own interests. If he were a good man, he would help his immediate family as well as himself, and if he were to serve the whole village or his entire clan, he would be regarded as a saint. But to work for any larger objective, whether provincial or national, was a sign of eccentricity or madness. As a Japanese sociologist has said of traditional rural society in his country, 'Beneath the surface of this seeming tranquillity, everyone is in frantic pursuit of his own selfish ends. . . . This selfishness must be converted into the kind of individualism which serves as the basis of rational co-operation for the benefit of all. Only then will our citizens ... grow to be the kind of people who willingly work for the democratization of their local and national governments.'[9]

The excitement of beginning this process, of planting the seeds of nationalism in simple minds, is part of the attraction of politics as a career in Asia. Nehru describes this in his book *Discovery of India*:

Sometimes as I reached a gathering, a great roar of welcome would great me: *Bharat Mata Ki Jai* – 'victory to Mother India!' I would ask them unexpectedly what they meant by that cry, who was this *Bharat Mata*, Mother India, whose victory they wanted? My question would amuse them and surprise them, and then, not knowing exactly what to answer, they would look at each other and at me. I persisted in my questioning. At last a vigorous Jat,* wedded to the soil from immemorial generations, would say that it was the *dharti*, the good earth of India, that they meant. What earth? Their particular village patch, or all the patches in the district or province, or in the whole of India? And so question and answer went on, till they would ask me impatiently to tell them all about it. I would endeavour to do so and explain that India was all that they had thought, but it was much more. The mountains and the rivers of India, and the forests and the broad fields, which gave us food, were all dear to us, but what counted ultimately were the people of India, people like them and me, who were spread out all over this vast land. *Bharat Mata*, I told them, you are in a manner yourselves *Bharat Mata*, and as this idea slowly soaked into their brains, their eyes would light up as if they had made a great discovery.[10]

But the difficulty is that the Asian politicians are in a hurry. The countries of Europe took four centuries to establish first a

*Member of the dominant caste in the Punjab province.

strong state, then internal security and law and order, then a sense of nationalism and finally democracy. But in Asia today these four political revolutions are telescoped into one, and people hope to consummate them in their own lifetime.[11]

The means of accelerating the building of a nation are now well known throughout the continent. Patriotism and solidarity are encouraged by propaganda, education and the use of the mass media. In 1968 the Singapore Government launched a song entitled 'Singapore We Love You' as part of a programme for 'the enhancement of national consciousness'. The best known ideological apparatus for nation-building was that which the fertile brain of Sukarno produced for Indonesia, with slogans such as NASAKOM (*Nasionalism*, *Agama* or religion, and *Komunism*, the three competing elements in Indonesian public life which Sukarno sought to drive in harness).[12] The dilemma is that the charisma required for this kind of leadership is quite opposite to the qualities of a good administrator.[13] In the immediate post-independence phase, Asia's leader-heroes – Nehru, Mao, Sukarno, Nu, Magsaysay – were brilliant coagulants but poor administrators, and only lately has it been recognized that both kinds of skill are required.

Meanwhile the weak sense of nationhood is everywhere apparent. As recently as a hundred years ago the Japanese Government confined foreigners to the immediate vicinity of the so-called Treaty Ports because it knew that the average Japanese lacked the independence to resist the predatoriness of the self-confident European.[14] The same anxiety supplies one reason for the restrictions placed on foreign travel and foreign missionaries today in China, Burma and India. I was once in Rangoon when the full confession of a Russian spy was published, revealing his transactions with many well-known Burmese who were named in the newspaper reports. I expected my Burmese friends to be indignant and angry, but instead they were sadly philosophical about the inevitability of foreign diplomats behaving in this way. Their only comment was that they could hardly refuse to allow any foreign diplomats to reside in the country. They took it for granted that many Burmese would succumb to pressure exerted by the sheer personality of an individual foreigner.

Prince Sihanouk of Cambodia once explained to his people

in a radio talk that he was trying to organize a new and independent newspaper which would veer neither to the American nor to the Chinese viewpoint on public affairs. 'It is impossible,' he added, 'to publish it immediately because I do not know where I can find a staff. I do not know who are our enemies and who are our friends because they have been able to buy many people. ... The other day I asked Prince Souvannareth – who is a Prince as I am and whom I trust – to bring me some people. However, it emerged that seven out of the ten had been bought by the Americans. ...'[15] An Indian journalist calculated that more than £125,000 had been spent by the Chinese, Russians, East Europeans and Americans to influence the voters of Bombay in the 1967 elections.[16] The lack of trust between the citizens of these new nations was most graphically seen in the notice recently displayed on the reception desks of government and commercial offices in Djakarta: 'Deposit Your Firearms Here.'

The national unity of the big countries of Asia is a question that stands on its own. The three great nation states of Europe (Britain, France and Germany) have an average area and population of about 150,000 square miles and 60 million people. China is almost *thirty* times larger than that, *thirteen* times as populous. India is eight times bigger in area, nine times bigger in population. The Republic of Indonesia could embrace two or three European nations of consequence in terms of both area and population. To put it another way, the Indian state of Uttar Pradesh and the Chinese province of Shantung are each larger than Britain both area and population. Madhya Pradesh and Maharashtra, Kwangtung and Hunan are comparable to such European nations as Spain or Italy. Szechuan province is bigger than Thailand, Andhra is bigger than Cambodia, Maharashtra would swallow up the entire Philippines. China, India, Indonesia, – these are the three Asian giants whose unity is, in Tibor Mende's phrase, a struggle of 'man against geography': their problems need separate consideration.

China has the largest population of any state in the world and yet paradoxically her unity problem is less than that of the other three Asian giants. At least there is a common language which is understood, though not without difficulty, from Manchuria in the north to the Himalayas in the south-west, and the written characters or ideograms are common to every corner of the land. Only the coastal regions between Shanghai and Canton in the south-east present serious linguistic departures within the main body of the Chinese population, and they are surrounded by Mandarin-speakers. China's relative isolation in world history has reinforced the sense of unity. But the provinces have acquired their various sub-personalities, and the periods when the central authority has collapsed (in the 1920s, for example, when warlords ran their own provinces or regions independently) have intensified provincial sentiment. One intimate observer of the Chinese communist scene believes that provincialism is now on the rise again as a reaction to the anaemic propagandistic culture purveyed by the Communist Party on a Chinawide basis, and also in response to the virtual closure of Chinese intellectuals' and artists' links with the outside world since the Sino-Soviet split of 1960.[17] The Cultural Revolution of 1966–8, with its anarchy and administrative breakdowns, probably accelerated this trend; the Party's leading Fukien province newspaper revealingly complained in 1967 that, 'A strong revolutionary centripetalism is what we need'.[18]

The economic aspect of all this is extremely important. The vice-chairman of the State Planning Commission revealed in 1958 that some areas were deciding on their own investment schemes: 'For these purposes they divert raw materials from key construction projects of the state, and in some cases even detain materials that are in transit.'[19] There was a notorious case in Fukien where the route of a new railway was altered from the central plan to suit the province's convenience,[20] and the First Secretary in Honan province was dismissed in 1958 for resisting the central Government's grain procurement demands.[21] Indeed, the import of costly Australian and Canadian wheat is explained by some observers as showing the need for the Peking Government to maximize its leverage over the grain-surplus provinces – which could otherwise hold it to ransom by withholding grain transfers to the cereal-deficit provinces and cities.[22] The central exchequer seems to depend on the provincial authorities for over half of its budget revenues, and public allegations have been made in Szechuan province that its First Secretary disposed of its important products – timber, grain, cotton and beef – in defiance of Peking.[23] Audrey Donnithorne concludes, in her magisterial examination of the Chinese economic system, that, 'Political and economic factors combine to make the province and its equivalents the key unit for economic development in China today.'[24]

The Communist Party has tried to insure against the risks of regionalism by putting outsiders into the higher echelons of provincial leadership and by maintaining its own standards of discipline.[25] But its first important purge in the Politburo in the early 1950s was of Kao Kang, who had allegedly turned Manchuria into his own little kingdom and treated with the Russians over Peking's head. Similar charges have been laid against some of the leaders disgraced in the more recent Cultural Revolution, notably the Mongolian Ulanfu. The danger is even greater in the extensive interior regions where articulate ethnic minorities live – Tibet, Inner Mongolia and Sinkiang, not to mention the southwest. The Chinese have handled their minorities better than the Indians or Indonesians have managed theirs, but there is still armed resistance in Tibet and tension in the Mongol and Muslim areas to the north.[26] China's dream of reintegrating Tibet into her own family after its seduction by the Western powers was unreal from the beginning.[27] The general problem was well stated by Liu Ko-ping, the communists' Muslim specialist, who wrote in 1958 that the idea of

separatism or secessionism, that is, the agitation for republics and a federation of republics ... exists principally among young non-Party intellectuals of the Mongolian, Korean, Hui, Uighur and other nationalities. But it exists in more serious proportions in a few national minorities where it is entertained not only by those outside the Party, but also by some within the Party, and not only by Party members in general but also by some high ranking cadres. They also seriously influenced a considerable part of the Party and non-Party cadres with the idea.[28]

The country where centrifugalism has attracted the most attention from Western journalists and scholars is India. Sir John Strachey, who knew the country intimately, used to begin his lectures about India at the end of the nineteenth century by saying: 'What is India? ... There is no such country ... India is a name which we give to a great region including a multitude

of different countries ... the differences between the countries
of Europe are undoubtedly smaller than those between the
countries of India. Scotland is more like Spain than Bengal is
like the Punjab.'[29] This is not exclusively a foreigner's view.
Jinnah, the founder of Pakistan, argued his case in the 1940s
for a new and separate Muslim state on the basis that, 'India is
not a national state, India is not a country but a subcontinent
composed of nationalities.'[30] When Toynbee described India as
'a society of the same magnitude as our Western civilization, ...
a whole world in herself,'[31] he was merely echoing the phrase of
the poet Rabindranath Tagore, that India's unity was 'a unity of
spirit'.

Nehru had consistently argued that India was one nation,[32]
but as prime minister of an independent India he was obliged
to recognize the force of the 'local nationalisms' within the
country to the extent of agreeing, against his real wishes and
better judgment, to the redrawing of state boundaries by the
criterion of language. British rule had left quite arbitrary borders
between the states of India, but by the 1960s the process of
reorganizing the country into 'linguistic states' had been virtually
completed. The only question is where the process should stop,
since each decision to bow to a linguistic lobby merely clears the
way for another one to pitch its tent outside the parliament.
Now that the Sikhs have been given their own state by the division
of the Punjab, politicians in New Delhi speculate about the campaign for a new state of Vidarbha to be carved out of the eastern
part of Maharashtra, and there are interests which aim to break
up the states of Uttar Pradesh and Madhya Pradesh.

The driving force for such reorganization is cultural and
political, but economic factors are also involved. There is a
wide disparity in the wealth and prosperity of the Indian states,
with income per head in Marahashtra, West Bengal or the
Punjab more than double that in Bihar. A recent report[33] pointed
out that more than half of the new industrial investment ap-
proved by the government over a $2\frac{1}{2}$-year period went to only
four states out of the then sixteen. Bengal and Bihar are at odds
over the development of the Damodar Valley (regarded as India's
equivalent of the Tennessee Valley Authority project in the
United States), with the two giant steel complexes of Durgapur

and Bokaro and huge amounts of electric power and irrigation potential on both sides of the boundary at stake.[34]

There were riots in Andhra in 1966 because the government refused to locate the country's next big steel mill at Vizagapat-nam,[35] and when New Delhi insisted on siting in Bihar a big new refinery to process oil from the Assamese fields, one Congress Party legislator proclaimed that, 'Every drop of oil in Assam is as sacred as a drop of blood of every Assamese. We cannot allow it to be sucked by others'. (In the end the government authorized two separate refineries, one in each state).[36] A final example of the drive for state autarky may be found in Kerala, where the communist-led state government, unable to get from New Delhi the rice supplies needed to meet its food deficit in 1967, asked for the use of some of the foreign exchange which the state's tea, rubber and coconut oil earn abroad.

Support for provincialism in India also comes from the less fortunate, less qualified or less enterprising members of the indigenous community who see jobs and power going to 'im-migrants' from other parts of India. In almost any Indian town it is possible to find traders, teachers, workers and professional men from many different states; indeed this has provided one of the concrete realities of Indian unity. But now the voice of the frustrated native is being politically organized.

An outstanding example can be found in Bombay, where only one man in three is a local Maharashtran. The Shiv Sena, formed a few years ago to protect the interests of this native minority, helped the local Congress Party to defeat the rebel Krishna Menon in the 1967 general election. A world-famous figure and former chief lieutenant of Nehru, Menon is a product of Kerala who speaks no Marathi and yet he had been returned with enthusiasm by the Bombay electorate until he became opposed by both the official Congress Party machine and the Shiv Sena. In the 1968 municipal elections the Shiv Sena gained almost one-third of the seats in the city. Its leader, Bal Thackeray, has explained that, 'Basically we are not against southern Indians. We want to see local people get a fair chance and an opportunity of jobs now monopolized by foreigners.'[37] Almost identical remarks could be cited by leaders of other local movements in Assam, Bihar and elsewhere.

'The separate regional patriotisms within India,' in the view of Selig Harrison, 'represent just as authentic expressions of nationalist spirit as the broader pan-Indian ideal.'[38] It is hardly surprising that they sometimes take the form of a demand for sovereign independence. Within Hindu India such extremism has so far been confined to the Dravidian south. The party which overturned the Congress in the state of Madras in 1967, the Dravida Munnetra Kazakham (DMK), had been founded on a platform of an independent Tamilnad. But its leaders had modified their stand on this by 1962, and co-operated with the Central Government in New Delhi as the Constitution required. They have since seen some of the younger and more extreme supporters forming a new National Liberation Front (NLF) to secure an independent Tamilnad.

It seems probable that most of the leaders of the various separatist movements will recognize the merits of belonging to a larger Indian Union once they are in control of their own state affairs. The smooth working of the federal machinery which binds the states together will gradually suffer as the old familiarity of the state leaders disappears. After Nehru, Shastri and Mrs Gandhi, there are no more all-India figures left in the Congress leadership, and some worsening of centre-state relations in the future seems inevitable. But this does not mean that India will break up into independent balkanized states.

The problem of centrifugalism was particularly acute in Pakistan, divided in half by a thousand miles of Indian territory* and united only by a common religion and twenty years of common history. From the very beginning national leadership was assumed by the West wing of the country. The East wing had no middle class: its interest, first in Islam and later in the idea of Pakistan, was in substance the protest of a neglected peasantry against absentee landlords and absentee capitalists who remained Hindu and patronized the city of Calcutta. 'East Pakistan is socially egalitarian,' Mushtaq Ahmad writes; 'its economy is characterised by a sharing of poverty. West Pakistan is socially stratified, distinguished by extremes of wealth and want.'[39] There is still a 40 per cent disparity in income per head between

*And three thousand *sea* miles – the equivalent of the voyage from Southampton to New York!

the two wings, in spite of the government's efforts to redress
the balance, and Bengalis complained bitterly that they produce
most of the country's valuable export commodities while the
other wing gets the bigger share of development projects.

Bengali students were rioting as early as 1951 for the recognition of Bengali as a national language. The 1956 Constitution
established an official equality between the two wings and their
two languages, while the 1962 Constitution went so far as to
invest the Central Government with a responsibility to remove
the disparity in living standards between the two wings. But any
movement in Bengal for more power *vis-a-vis* Karachi used to be
seen from the West wing as the precursor of secession, and of possible reintegration of East and West Bengal (even as a separate state,
independent of both India and Pakistan). The Central Government
did not help its case by leaving the East wing in the protection of
a single division of troops during the 1965 war with India.

In 1966 a leading East wing politician, Sheikh Mujibur Rahman, announced a six-point charter of survival for Pakistan as a
whole, which included the ending of central control over finance
and foreign trade, together with the creation of separate currencies and separate militias for each wing.[40] 'I do not like to
be a colony of anyone any more,' Mujibur declared.[41] Still
dependent on the West wing for technical and professional
skills, in spite of their insistence on the development of Bengali
culture and the Bengali language, most thoughtful East Pakistanis
have until quite recently preferred a back seat in Pakistan to a
possible back seat in India or in a United Bengal. The memory
of centuries of Hindu oppression was stronger than resentment
over the more recent excesses of Sindhi or Punjabi *satraps* sent by
Karachi. But Mujibur's victory in the 1970 elections made the
separatist movement irresistible,[42] and West Pakistani's crack-
down on Bengali intellectuals and politicians in 1971 made an
independent and sovereign *Bangla Desh* inevitable.

Indonesia spreads over more than three thousand islands and
contains more than three hundred distinct ethnic groups. After
independence the government tried to impose provincial
borders across the ethnic divisions, but was eventually obliged
to acquiesce in the re-organization of 'linguistic states' in Sumatra. Within a decade of independence regional rebels were

troubling the Central Government – extremist Muslims in
Sulawesi and the Lesser Sundas, and Melanesians in the interior
of Ceram fighting for their 'Republic of the South Moluccas'.[43]
The most serious of these uprisings were suppressed by the
army in the early 1960s but some resistance continues in almost
every province. A special difficulty is in prospect in West Irian,
only recently acquired (*via* the United Nations) from the Dutch
and containing a population ethnically different from and
culturally inferior to the other parts of the Republic.[44] One of
the underground leaders of the 'Papuan Independence Movement' complains that 'the Indonesian Government . . . are
many times more colonial than the Dutch',[45] and it may prove
impossible to bring the Irianese willingly into the Indonesian
family.

The provinces have strong economic grievances, too, with
Sumatra supplying more than half of the country's exports
and the densely populated Java hogging four-fifths of the
country's imports.[46] In practice this inequity is alleviated by
widespread organized smuggling. Under the Mokaginta Plan
of 1966, Sumatra was allowed to retain a reasonable proportion
of its export earnings for its own investment projects, but it
remains to be seen whether this formula will really solve the
problem. The upheaval and administrative breakdowns which
accompanied the downfall of Sukarno in 1965-6 have intensified
regional distrust of the centre, and it cannot be assumed that the
permanent political unity of Indonesia is assured.

The failure of these three giants incontrovertibly to consolidate
their unity is not inevitable, however, and there is another view
that, 'The peoples of South Asia may have struck lucky, stumb-
ling by accident on a truly up-to-date political device, the large
multi-lingual state; something enabling them to short-circuit
what hitherto have been the standard processes of history. . . .'[47]
The motto of the Indonesian Republic, *Bhinneka Tunggal Ika*
('Unity in Diversity') and the definition of China in her constitution as a 'unitary, multi-national state' are goals which the
Asian giants may realize,* enjoying the hindsight that the
Europeans lacked. But short cuts are proverbially unreliable

*At the cost, however, of a number of restrictive conventions which
must constantly irritate – that the prime minister of India always comes

and it would seem better to suppose that Asians are likely to
choose more or less the same sort of size of political unit, normally based on ethnic or linguistic exclusivity, already found
efficacious by the Europeans.

The difficulty is that as the villager – perhaps the son or
grandson of the one first fired by Nehru's oratory – becomes more
involved with national life, more in contact with people from
other ethnic groups speaking unfamiliar languages or dialects,
he must become more conscious of his own ethnicity, more
aware of the differences between the privileges of other groups
and his own, so that the very process of making him aware of
the larger India or the larger Indonesia to which he ought to
belong paradoxically strengthens his need and his desire to seek
protection in a smaller, more manageable, more effective group.
'It may well be that ethnic loyalties in a politicised and in-
vidious form will grow in intensity before national loyalties
triumph.'[48]

Chauvinistic nationalism of the kind familiar in Europe is
certainly on the increase in Asia, as recent Sino-Indian and
Indonesian-Chinese relations show. The Vietnamese youth who
called in the Saigon Student Union a few years ago, to thunderous
applause, for the American bombing of China as well as the
installation in Saigon of a free Vietnamese Government independent of the USA may be regarded as a symbol of this.[49] No
European communist is in any more doubt that Asian communists
are at least as much Asian as they are communist, possibly more
so. Ho Chi Minh himself confessed that, 'At first, patriotism,
not yet Communism, led me to have confidence in Lenin, in
the Third International',[50] and the Sinicization of Marxism under
Mao has become a special study of its own. Even the Mongolian
communists had to be chided by Moscow for their celebration
of the eighth hundred anniversary of Genghis Khan: 'It is true',
one of the Mongolians' leading historians had ingenuously
written, 'that Genghis Khan invaded and conquered many
countries of Asia and Europe. However, even these reactionary
acts do not diminish his stature as a historic figure nor his contributions to social development.'[51]

from Uttar Pradesh state, for instance, or the president of Indonesia from
Java.

In 1967 an Indian Nazi Party was inaugurated with a policy of dictatorial government for India for two decades to make her the strongest power in the world, after which British influences would be entirely rooted out and the territories occupied by China and Pakistan recovered.[52] Indonesian extremists dream openly of an *Indonesia Raya* (Greater Indonesia) enveloping Malaysia, Southern Thailand, and the Philippines; Cambodia and Laos both fear Vietnamese and Thai expansionism; and the whole of South-East Asia is occasionally troubled by imagining the destiny which the Chinese are privately designing for the sub-continent.

One concrete product of these fears is the Asia-wide movement towards the indigenization of commerce and industry. This has been carried furthest by Indonesia and Burma, where Chinese and Indian traders (and the efficiency of the national economy) have been the chief victims.[53] But even unrevolutionary Malaysia has a Cabinet Committee to plan the Malaysianization of trade and industry, and a public trust to train Malays in the requisite skills. The link between economic progress (or home management) and nation-building is succinctly described by M. N. Srinivas, the leading Indian sociologist:

> Kinship obligations are so strong that they tend to prevail over civic morality ... Even those who have to profess publicly their belief in egalitarianism have strong kinship loyalties. This results in a divergence between their beliefs and conduct. When such a divergence is widespread, people tend to be cynical. And cynicism is not the proper soil for rousing the necessary enthusiasm in the people for the Five-Year Plans.[54]

So one comes back to the basic social changes which lie behind the superficial development of Asian nationalism, and may force it into unexpected directions. Anil Seal, the historian of Indian nationalism, declares:

> By the side of the vast swell of aspiration and rivalry which has hurled it forward, the political readjustments of independence seem of small account. These nationalisms have been merely the swirling surface of the waters, below them pulse the tides of social change, pulling Asia no man knows where.[55]

Chapter Two

Homo Religiosus

A Frenchman has described the Asian as 'above all *homo religiosus*'.[1] But religion means different things to the average Asian and the average European. Buddhism is in some aspects atheistic, Confucianism and Shinto are concerned with social morality and ancestor worship rather than religious belief, while the Hindu pantheon houses 300 million gods. Most Asians do not associate religion with logical reasoning, and they are intellectually more tolerant about it than Westerners. A recent survey of more than a hundred Japanese universities showed that 'at least 70 per cent of the students ... consider religion as something purely subjective and relative, ... fully man-instituted to fill the deepest psychological needs of the human heart.' Only 8 per cent of the students admitted to some kind of faith.

The Japanese Ministry of Education publishes annual figures of membership in religious organizations; in a total population of just over 100 million, the most recent list shows 80 million Shintoists, 79 million Buddhists and 7 million others including Christians. A footnote explains that 'the total membership figure exceeds the total population of Japan because Shinto and Buddhist affiliations are not mutually exclusive and many people consider themselves as followers or members of both religious groups.'[3] I have come across a Japanese who described herself as 'Christian-Buddhist-Shintoist'.

Astrology is taken very seriously in many parts of Asia, and an Indian finance minister, Morarji Desai, has stated, 'I firmly believe that the law of *Karma* governs the universe, and therefore I believe in astrology as a science ... One's destiny is the sum-total of the consequences of one's past actions ... It stands to reason ... that one's destiny is capable of being charted in advance by a good astrologer.'[4] Many Asian presidents and prime ministers take astrological advice, and both India and

Burma had their independence from British rule declared on a day and hour (twenty minutes past four in the morning, in Burma's case) chosen by the students of the stars.

ASIA'S MAIN RELIGIONS
Approximate distribution in 1969 by millions of adherents

	Hindu	Confucian	Muslim	Buddhist	Christian
Cambodia	—	—	—	5	—
Ceylon	2	—	1	6	1
China	—	300	25	150	3
India	370	—	48	4	13
Indonesia	—	—	84	1	6
Japan	—	—	—	55	1
Malaysia	1	—	3	4	1
Pakistan	1	—	85	—	1
Philippines	—	—	2	—	26
Thailand	—	—	1	25	—
TOTAL	374	300	249	250	52

Based on data from *World Christian Handbook* 1968 and other sources.

In 1967 Indian astrologers warned that the entry of Jupiter, the source of intellect, into the realm of Leo, source of life, threatened quarrels, death and sterility, and couples were urged not to enter into marriages during the thirteen-month period affected by this conjunction. The modern school of astrologers under Pandit Goswami Girdhari Lal Shastri (General Secretary of the Astrological and Astronomical Society of India, counsellor to the prime minister and officiator at Nehru's funeral rites) advised that it was only the six weeks in the middle of the thirteen-month period which were to be avoided.* There is keen rivalry between the modernists who use telescopes and the traditional astrologers who accuse them of 'perverting our sacred scriptures with foreign ideas'.[5]

In Japan 1966 was the year of Hinoeuma, the Fiery Horse, and the fortune-tellers predicted that girls born in that year would be so strong-willed that no one would marry them: it was reported that the birth rate in the whole country dropped by 30 per cent in response.[6] Westerners should not feel superior about all

*The sceptics said that this was to shorten the period in which *gurus* might have to suffer from fewer wedding officiation fees.

this, since astrology has a following in the West too (a British practitioner urges investors to check the astrological sign under which companies are registered).[7]

Astrology need not be too demanding when it comes to decisions on important public affairs: when a foreigner asked President Suharto's Western-educated economic advisers whether they felt themselves to be competing with the *guru*, or mystical sage, whom he frequently consults on important matters, they replied, 'It's easy; Suharto asks us about economics and he asks the *gurus* about timing.'[8]

The British people, being Christians, sometimes forget the religious wars of their own history and today consider religion as a private and personal matter between man and God. This can never be the case in Hinduism and Islam, for both these religions are definite social codes which govern not so much man's relations with his God, as man's relations with his neighbour. They govern not only his law and culture but every aspect of his social life, and such religions, essentially exclusive, completely preclude that merging of identity and unity of thought on which Western democracy is based . . .[9]

This is why conversions from one religion to another cause such difficulty. The conversion of one man can be felt as a threat or betrayal by an entire community, and riots and murders can sometimes ensue. The role of religion in the social and intellectual revolution in which so many of our generation of Asians are involved, and the personal tragedies which it can precipitate, can be surmised from the recollections of a young Indonesian who was the first in his rural family to acquire a modern, Western-influenced education:

I still remember how as a very conceited young man, enthralled by the new knowledge I had just acquired in school which in any case I had not properly assimilated – I wounded my father very deeply by not understanding the possible consequences of my words in such a strained atmosphere. One day, when I was about twenty-three, I found myself talking to him quite freely about the theories of the nineteenth century philosophers on such topics as evolution and the rise and fall of the great religions. My words cut my father to the heart; he understood that he would never now be able to eradicate these ideas from his son's mind, and so with a heart filled with an inexpressible grief and with tears pouring down his face, he said:

'Ah, my son, we are not only divided in this world, but we shall never meet again in the next. Our Gods are different, and our worlds hereafter will be different.'[10]

Yet the Asian religions are not organized to challenge the state as the churches sometimes did in Europe. The *mullahs*, bonzes and priests tend to act autonomously and quarrel with each other rather than co-operate in common purposes. There is thus a better chance in Asia today than there was in Europe at the time of nation-building for politics and religion to be kept formally distinct.[11] Pakistan was constitutionally an 'Islamic' state, but the other Muslim countries have avoided this, and freedom of religion, coupled with the secularity of the state, is guaranteed in most Asian constitutions. His attempt to make Buddhism the state religion in Burma was one of the reasons for U Nu's removal from office in 1962.

The standard political judgment on the impact of religion is that of Gunnar Myrdal, that it 'usually acts as a tremendous force for social inertia. The writer knows of no instance in present-day South Asia where religion has induced social change.'[12] The best known example of the reactionary function of religion is probably that of the riots in New Delhi at the end of 1966 on the question of cow-slaughter. The cow is considered sacred by Hindus, and although some reformers argue that the ancient scriptures do not prohibit their slaughter,[13] Hindu extremists want the government to make it illegal. Their campaign culminated in a demonstration by several hundred thousand people, led by naked *Sadhus* with ceremonial tridents, who set fire to buses, surrounded the house of the president of the Congress Party and caused many deaths in the *mêlée*. One of the four *shankaracharyas*, the high priests of Hinduism, fasted for seventy-three days in support of the campaign, and the Government went so far as to arrest and imprison him. The religious injunction against killing cows has produced an enormous population of ill-nourished and economically useless cattle which the modernizers in India would like to transform into a smaller number of well-tended, healthy, productive livestock. But the *gurus* thwart them.

Pakistan faced not dissimilar tensions. The government set up an official Islamic Research Institute to advise it how the country should be made an Islamic state and how to interpret the teachings of the Koran 'in such a way as to bring out its dynamic character in the context of the intellectual and scientific progress of the modern world'.[14] But the traditional *ulemas* of the mosques opposed the Institute's efforts to defend the modern banking systems from the Koranic prohibition of usury, and its justification of the mechanical slaughter of animals in modern conditions. Its director, Dr Fazlur Rehman, was obliged to resign in 1968 when his questioning of the revelation of the Koran to the prophet Mohammed aroused a storm of protest.[15] By concentrating on such issues the religious leaders would seem to be inviting their own decline. As one observer says of Indonesia, 'Without advocating land-redistribution, without attacking poverty in an energetic way and wagering its spiritual strength on the side of the under-privileged, Islam will never be able to hold its own.'[16]

All too often the priests seem to fight for the retention of their own privileges. When Buddhist monks attacked Government offices and courted arrest in Burma, their resentment was primarily against the Government's attempts to end the abuses of the priesthood (including, for example, free supplies of luxury goods from government shops).[17] The most notorious – though not the most typical – Buddhist monk of modern times is perhaps the Ceylonese Buddharakkhita, who by sheer force of personality became a leader of the Buddhist resurgence in the 1950s, helped his family to acquire a shipping line and numerous other business interests, and was convicted as the arch-conspirator behind the assassination by another monk of the prime minister, Solomon Bandaranaike.[18] Indeed, religious sentiment is often exploited by right-wing politicians as an unashamed weapon against the left. The wholesale slaughter of communists in Indonesia in 1966 was largely the work of KAMI, a coalition of Muslim and Christian student organizations encouraged by army officers to stem Marxist influence, and Hindu revivalism in some parts of India is supported by Congress Party leaders for the same reason.[19] The obverse of this phenomenon can be seen in China, where one rural reaction to the ideological fervour of the communists' Cultural Revolution was a revival of religious practices.[20]

Religion can nevertheless be a vehicle for some kinds of

social change. The mass conversion to Buddhism of ten million ex-Untouchables in the past decade or so affords one example. 'I was born a Hindu,' declared their late leader, Dr Ambedkar, 'but I will not die a Hindu,' and his example of conversion has been followed by more than 10 per cent of these unfortunates whose legal liberation has not yet brought social acceptance, and for whom a new religion can mean a new start in life.[21] The Buddhist movement in Ceylon had implications for social reform. Its leaders' report, *The Betrayal of Buddhism*,[22] led the Bandaranaike Government of 1956 to seek to restore Buddhism to its 'rightful place', by creating new universities and a Ministry of Cultural Affairs: these enhanced the power of the abbots and leading monks (including Buddharakkhita), but they also in the end brought modern education within the reach of a larger proportion of ordinary un-Westernized Ceylonese who had previously been excluded from the Christian-dominated colonial education system.

Religion can also express a reaction, not so much against the *idea* of progress and social change, as against its particular *form* and *speed*. The so-called new sects of Buddhism in Japan fall into this category.[23] The best known is the *Soka Gakkai* (Value-Creation Society), which began before the war as a small sect but expanded in the post-war years as a haven for people who feel insecure amidst the rapid modernization going on all around them – particularly the self-employed, unorganized craftsmen and labourers, farmers and fishermen, older housewives and the younger generation. It specializes in miraculous cures of ailments, mass prayers and meetings, and a quasi-parental relationship between existing members and the new converts whom they are encouraged to bring in. *Soka Gakkai's* aim is to transform society by personal human change (unlike the Marxists, who seek institutional change). It has now produced its own political party, which won 10 per cent of the popular vote in the 1968 parliamentary elections. The *Rissho Koseikai* is a rival sect of Buddhists which took the lead in the early 1950s in forming with numerous other groups the *Shin Shuren* (Federation of New Japanese Religious Organizations) as a counter to the *Soka Gakkai*.[24]

These sects offer comfort to those Japanese who regret the

decline of hierarchy, of calm, of the sense of belonging in modern industrial society. In the West we might expect such reactions to the tensions of modern life to take a political rather than religious expression, But Richard Beardsley describes the new sects as 'pre-political reactions to change', similar to earlier movements among Westerners 'when tension-ridden socio-cultural change has awakened them to expectations of better lives but not yet taught them political approaches to achieving them'.[25]

There are some Asian situations in which the reformers pray religion in aid of progress. Some Westerners might think of Buddhism as too passive for this role, but, 'on his way to the next world, a Buddhist priest has responsibilities in this one',[26] as a Vietnamese bonze has explained. Thus U Nu in Burma supplied his people with modern industries, free vitamin pills and official translations of Dale Carnegie's *How to Win Friends and Influence People*, without ceasing to claim that he was following the Buddha's teaching. The Buddhists in Communist China have taken the strongest line against Buddhist withdrawal from the world. Chu-tsan, one of their leaders, has claimed that,

Rebirth in the Western Paradise is for the sake of reforming this human world in the East ... becoming a Buddha in an ivory tower of leisure and contentment ... is just another pastime and opiate of landlords, bureaucrats and petit bourgeois when they are surfeited with wine and food. It has nothing at all to do with Buddhism.[27]

Another of China's 'Red Buddhists' has insisted that, 'The First Five-Year Plan is the initial blueprint for the Western Paradise here on earth',[28] and Chinese monks were urged to 'join the army directly and learn the spirit in which Shakyamuni as the embodiment of compassion ... killed robbers to save the people. ... To wipe out the American imperialist demons that are breaking world peace is, according to the Buddhist doctrine, not only blameless but actually gives rise to merit.'[29] When an English Buddhist asked an eminent Chinese monk about communist brainwashing, the latter replied:

We do not understand why one who professes to be a follower of the Buddha should be so terrified by the term 'remoulding' and joins in the clamour against it as 'brainwashing'. In fact, if dirt is found in one's thought (just as it is on one's body), what harm would it do to advise him to have a wash?... After all the question is with regard to what things are to be washed off ... The things that we advise people to wash off are: concern for individual interests at the expense of the collective interests; concern for immediate interests at the expense of long term interests – in other words, lack of patriotism, disdainfulness towards the masses and the like thoughts, that are concrete manifestations of greed, hatred and stupidity.[30]

A religious basis for modern interventionist policies is sought not merely by the communists but by the many other Asian leaders who profess some form of socialism. Prince Sihanouk, who suppressed his country's communist party, offered instead what he called 'Buddhist Socialist Nationalism', insisting that 'Buddhism is socialist in its fight against social injustice ... one often forgets that Buddha was a revolutionary preaching in a feudal society love of one's neighbour and equality among all living beings. ...'[31] Rajagopalachari, the Hindu statesman, has declared that, 'the *Gita** lays down in a unique manner the socialist doctrine in terms of religion',[32] and Sukarno once remarked: 'I am attached to socialism because I am attached to Islam. I am attached to socialism and I fight for it, as an obligation toward God.'[33]

Religious forces have now begun to enter Asian politics in a more organized way than before. One of the main factors in the overthrow of President Diem of South Vietnam was the United Buddhist Church, which in the early 1960s developed a militant political orientation and achieved much in the educational and social welfare fields. But factionalism has now reduced its power, the Buddhist leaders in Vietnam being divided not merely over personalities and the niceties of religion but on the fundamental question of the appropriateness of any kind of political activity. Vinoba Bhave and Jayaprakash Narayan in India carry on the Gandhian tradition of reformed Hinduism in the field of voluntary land reform and social welfare.

In Japan the most successful of the new Buddhist sects, the *Soka Gakkai*, has formed its own political party, the *Komeito* (Clean Government Party) which has had remarkable success at the polls in recent years but which is formally distinct from

*Bhagavad Gita, the classic Hindu scripture.

its religious parent. The same goes for the *Jan Sangh* of North India and the *Dravida Munnetra Kazakham* (DMK) in Madras state, both of which had their origin in religious or caste organizations but separated from them as soon as they had a real prospect of gaining political power. In state office after the 1967 elections, both have followed more moderate and less sectional policies than their origins would have suggested. The *Jan Sangh*, though associated with reactionary and militant elements of Hinduism, actually invites and accepts Muslim members. There are also important parties in Indonesia, Malaysia and Pakistan which are based on religious exclusivity.

The social character of religion invests it with the potential for violence: the half million who died during the rioting and disorder that followed the partition of India and Pakistan in 1947,[34] and the quarter of a million who were killed in cold blood in Indonesia in 1965–6 after the unsuccessful pro-communist *coup*, were all victims of disputes that had a religious origin. When Bertha Hertog, a Dutch girl left during the war with Muslim foster parents and converted by them to Islam, was ordered by a Singapore court in 1950 to be returned to her Dutch parents, there were three days of religious rioting in which many died. Such emotions, if pent up and released on a large scale, can disrupt the new nations of Asia, especially if the majority religion succumbs to intolerance. The Muslims who would like to make Indonesia a theocratic state would oblige the Christians and Hindus of the eastern islands to secede, and comparable observations could be made about India, Pakistan, Burma, Vietnam, Malaysia, and the Philippines. The Muslims and Christians fought each other on the Philippine island of Jolo twenty or so years ago, and there have been more recent clashes between these rival faiths in both Indonesia and the Philippines.

Christianity suffers in the nationalistic Asia of today from its association with the colonial powers. Hindu leaders have launched a 'Save India from Christian Imperialism Conference', warning their countrymen of the 'evil designs of Christian powers to subjugate India again through cultural conquest'.[35] The Hindu organizations identify foreign missionaries as 'political agents of foreign powers', and refer scornfully to 'conversion by milk powder'. Muslims in Indonesia are resentful of recent Christian proselytizing successes in that country, with conversions at the rate of 250,000 a year since the communist setback of 1965.[36] They call them 'rice Christians'. Buddhism in South Vietnam and Islam in the Philippines become natural vehicles for political opposition to the Christian élites in power in those countries. Yet there are more church-going Christians in Asia than there are in Britain, with a total membership of some sixty million[37] and including such famous converts as Chiang Kai-shek. In the Philippines the Catholics are in a majority over the Muslims.

It is the missionaries who are probably most to blame for this lack of sympathy for Christianity. George Patterson, who was himself once a Plymouth Brother missionary in China, had this to say of his colleagues:

Missionaries everywhere bowed and scraped to the petty whims of any ragged local functionary in their anxiety to preserve their own and their Mission's position from becoming involved in the possible stigma of indulging or interfering in politics. This fear arose out of an unconscious guilt complex through owning, in a country that was not their own, property and land held often on dubious deeds and founded on even more dubious treaties permitting them to be there in the first place. Rarely mixing with or showing interest in the people except for personal and professional reasons, they wore an air of superiority that more often than not became a denunciation of everything Eastern and a dictatorial insistence that the Western way of life was the one possible for the Christian, in religion, in culture and very often in governmental structure and administration.[38]

It is true that the Chinese are congenitally sceptical of proselytizers: 'to travel abroad and live among strangers, not for profit or advantage, but merely to alter their religion and substitute another, equally steeped in the supernatural, and thus, to the educated, equally unsophisticated, seemed a most improbable explanation. It was much easier to believe . . . that the missionary was the agent of some foreign power.'[39] But even elsewhere the missionary, however sincere, tends to be a poor ambassador, especially since he sees his main opportunities among the neglected or underprivileged sections of the country where he works: the championing of these causes is at best embarrassing to the country's nationalist and infellectual leadership and at worst becomes political dynamite – as Michael Scott found in Naga-land.[40] Of course this is also true for, say, the few Buddhist and Muslim missionaries in India. American and other Western missionaries have been expelled from almost every Asian country, even recently from Malaysia. The general trend is towards Asianization of the churches and missions, a policy which the Chinese communists have carried to the extreme of forbidding any foreign money or personnel to assist the 'patriotic' Chinese Christians who are still allowed to worship and maintain their churches.[41]

If religion in Asia has a social rather than a personal function, it also has an international role. The Islamic countries (Pakistan, Indonesia and Malaysia) are the most amenable to concerting their foreign policy on religious lines, and the Malay party in the ruling Alliance Government of Malaysia has called for a Commonwealth of Muslim nations. The Regional Co-operation and Development between Pakistan, Iran and Turkey is the only institutional expression of this so far, but Pakistan gained wide-spread support from other Muslim nations during the 1965 war: it seems that Indonesian military help was at one point dispatched while Iran considered embargoing oil shipments to India. Malaysia was an exception to this, having a resident Indian minority (mostly southern Hindus) and remembering Nehru's unfailing support during and after her independence negotiations. Some of the Malay politicians wanted their Government to abandon its neutrality in the Kashmir war, but they remained in a minority and Pakistan finally broke her diplomatic relations with Malaysia on this issue.[42]

The idea of Muslim solidarity took a beating during the military confrontation between Malaysia and Indonesia in the early 1960s, but once this was over it was possible for a Philippine journalist to report that the Malaysian prime minister had 'secretly been attempting of late to line the Indonesians up on their side against the Christian Filipinos using the Muslim faith as their common denominator.'[43] Asian religionists have also taken to demonstrating in sympathy with their co-faithful abroad, a recent example being the barracking of the emperor Haile Selassie at Djakarta airport in protest against Ethiopian perse-cution of Muslims.

The Buddhist countries, lacking the international organization of Islam, do not act together in the same way. There is a World Fellowship of Buddhists which meets every three years with a headquarters in Bangkok, but this has become ineffective because of a split between the communist-controlled delegations and the rest. The American-Taiwanese-Thai-dominated Eighth Conference in Chiengmai in 1966 voted to 'refrain from involving itself in politics'.[44] Some international proselytizing is conducted from Rangoon, Colombo and Bangkok (and to a lesser extent from Japan), but on a rather small scale. There also tends to be tension between the relatively passive Asian Buddhist and the kind of Western convert who wants to draw up a creed acceptable to Buddhists everywhere and to organize Buddhist activities more closely and more purposefully.

There are political overtones to all this: the Chinese communists have often sought to convoke international Buddhist conferences to support their foreign policy line of the day, for example by protesting against American intervention in Vietnam, but with decreasing success. In 1966 the Government of Ceylon sent a mission to Vietnam to investigate the political clash between one group of ambitious Buddhist monks and the Saigon Government with a view to reconciling them. But I know of no case where a government has based an important foreign policy decision towards another country on the fact of its being Buddhist or not.

Hinduism is concentrated in India, but is not a seriously proselytizing religion, although it has been attracting intellectual adherents or sympathizers ever since Swami Vivekananda's dramatic address in Chicago in 1893, and the *Arya Samaj*, (a modern reform group which makes no caste distinctions) is converting Africans to Hinduism (from Christianity) in Kenya.[45] Hinduism also extends wherever Indians live abroad, and King Mahendra of Nepal has told his people:

Today we can protect and advance our nation and national society only if all of us cease to have any shyness or scruples about calling ourselves Hindus, but march forward to protect, strengthen and develop Hindu society and revitalize *Dharma*. It has become absolutely necessary for all Hindus to realize this fully for the welfare of mankind.[46]

Chapter Three

Classes and Castes

WHEN Michael Field was the *Daily Telegraph* correspondent in Bangkok, he used to have a drink now and again with an official of the Soviet Embassy there who was interested in expressing the situation in Thailand in Marxist terms. Over a bottle of Georgian wine one day the Russian asked, quite seriously: 'Do you think it might be described as a semi-colonial, comprador economy in which the national bourgeoisie is evolving from a feudal-paternalistic framework into primitive pre-monopoly capitalism, but coming quickly under the control of imperialistic monopoly finance-capitalism?'[1] Many scholars, both Asian and Western, have insisted that the societies of Asia do not admit to the class distinctions of Europe, and that Marxist analysis cannot be uncritically applied to the complex social relationships of countries where the family or clan is the basic unit, where loyalties are vertical rather than horizontal, where villages enjoy considerable autonomy and where modern industrialization has only just begun.

It is true that all Asian societies have a tiny traditional élite composed of the larger landowners, money-lenders and merchants, scholars, government officers, priests and the ruling aristocracy surrounding the local court or seat of government, while the rest of the population is largely the peasantry. To many Westerners this traditional face of Asia, still visible beyond the centres of big cities, evokes memories of the feudalism of medieval Europe. But Liang Shu-ming, the Chinese philosopher of this century who disputed the validity for China of European class distinctions, also showed that feudalism as a system of ownership in China had ended two thousand years ago,[2] and European patterns of historical development can no more be imported into the Asian scene than European categories of social analysis. To dismiss the traditional basis of Asian life as 'feudalistic' and thus indefensible in modern times is to misunderstand its subtleties.

Even the big cities such as Shanghai and Calcutta have not produced the kind of proletarianized urban society that now dominates the West: traditional rural relationships and loyalties tend to be maintained even within the urban framework.[3] It is thus possible for leaders to attempt to organize city life in ways which give preference to the traditional values of the people involved. Gandhi organized the textile workers of Ahmedabad on the basis of accepting the management of the mills as trustees of the enterprise on their behalf instead of confronting them as class enemies. The communists in China had little difficulty in controlling factory workers and trade unions because the vertical line of loyalties expressed in the concept of hierarchy comes far more easily to the product of Chinese civilization than the horizontal line of loyalties expressed in the idea of egalitarian solidarity. The paradox is that Mao Tse-tung preaches equality and seeks to develop the Chinese personality towards it, and yet he relies for his organizational success on the quasi-feudal sense of deference to authority and unquestioning acceptance of political leadership so deeply ingrained in the Chinese.

Similarly in Japan the trade unions have never followed the path which their American patrons and supporters had charted out for them. They prefer to be what we call 'house unions', that is unions organizing only the labour within one single large enterprise or group. Strikes are almost unheard of, though they can be extremely violent when they do occur. The attitude of union leaders toward management would strike the average Western proletarian as either shamefully timid or else suspiciously cooperative, although it is now being seen in Britain, where poor management-labour relations begin to threaten the national livelihood, as a model worthy of imitation.

But the timidity is merely the acceptance of a different set of rules which the management in Japan normally observes, for its part, by according to labour recognition of its own dignity and self-respect. The welfare benefits given to workers by the big Japanese employers (and also by Chinese capitalists in Hongkong, Taiwan and Singapore) are the envy of the visiting Western trade unionist, though he tends to scorn them as substitutes for respectable wage levels, ignoring the possibility that the cultural tradition makes people prefer this way of handling industrial relations. Japanese employers give their labour force special outings, organized holidays and entertainments, and facilities of all kinds. An electronics factory in Kyoto issues its 750 young women employees with an outfit which it paid Pierre Cardin $15,000 to design.[4] It is perhaps not surprising that, in spite of the Marxist intellectuals' clamour for 'class struggle', 87 per cent of the Japanese regard themselves as being 'middle class'.[5]

One of the least defensible class distinctions shared traditionally by both China and India (though not by Japan) is the deep-seated contempt of the educated class as a whole for manual work. This is why so many Asian students in the West prove incapable of helping with the washing-up or mending a light fuse: they have never acquired these simple kinds of manual dexterity. 'Indian men,' an Indian sociologist observes, 'are generally illiterate with their hands.'[6] In India this means that management and clerks are reluctant to dirty their hands, and that enterprises have to be, by Western standards, overmanned. In China the communists have declared total war against this tradition, at the cost of consigning technical experts and creative intellectuals to long periods of manual labour in factory or farm.

Ultimately, Mao Tse-tung hopes to establish as the norm in China the 'all-round man', neither rural nor urban, neither agricultural nor industrial, neither intellectual nor plebeian, but a mixture of all with the capacity to turn himself to anything that is needed and to see the interests of the nation (indeed of mankind) above those of his own locality and group. Unfortunately any government of China, and any party seeking to alter its politics, has to work through some kind of bureaucracy, whether political or administrative. This, as Jack Gray has said, is 'the class which Marx forgot: the bureaucracy, which may own nothing and enjoy everything'.[7] It clings very stubbornly to its group privileges and its hierarchies, and it became the chief target of Mao's Cultural Revolution in 1966-8.

The People's Commune, the new institution which Mao developed in China in 1958, encourages the peasant to see farming and industry as both within his grasp: this was the virtue of the otherwise wasteful backyard steel furnace campaign in the Great Leap Forward. The development of small-scale rural industries in the countryside has become a fixed policy of the Chinese

communists. But the Cultural Revolution showed that the collectivization of the communes had not brought class differentia-
tions to an end. The Party ideologists must constantly struggle to
prevent control passing back into the hands of the richer and
more industrious peasants, the 'kulaks', who are the natural
leaders and the pioneers of 'spontaneous capitalism'.

In India the rural revolution is less dramatic, although the
attempt has been made in the past decade to introduce a new
pattern of rural self-government based at the lowest level on the
elected village *Panchayat* or committee. The situation varies in
each state, but most of the *Panchayats* have responsibility for
social welfare and civic amenities, and in future the slightly higher
level of district *Panchayats* may also be given responsibility for
economic development projects. They have been given some
direct revenues, and in a few states they have some executive
functions. But the *Panchayat* movement has not been widely
successful, the peasants being on the whole unready to take up
such new responsibilities and becoming easy prey of local
politicians.[8] A similar fate overtook the Basic Democracies
movement in Pakistan.[9]

If the class struggle seems somewhat elusive and shadowy in
Asia, there is another institution which bears comparison with
class but which is of far greater antiquity. As Michael Young
observed in *The Rise of Meritocracy*, 'The soil grows castes; the
machine makes classes.' Caste is a very old social institution
peculiar to India and in lesser degree to neighbouring countries
influenced by Indian culture. It is so deep-rooted that it operates
even within the Jewish, Christian and Muslim communities in
India.

It differs from class in that one cannot escape from the caste
into which one is born: there is far more mobility between classes
in Europe than there is between castes in India. The advantage of
the caste system is the sense of security which it creates about
one's place in the community and in the world at large, and the
cohesion which it imparts to the enormous and otherwise heterogeneous Indian population. It is in part an extended family or
clan system. 'You can't be without a community,' one foreign
observer explains. 'Without a community, it is awkward for a

man in all his relationships. This is the culture of the country. In India you have got to be connected.'[10] If one read 'organization' for 'community', the remark could equally apply to Communist China and even – with a generous stretch – to Japan.

The caste system is ardently defended by all but the most Westernized Indian intellectuals, and Ananda Coomaraswamy claimed that, 'Even with all its imperfections Hindu society as it survives will appear to many to be superior to any form of social organization attained on a large scale anywhere else, and infinitely superior to the social order which we know as "modern civilization".'[11] It accepts what Coomaraswamy calls 'the natural inequality of men' and provides 'a very nearly ideal combination of duty and pleasure, compulsion and freedom'.[12] These words were written more than half a century ago, but there are Indians today who express similar feelings. Thus Nirad Chaudhuri, the liveliest of India's own critics, cries out to the would-be abolishers of caste: 'Please do not pulverise a society, which has no other source of cohesion, into an amorphous dust.'[13] In modern India, as in Ceylon, leadership in society – in politics, in business, in the professions – is open to all castes, and cases of able men being frustrated by their caste origin are becoming fewer.

But the ritual and purely religious aspect of the caste system is less easy to defend. Acceptance of inequality is one thing, but the idea that one can be polluted by contact with an inferior, and needs to undergo ritual purification to render the contamination harmless, is offensive to modern values. Strict adherents of Hinduism are obliged to regulate their everyday life in the minutest detail, and to observe countless prohibitions and restraints in diet, clothing, time-table, social relations – even in sex life. Orthodox Brahmins (the highest caste) in Tanjore are allowed to make love only on Fridays.[14] But this ritual aspect of caste is the most vulnerable to modernization, and it is tending to be relaxed rather rapidly, although one must remember that the caste system in India is still gaining new members (by the process of 'Sanskritization' of the millions of tribal people in many areas of India who have not yet been absorbed into Hinduism).[15]

The degree of social immobility imposed by the caste system, as it is practised today, is a matter of controversy. Some Indians

feel that caste has become a scapegoat for the social immobility
into which British rule unwittingly froze it,[16] and that left to
itself the system has adequate powers of flexibility.

Indeed, the question is less and less frequently posed in this
way. Social scientists, whether Indian or foreign, start these days
from the premise that the caste system is the fixed core of Indian
society, and seek to discover how it responds to the new demands
of economic and intellectual change; they no longer discuss it as
if it were something that could be replaced by an entirely different
system. As Professor M. N. Srinivas, the *doyen* of Indian sociologists, has insisted: 'Caste is so tacitly and so completely accepted
by all, including those most vocal in condemning it, that it is
everywhere the unit of social action.'[17] Indeed he goes on to say
that, 'There is a good case for arguing that caste-consciousness
and organization have increased in modern India. Witness for
instance the proliferation of caste banks, hostels, co-operative
societies, charities, marriage halls, conferences and journals in
Indian towns. . . .'

The impact of caste loyalties on Indian politics has been very
closely studied in recent years. Jayaprakash Narayan, India's
most respected Gandhian politician, says that, 'Caste is the
biggest party in India.' Another Indian writer explains that caste
'has now actively entered the arena for the competitive distribution and redistribution of material rewards and social and political
perquisites among different social groups'.[18] But the caste system
does not remain unaffected by this growing involvement in
modern politics. Another Indian scholar concludes that 'pri-
mordial and parochial ties and loyalties to tribe, caste or religion
can never be uprooted through a policy of political ostracism, nor
can they be broken merely by legislation; but they begin to erode
and weaken and are modified when exposed to and drawn into
the political process.'[19]

Indian Marxists explain their country's politics in terms of the
struggle between classes. The first major assault on this position
was made by Selig Harrison who, in his book *India, the Most
Dangerous Decades*, argued that caste was a more important
factor in Indian party politics than class. Harrison was generaliz-
ing, however, from the particular case of the State of Andhra, and
subsequent studies show that it is wrong to suppose that caste

factors are exclusive or overriding in elections throughout India.

A study of a village in the Punjab showed that members of a given caste group voted for different candidates and parties, depending on their own economic circumstances and the severity of their family feuds within the caste.[20] Factionalism and personal ambition were found to be more important factors than caste in the complex affairs of the Bihar Congress Party.[21] The fact is, as one scholar has noted, that, 'Few politicians in India can afford to court a single caste, for in most constituencies no single caste community so predominates as to command a majority alone.'[22]

The impact of caste on mobility within the Indian economy has been less thoroughly studied. A remark by an ordinary Indian factory worker suggests that it is considerable: 'The managing director is born in a rich family of a high caste because of his meritorious deeds in the previous birth; he is continuing his good deeds in this birth by giving wages and salaries to all these employees. It is as though God had ordered him when he was born: "Go to the earth, start a big factory and support all these people".'[23]

Louis Dumont argues in his book *Homo Hierarchicus* that the caste system is capable of accommodating the modernization of India without losing its essential character, and he may be right. A similar conclusion emerges from the work of Lloyd and Susanne Rudolph, who feel that caste will remain the framework within which the inequalities of the old order and the ancient hierarchies will be destroyed.[24] Perhaps the ultimate test of the resilience of the caste system will be the fate of the eighty million or so 'ex-Untouchables' who occupy the lowest rung on the Hindu ladder. These are the people whose humiliations were so movingly depicted in Mulk Raj Anand's novel *Untouchable*, whom Gandhi renamed *Harijans* (Children of God), and whose traditional untouchability was firmly abolished by law in the Indian Constitution.[25]

Twenty years of legal change have not, however, removed the social discrimination which the ex-Untouchables must endure, and in this respect, their position has been compared with that of the American Negroes.[26] You can still find villages and towns in India where the higher castes will say openly of the ex-Untouchables: 'Today they want to use our wells, and tomorrow they will want to marry our daughters.' The fact that about ten million of them have now been converted to Buddhism, following the example set by their late leader, Dr Ambedkar, some fourteen years ago, suggests a strong disbelief in the capacity of the Hindu system to break the Untouchable barrier.[27] But Dr Ambedkar himself was able to reach the highest ranks of the Indian political ladder, and there is no doubt that the position of the *Harijans*, especially their access to temples, roads and wells, is improving year by year.[28]

It is, of course, unfair to think of India as the only society guilty of discrimination. Even within Asia there is the curious and little-known case of the *Eta*, the Japanese outcasts. These are people whose pursuit of such *taboo* trades as slaughtering, tanning and leatherwork invested them with an inferior social status said to be traceable to early Buddhist influence. In the nineteenth century the *Eta* (the name means 'filth-galore') were physically segregated in urban ghettoes or rural districts. They were legally emancipated by Imperial Decree in 1871, but social discrimination has continued and in 1946 an All-Japan Committee for the Emancipation of Segregated Communities was formed to protect the interests of these three million unfortunates.[29] If Japan, so egalitarian in other respects, can tolerate this surprising pocket of social discrimination, one should perhaps be slightly less impatient with India, where the sense of hierarchy remains so strong.

Chapter Four

Conflicts of Culture

ALL the great Western thinkers have sought to explain Asia's vulnerability to Westernization and to Western imperialism. Karl Marx found difficulty in fitting Asian societies into his world-view, according to which slavery leads inexorably first to feudalism, then capitalism and finally socialism: he wrote with some bafflement of the 'Asiatic mode of production' as if it did not really fit with these. For Hegel, 'China and India lie as it were outside the course of world history', and for von Ranke they belonged to 'the nations of eternal stagnation'. Max Weber found Asia lacking in the 'Protestant ethic' which has been the magic ingredient in Europe's surge forward. Karl Wittfogel in *Oriental Despotism* painted a picture of simple village communities overlaid by tyranny. Asian sociology is not in fact reducible to any of these neat categories,[1] but the impact of Western power and Western ideas on Asia has been traumatic. Her intellectuals are still struggling to recover from it, to discriminate between the desirable and undesirable elements of alien influence, to digest the one and vomit the other. In many cases, especially among the first generation to be fully exposed to foreign cultural influence, the encounter has brought bitterness and loneliness and personal tragedy.

This 'spiritual breakdown' of the man whose native values are suddenly assaulted and intellectually undermined before he has the chance of re-building his life and personality on another set, has been documented in such novels as *Kokoro* ('Heart'), by the Japanese Natsume Soseki,[2] and *Salah Asuhan* ('Wasted Education'), by the Indonesian Abdul Muis. The extreme case is where a man's entire education is conducted, for the first time in his family's experience, under an alien culture and in a foreign language, as happened in all the countries that fell under European rule. 'A single generation of English education suffices to break the threads of tradition and to create a nondescript superficial being deprived of all roots . . .'[3] Nor is this confined to the first generation. The youngest and most recent Indian to describe his experience of cultural alienation came from a family which was already Westernized, yet he laments that,

> The deepest tragedy of British rule in India is that it succeeded in producing individuals like me who can neither feel an identity with their own people nor accept the glare, the steel-muscle concept of human life as it exists in America and which seems slowly to be gripping the whole West.[4]

Even a country like Japan, which did not have to submit to colonialism, found, in Yoshida Shigeru's words, that 'a kind of moral vacuum was the price that had to be paid for the introduction of an alien culture'.[5] The wholesale reorganization of Japanese education by the Meiji reformers a century ago provided an early example of the near-impossibility of striking a constantly satisfactory balance between indigenous tradition and alien innovation. After the Meiji Government had investigated the school systems of Europe and America it adopted, in the famous *Gakusei* (Education Decree) of 1872, a system based on these models. The decree explained that the existing schools benefited mainly the upper classes of society and were in any case defective: 'Much time was spent in the useless occupation of writing poetry and composing maxims, instead of learning what would be for the students' own benefit or that of the state.' But within a few years the government found it necessary to put a brake on the spread of these European-inspired ideas. Its introduction on the principles of education issued in 1879 admitted that the earlier call to destroy old customs and search for knowledge in other parts of the world had led to a decline in morals and manners. It added:

> Although the advantages of Western culture were adopted, and resulted in spectacular effects for the moment, once it leads to a tendency to neglect benevolence, responsibility, loyalty and fidelity and becomes merely a competition to introduce Western manners, there is fear that in the future no one will know responsibility between the Emperor and his subjects. This is not the true motive of education in our nation. Therefore, henceforth, we shall make clear the virtues of benevolence, responsibility, loyalty and fidelity based on the precepts

of our ancestors. In the teaching of morality the Confucian morality will be primary. Men will furthermore respect faithfulness and good manners.[6]

But influences of the kind which the West brought to bear on Asia, like those that Europe had received from other civilizations earlier in its history, cannot be stemmed by an emperor's signature, and even today it is possible for a senior Japanese educator to observe that his country still lives in a 'self-admitted moral vacuum'.[7]

Many sensitive Asians caught in this cultural trap have spoken of the sense of displacement which they suffer. Jawaharlal Nehru, who was educated in the manner of the English upper classes at Harrow, Cambridge and the Inner Temple, wrote in his autobiography:

I have become a queer mixture of the East and the West, out of place everywhere, at home nowhere. Perhaps my thoughts and approach to life are more akin to what is called Western than Eastern, but India clings to me, as she does to all her children, in innumerable ways; and behind me lie, somewhere in the subconscious, racial memories of a hundred, or whatever the number may be, generations of Brahmans. I cannot get rid of either that past inheritance or my recent acquisitions. They are both part of me, and, though they help me in both the East and the West, they also create in me a feeling of spiritual loneliness not only in public activities but in life itself. I am a stranger and alien in the West. I cannot be of it. But in my own country also, sometimes, I have an exile's feeling.[8]

The pressure to adopt Western values was irresistible. Macaulay, who joined the Indian Government in 1834 and charted its education policy, stated unequivocally that the schools and colleges which the British Raj was beginning to establish in India were meant to produce 'a class of persons Indian in blood and colour, but English in taste, in opinion, in morals and in intellect'. Even today this would be accepted by many a well-to-do Asian father as the ideal for his eldest son, as it was for Lee Kuan Yew, the prime minister of Singapore, whose father sent him to Cambridge to become 'the equal of any Englishman – the model of perfection'. Lee obliged by winning a double first, but confessed: 'I cry with Nehru when I think I cannot speak my mother tongue as well as I speak English.'[9]

Although there was pressure, economic and social, both official and from the family, to enter the intellectual world of Western thought and 'drink foreign ink', it was not a case of the first pioneers' being reluctant. At first sight the attractions of Europe were dazzling and exciting. Sir Surendranath Banerjea, the Indian National Congress leader at the beginning of this century, observed:

Our fathers, the first-fruits of English education, were violently pro-British. They could see no flaw in the civilization or the culture of the West. They were charmed by its novelty and its strangeness. The enfranchisement of the individual, the substitution of the right of private judgment in place of traditional authority, the exaltation of duty over custom, all came with the force and suddenness of a revelation to an Oriental people who knew no more binding obligation than the mandate of immemorial usage and of venerable tradition.[10]

Even now Dom Moraes, the Indian poet, Fou Ts'ong, the Chinese pianist, and Yoko Ono, the Japanese artist, all prefer to live outside their land of birth, and Paris, Amsterdam, San Francisco and Geneva are full of intellectual exiles from Asia. They are the exceptions of course; most Asian intellectuals stay at home, either because they have to or because they prefer to nurse their cultural schizophrenia in a familiar rather than an unfamiliar milieu. Many of them come to terms with their own tradition after the initial exposure to Westernization: Nirad Chaudhuri writes that over his sixty-five years he had seen 'at least five shoals of Hindu tadpoles shedding their Western tails and becoming Hindu frogs'.[11]

The typical pattern of reaction to Westernism in an Asian society was first to ignore, then to begin to imitate certain selective ingredients of it. Raja Rammohun Roy and Sayid Ahmed Khan of India, Yen Fu of China, were the outstanding representatives of this phase. It was succeeded by a division between those who, like Liang Chi-chao and the Meiji reformers in Japan, advocated a sharp break with tradition and an almost wholesale absorption of Western culture, and those who like, Sri Ramakrishna and Iqbal, sensed the moral deterioration which accompanied the innovations and preferred to reassert the ethical superiority of the indigenous tradition. But this division in turn became blurred as more and more Asian leaders developed their own synthesis of Asian and European culture, as Gandhi, Sun Yat-sen, Jinnah, Nehru and Mao Tse-tung all did.

The relationship between a Westernized Asian and his own country, his own traditions, has never been better described than by Nehru in his will, where he explained how he wanted his funeral to be arranged:

My desire to have a handful of my ashes thrown into the Ganga at Allahabad has no religious significance, so far as I am concerned. I have no religious sentiment in the matter. I have been attached to the Ganga and the Jumna rivers in Allahabad ever since my childhood and, as I have grown older, this attachment has also grown. I have watched their varying moods as the seasons changed, and have often thought of the history and myth and tradition and song and story that have become attached to them through the long ages and become part of their flowing waters. The Ganga, especially, is the river of India, beloved of her people, round which are intertwined her racial memories, her hopes and fears, her songs of triumph, her victories and her defeats. She has been a symbol of India's age-long culture and civilization, ever-changing, ever-flowing, and yet ever the same Ganga. She reminds me of the snow-covered peaks and deep valleys of the Himalayas, which I have loved so much, and of the rich and vast plains below, where my life and work have been cast. Smiling and dancing in the morning sunlight, and dark and gloomy and full of mystery as the evening shadows fall; a narrow, slow and graceful stream in winter, and a vast roaring thing during the monsoon, broad-bosomed almost as the sea, and with something of the sea's power to destroy, the Ganga has been to me a symbol and a memory of the past of India, running into the present, and flowing on to the great ocean of the future. And though I have discarded much of past tradition and custom, and am anxious that India should rid herself of all shackles that bind and constrain her and divide her people, and suppress vast numbers of them, and prevent the free development of the body and the spirit; though I seek all this, yet I do not wish to cut myself off from that past completely. I am proud of that great inheritance that has been, and is, ours, and I am conscious that I too, like all of us, am a link in that unbroken chain which goes back to the dawn of history in the immemorial past of India. That chain I would not break, for I treasure it and seek inspiration from it. And as witness of this desire of mine and as my last homage to India's cultural inheritance, I am making this request that a handful of my ashes be thrown into the Ganga at Allahabad to be carried to the great ocean that washes India's shore.[12]

An early, if naïve expression of the ideal synthesis was the slogan *Toyo Dotoku, Seiyo Geijutsu* ('Eastern morality, Western science') of the Japanese philosopher Sakuma Shozan. 'Acquire mechanical arts from others, retain righteousness, sympathy and filial piety as our own,' advised another Japanese thinker. While the material achievements of Europe, from electricity to the railway, were admired and envied, the indiscipline and moral laxity of Westerners was despised, and these feelings persist today. One of India's leading novelists recently wrote that, 'the prospect of drifting into the moods, attitudes and habits of acquisitive Western civilization seems frightening. . . .'[13] The West emphasizes material progress and efficiency, and its political theory is based on the premise that society exists primarily to satisfy the individual needs and demands of all its members. To the Asian such an outlook still seems too crude and calculating. He prefers to talk in more explicitly ethical terms. Many Japanese did not think it unusual or embarrassing when their present prime minister pledged that the spirit of 'human love' would be the main theme of his new cabinet, or that he should declare that, 'lack of spirit is more dreadful than economic crisis'[14] (the Chinese communists also excel in such moralistic language).

Indeed the beginnings of puritanism are to be found throughout Asia today, with the significant exception of Japan. A taxi driver and a girl were recently given five lashes and a week's hard labour for kissing in public in Karachi, and a dance band was arrested in Djakarta a few years ago for singing Beatle songs.[15] The Chinese communists are liable to take direct physical action against teenage rebels in Shanghai wearing winklepickers or stovepipe trousers, Indonesian soldiers arrange compulsory public haircuts for long-haired students, and the visiting European or American hippie tends to be unceremoniously clapped in jail in Bangkok and some other Asian cities. When Viscount Montgomery chided Mao Tse-tung for making China a 'closed shop' to foreigners, Mao explained that the Western peoples brought with them a laxity in moral standards which might impede the high standards he was trying to reach in China - adding that where the West goes moral standards deteriorate.[16] A Burmese official has explicitly stated: 'We would rather do without the foreign exchange than have the corruption tourists would bring.'[17] Prince Sihanouk once summarized his foreign policy in the phrase: 'Like a virgin Cambodia does not want to be approached by anyone.'[18]

But the dichotomy between Asian spiritualism and Western materialism is now thoroughly discredited, as Raghavan Iyer's book *The Glass Curtain Between Asia and Europe* shows. When Tibor Mende asked Nehru about this, he replied, 'I won't put it that way, that Indians are "more spiritual". I would say that a static society talks more about so-called spitituality.'[19] The best of the Japanese thinkers of the past hundred years – Kotoku Shusui, for instance, or Fukuzawa Yukichi – have seen no East or West in moral values. Sjahrir, the Indonesian socialist revolutionary, wrote:

We must extend and intensify life, and raise and improve the goals towards which we strive. This is what the West has taught us, and this is what I admire in the West despite its brutality and its coarseness. I would even take this brutality and coarseness as accompanying features of the new concept of life that the West has taught us. I would even accept capitalism as an improvement upon the much famed wisdom and religion of the East. For it is precisely this wisdom and religion that make us unable to understand the fact that we have sunk to the lowest depths to which man can descend: we have sunk to slavery and to enduring subjugation.

What we in the East admire most in the West is its indestructible vitality, its love for life and for the fulfilment of life. Every vital young man and young woman in the East ought to look towards the West, for he or she can learn only from the West to regard himself or herself as a centre of vitality capable of changing and bettering the world.

The East must become Western in the sense that it must acquire as great a vitality and dynamism as the West. Faust must reveal himself to the Eastern man and mind . . .[20]

At the heart of the dilemma posed by Westernization is the conflict between the traditional family system and the need for emancipated individualism. Lin Yutang declared that under the Confucian system 'the family became a walled castle outside of which everything was legitimate loot'.[21] One of the common tragedies in Communist China is when a man is torn between the traditionally overriding obligation to his parents and the new demand to uphold the morality and law of the state, for example where his father evades a tax or is discovered dabbling in the black market. The novelist Lao She says:

> In the old days, Chinese people specialized in 'son covers up for father, father covers up for son'. So everyone covered up, and truth and justice were hidden away beyond the hope of discovery. Today the father-son relationship can no longer bury the truth beneath it.[22]

Everywhere in Asia the family reigns supreme and usually stands before the law. The anthropologist who called the Philippines 'an anarchy of families' could have been speaking of almost any Asian country. So the communists in China and the new nationalist governments in India and South-East Asia have all sought to legislate away the supreme power of the family, to clear the path for a society of more autonomous individuals more easily able to relate to and deal with each other in all the complex ways which modern life demands across the narrow frontiers of the blood family.

But the reformers are resisted. Because of his unchallengeable prestige, Nehru was able to have incorporated into the codification of Hindu law in the 1950s a number of important changes far ahead of public opinion, giving women, for example, the right to inherit property and divorce. Now that he is dead, legislators are beginning to press for amendments which would deprive women of these rights. Similarly in China the *avant-garde* marriage and divorce laws of the communists met with widespread resistance.[23]

Provincial Japanese politicians are expected to lend their name or presence to marriage-broking among their constituents, and in a Japanese regiment or firm every officer or executive knows the full details of each of his men's family situations and problems.[24] We in the West sometimes smile at the idea of an arranged marriage, but where the family is the only valid unit of society the individual is bound to put his family's needs before his own pleasure. When a family plans the marriage of its eldest son, it thereby seeks access to the assets of another family, and the result of the union may range from the availability of new sources of investment funds for the family enterprise, the working off of an onerous debt, the rationalization of fragmented land holdings, the acquisition of new unpaid labour for the family farm or an *entrée* into more influential political circles. For the son to wreck such careful plans on the grounds that he is not attracted to the girl is regarded as a wicked and almost blasphemous betrayal.

The habit of obeying one's parents persists so strongly that the chief minister of an Indian state resigned in 1968 because his mother disapproved of his activities and ordered him to give them up. 'Being the only son,' he explained to his party colleagues, 'I am not in a position to disobey her. In fact I have never done so in my life.'[25] In most Asian cultures it is the custom to be extremely indulgent and permissive in bringing up young children, so that they feel totally secure in the family's warm embrace. This means that as adults they fear above everything social rejection or the sense of not belonging. So dissent and non-conformity become almost a psychological impossibility.

In this sort of society all relationships are modelled on those within the family, so that political parties tend to be a cluster of patron-client relationships. A local landowner or priest who wishes to enter provincial or national politics offers himself as the patron of the peasants in his district. Like a father, he secures for them government development projects and. tax exemptions, and, like sons, they vote for him at elections and put their disputes to him for arbitration. Asian politics thus tend to be non-ideological, and law merges into conciliation.

In the West the legal system has been devised to meet the needs of autonomous individuals, and the court judges between equal adversaries. In Asia the court is expected not merely to judge but to conciliate, in the manner of a father, and the Western legal system has thus proved unsuitable. 'The British law procedures of the present Indian courts are not serving the purposes of expeditious settlement and preservation of resources as well as the mediatory methods of the traditional Indian legal system. . . . .'[26] Japan has gradually reverted to conciliation after the Meiji reforms which introduced a Western legal code, and in 1948 conciliation was made a compulsory prerequisite to litiga-

tion in the family courts.[27] The whole philosophy of *Satyagraha*,
Gandhi's technique for using non-violence and non-co-operation
in the resolution of conflicts, is rooted in these non-Western
values.

If the family is the pillar of Asian society, nature is the face
of the greater external world in which society exists. In most
Asian philosophies and religions man appears as a part of nature
rather than an antagonist against it. There are no Canutes, no
Fausts, no King Lears in Asian literature; hence the reservations
which many Asians feel about the thrusting Western urge to
gain control of the environment, hence the *frisson* of daring
and of *hubris* which ran through China when the communists
launched the Great Leap Forward with the slogan, 'Demand
Grain from Nature, and Declare War against the Great Earth'.

The idea of keeping the best of the native old and mixing it
with the best of the alien new is psychologically important in
Asia because it helps to fend off the demoralizing suspicion that
Asia is doomed for ever to follow in the footsteps of the West,
never again to seize the initiative to contribute substantially to
world culture. A whisper of this despair is heard in the lines of a
recent article in the *Peking Review* on science in China: 'We
cannot just take the beaten track traversed by other countries
in the development of technology and trail behind them at a
snail's pace. We must break away from conventions and do our
utmost to adopt advanced techniques in order to build our country into a powerful modern socialist state in not too long a historical period'.[28]

When the president of Peking University was seeking fifty
years ago to convince suspicious traditionalist scholars of the
need for China to have modern Western-style universities, he
explained that they would meet not only the demand for learning
about European culture itself but also 'the necessity of making
further discoveries on the basis of European culture': it was not
enough to preserve the essentials of China's national culture,
'it is also necessary to use scientific methods to expound the real
nature of our national essentials'.[29] The Indian, Chinese and
Japanese winners of Nobel prizes in the scientific field are the
evidence that Asia can excel – and will increasingly excel – in all
modern activities. But the anxiety remains that these are activities

in which the West will always be able to claim the original
initiative.*

Hence the drive to find contexts in which Asia can plausibly
be seen at the centre instead of at the fringe of the world. The
Japanese militarists in 1937 urged their school-children and
students to support Japanese ideals, 'not only for the sake of
our nation, but for the sake of the entire human race which is
struggling to find a way out of the deadlock with which individualism is faced. Here lies our great cosmopolitan mission'.[30] A
generation later there are Japanese intellectuals who see their
country as the honourable pioneer of a new kind of institutionally
pacifist 'United-Nations' nation, renouncing military activities.
Gandhi was told by Tolstoy, in a letter, that his *Satyagraha* was
the most important work being done in the whole world, and
that all Christian and other nations would eventually take it up.
This prediction, alas, has failed, but I have heard a senior Indian
planning officer describe India's mixed economy as the central
ideal towards which the capitalist and communist systems were
each approximating, and Jayaprakash Narayan has said: 'I
think we should achieve in our country a synthesis ... between
science and spirituality. There is no other country in the world
which is perhaps more fitted to do this. I am not a chauvinist,
I am not even a nationalist in the ordinary sense of the term ...
but it is a conviction with me. ...'[31] In China (whose very name,
Chungkuo, means 'central state') the Sinocentric world vision
has a long history, and Mao Tse-tung could echo it during the
Cultural Revolution when he said that, 'China is not only
the political centre of world revolution but should become the
military and technical centre.'[32]

Such claims may seem fanciful even to those who advance
them, but there are practical ways in which Asia can assert its
differences, for example by abandoning the Western calendar.
Ceylon rejected Sunday as the official weekly day of rest and
replaced it with the Buddhist *poya* days, which yield only forty-
nine week-ends a year and are thus somewhat inconvenient.

---

*This presumes a very short view of history, of course, since there were
important Chinese, Japanese and Indian scientific and mathematical
innovators in the seventeenth, eighteenth and earlier centuries: see, e.g.,
Needham, *Science and Civilisation in China*.

The need to burst out of what Richard Hensman, the Ceylonese Christian, calls the West's 'asphyxiation' of Asia[33] has led China, Burma and one or two other countries to refuse to allow the philanthropic Western organizations – the British Council, the Ford Foundation – to operate in their territory, and even to reject foreign aid.

The search is for something distinctive to give to modern world culture, not merely good imitations of Western ideas or forms. Munakata Shikō and Affandi, Zao Wouki and Jamini Roy, are hailed in Western salons as superbly imaginative practitioners of modern painting, but no twentieth-century Asian artist has yet founded a new world school. Asian painters ask themselves whether their goal is merely 'a share in a luxury trade which, considering the self-destructive mood of European art, may well be near its end'?[34] Many young Indians felt flattered when George Harrison began to use the *sitar* in Beatle songs in 1965, and went to Bombay in the following year to learn more about this traditional Indian instrument. John Mayer, the Indian composer, has created a following for his particular blending of traditional and modern styles in what he calls 'Indo-Jazz',[35] and Takamitsu, the Japanese composer, now exerts much influence in Western musical circles. Sakamoto Kyu, the Japanese pop idol of the early 1960s, actually joined the Western hit parades with his song, which in the West was given the title *Sukiyaki*.

All this helps to reassure Asians that they are not destined to lose their identity in the world's race towards Westernization – or towards modernization, as scholars now prefer to call it in deference to the fact that the diffusion of the modern world culture which originated in the West 'has reached a point, and the culture has achieved such a dynamics of its own, that the culture can no longer be claimed entirely by the West'.[36] The secrets of traditional Chinese acupuncture and moxibustion, as well as of *ayurveda*, the Indian homoeopathic medical system, are providing Western doctors with some surprises, and the ancient Asian pharmacopoeia is by no means outdated or overtaken by the Western. 'The Chinese traditional medicine', declared one specialist, 'can cure a number of diseases that Western medicine is unable to deal with efficiently'.[37]

In the political field the Maoist experiment of 'ruralizing' industry – of industrializing without creating the attendant horrors of uncontrolled urbanization – is perhaps likely to meet the fate of the Gandhian experiment with non-violence, since both require an unusual degree of unselfishness, public spiritedness and altruism. But each will be honoured as honest contributions to the effort to save mankind from the atomization of modern life, and each has inspired a select following throughout the world, including the West, of people through whom they continue to exert an influence. The recent cult of Mao among Western student rebels is partly fad, partly a demonstration against their respective establishments, but partly also a reflection of the relatively longer survival of idealism in China's communist message – by comparison, at least, with the European Marxists either side of the iron curtain.

It is no accident that the modern Asian art which exudes the freshest, strongest non-Western flavour springs from the country which insulated itself the longest from early Western influence and then undertook its own modernization without the unwanted intrusion of Westerners. The artistic genius of Japan has produced world masters in our day in two notable fields, architecture and the cinema. The buildings of Tange Kenzo's National Gymnasium in Tokyo and Yamasaki Minoru's Northwestern National Life Building in Minneapolis are certainly among the most beautiful and inventive of twentieth-century structures, while the films of Kurosawa, Mizoguchi and Ozu (directors of *Rashomon*, *Ugetsu Monogatari* and *Tokyo Story* respectively) have delighted the world. Of Kurosawa's ability to realize an image of man as first and foremost an animal, one European film critic has commented: 'He re-creates an old conception of the hero, pre-Roman, and possibly to be found only in Asian art....'[38] It is by being true to the best in their own tradition that Asian artists will rediscover their genius.

It is easy to list the few 'successes' of our contemporary Asian culture, impossible to list all the cases where Westerners still predominate. The position was stated most brutally by V. S. Naipaul, the West Indian writer who observes India from the dispassionate distance of two generations. Professing to see a widening gap between India and the West, not only in material development but also in sensibility and wisdom, he concludes: 'The West is alert, many featured and ever-changing; its writers and philosophers respond to complexity by continually seeking to alter and extend sensibility; no art or attitude stands still. India possesses only its unexamined past and its pathetic spirituality ... India is simple, the West grows wiser'.[39] Some analysts of the philistinism, violence and insensibility of the Chinese Cultural Revolution would include China in such strictures.

The sense of forever trailing behind the West's lead is heightened by such statements as that of Thorkil Kristensen, secretary-general of the Organisation for Economic Co-operation and Development (OECD), who, in the course of a discussion of the economic problems of the developing countries of Asia and elsewhere, defended the Western governments' spending more on such domestic activities as public health and urban renewal while giving comparatively little in foreign aid, in the following terms:

It should not be forgotten that in all the fields mentioned ... it is the mission of the developed countries to be the pioneers of mankind. ... What is done in the developed countries in order to get the strong forces and the complexities of modern society under control is therefore of great importance for the presently less developed regions, even if in the short run it means that development aid must compete with many requirements of various kinds within the rich societies.*[40]

Some Western scholars feel that Japan, the 'new Far West,' is the test case of the modernization-Westernization dilemma, and that the signs already reveal an eventual 'landslide into Westernization'.[41] But many Japanese oppose this view. 'It is not the way of the world', said Yanaihara Tadao, the educationalist, 'that Japanese society should become exactly like that of the West. World culture is to be enriched by the peculiar characteristics and differences of the cultures of various peoples in the world'.[42] The consensus among Asian intellectuals is, most probably, that enough of the traditions will be retained to prevent a collective loss of cultural identity (also that Western societies may, because of the strength of their own peculiar traditions, begin to depart more obviously from the shifting world norm

*It was statements of this kind by Soviet leaders that helped confirm the Chinese in their rejection of Russian patronage.

and thus have less claim to possess the criteria by which other societies should be judged).

But the sense of regret that so few Asian strands have so far been woven into the modern world tapestry remains. Tanizaki Junichiro, the Japanese novelist and author of *Some Prefer Nettles* and *The Makioka Sisters*, once mused on the simple fountain-pen, the Western invention from which writers everywhere profit today: if it

had been invented by the ancient Chinese or Japanese, it would surely have had a tufted end like our writing brush. The ink would not have been this bluish colour, but rather black, something like the India ink, and it would have been made to seep down from the handle into the brush. And since we would then have found it inconvenient to write on Western paper, something near Japanese paper – even under mass production, if you will – would have been most in demand. Foreign ink and pen would not be as popular as they are: the talk of discarding our system of writing for Roman letters would be less noisy.... But more than that: our thought and our literature might not be imitating the West as they are, they might have pushed forward into new regions quite on their own. An insignificant little piece of writing equipment, when one thinks of it, has had a vast, almost boundless, influence on our culture.... (Having) come this far we cannot turn back.... (But) ... It is not impossible that we would one day have discovered our own substitute for the trolley, the radio, the airplane of today. They would have been no borrowed gadgets, they would have been the tools of our own culture suited to us....[43]

Chapter Five

The Language Battle

WHEN the prime minister of Singapore, Lee Kuan Yew, first arrived as an undergraduate at Cambridge, to be met with the usual question, 'Where are you from?' he used sometimes to reply: 'I come from a place where 95 per cent of the people don't speak English, but where all the traffic signs say "Halt".' The distant observer might imagine that this kind of language problem would have found its resolution with the end of colonial rule and the emergence of indigenous governments able to address the people in their own language. In fact, however, Asia's language problems have intensified with independence.

The brave words of two Singhalese writers, 'We belong to one nation. . . . Differences in language do not prevent us from being a nation',[1] typify the nationalist urge to overcome the divisiveness of multi-lingualism. Yet a Ceylonese citizen was killed in 1966 when a government decision on the relative official status of Singhalese and Tamil caused rioting in the streets. In the late summer of 1967 over a hundred Indians died in riots at Ranchi over the question of the use of Hindi versus Urdu – more than lost their lives in the local famine that year. Five southern Indians, including a postman, a headmaster and a farmer, burned themselves to death in 1965 in protest against the threatened abandonment of English as an official language in India, and many more were killed in rioting in Madras. When at the end of 1967, under this kind of pressure from the south, the Government introduced in Parliament an amendment to the Language Bill perpetuating English as an associate official language, the north Indian advocates of Hindi as the sole official language rioted in turn for ten days: English signs were ripped down, an American woman had her hair pulled in a New Delhi street, and several opposition state ministers were arrested. When the news reached Madras, southerners set fire to trains and physically threatened north Indians in the streets. Language is literally a burning issue in parts of Asia today.

Despite the transfer of power from European hands, the languages of colonialism do live on. When the nations of Asia and Africa met in 1955 at Bandung to celebrate their freedom and proclaim their common outlook on world problems, twenty-five prime ministers spoke in English, and three in French, throughout the conference. Only one spoke in his own tongue, and that was Chou En-lai, who was criticized for being unco-operative and slowing down the proceedings. Almost every important communication between any two governments in Asia today is in English (the main exceptions being Vietnam, Laos and Cambodia, which use French).

Naturally the newly independent governments endeavoured to reduce the use of European languages and promote the local vernacular tongue in its place. The Burmese Government, for example, ruled that Burmese should become the medium of instruction at the University of Rangoon, but within months the order had to be rescinded because there were not enough teachers able to use Burmese at the intellectual level of university lectures, and not enough Burmese-language textbooks (or Burmese translations of foreign textbooks). In 1966, of the twenty thousand books published in India almost two decades after independence, half were in English and only 15 per cent were in Hindi, the language which the Government is grooming eventually to succeed English as the country's *lingua franca*. About a quarter of the newspapers that circulate in India are in English, and it is usually estimated that English is still spoken by the ten million or so upper crust – professional men, politicians, administrators, businessmen, and many intellectuals and teachers.

Readers' Digest surveyed several Asian cities in 1966 and found that two-thirds of the population in Manila and Singapore spoke or read English: the proportion was 40 per cent in Bangkok, 14 per cent in Taipei, 10 per cent in Tokyo and 9 per cent in Seoul.[2] A Soviet scientist temporarily assigned to Peking and having to communicate all too often through interpreters, said of one encounter with a Chinese colleague, 'to my great joy, it turned out that he spoke English'.³ There are weighty reasons for the resilience of English in post-colonial Asia. The Indian Secondary Education Commission reported in 1953 after investigating the language question:

As a result of historical causes, English has come to be the one language that is widely known among the educated classes of the country. It was stressed by some of our witnesses that much of the national unity in political and other spheres of activity has been brought about through the study of English language and literature and modern Western thought by all educated Indians. They also stated that the present position of India in the international sphere is partly due to the command that educated Indians have acquired over English. Many eminent educationists and scientists have, therefore, expressed the opinion that under no circumstances should we sacrifice the many advantages that we have gained by the study of English. They hold that in matters pertaining to education, sentiment should not be the ruling factor and that what was most urgently needed was that our youth acquire knowledge from all sources and contribute their share to its expansion and development . . .⁴

But the quality of the English being taught, even in India and the Philippines where it has a long history and a firm hold, is declining. A Philippine journalist comments:

Because of their lack of command of English the masses have got used to only half-understanding what is said to them in English. They appreciate the sound without knowing the sense ... Thus we find in our society a deplorable lack of serious thinking among great sections of the population. We half understand books and periodicals written in English. We find it an ordeal to communicate with each other through a foreign medium and yet we have so neglected our native language that we find ourselves at a loss in expressing ourselves in this language.⁵

The same problem attends the survival of Dutch in Indonesia, Spanish in the Philippines, and French in Vietnam, Cambodia and Laos.

But these foreign languages cannot be a permanent substitute for the vernacular. UNESCO stands for the view that: 'It is axiomatic that the best medium for teaching a child is his mother tongue. Psychologically, it is the system of meaningful signs that in his mind works automatically for the expression and understanding. Sociologically, it is a means of identification among the members of the community to which he belongs. Educationally, he learns more quickly through it than through an unfamiliar language medium.'[6] The need to use and support the mother tongue was recognized in another Indian report, this time by the Committee on Emotional Integration, which in 1962 concluded that:

Having Indian languages as media of instruction from the lowest to the highest stage of education is a matter of profound importance for national integration. There is urgent need to remove the gulf that has existed between the masses of the people and the intellectual elite. For centuries Indian intellectuals had to work in some common language, first Sanskrit, then Persian and recently, English. The gulf between them and the masses of the people has, therefore, persisted. Only the adoption of regional languages right up to the university level will help to remove the gulf. We wish to endorse and emphasise what the National Integration Council said at its recent meeting (July 1962): 'India's university men will be unable to make their maximum contribution to the advancement of learning generally and science and technology in particular, unless there is a continuous means of communication in the shape of the regional languages between its masses, its artisans, technicians and its university men. The development of talent in the country will also, in the view of the Council, be retarded unless regional languages are employed as media of instruction at the university stage.'[7]

The difficulty is that so many of Asia's mother tongues are inadequate in vocabulary or in their degree of sophistication for use in the higher realms of learning, especially in science and technology. A senior official of the *Sahitya Akademi*, India's National Academy of Letters confesses:

To be frank, no Indian language is adequate for the teaching of modern sciences beyond the matriculation or intermediate examination level, as the majority of Vice-Chancellors of Indian universities confess. Whether law could be administered, or medicine dispensed, are also questions which are open to two opinions.[8]

In many Asian languages it is a matter of controversy or un- certainty how best to express such ideas as 'nuclear physics', or 'logical positivism', or 'proportional representation'. Those who need to use such terms are precisely those already educated in English or some other foreign language. When I was teaching at a Bengali university I spoke English, and those of my colleagues who tried to do justice to the syllabus using exclusively Bengali found that the strain of unfamiliarity and the verbal ambiguities, added to the necessity of incorporating large numbers of English words into the Bengali sentences because there was no local equivalent, made it almost impossible. Most creative writers in Asia today are minting not merely sonorous phrases but completely new words, and until a corpus of modern literature has been built up and a literary consensus reached on the most important new expressions, lecturers and drafters of memoranda will continue to experience difficulty.

There are academies at work in New Delhi, Djakarta, Kuala Lumpur, Karachi and many other cities investigating and recommending possible translations of modern and foreign expressions. If this sounds a little forced, it might be recalled that Finnish was similarly developed, over a mere century, out of local dialects with little written literature, to meet the demands of a new and vulnerable nation. Even if the vernacular is ready for its newly expanded use in universities and laboratories, there is the practical problem of supplying the vast numbers of trained teachers and textbooks that are required. After two decades of independence, less than half of India's legal code is translated into Hindi, and the facilities of the official translation services are strained by keeping up with their existing work, without adding all the new textbooks which ought ideally to be entering the schools every year.

All these problems become compounded where there is more than one vernacular language, as is the case in India, Pakistan, China, Ceylon, Burma, Malaysia, Indonesia and the Philippines. The West is familiar with the tensions which competing languages can produce from the recent history of Belgium and Canada, but these two cases pale into insignificance alongside India's, where the 1961 census listed 1,549 separate languages or dialects, or Indonesia's where there are at least fifty.

Most of the hundreds of Indian languages, let it be hastily clarified, are tribal tongues spoken by very tiny communities. But at least sixty of them are each spoken by more than ten thousand people. Roughly 45 per cent of the population of

India speaks either Hindi or such allied and more or less mutually intelligible languages as Urdu or Punjabi. But the next most important language, Telugu (the tongue of the state of Andhra), claims only 10 per cent of the Indian population, and it is closely followed by Bengali, Marathi and Tamil (the languages of Bengal, Maharashtra and Madras respectively) with 8 per cent or 9 per cent each. Sanskrit, the ancient language from which many of the present ones derive, is still the vehicle of the priests, and English remains the principal language for inter-state communication. It would be possible to draw a parallel between this situation and that of Europe, but only, as Professor Morris-Jones has observed, if it were to be imagined that the political unity of the Roman Empire survived, that the *lingua franca* of the administrative *élite* was, shall we say, Chinese, and that the priestly culture used ancient Greek.[9]

The constitution adopted by India at her independence laid it down that Hindi would replace English as the official language of the country in 1965. But the change would have meant that the Hindi speakers of north India would enjoy an innate and unfair advantage over other Indians when competing for government and private employment in offices where the official national language is used. Conversely the south Indians who had invested so much of their lives acquiring English would now be handicapped by having to learn Hindi. Fifteen years was not long enough to allow a peaceful transition by southern educational interests to the new second language. In the end the government compromised: English was retained indefinitely as an associate national language, and civil service examinations were to be held in all of the country's sixteen principal languages. The *Jan Sangh*, representing the conservative Hindus of north India, accepted this but agreed to give English only another ten years. The settlement cannot be a final one: the Madras Assembly has resolved to abolish the teaching of Hindi and refused to issue a Hindi stamp at the post offices. The north is impatient to give Hindi its due, but its pressure on the south makes it less and less easy for southerners to accept the change gracefully.[10]

Pakistan had similar problems, on a smaller scale. It took rioting and shooting for the Bengalis of East Pakistan to get their language accepted as an official equal to Urdu, the *lingua franca* of the dominant West wing, and even within the West wing there is tension between the speakers of Sindhi, Punjabi and the north-western tribal tongues, spurred on by the Bengali example.

China is relatively lucky in that all Chinese languages and dialects (those spoken by 95 per cent of the population) are written in the same ideographic form and that the main language – known to Westerners as Mandarin, to Chinese as *Kuoyu* – is more or less understood from north to south. Even so, Chairman Mao has broadcast to his people only once (and that for merely a few seconds) because his heavy regional Hunanese accent would be barely intelligible to the majority of listeners and would detract from his image as a national father-figure. Even the suave Chou En-lai is understood with difficulty by those unfamiliar with the speech of his native Chekiang province. There is a quite different linguistic patchwork in the southern coastal areas between Shanghai and Canton, where the languages are as different from Mandarin as Portuguese and Rumanian are from French (and it was from these coastal areas that most of the overseas Chinese originally hailed: hence their linguistic confusion). The plan is to steadily popularize the Mandarin speech of the Peking dialect, but no rigid timetable has been set for this.

In Indonesia the dilemma of having the national language identified with one region, whose dominance of the country as a whole is resented, has been avoided. Javanese is the most widely spoken vernacular, but it so happens that Malay, the language of the coastal peoples in the areas where the successive waves of foreign conquerors (Indians, Arabs, Europeans) tended first to break, became for that reason the *lingua franca* of the whole archipelago. The nationalists chose it as their national language and their symbol of freedom as early as 1928, naming it *Indonesia Bahasa*. It has by now had time to mellow, to grow and proliferate as a language and is perfectly viable in spite of its lowly status (it was not the language of scholarship until very recently).[11] Inevitably, because of the speed with which it has been developed, it does contain some elements of artificiality, and there are complaints now that it is becoming somewhat Javanized[12] – but that is probably inevitable, given the numerical preponderance of the Javanese. But when former President

Sukarno boasted: 'Can I not justifiably express pride in the fact that whereas India is now battling over a unitary language and China has not yet a unitary language, my Marhaens,* spread over 10,000 islands, all speak *Bahasa Indonesia!*' there was substance to his claim.[13]

The choice of Malay also means that Indonesia shares with Malaysia the same official language, and the two countries co-operate in standardizing their spelling and their new words. In Malaysia itself the tussle is a triangular one between English, Malay and Chinese. Following the Indian pattern, Malay was designated to succeed English within ten years of independence, but in practice the effect of this was miminized. A Malay official recently made a public protest against a tri-lingual notice displayed outside the Ministry of Finance (headed by a Chinese): the Government defended it as practical, since some citizens wanting access to that department were literate in only one of these three languages. Out of deference to the Malays' political power, Malay is now learned as the first or second 'foreign' language by almost all Malaysia's Chinese and Indian schoolchildren. But, as a Malay politician has complained, Malay lacks 'economic value' and remains relatively neglected. Those keen to get ahead in government, in business or the professions, still tend to regard English as the most important proficiency to have.[14]

The main solutions to these various Asian language problems may thus be summarized as that of the 'two-language' formula and that of the 'three-language' formula. The Cantonese child learns Cantonese at home and Mandarin at school, the Balinese boy speaks Balinese at home and learns *Bahasa Indonesia* at school. But for many millions of schoolchildren in India and Pakistan, three languages have to be mastered: the mother tongue first, then Hindi or Urdu (if different from the mother tongue), and finally English. 'In the present-day world,' Prime Minister Mrs Indira Gandhi recently exhorted, 'we cannot afford to live in isolation. Therefore there should be three languages – regional, national and international'.[15] But this is a grave burden on a strained and under-financed educational system as well as on children already exposed to a tempo of social and economic change unprecedented in history.

*A common Indonesian name, the equivalent of Smith or Jones.

In some extreme cases more than three languages have to be learned: the Pakistani Sindhi, for example the present President Z. A. Bhutto, would have acquired Sindhi at his home, Urdu and English at school. If he came from a devout family he would also have learnt Arabic in order to read the Koran, and if he were as patriotic as the Government at one time apparently expected him to be, he would have learnt Bengali (as the equal national language alongside Urdu) into the bargain – a total of five distinct languages employing three totally different scripts. A survey of Malaysian university students a few years ago showed that most of the Chinese students spoke at least four languages – English, Malay, Hokkien and Cantonese (again, for those who wanted to write, two or three entirely divergent scripts).[16] The British student who can go all round the world and into every discipline without ever needing to be fluent in another language, does not appreciate his good fortune.

So far the language problem has been discussed as one of speech, but the question of script can also cause trouble. The ideograms of China and Japan are the product of a leisured society, and they mean that a child has to put twice as much time and energy as a European into acquiring the mechanical means of expressing all his thoughts on paper. There is the world of difference between 40,000 separate characters* and 26 separate letters of the alphabet. Some scholars in both Japan and China therefore urge the adoption of the roman alphabet (as Vietnam, which had also inherited the ideograms, has gradually done over the past two or three hundred years). But the snag in China's case is that Chinese spelt in roman letters would rely more on the sound than the picture to convey the meaning – and so would remain largely meaningless to all but the speakers of the Pekinese Mandarin dialect. To romanize would speed modernization but threaten national unity – that is the dilemma of the Chinese leaders.[17]

---

*No one learns all 40,000 characters: a scholar remembers about 10,000, an undergraduate about 6,000, the average reader of a newspaper only 3,500 or so. The ideograms have recently been simplified in both China and Japan. Korea has invented its own script. This whole question has presented a fascinating challenge to the designers and inventors of typewriters for use in China and Japan.

Even in India it has been argued that the best thing would be to 'go latin', so that Indians can more easily learn to write and read in the other regional languages.[18] But Vietnam, Malaysia and Indonesia are the only South and East Asian countries whose official language is officially written in roman letters.

Chapter Six

Racial Pride and Prejudice

'WHAT they are trying to do,' Prince Sihanouk of Cambodia recently said of the Anglo-Saxon powers, 'is to weaken the Yellow race so as to prevent it from harming them, so that they can implant themselves into the skin and flesh of the Yellow race and the water and land of Asia, which belongs to the Yellow race.'¹ During the past century of the Western ascendancy, most articulate Asians have become concious of not belonging to the 'white' race,* although this division of mankind along the colour spectrum becomes more and more unreal the longer one considers it. The Chinese communists may have made a very important contribution to world understanding by portraying, in their numerous propaganda posters extolling the solidarity of the working people of the whole world, the Caucasians as either pink or puce – so that there is no race to be labelled as white.

So compelling has the Western ascendancy become, however, that a leading Indian writer professes to believe that his country-men are 'Europeans enslaved by a tropical country', whose only future is to 'recover at least our old European spirit'. He calls on Indians to 'cease to think of yourselves as Orientals, and never admit that there is any mental bond between you and true Asiatics'.² The last emperor of China recorded how frightened he was as a boy of his English tutor, Mr Reginald Johnston, because of 'the clarity of his blue eyes and the yellowish grey of his hair'.³ The consciousness of inferiority, and its identification with racial differences, find expression in Asia, as within the multi-racial societies of the West itself, in sexual jealousy.†

*There is one indigenous group of Caucasians in Asia, namely the *Ainu* of Japan, who are dying out but still present a fascinating challenge to the anthropologist.

†Conversely to the usual myth (that the darker-skinned are better sexually endowed), the Chinese use for their European visitors, in addition to such predictable epithets as 'big-nose', 'hairy one' and 'red-face', the more unexpected one of 'big-penis'.

The late President Sukarno, one of Asia's most famous lovers, confessed:

> I was very much attracted to Dutch girls. I wanted desperately to make love to them. It was the only way I knew to exert some form of superiority over the white race and make it bend to my will. That's always the aim, isn't it? For a brown-skinned man to overpower the white man. It's some sort of goal to attain. Overpowering a white girl and making her want me became a matter of pride. A handsome boy always has steady girl friends. I had many. They even adored my irregular teeth. But I admit I deliberately went after the white ones.[4]

Asians are as capable of colour prejudice as Europeans,[5] and share the same idealized preference for paler pigmentation. The advertisements for marriage partners which fill the columns of Indian newspapers invariably indicate a predilection for lighter skins, and the Japanese distaste for Negroes is so strong that the unfortunate illegitimate children of American Negro soldiers and their Japanese girl-friends are segregated, usually in remote rural districts, so that they do not have to run the gauntlet of Japanese society.[6] A Japanese schoolteacher, who had encouraged his class to seek pen-pals in an American school, caused a stir in Tokyo's foreign community, though not among the Japanese themselves, by explaining to his opposite number across the Pacific Ocean that his boys wanted to correspond only with white children, not with black.[7] There have been cases of Negro officers in the American army in Vietnam seeking transfer because of the open discrimination practised against them by Vietnamese officers.[8]

East Asia's contact with black Africans is very recent, although the Chinese traded in East Africa (and received a giraffe as a gift to the emperor by an Embassy from the Kenya coast) as early as the fifteenth century. K'ang Yu-wei, the celebrated Chinese reformer, elaborated at the end of the nineteenth century a racial philosophy which makes strange reading today. The Caucasian and the Mongoloid peoples, whom he called, rather charmingly, 'silver and gold', would eventually merge into one race,* which would rule the world as the brown and black people

*The Japanese nineteenth-century reformer, Inoue, also urged miscegenation between Japanese and Europeans.

became annihilated through famine, disease and warfare. 'The black people, however, are a really difficult problem, owing to their extreme ugliness and stupidity. Promoting mixed marriages with them is next to impossible. The only solution is to remove them wholesale to Canada, Sweden and Norway, to occupy the empty lands there. This, plus improving their food and clothing, will result in their becoming brown after two to three hundred years. . . . Thus in 700 to 1,000 years, the blackest African negroes will be transformed into white persons.'[9]

Even today Ghanaian students in both India and China complain of their hosts' racial prejudice,[10] and the Afro-Asian honeymoon, which began with the Bandung Conference in 1955 has failed to mature into a successful relationship. An Indian journalist who covered many of the Afro-Asian conferences concluded that, 'The Asians found the Africans jejune and over-emotional, and the Africans found the Asians hide-bound and patronising.'[11] Even at UNCTAD (the United Nations Conference on Trade and Development) the Africans and the Asians find it increasingly hard to make common cause against what the Cambodian Government once called 'the arrogance of the over-developed white countries'.[12]

There are noble exceptions to these prejudices, which are also on occasion overcome by the forces of ideology. The Chinese communists have been reported as lobbying African delegations to support their anti-Soviet stand at Afro-Asian meetings in the terms, 'We blacks. . . .'[13] Technicians from both China and Taiwan have made a good impression in many African countries, and the Chinese communists are particularly respected for accepting local rather than inflated foreign living standards. In an international milieu an Indian or a Pakistani finds it easy to identify himself on the black side of the fence: Tariq Ali speaks in London on Black Power platforms, and Dom Moraes gave a BBC television programme under the title, 'One Black Englishman'.*

One community which finds itself caught in the middle of all this is the Eurasian, in whom European and Asian blood is

*But Chinese in Hongkong did not conceal their satisfaction when the South African Government accorded 'white' status to visiting Chinese merchants a few years ago.

mixed. There are distinguished and successful individuals of mixed parentage, including Prince Chula of Thailand (who has a Russian mother) and Han Suyin (who has a Belgian mother). But there are also substantial communities of many thousands, such as the so-called 'Indos' of Indonesia and the Anglo-Indians of India, who have become, over several generations, almost a new caste, jealous of their social superiority over the fully indigenous but constantly rebuffed by the fully alien.[14] One of them thus describes the problem of being an Eurasian in India:

I asked one of my schoolteachers what 'Eurasian' meant but she blushed deeply and passed me on to the Headmaster who said I would understand when I was older but that I must always remember that Jesus loved me. He then showed me a picture on his wall of the Founder of Christianity welcoming a great concourse of persons who pressed upon Him from every side each dressed in pointedly national costumes. I examined this attentively hoping to find a Eurasian who (as I knew from my reading) would be identifiable by his dirty ducks and battered topee. No figure answered to this description. This interview left me with the impression that Eurasians were such abandoned people that they found no place even in universal charity.[15]

Now that independence has come, these people have undergone further humiliations: some of them settled in Holland or Britain, but most could not afford to do this. Their leaders are represented in both the Indian and Indonesian parliament, and the Anglo-Indians' stock went up in 1965 because of their courage and military exploits in the war against Pakistan.

Relations between the races indigenous to Asia are complicated by the very different attitudes taken toward race. For the Chinese and Koreans the *jus sanguinis* is traditionally respected, so that all the offspring of the race, wherever they are born or reside, and for however many generations their line has been in exile, are legally citizens of the state and entitled to participate in its elections. Since there are more than fifteen million Chinese permanently resident abroad, and many of these have now acquired foreign citizenship,[16] this is becoming more and more a formality, an expression of sentiment. But the welfare of the overseas Chinese, especially those in South-East Asia, is regarded as a serious responsibility by the Peking Government – and by its Kuomintang rival in Taipei. In the last few years Chinese citizens have been killed in cold blood (some even disembowelled) in Indonesia, a Chinese businessman has been executed for black-marketeering in Saigon, Chinese shops have been wrecked in Rangoon and traders have been forced to remove their Chinese signs in Manila. The overseas Chinese community, which is hated and envied for its enterprise and money-making skills, and which other Asians have compared with the Jews, naturally seeks the help of the Chinese Government whenever its interests are attacked.

The Peking Government has officially advised these overseas 'kith and kin' to assimilate into the societies where they have lived (in some cases for many generations), to adopt local customs and even the local religion, and to take up local citizenship with all that this implies. Most of them have already struck out on this path, and their children are tending more often than not to attend schools where the local language is the medium of instruction, so that their cultural link with China is vastly weakened.[17] But there is still a minority of overseas Chinese who, true to the literal meaning of the name which they give themselves (*Hua-chiao*, or 'Sojourning Chinese'), reject assimilation, and it is they who cause the political difficulties.[18] In Thailand, where assimilation has perhaps gone furthest, almost everyone in public life, from the king downwards, acknowledges at least one Chinese ancestor, though he may go back several generations. Indeed it has been argued that the Thai Chinese possess a double identity – as Chinese, but also as 'South-East Asians' – which could become a pattern for the whole area.[19] The overseas Chinese are already as distinct from the Chinese in China as the Australians and Americans are from Britain,[20] and they could in the long run become, as a highly cosmopolitan and communication-minded group, a powerful force for the infant sense of unity in South-East Asia.

There are also large numbers of overseas Indians, in Africa, America and Britain as well as in Japan and South-East Asia, who have become in some instances the objects of envy and resentment.[21] But the sense of belonging to the Indian state, as distinct from the Indian cultural tradition, does not survive for very long on foreign soil, and the Indian Government is not swayed by the blood tie. Overseas Indians are encouraged even more firmly than overseas Chinese to assimilate, and the government has refused to accept the responsibility of automatically taking back into Indian life any Indian rejected by his host country, whether it be Singapore coping with the rundown of the British military base or Kenya seeking to Africanize its commerce. (It is almost inconceivable that any Chinese Government would ever renounce such responsibility for the overseas Chinese). 'Indian citizenship', the Indian High Commissioner in Singapore told Singaporean Indians who wanted to abandon their local citizenship and return to India, 'is not a commodity that can be bartered or cast off like a wornout coat and be pulled out of moth-balls for the convenience of the individual'.[22]

But repatriation is not a solution to the problem; it is at best a palliative for a very small part of it. There are two examples of large-scale attempts to repatriate, from Indonesia and Ceylon. After China and Indonesia had signed a treaty in 1959 governing the status of the overseas Chinese in Indonesia, several thousand of them voluntarily returned to China on special ships. But repatriations reached only 160,000, a mere 5 per cent of the total, in the seven years that followed the treaty. A further 55,000 were reported to have left Indonesia for Singapore, Thailand, Hongkong, Taiwan and other destinations by the end of 1967.[23] In Ceylon the citizenship of almost a million Tamils, whose ancestors came from South India a century and a half ago to work the European plantations, is in dispute. The governments of India and Ceylon agreed in 1964 that more than half of them could be repatriated to India, and the arrangements for this came into effect in 1967. But the actual mechanics of selecting which people should go, of reassuring those remaining that they would not suffer new discrimination, and of supplying the foreign exchange for the repatriates to take their savings back with them has proved almost insuperable.[24] By the end of 1968, when Enoch Powell was citing the Indo-Ceylonese agreement as a precedent for Britain to use in repatriating immigrants from India and Pakistan, only six thousand Indians had actually left Ceylon.[25]

There are other racial minorities apart from the Indians and Chinese. Indonesia has a community of 200,000 Arabs,[26] Thailand has about 75,000 Vietnamese refugees living in the north[27] and perhaps ten times as many Malays in its southern provinces. There are Cambodians in Vietnam, Koreans in China and Japan,

Mongolians in China and the Soviet Union. All of these minorities get into trouble of some kind when relations between their host country and motherland are strained, and they are often suspected of potential sabotage, of being a 'fifth column'. There is even one country, Malaysia, which could be said to be entirely composed of racial minorities, since the Malays themselves account for less than half of the population: the Chinese make up 40 per cent and there is a substantial Tamil population as well (for the same reason as in Ceylon). The Malays were there first, but in very small numbers, and their present level of population has been made possible by the large-scale immigration of Malays from Sumatra before it became part of independent Indonesia. The national unity of Malaya is thus first and foremost a problem in racial tolerance.[28] The first prime minister, Tunku Abdul Rahman, is himself of mixed blood (his father was a Malay Prince, his mother a Shan Princess from northern Thailand), is dedicated to racial harmony and has adopted Chinese children into his family. But the political awakening of the Malay population will make it increasingly difficult to maintain this harmony, as the post-election riots in Kuala Lumpur in May of 1969 suggested.

China herself embraces some forty million citizens who are not of the Han race, and some of them have a tradition of resisting Chinese rule. The Uighurs of Sinkiang and the million or so Mongols of China's Inner Mongolian Autonomous Region provide two of the most interesting examples of this, but the case which has appealed most to the Western imagination is Tibet. The Tibetans, though themselves divided into a number of quarrelsome tribes, are racially and culturally distinct. By tradition, the Dalai Lama is Tibet's god, king and chief priest all at once, but no Dalai Lama of modern times has been able unequivocally to establish international acceptance of his country's sovereign independent status. Tibet was regarded in the eighteenth and nineteenth centuries as within the Chinese sphere of influence, and this was explicitly recognized by the British Government of India in the Simla Convention in 1914. But the Chinese Government was too weak to maintain its forces in Tibet during the period 1913–50, and there was some indignation when the communist regime sent its army into Tibet in 1950. The Dalai

Lama tried to co-operate with the Chinese, but the traditional racial and cultural animosities combined with new class tension (the Chinese favouring the emancipation of the serfs and abolition of the monks' feudal privileges) to plunge Tibet into rebellion in 1959. The International Commission of Jurists has published a report by an Indian lawyer which admits a *prima facie* case of genocide on the part of the Chinese against the Tibetans. The evidence for this is unsatisfactory, and it is unlikely that Peking intends systematically to reduce or destroy its minority nationalities. But its rule is still not fully accepted in Tibet, where its position is in effect a colonialist one.

The extreme example of a majority race harassed by its minorities is Burma, where the Burmans have not only built up pressure against the 500,000 Indians and 300,000 Chinese who between them were controlling the entire economy and retaining most of its profits, but have also fought sustained insurrections by Shan, Karen, Chin and other inhabitants of the interior who resented being handed over to the Burmans by the British. It is these thirty million or more hill peoples in that whorled thrust of mountainous country that juts into South-East Asia from the central Asian plateau, who present the greatest political poser, affecting not only Burma but also India, Pakistan, China, Thailand, Vietnam, Cambodia, and Laos.* The Indian, Chinese and Burmese armies have been fighting rebel Nagas, Khambas, Shans, Mizos, Karens, Chins and others on and off for the past fifteen or twenty years. They live in areas that are difficult of access and beyond the capacity of any of the governments concerned to maintain in permanent civilian administration. The people refuse to identify with any of the states surrounding them. Phizo, the underground leader of the Nagas, has declared, 'We are not Indians and will never become Indians',[29] and although some of the Nagas have accepted arms, training and support from China, they are well aware of the attendant risks and will not exchange one unwanted patron for another.[30]

From time to time there is talk of new independent states being carved out of these troubled tracts. Nagaland has already been

---

*Tribal people, some of them still in the Stone Age, provide political and administrative challenges, comparable to colonialism, in the Philippines, Indonesia and south-central India as well.

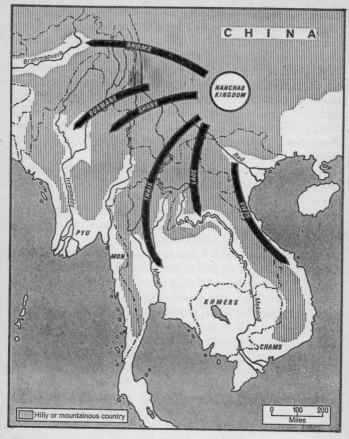

Major tribal movements into South-East Asia in the centuries immediately preceding the European colonial era.

accorded full statehood within the Indian union, the Burmese
have offered some degree of federal autonomy to their minorities, and the Chinese communists officially treat the minority
areas as autonomous – although this is always stage-managed so
that the interests of both Chinese nationalism and communism

are safeguarded.[31] But federal autonomy within the existing
national boundaries may not be enough, since the biggest and
most assertive minorities straddle the present frontiers. There are
Nagas in both India and Burma, Meos in both Laos and China,
Arakanese in Bangla Desh and Burma. These people were, after
all, organized by the Western allies in the Second World War to
harass the Japanese throughout the area, and more recently the
Montagnards of Vietnam have been built up by the French and
Americans (against the real wishes of many in the Saigon
Government of the day) to fight the Vietnamese communists. In
the past two or three years embattled tribal guerrillas have begun
to co-operate with each other across these frontiers. The Shan
rebels fighting the Burmese army retire into Thailand for sanc-
tuary and replenishment, and the Nagas of India cross Burmese
territory to receive training and arms in China. Their activities
are further complicated by the existence in Laos (and formerly
Burma) of several thousand Chinese Kuomintang troops, and by
the centuries-old trade in the opium grown in these hills – a trade
which has created vested interests that constitute a powerful factor in the area's politics and economics.[32]

A recent visitor to these areas reports the 'rapid growth of cultural and political consciousness among the major ethnic groups,
and the gathering momentum of co-operation and co-ordination
among them'.[33] Under the leadership of the Nagas (who now
have more than three thousand university graduates) and the
Shans, this movement will perhaps become the single most taxing
political headache shared by all the countries in the area. Proposals have been reported for an independent Chinland formed by
pieces of Burmese, Pakistani and Indian territory,[34] and Mao
Tse-tung is said to have encouraged in the early 1950s a movement
for the Thai minorities in Laos, North Vietnam and Southern
China to come together and constitute a new sovereign buffer
state on China's border.[35] More recently the idea has been can-
vassed of a 'loose confederation of freely co-operating medium
sized nation-states', or of these peoples' finding their political
destiny in a 'new intermediate form of state'.[36]

If any of the existing countries had to be the anchor for such a
loose grouping, some would say that Thailand qualifies best,
being ethnically closer to many of the peoples and with a better

recent record of peaceful dealings with them. But the growth of communist subversion on Thailand's north-east frontier has forced the Thai Government into a more active role in its previously neglected distant border areas, and the Meos, Yaos, Karens and others in the Thai north are now subjected to the invasion of Thai administrators, Buddhist missionary-monks and American anthropologists in their hundreds.[37] Given the contempt of the urbanized Thai for the hill tribes, it is doubtful if the hill peoples will in the long run be any more enamoured of Thailand than of Burma, India, China or the rest.

There are many more conflicts in Asia which derive much of their intensity from racial differences. The Afghan-supported movement for the creation of a separate state of 'Pakhtoonistan' out of parts of Pakistan's north-western regions is one.[38] The continuing rebellion of some Tibetan tribes against Chinese communist rule is another.[39] As political consciousness spreads there will be further examples brought to the world's newspaper headlines.

Chapter Seven

Ambiguous Borders

THE presumption of the European colonial powers in fixing with premature exactness the frontier system of modern Asia was a prime cause of many of today's disputes. The Europeans found Asia in a relatively fluid condition; its geo-political divisions were far from clear-cut and there were vast tracts of doubtful sovereignty. But the British and the French needed to be as certain of each other's frontiers in Asia as they were in Europe, and the vagueness which had been permissible on the pre-colonial maps of Asia[1] was negotiated almost out of existence during the late nineteenth century.

The ebb and flow of ethnic and cultural waves could not, however, be halted by colonialism. The historical processes which were already in train when the Europeans arrived continued, almost unnoticed, under their stewardship. In South-East Asia the Burmans, Thais, Vietnamese and Laotians were all more or less recent arrivals when the Dutch and Portuguese ships first touched there. Participants in the great southward movement of populations from China through the archipelago into the Indonesian islands, a progress which is the central theme of the region's pre-history, these peoples were themselves colonizers in the course of extending their sway when they had to submit, in varying degree, to European power.[2] The Vietnamese finally conquered the Cham people in what is now South Vietnam less than three centuries ago. The Burmans are still endeavouring to consolidate the authority in theory bequeathed them by Britain over the Chins, Karens, Shans and other nationalities within their borders. Thailand is today pursuing the drive to de-Malayise and Thai-ise the 750,000 or so Malays who live on the Thai side of the Malaysian-Thai border. Many tribal peoples in India are even now absorbed into the Hindu body by the process of 'sanskritization'.[3]

Although a certain amount of colonization and resettlement is carried out by the Chinese and North Vietnamese in their hill-tribe areas, and the minorities in Burma are mostly in active rebellion against the Burmese government, these are cultural rather than physical pressures. The analogy in Britain would, I suppose, be the process by which the Scots and the Welsh are being progressively anglicized. But the physical movement of people goes on within the tribal areas of South-West Asia. There are tribes in northern Thailand which crossed from the Chinese province of Yunnan within living memory.

When the Europeans left Asia after the Second World War, the new nationalist governments had to decide whether or not to accept the frontiers drawn by alien masters. It might theoretically have been possible for them to have co-operated in a continent-wide examination and renegotiation of boundaries, based on their own needs. But the intra-Asian relationships were too fragile for such a task and in practice the forces of nationalism which had fought for independence of European rule took as their next goal, after independence, the preservation of the maximum territorial sovereignty bequeathed them by their own particular metropolitan power. The Indonesian freedom fighters could no more stomach the idea of West Irian's becoming separate from the other constituent parts of the Dutch East Indies than Nehru could accept the loss of Kashmir or the Malaysians the questioning of Sabah's status by the Philippine government. Ho Chi Minh opposed the repartition of Vietnam as vigorously as Nehru fought the idea of Pakistan, and both rested their case implicitly on the imperial precedent: Vietnamese and Indian unity reached their apex under European rule.[4]

It was assumed without a second thought by Indian intellectuals in 1947 that every inch of territory administered or claimed by the king-emperor George VI on 14 August became, bar the two wings of Pakistan, an inalienable and universally accepted part of the independent Indian Republic on 15 August. There was an unmistakable note of jingoism in Nehru's declaration in the *Lok Sabha*, the lower house of India's parliament, that, 'so far as we are concerned the McMahon Line is the frontier – firm by treaty, firm by usage and right, and firm by geography'.[5] That Chinese officials in Peking, heirs to decades of intricate diplomacy with Britain over this frontier, might disagree came as a shock in New Delhi.

During the 1890s British and French colonial administrators fixed the precise alignment of most of South-East Asia's land boundaries, including Thailand's. The Thais were alone in resisting Europe's direct embrace, but the price they paid for their freedom was a progressive diminution of territory in favour of the more powerful and persuasive colonial regimes all around them. When the Europeans began to conquer South-East Asia they found Thailand in the ascendant under a remarkably strong royal family which still sits on the Siamese throne. By contrast the rival South-East Asian powers of Cambodia and Burma were weak and divided, and the Vietnamese also proved incapable of resisting French imperialism. The effect of Anglo-French colonialism was thus to save Cambodia from extinction, to create Laos almost from scratch as a separate state, and to enlarge the area of Burma, Vietnam and Malaya – all at Siamese expense.

Some of the frontiers delineated during all this were artificial in the extreme. The Burma-Laos border along the Mekong River affords an example of what Alastair Lamb calls 'boundary engineering':[6] agreed to by British and French officials in 1896 to suit their own purposes, it has no basis in tradition and might well have become an issue between the nations concerned (including Thailand and China, divided only by this narrow neck of highland where Burma and Laos meet) had any of their central governments got the area under continuous firm control.

For it must be remembered that most of the terrain where the actual or latent border conflicts lurk is either uninhabited, inaccessible, or unadministered. We are not dealing with areas like the Saar or Alsace-Lorraine, where large communities live and have, at any given moment of recent history, been served by a modern administration and participated economically in a nation-wide market. The Aksai Chin region of Ladakh which is so bitterly disputed between China and India is totally without permanent inhabitants, and a bleaker or less hospitable fifteen thousand square miles could scarcely be imagined. India's North East Frontier Agency (NEFA), the other major bone of contention in the Sino-Indian border tussle, is thinly inhabited by tribal peoples who are not historically linked with either side and were part of no modern nation state at all until the cartographers shanghai-ed them into one.

The same could be said of much of the central whorl of the South-East Asian mountain system where the nationally un-affiliated tribes predominate. The Thai Government has only recently begun to interest itself in its furthest frontier regions, and the authorities in Rangoon have only occasional patrolling in most of the Burmese borderlands. When the Sino-Burmese border was demarcated on the ground in 1960 the Burmese personnel had to go in by helicopter and small plane. Even if an army detachment marches through a tribal border region every now and again, this may be the sole contact which its inhabitants have with their 'governments'. Roads, schools, posts, electricity, clinics and the like are still unknown to many a hill-villager in Asia.

In the light of these general remarks some of the particular frontier problems of Asia can now be examined, beginning with the continent's most artificial border – that between India and Pakistan, devised in a hurry to allow the Attlee Government of Britain to get off the imperialist hook in India. When it finally became apparent in 1946 that Jinnah and Nehru would not work together to lead a united India, a Commission was set up under Lord Radcliffe to settle where the division should be drawn between the two separate states of India and Pakistan.

There was no traditional basis for this and the line that emerged inevitably failed to meet all the conditions of a satisfactory frontier. It separated the East Bengali jutefields from the West Bengali jute mills, cut the road and rail links between the two Indian states of West Bengal and Assam, and contained numerous irritating enclaves on either side, all in the interests of dividing the mainly Muslim areas from the mainly Hindu areas with the least possible local dislocation. It contained such minor ambiguities as the Rann of Kutch sector (which almost provoked military conflict in 1965)[7] and, even more important, it left equivocal the status of the so-called princely states which legally could not be directed by the British Government to join either India or Pakistan. In practice most of the maharajahs were cajoled into a sensible accession by the charm of Mountbatten, the last viceroy, and the forcefulness of Vallabhai Patel, Nehru's lieutenant. But the two important states of Hyderabad and

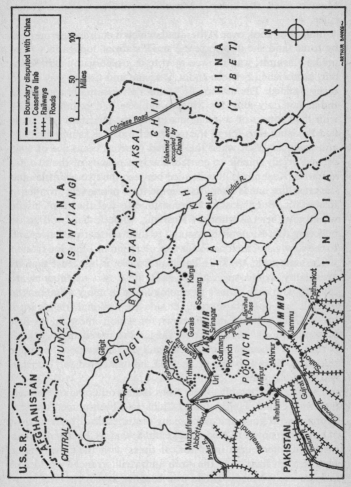

Jammu and Kashmir state, disputed between India, Pakistan and in part China.

Kashmir refused. The former had a Hindu population under a Muslim ruler, the latter a Muslim population under a Hindu ruler.

India soon took over Hyderabad, which it entirely surrounded, by force (and she also took the small state of Junagadh which, unlike Kashmir, was allowed to vote in a plebiscite). But Kashmir, sandwiched between India, Pakistan and China, was not so easily decided. The unpopular Maharajah eventually acceded to India, but only after his Muslim subjects had begun to rebel, with the support of co-religionists from the Pakistani side. India and Pakistan thus found themselves at war in Kashmir in 1947, and again in 1965, when the United Nations cease-fire of 1948 proved briefly unable to contain the frustrations of the two adversaries. Kashmir is now divided between the two countries and the cease-fire line is likely to become their permanent frontier in this sector. But Pakistan will continue to feel that a plebiscite would give her the whole of Kashmir, while Indians will go on believing that Kashmir is essential to their northern defences and to the survival of their nation as a secular, or multi-religious state.[8]

Kashmir aside, the Indo-Pakistan frontier is less tense than its artificiality would suggest. At least these two neighbours are familiar with each other's psychology, and in many instances the officials and politicians on either side are personal friends from pre-1947 days. It was not unknown for senior officers in the first Kashmir war of 1948 to fly over the lines to the enemy's cocktail parties, the 'enemy' being a colleague who had worked by your side until, forced to choose in 1947, he had opted for Pakistan and you for India.

This factor is notably absent from India's other major frontier, that with China. Unlike India, China had been unified under a strong central government for many centuries prior to the arrival of European power in Asia. Unlike India, again, China had had no sustained intercourse in historical times with the other major centres of civilization in the Arab and Mediterranean world and in India itself. Nor did China ever become, save for a brief interlude under the Mongol dynasty, a serious maritime power. For the Chinese emperors, therefore, the frontiers were areas where Chinese civilization ended and the barbarians began. The only problem was the tendency for some of the barbarians, notably the Tibetans, Mongolians and Manchurians, occasionally to invade China. For centuries the Chinese relied on a two-tier defence strategy against this threat: a buffer belt across central Asia in which China exercised some influence short of direct administrative responsibility (the tributary system) and was therefore able to get early warning of invasion plans and a chance to thwart them before they started, and the Great Wall to stop the hordes once they had marched.

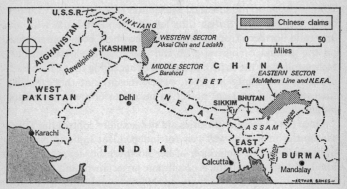

The Sino-Indian boundary.

In the nineteenth century China came into the entirely new situation of being surrounded by hostile European imperial systems – Russian to the north and west, British to the south-west, and French to the south. It was no longer enough to maintain a twilight zone of tributary states, and the Chinese imperial government tried in its final decades to establish direct rule in its most vulnerable frontier regions, Sinkiang and Tibet. But it was too weak fully to succeed in these endeavours, and the first forty years of Republican government after 1912 were no better. Only when the communists finally expelled the Kuomintang of Chiang Kai-shek in 1949 did it become possible for the central government of China to attend to its western frontiers. By that time Mongolia had, with Russian help, established itself as an independent nation, but Sinkiang remained Chinese and Tibet soon yielded once more to the Chinese armies.

Meanwhile the British in India were also finding it necessary to assert direct rule rather than mere influence in the northern Himalayan regions vulnerable, as they thought, to Russian infiltration. They steadily eroded the frontiers of traditional Tibetan influence, vainly sought Chinese agreement to a border line through the middle of the Aksai Chin plateau of Ladakh, and progressively extended their administration into the hill-tribe areas of NEFA (a process which was still going on in 1947 and was continued by the Nehru government thereafter), obtaining Tibetan assent to the so-called McMahon Line which the Chinese today dispute. The British thus left independent India with an uncertain northern frontier which had nowhere been demarcated on the ground or agreed with the neighbouring government.[9] Nehru followed the British precedent of accepting that China had ultimate sovereignty in Tibet, which meant that the Tibetans themselves had no legal power to negotiate border agreements independently.

Since the Chinese authorities did not actually control the Tibetan border in 1947 it was easy for independent India to proceed unilaterally with a definition of her northern border; the occasional protests of both the Kuomintang government and the Dalai Lama against Indian activity in NEFA and Indian 'cartographical aggression' were not taken seriously. But in 1950 the Chinese re-asserted their power in Tibet and began to administer and patrol the Indian border regions again for the first time since 1912. At the same time the old Kuomintang maps began to appear in Peking under a communist imprint. When Nehru raised the question with Chou En-lai he was told that these were the old maps being reprinted and that they would be duly revised as soon as possible. It did not occur to the Indian prime minister that the Chinese could with equal justice have asked him about *his* maps, which also reproduced the previous imperialist government's claims without prior consultation with the neighbour concerned.

The tragedy was that both the Chinese and the Indians assumed that their respective claims were correct and that the only problem was to convince the less well-informed other side of this. The Chinese had the added difficulty that these borderlands had not been administered by a Chinese government for almost forty years, and it took time for the communists to assess the problem, assemble the facts and decide on a policy. Since they suspected Nehru of being a British stooge (until his efforts in the Korean negotiations in 1951 and 1952 persuaded them, temporarily, of his integrity), it is understandable that they played for time. Gradually, as the 1950s rolled on, the rival forces took up their positions in the disputed areas, and in the mid-fifties the first armed clashes occurred. By then Indian opinion and Nehru himself had been offended by the bullying attitude of Peking towards Tibet, and the Tibetan Revolt of 1959 crystallized the Indian sense of disillusion with China. At the same time it became known that the Chinese had built a road across the disputed Aksai Chin and that India had only come to learn of it a year later after maps published in Peking had shown it.

The armed clashes naturally increased after 1959 when the Chinese had to guard the border far more rigorously than before to prevent Tibetan guerrillas from escaping or returning with new supplies. With this incentive the Chinese made the most headway to begin with in completing the physical administration of their claimed border areas, but the Indians made a comparable drive in the summer of 1962 when Nehru ordered the Indian Army to expel the Chinese from N E F A and 'recover' the lost ground in Ladakh. Faced for the first time with a concerted Indian military thrust into what they saw as their own legitimate territory, the Chinese counter-attacked in October and inflicted a humiliating defeat on the Indian forces. The fighting was restricted to the disputed areas, neither side venturing into territory which it had not previously claimed as its own.[10]

Since then there has been frequent sabre-rattling along the cease-fire line but no evidence that either side seriously intends to put it to another military test. Like the ceasefire line in Kashmir, it will in all probability become permanent. It gives the Chinese the Aksai Chin road which, because of the vast desert to the north, is their only practicable link between Tibet and Sinkiang, and it leaves most of N E F A (with the exception of a few small districts where the Indian case is not at all conclusive) to India. It hurts Indian pride more than Indian national interests, and is as good a border as we are likely to get in this intractable Himalayan area. It will be a source of minor tension for a long time to

Two extreme views of China's historical frontiers, as set out in books published in Peking in 1925 and 1954.

come, as the Chinese alarums during the Indo-Pakistan war of 1965 showed, but time is on the side of its eventual acceptance.[11]

Meanwhile the Chinese took pains to negotiate their other southern frontiers. Border agreements were made with Burma in 1960, Nepal in 1961, Afghanistan and Pakistan in 1963, and most of these boundaries were subsequently the object of joint demarcation with pillars and posts on the ground. These treaties (and another with Mongolia in 1962) are cast in the Western mould as contracts between theoretically equal parties, and as evidence for or against China's acceptance of her present borders they have more weight than the old historical maps still published in Peking showing the furthest extent of the Chinese empire and its tributaries in its heyday.

But China has one more border which remains disputed, and that is the longest which any two nations in the world share: her Soviet boundary. Like her other borders, this is the product of a series of 'unequal treaties' which the European imperialist powers forced on China during the nineteenth century and which the communist government said from the start it would examine and then 'recognize, abrogate, revise or renegotiate' according to their respective contents. Chinese resentment against Russian imperialism was suppressed during the Sino-Soviet honeymoon of 1949–60, but it has since surfaced and shown itself as, if anything, even more bitter than the remaining animus against West European imperialism (which has, after all, vacated its principal Asian conquests).

Mao Tse-tung has said that the Chinese have not yet presented their account for past Russian encroachment, although none of the areas taken by the Tsars contained resident Chinese communities, and the official position of Peking is still that the current border is in general an acceptable basis for settlement. Border negotiations were held in 1964–5 and again in 1969, but inconclusively. Given the three facts, that the two governments are now actively colonizing and developing these borderlands (which have considerable economic potential), that their rivalry for influence in central Asia and in the world at large is unlikely to abate, and that there are minority nationalities (including Mongols and Kazakhs) who bestride the frontier, it is hard to escape the conclusion that this border is going to be a source of tension for many decades to come. The minor clashes over a small island in the Ussuri River near Vladivostok in 1969 were only a curtain-raiser for further fights, but whether the Chinese will seek seriously to vary this frontier in any important respects is another matter.[12]

So much for the frontiers of India and China, the two giants of the Asian mainland. South-East Asia has not thrown any major border disputes into the world headlines since the war, although the Vietnam conflict is partly over the question whether the seventeenth parallel is an international frontier between the two

separate sovereign states of North and South Vietnam, or a
cease-fire line in a civil war within the single state of Vietnam for
which two factions are still fighting. But the potential for conflicts
can be illustrated from the case of the Preah Vihar temple, an
ancient Khmer monument, for the jurisdiction of which Cambodia and Thailand went before the International Court of Justice at the Hague in 1962.

As we have seen, Thailand was on the road to expansion when
the Europeans came along to thwart her. Without British and
French resistance, Thailand would today be ruling considerable
areas of northern Burma, Laos, Cambodia and northern Malaya.
Indeed, during the short-lived Japanese stewardship of South-
East Asia in the early 1940s the maps were redrawn to give Thailand two Shan states of Burma, a good portion of Laos, four
Malay states and two Cambodian provinces. All this was undone
again in 1945, but it can readily be imagined what irredentist
sentiments lurk not too far below the surface of Thai nationalism.
In fact Thailand's relations with her neighbours are rather good:
there is considerable official co-operation on border matters with
Burma and Malaysia (on account mainly of the rebellious Chinese
and dissident minority nationalities active in those two border
regions), while Laos is regarded as a junior cousin rather than a
foreign state.

But Cambodia, which the brilliant though hypersensitive
Prince Sihanouk saved from extinction after the French withdrawal, is a different matter. For Cambodians there are only two
threats to their sovereignty, and these are Thai and Vietnamese
nationalism. As a matter of geographical fact Cambodia abuts on
South rather than North Vietnam, and, since the two governments in Saigon and Bangkok are allies in the US-led anti-
communist front in South-East Asia, the Prince needed all his
agility and bravado to keep his tiny state on the map. His strategy
is to follow a neutralist or non-aligned policy with the explicit
backing of China and North Vietnam, the two powers most inimical to Thailand and South Vietnam. But he was unable to
overcome the refusal or reluctance of the Thais and South
Vietnamese to give final recognition to their Cambodian frontiers bequeathed by French colonialism. Vietnam disputed some
islands off the coast, while Thailand disputed the Preah Viher

temple – and Cambodians saw both claims as the thin end of the wedge.

The International Court awarded the temple, through the middle of which the border agreed in the Franco-Thai Treaty of 1904 appeared to run, to Cambodia by a majority verdict.[13] The Thais had grudgingly to accept this decision, but there have been small-scale clashes since then in the temple area and elsewhere along the Thai-Cambodian border. Vietcong fighters in South Vietnam have long taken refuge in some of the less intensely administered border areas of Cambodia when the Americans or the South Vietnamese forces pressed them too hard, and now that both the latter have openly pursued them into Cambodian territory, this border is untenable.

Even Cambodia's border with her third neighbour, Laos, has been the subject of infiltration by tribal people with the support of the Laotian and, so Sihanouk declared, Vietnamese communists, whose dislike for the Cambodians, combined with their anger over Sihanouk's unashamed repression of his own local communists, occasionally prevailed over the former official Hanoi-Peking line of diplomatic co-operation with Sihanouk. In these circumstances Sihanouk appealed to the great powers to recognize his frontiers and guarantee his country's territorial integrity. But the powers, both capitalist and communist, finding that their local allies in the region had emotional reservations about Cambodian territorial integrity, were understandably slow to respond, ultimately doing so with varying degrees of verbal ambiguity. The Cambodian frontiers are now the most vulnerable in Asia.[14]

Off the mainland of Asia the main difficulty regarding frontiers has been with Indonesia, although Ceylon is now quarrelling with India over an islet called Kachchativu, the two small islands of Kunashiri and Etorofu are disputed between Japan and the Soviet Union,[15] and the almost uninhabited Paracel Islands in the South China Sea are simultaneously claimed by South Vietnam and China.[16] The Indonesian questions do not strictly speaking concern the disputed alignment of a land frontier but rather the disputed sovereignty of certain islands or parts of islands at the fringe of the Indonesian Republic. The West Irian question comes within this category. Indonesian nationalists regard it as part of their republic because it was formerly administered along with what is now Indonesia by the same Dutch colonial authority. In 1962, after a long diplomatic battle against Holland in which American anti-colonialist sentiment was of crucial help to President Sukarno, Indonesia won the jurisdiction of West Irian from the Dutch (who had continued to rule it as a colony after Indonesian independence). But the United Nations, which was made the forum for this handover, insisted on an eventual plebiscite for which Indonesia finally substituted a rigged 'expression of opinion' in its favour.

In actual fact the Indonesians were disappointed to find that West Irian was the home of extremely primitive tribesmen who had nothing in common with themselves and were so hostile to their new rulers that only national pride keeps the Indonesian flag flying there. One might note in passing that West Irian provides Indonesia with its only important land frontier, since the other half of New Guinea is administered by Australia. But even when Australian-Indonesian relations were at their lowest point, this frontier was not challenged, and there is now considerable cooperation between the two sides. The Australians are grooming Papua and New Guinea for independence, however, and if the Indonesians should insist on repressing any eventual desire on their side of the island to go with an independent East New Guinea rather than Indonesia there is the likelihood of trouble.[17]

Similar difficulties remain unresolved in northern Borneo, or Kalimantan. The formerly Dutch part of this vast island, inhabited in its central areas by primitive indigenous tribes but with Malay and Chinese settlements in the coastal areas, has all along been in the Indonesian Republic. But the disposition of the ex-British part in the north – the two former colonies of Sabah (British North Borneo) and Sarawak (where the Brooke family of White Rajahs once held sway), together with the theoretically independent Sultanate of Brunei which is under strong British influence still – has proved less easy. None of them had been ruled from Singapore or Kuala Lumpur in colonial times, and so they did not automatically follow Malaya into independence in 1957. As with Irian, though to a far lesser extent, these territories were considered unready for independence and even in 1963, when the British finally decided to leave, their viability was questionable. There had been talk of their federating to form one northern Borneo state, but there was not even enough familiarity or trust for that, and in the end Sabah and Sarawak reluctantly agreed to enter the Malaysian Federation, which was simultaneously enlarged by the addition of Singapore.

This was the only formula minimally satisfactory to all the parties; the Malays ensured that the Chinese would not have a numerical majority (which they would have had in a Federation confined to Malaya and Singapore), the indigenous people of Sabah and Sarawak had the benefit of belonging to a unit of viable size with the same British colonial traditions, and the British were able to complete in all important respects (Hongkong being a special case) their decolonization programme in Asia. But there were difficulties also. The Dayaks, Dusuns and other indigenous peoples of northern Borneo dislike the Malays and were suspicious of their new masters. The expulsion of Singapore from the Federation in 1965 raised grave doubts about the capacity of the Chinese and the Malays to co-exist politically in the same state. Finally, the way in which both the Malayan and the Bornean leaders had to be pressed by Britain into accepting the federal solution suggested, particularly to those who were already suggestible in this direction, that this was an imposed solution which failed to meet the real wishes of the people concerned.

There was never any referendum or plebiscite in northern Borneo, although elections before and after the new Federation came into existence confirmed in office the political parties or coalitions favouring it. The suspicion of foul play fell on eager ears in Djakarta, where Indonesian nationalists had learnt to distrust all proposals by a colonial power for the subsequent destiny of its empire. President Sukarno never explicitly laid claim on behalf of Indonesia to Sabah and Sarawak. He did, however, throw his country behind the northern Bornean opponents of Malaysia (ironically these were, in the main, disaffected left-wing Chinese residents) and prosecuted for four years a confrontation against Malaysia that involved guerrilla fighting in the Bornean jungles and even the landing of guerrilla troops on peninsular Malaysian soil itself. The *konfrontasi*, as it was called, suited Sukarno's foreign policy and domestic needs at the time, but it never showed signs of succeeding and in the end it became one of the issues which led the Indonesian army leaders to over-throw Sukarno. Since the Suharto regime assumed power in 1965–6 there has been no further talk of backing dissident elements in Malaysia.

But the lifting of Indonesian pressure brought into the open another threat to Sabah, namely an old Philippine claim which President Macapagal had brought into the limelight in the early 1960s. At one point in its colourful history Sabah had been 'bought' from the Sultan of Sulu whose remaining possessions form part of the Philippines. His supporters argue that the 'purchase' was in fact a 'lease', and that residual sovereignty remained with him – and thus, by the logic of modern nationalism and the nature of Philippine politics, with the government in Manila. This became during the 1960s a fine rallying cry for Philippine nationalism, although in their more rational moments the Philippine leaders, like their Indonesian counterparts, would concede that a referendum or plebiscite among the people concerned is the only test that ought to matter. Unfortunately the Malaysian leaders decided early on that if they agreed to a plebiscite they would demonstrate their own lack of confidence, and for the same reason they have rejected the Philippines' suggestion to put the matter to the International Court. The sovereignty of Sabah has thus shown its potential of leading to armed conflict, first between Malaysia and Indonesia and then between Malaysia and the Philippines, although ultimately, as the Malaysians consolidate their position in Sabah, they ought to be able to offer their opponents a face-saving solution.[18]

These conflicts of interest over frontier alignments and over the sovereignty of marginal areas at the edge of the new post-colonial states constitute an extremely important factor in contemporary Asian politics. They are accentuated by the failure of most of the governments fully to control and administer the more distant, difficult and ethnically different areas of their countries. This deficiency is gradually being remedied, but only as part of another process, the cultivation of a modern sense of nationalism, which in turn renders the rational resolution of such conflicts less easy.

Chapter Eight

The Agricultural Base

THE people of India, Jawaharlal Nehru wrote towards the end of his life, were 'very fine people, very capable people, very intelligent people, but people who have functioned for ages past in certain ruts of thought and action. Take our peasant; it is a matter of amazement and shame to me that any peasant should go about today with a plough that was used in Vedic times. There has been no change since then. It should have been a museum-piece; yet the fact is, it is there. It astonishes me.'[1] You can still go to the shining new steel mills of India and see in their shadow the pathetically skinny Indian peasant guiding his three-thousand-year-old wooden plough through the parched soil.

The central issue in the Asian modernization drama is that of agriculture, the traditional source of livelihood of some 70 per cent of the population and still for most countries the largest single source of wealth. The methods by which rice, wheat and other crops are grown in most parts of Asia are extraordinarily old-fashioned. Irrigation systems have been developed in many Asian civilizations (an outstanding example may be found near the ruins of Angkor Wat in Cambodia, where at the beginning of this century French engineers had merely to recommission ancient works). But chemical fertilizer and pesticide, modern machines, electricity and the breeding of better strains of seeds, were only introduced in many Asian villages within the past ten years, if at all.

The urgency of the agricultural revolution in Asia stems from the two facts of widespread malnutrition and recurrent famine. The extent of malnourishment in Asia is controversial. Professor Colin Clark argues[2] that the United Nations Food and Agricultural Organization (FAO) has consistently exaggerated it. Certainly the early post-war assumptions have changed: for one thing, it is now recognized that calorie needs vary with body weight, and that fewer calories are needed in a warm climate than in a cold one, so that the norm for Europe is not necessarily the norm for tropical Asia. The best estimate is that the average daily calorie intake in Asia today is around 2,050, which is too close for comfort to the minimum requirement defined by the United Nations. The average naturally conceals even worse departures from the desirable minimum: an American scholar has estimated that one Indian in three is eating below the 1,600-calorie level, which is only five-sixths of the FAO standard for India of 1,936, and an Indonesian writer calculates average consumption in Java at only 1,650 calories.[3]

The average Asian diet is particularly deficient in protein. It was possible to calculate only six years ago that the entire meat production of Asia (with some 1,800 million mouths to feed) was only marginally bigger than Australia's (with only 12 million). U Nu, the Burmese leader, hoped to transform his countrymen by a nationwide issue of vitamin pills, but was frustrated by the administrative, economic and educational difficulties his scheme encountered. The typical teenager in Japan today stands at least four inches higher than his grandfather did, and this is attributed chiefly to the popularization of milk, eggs and butter and the greater consumption of meat, particularly in the last twenty years. But that teenager's counterpart in China today is still lucky to get meat once a week: too many of Asia's millions still have little to enrich their twice-daily rice-bowl.

This kind of malnutrition is often imposed on the next generation, since peasant women in many parts of Asia almost starve themselves during pregnancy in order to keep the foetus small and render its delivery easier. And until 1968 there was little discernible change in this depressing picture. The United Nations Economic Commission for Asia and the Far East (ECAFE) has calculated that average calorie and protein consumption per head was still, in 1964, below the pre-war level in Asia.

Much of this undernourishment can be overcome by education. People in Kerala, the South Indian state, have almost starved when rice was short and yet failed to take advantage of the nutritious fruits and vegetables all around them or the fish which their neighbours bring in from the sea – because they are not accustomed to such foods.[4] But sheer quantitative inadequacy of food harvests is the main cause of malnutrition, and until a year or two ago there was no lack of voices to prophesy a worsening of the Asian dilemma. 'Unless drastic measures are taken to increase food production in this region,' said Dr B. R. Sen, then Director-General of the FAO, a few years ago, 'the precarious balance that now exists will break down, and famines will begin to appear around 1980.'[5]

Famine is not, of course, a new thing in Asia. The Chinese Government in imperial days used to include an official famine factor when calculating the population's normal death rate, and no fewer than 1,828 famines are recorded in Chinese history. The Bengal famine of 1943 took about two million lives, and so did the big floods on the Yellow River in northern China in the 1930s. There have been cases of actual starvation in Orissa, Bihar and Uttar Pradesh, three states of north-eastern India, as recently as 1966–7, and desperate food shortages have occurred during the 1960s in some parts of Indonesia and China, driving people to eat bark, insects and grass in order to survive: even cases of cannibalism are recorded. There was rioting in Kerala in 1966 when the daily rice ration was cut from 6 to 4 ounces; indeed food riots and looting of grainstores was common in many parts of India during 1966–7.

Behind the crop failures which lead to famine stand the two terrors of the Asian farmer, flood and drought. Crops require the application of water, neither too much nor too little, at certain stages of their growth. If the rains come too early or too late, if they continue too long or if they are unusually heavy, then crops can either shrivel into the ground or be washed out of the fields. Those who live in temperate climates where the variation in rainfall is limited do not realize how lucky they are. In Asia only a well-planned, sustained and expensive programme of water conservancy (strengthening the river banks, reafforestation to prevent soil erosion, measures against silting, systems of irrigation and drainage canals) can provide some minimal protection against the vagaries of the rain. The Chinese even have a plan to divert the surplus waters of the mighty Yangtze to moisten the dry wheat plains of northern China, a project which will take generations to achieve.[6]

In these modern times flooding or drought does not lead to mass starvation, as the Chinese Government proved in 1959–61

and the Indian Government in 1966-7. But it does interrupt the
effort to increase farm yields. In the summer of 1954, when the
Yangtze burst its banks, soldiers formed human walls to contain
the breaches in the dykes, and still ten million people had to flee
their homes. 'Under the present Government no human lives
are lost in such disasters,' the communist press boasted, but the
damage done to the campaign to raise agricultural output can be
imagined.

During the first half of the twentieth century Indian production
of foodgrains probably expanded by an annual $\frac{1}{2}$ per cent, on
average, and this was typical of other countries too. From the
early 1950s, after the restoration of peace and consolidation of
the new nationalist governments, the tempo of improvement
quickened. The United Nations statistical indices show an improvement of some 30-40 per cent in agricultural harvests in
Asia during the decade 1955-65.[7] But the figures began to fluctuate badly, and their overall trend to stagnate, during the
1960s.

The common experience of the Asian governments was that
their initial efforts to increase farm output succeeded rather well.
It was not at first appreciated that the annual crop increases were
more the result of the return to peacetime conditions after the
Second World War (and, in China's and India's case, after the
additional turmoil of civil war and partition) than of any encouragement by the governments. By the end of the 1950s harvests had more or less regained their pre-war levels and even improved on them, but it then became clear that more expensive
investments would have to be made in order to maintain the
momentum.

During the first six years of the decade of the 1960s the
FAO estimated the average annual growth in foodgrain harvests in Asia at a mere 1 per cent, and as late as 1967 it was still
possible for the president of the Asian Development Bank to
state that Asian food production in the preceding twelve months
was rather less than the pre-war level.[8] By the mid-sixties the gravity of the situation was recognized throughout Asia. The Chinese
communists relegated heavy industry to a role below that of
agriculture, which is now described as the foundation of China's
national economy:[9] industrialization proceeds, but with a lower

priority and with special emphasis on 'agro-industries', that is to say, the industries which directly support or exploit agriculture. Similar priority is being given in India and elsewhere to the manufacture of chemical fertilizer and irrigation pumps on the one hand, and to the processing of crops in rice-mills and similar enterprises on the other.

The down-grading of heavy industry was doctrinally painful to the Chinese communists, who are still chided by European Marxists for this heresy, and the anti-egalitarian aspects of the new agricultural drive were distasteful to intellectuals in both China and India. In the interests of increasing total national production of foodstuffs, investment began in the 1960s to be concentrated on areas able to make the best return on it, which were also the areas needing help least. Social justice required a levelling-up by giving special help to the poorly provided areas, but the need to get bigger harvests quickly required the throwing of good money after good, and letting the really backward regions wait a few years before getting comparable attention. Indian socialists liked this no more than the Chinese communists, but the cruel dilemma was resolved in both countries in the same realistic way.

A similar conflict between social ideals and economic reality characterizes the debate about land reform, an improvement which virtually every Asian government has tried to make. Before the war absentee landlords in many parts of the continent owned a large proportion of the farmland, and tended to neglect it. The worst instances of share-cropping, the system by which a peasant had to deliver a sizeable share of the harvest to the landlord in lieu of rent, were restricted to a few areas, and it happens that these were also the main areas where communism made a serious appeal: in Luzon in the Philippines, parts of Java, the two Vietnam deltas and northern China.[10]

But share-cropping aside, the enterprising peasants throughout Asia were often frustrated by their landlords' lack of interest in technical improvement, by the high rents they had to pay,[11] and by the extortions of local moneylenders who often worked closely with the landlord class and sometimes played both roles at the same time. As Dr Sen of F A O argued to the World Land Reform Conference in 1966, this kind of measure is 'most vital to

boosting agricultural productivity. As in other fields of investment, a continuous state of uncertainty about the future of land
rights dissuades people from putting forth their best in terms of
capital and labour.'

Japan's post-war 'miracle' owes much to the American-
imposed land reform of the occupation years,[12] and it is no accident that Taiwan, the show-piece of developing Asia, is the only
other country in the continent to have completed a 'Land to the
Tiller' campaign.[13] In India, where land reform was dear to
Nehru's heart but where actual implementation is slow, over half
of the farm land is still owned by one-eighth of the population,
and a rural élite numbering only 1 per cent of the total inhabitants
own 20 per cent of the land.[14] Similar remarks could be made of
the Philippines and one or two other countries.

Yet there is some concern in Japan and Taiwan lest the land
reform perpetuate an undue fragmentation of the holdings below
the level of economic viability, and the conclusion of one expert
with no ideological axe to grind is that further land reform
throughout India would not necessarily boost output. A strictly
equal division of land would make every holding uneconomic,
and about 80 per cent of the land is already owner-cultivated: 'I
am inclined to estimate that at least two-thirds of the land is par-
celled up into economic holdings or holdings that might be economic if certain additional facilities were provided.'[15]

In the communist states the land reform was followed by co-
operativization and collectivization. China introduced the
People's Commune in 1958 as the ultimate model for socialist
agriculture and rural organization in an Asian context, but it has
not made many converts elsewhere. The commune is a kind of
federation of perhaps a hundred villages containing around fifty
thousand people. It is not only the highest unit of agriculture but
also the lowest unit of government, incorporating political, military, judicial, fiscal, and industrial functions as well as farming. It
offers the possibility of large-scale mobilization of manpower,
notably for public works and water conservancy, and also a
means of harnessing peasant energies during the agriculturally
slack seasons.[16] As an institution it has its critics even in China,
and its popularity reached a low point in the early 1960s, but it
does have something to offer and seems unlikely to disappear.

The consequences of collectivization are still disputed by scholars; it allows public works to be carried out on a scale impossible for owners of small holdings, and one impartial observer concluded, of a collectivized village in eastern China just before the communes came, that the loss of incentive was 'much out-balanced by organizational and technical gains.'[17] Yet the diminution of incentive is there, and only an ultra-optimist could expect the acquisitive instinct of an Asian peasant to be destroyed by the relatively short period of propaganda and education which the communists have been able to provide in China, North Vietnam, North Korea or Mongolia.

Then the whole question of the lengths to which collectivization should be pushed in China's villages was central to the conflict within the communist leadership that became bound up with the Cultural Revolution of 1966–8.[18] Liu Shao-chi, for more than twenty years the second most powerful man in Communist China but named in 1967 as the leading opponent of Mao Tse-tung's radical brand of socialism, is alleged to have been lukewarm about the collectives from the very beginning: 'No collectivization without mechanization' was one of his slogans, his critics now assert, and he argued that: 'only when 70 per cent of the peasant households own three horses will it be possible to establish collective farms.'[19] The 'revisionist' opponents of Mao feel that the surviving private sector in Chinese agriculture must be preserved from the onslaughts of the fanatical ideologues, and that some degree of diffusion of responsibility and market incentive* is essential if production is to be increased.

As on the question of geographical allocation of investment, so on the nation-wide compromising of social justice in the interests of production, most planners and politicians in both India and China (though not Mao himself and his clique) are

---

*Pricing policy is also a vital element in farm incentives. The Burmese government pegged the price of rice at its 1948 level for many years in order to protect the consumer and prevent inflation, and this was one explanation of the fact that by 1960 the production of rice and the area sown to it were still less than they had been pre-war. Later the military government tried to nationalize the rice trade but had to retreat before the subsequent chaos. Government pricing policy in both Pakistan and India has shifted during the past ten years or so to ensure that the farmers have a tangible incentive to produce more.

regretfully resigned to a situation where improvements in agriculture are bound to benefit the already better-off rather than the poorest peasants. The short term has to take precedence over the long. Tomorrow's crisis of the widening gulf between rich and poor in the countryside will have to be faced by tomorrow's leaders, while today's grapple with the challenge of feeding the politically explosive 10 per cent who live in the cities.

Peasants nurse considerable resentment against the townsmen and city-dwellers whose life seems so incomparably better than theirs, and the predilection of enterprising or intelligent young peasants for making their way to the cities, where more opportunities present themselves, has caused a gross imbalance. During the Cultural Revolution in China one group of peasants near Shanghai put up a giant poster listing thirty-five grievances, all concerned with the gulf between town and country. The countryside lacked teachers, hospitals, administrative offices, decent housing and newspapers. Rural workers' wages were a mere fraction of their urban cousins', and they had to provide their own tools and share-capital when entering a commune. They had to pay high prices for chemical fertilizers, and enjoyed no pension system. They had funds distributed only once a year, and even marriage was a problem because the girls ran after the better-paid urban workers.[20] After eighteen years of communist rule, dedicated in part to the abolition of these rural-urban tensions, they still represented political dynamite, and in India they are far worse. Michael Lipton writes of 'the urban bias that turns education into a vast funnel for removing the best rural brains to urban jobs' in India.[21] There are parts of Asia, the north-east provinces of Thailand for example, where people have hardly heard of the government and have certainly not until a year or two ago benefited from any public works such as roads, radios, schools, hospitals or irrigation canals, and it is hardly surprising that loyalty to the government is minimal in such areas or that they are so vulnerable to communist or any other kind of subversion.

In fact, of course, the fate of the unsuccessful urban population is a miserable one. Anyone who has seen the suburbs of Calcutta or Shanghai will sympathize with Han Suyin's condemnation: 'In Asia the city has become in a sense the *étouffoir*, a senseless megalopolis drawing the hungry millions of the country into a horrifying belt of slums round its glittering, moneyed core.'[22]

A group of Anglo-American experts concluded of Calcutta: 'We have not seen human degradation on a comparable scale in any other city in the world. This is one of the greatest urban concentrations in existence rapidly approaching the point of breakdown in its economy, housing, sanitation, transport and the essential humanities of life. If the final breakdown were to take place it would be a disaster for mankind of a more sinister sort than any disaster of flood or famine.'[23]

The Chinese communists dream of merging the rural and urban worlds, making them interchangeable and turning the peasantry, as the *Guardian* once put it, 'into an industrial proletariat without urbanizing it, as both the West and Russia had to do in their own industrial revolutions.'[24] Simple factories are brought to the peasant through the commune (which is meant to become virtually self-sufficient in basic manufactures), while city-dwellers are sent down to the farm to learn how the other half lives and help it widen its horizons. 'We are not going to build any more cities,' one of the Chinese planners has stated.[25]

These dreams seem still far from reality. What E. F. Schumacher[26] has called the 'immiserization' of Asia's urban centres can conceivably be prevented from getting worse, but can hardly be undone. Luckily the necessity to make concessions to the peasants in order to secure bigger harvests seems to be reversing the trend. These days rural leaders have more political influence than before. It was largely the rural vote that toppled the Congress Party from office in so many Indian states in the 1967 elections, that keeps the conservative Liberal-Democrats in power in Japan, and that allowed Mao Tse-tung to overthrow, at least for a time in 1967–8, the urban-based leadership of the Chinese Communist Party apparatus.

Meanwhile the revolution in agricultural technology proceeds throughout the continent. Only one-third of Asia's land area is arable, but in most countries it has been found possible to extend the acreage sown to crops by a small proportion, and also to increase the extent of double-cropping (even, in some well-endowed areas, treble-cropping) on the same piece of soil. The land ratio still represents an obstacle to progress: Asians enjoy only half the average human being's share of arable land. The most important contribution to bigger harvests has therefore been to increase the yield from each acre.

The average cereal yield in Asia in 1965 was under 2 tons per hectare (less than half the European or North American yields), according to a UN survey,[27] but performance ranged widely from only 1 ton in India to more than $3\frac{1}{2}$ tons in Taiwan. You get more weight of rice out of a field than wheat (which is one reason why China is not quite so unhappy as might at first sight appear in exporting one million tons of rice a year and importing five million tons of wheat). But even for rice the variation is startling: 5 tons per hectare in Japan, 4 in Taiwan and South Korea, only $1\frac{1}{2}$ in India, Pakistan, Burma and Thailand. Clearly there is a good margin for improvement.

This is achieved by better education of the farmer, and by providing him with four new inputs: chemical fertilizer and pesticide, artificial water supply, new and better strains of seed, and improved machinery with electrification. The vast majority of India's and China's farmlands are deficient in nitrogen and phosphorus, and more than half of India's lack potash. Traditionally the East Asian farmer uses human excrement to manure his fields, which is why they smell so nastily to a European nose. But the traditional organic manures are insufficient, and future increases in yield must come from the application of chemical fertilizer. The ground to be made up may be gauged from the fact that in Taiwan in 1965 the average per-hectare application was over 250 kilos, whereas in Indonesia it was only $8\frac{1}{2}$ kilos, in Pakistan only $5\frac{1}{2}$ kilos and in India a derisory 5 kilos.[28] It is only since the mid-sixties that either China or India has seriously campaigned for bigger use of expensive chemical fertilizer. Once it catches on, the demand can snowball, and in India there is now a black market in fertilizer.

Irrigation is gradually spreading, but still less than one in three of Asia's farm acres are irrigated (and in India only one in five). This is especially important for rice, which needs to be grown wet, but it is essential for all crops if the full benefit of fertilizer and better seed strains is to be obtained.

Mechanization is nowadays less popular with planners because it is so costly, and because the one thing which is not short in

Asia is manpower. One of the complaints which the Chinese communists made about Soviet aid was the Russians' stress on introducing tractors which were not widely helpful on China's hilly, canal-crossed and densely populated ground.

It is the new seeds which are attracting the limelight at the moment. Very little work had been done on this in Asia (except in Japan) until 1960, when the International Rice Research Institute was established at Los Baños in the Philippines by the Rockefeller and Ford Foundations of the USA. These two philanthropic institutions had achieved considerable success in Mexico in the 1940s and 1950s in developing new wheat strains, and during the 1960s they turned their energies to rice. Soon the Institute perfected a hybrid of an Indonesian strain and a dwarf Taiwanese rice which was responsive to nitrogen, matured quickly and did not grow too tall (tall rippling crops being vulnerable to rain and wind). It was called IR-8. Now in widespread use throughout Asia, this new 'miracle' rice is producing yields two, three or even four times larger than the traditional strains.[29]

Progress is never, of course, easy: new strains have their initial problems and can only be proved over a long period of time. Besides, the bumper yields can only result where minimum amounts of fertilizer and water can be assured, and this means that they can succeed only in a minority of Asia's farms (and that the gulf between the good and bad farm areas is bound to yawn even more widely). But the initial success of these new seeds has been enough to convince India that famine *can* be defeated, and they have transformed the agricultural atmosphere throughout the continent.

There is a Maharajah's son in Mysore, a Cambridge economics graduate and an elected local legislator, who has raised yields of sorghum, an important cereal, by five to ten times on his estate through the use of new hybrid seeds,[30] and many other particular examples of success could be quoted. Even a cautious prediction would now put the average annual increase in foodgrain harvests in Asia at around 4 per cent over the next decade (well in excess of the population growth), and one does not have to look far for more optimistic experts.

It is one thing to grow more food, quite another to see that it is all safely stored for human consumption. When the experimental farm of the International Rice Research Institute in Los Baños began to produce tangible results with its new hybrids, it was invaded by rats. The Institute's answer was to put up electrified low wire fences at a cost of $55 per acre (and a catch of one rat per acre every thirty-six hours).[31] The average Asian farmer cannot afford such protection, and India's Central Food Technological Research at Mysore has estimated that as much as half of the country's entire food production is destroyed by rats* (which alone account for a quarter), birds, insects and rot.[32] This represents damage to the tune of over £12 million a day, and there is little chance of reducing it dramatically. Storage is expensive and so are anti-pest devices.

The Chinese communists used to organize nation-wide campaigns to wipe out sparrows, by beating gongs to prevent their sleeping, and almost 2,000 million of them were claimed killed in 1958. But the campaign was followed by a plague of destructive caterpillars, and it was realized that the cycle of nature is not so easily interfered with. The sparrows were reprieved, but the authorities still organize campaigns against rats.

Meanwhile Asia continues to be a large food importer. It is importing more than 20 million tons of wheat annually, and since 1964 has become a net importer of rice in spite of producing 60 per cent of the world crop. Most of this wheat and rice comes from North and South America and from Australia, and a very large proportion of it has been supplied free (or with very liberal repayment terms) under American aid. It was such shipments that saved numerous Indians from starvation in 1966–7. But India is having to pay the equivalent of half of her total export earnings, China and Pakistan a quarter of theirs, merely to obtain food for consumption, and this is obviously unsatisfactory when the long-term need is for machinery and industrial materials to break the vicious circle and speed Asian development.

There is also a nagging anxiety lest food aid actually aggravate this problem. 'The availability of Public Law 480 farm products,' says one American writer, 'has not only made it possible for

*There is a temple in Rajasthan where rats are sacred, and devout Hindus pamper them with grain.

these governments to be complacent about agriculture, but it has also impaired the economic incentives for agricultural production in those countries.'[33] Or, as the radical Indian newspaper *Patriot* put it at the time, less fairly but more graphically: 'Every grain of American wheat kills a grain of wheat that could grow in an Indian field.'[34]

This particular dilemma is being cruelly resolved by the sharp fall in the West's surplus food stocks since 1961. The Americans are now wanting hard currency for their food shipments, and have insisted on their Western allies' contributing more to the food aid programmes. Although the American farmer remains the world's best hope,* he is at the most going to be able to supply one-eighth of non-communist Asia's likely food deficit in the 1980s.[35] This fact has done more than anything else to lend urgency to the agricultural programmes of the Asian governments.

Agricultural problems embrace more than foodgrains. Cash crops and plantation products of various kinds, ranging from tea and sugar to spices and rubber, are also extremely important to the Asian economies, both as a means of livelihood to farmers and as sources of foreign exchange earnings. These products, together with minerals, were the original cause of Europe's attraction to the Orient, and their commerical development (even, in some cases, introduction from other continents) was often the work of European entrepreneurs over the past century or so.

Most Asian countries are still dependent on primary commodities for their export cheque: Ceylon relies on tea, rubber and coconuts for 90 per cent of her export earnings, Malaysia on rubber and tin for 60 per cent of hers. Unfortunately for them the modern international trading system ensures that these commodity prices are constantly tending to fall, while the price of the manufactured goods which Asia buys from the West in return tends to rise. This is the penalty of depending on commodities which are relatively perishable (always a factor in the buyer's favour), have little margin for improvement since they are more

*The American farm worker produces more than fifty times the weight of food that his Indian counterpart can produce (and twenty-five times the Japanese).

or less in their natural state, often fluctuate ungovernably in the amount of annual production, and are increasingly liable to lose favour with consumers in favour of cheaper synthetic substitutes (nylon for bristle, plastic for jute, chemical compounds for rubber and so forth). Over the seven years to 1965 the developing countries in ECAFE exported 27 per cent *more* of primary products by weight, but saw a drop of 9 per cent on the prices they fetched.[36]

The stabilization of commodity prices has proved an elusive goal of the Asian (and other developing countries') governments, since it requires the West to sacrifice a degree of the dynamism that informs the international capitalist economic system, and demands also a level of collective self-discipline on the Asian side that is nowhere in sight. Furthermore, Asian agriculture is so old fashioned that European and American farmers, in spite of their wildly higher labour costs, are proving embarrassingly competitive in a number of products formerly the preserve of tropical producers: soya-beans and rice, for example.

Asia's share in world exports of crude materials of all kinds slumped by a third in the decade 1955–65, a recent UN survey finds, and this loss is compounded by the discrimination which many Western countries operate in favour of their own farmers. Thailand provides an example of a country which has rather successfully diversified its agricultural exports to become less dependent on a few crops. But as the 1967 United Nations *Economic Survey of Asia* remarked, 'Economic development is, after all, difficult enough without having to be burdened by the additional task of developing new export products while more traditional outputs are available but either hampered in their access to foreign markets or subjected to sharp declines in value. ...' In Malaysia the fall in the world rubber price over twelve months has recently caused a loss of some £50 million in export earnings, and a similar drop in tea prices cost Ceylon £18 million in one year. Such fluctuations are completely beyond the producers' control, and are unpredictable; every time this kind of thing happens, the government concerned has to make further agonizing cuts in the country's development programme. Similar examples could be cited from every Asian country. Small wonder that the long-term escape from penury is seen in industrialization.

Chapter Nine

Industrialization

'INDUSTRIALIZATION,' wrote the *People's Daily*[1] of Peking on the inaugural day of China's First Five-Year Plan, 'provides a guarantee that our people shall no longer be exposed by imperialism to treachery and humiliations, and shall no longer live in poverty.' The order in which these two goals are listed might at first sight seem surprising. The Asian nationalist regards the creation of modern industries as the most significant and satisfying part of the economic development process, and is often more conscious of their psychological value in removing an important cause of his inferiority complex *vis-à-vis* Europe and America, than of their contribution to raising his compatriots' standard of living.

In the longer term, only industrialization can free the underdeveloped countries of Asia from costly dependence upon non-Asian suppliers of technology and machines. The Indian Fourth Five-Year Plan works on the premise 'that in the context of an unfavourable land-man ratio, capital enrichment of the Indian economy could not proceed very far within the bounds of an essentially agrarian economy, and that, beyond a point, capital enrichment necessarily meant industrialization'.

The roots of modern industry go some way back into the nineteenth century, at least for the three big countries of India, China and Japan. Dwarkanath Tagore, the poet Rabindranath's grandfather, acquired India's largest coalmine in 1836, and Jamsetji Tata opened his pioneering modern cotton mill in Nagpur on the same day in 1877 that saw Victoria declared Empress of India.[2] Japan's first modern textile mill was founded in 1867 by the lord of Satsuma, while her first modern steel mill, the Government-owned Yawata Iron Works, was commissioned in 1901. The Tata steel mill at Jamshedpur in eastern India started seven years later, and steel has been made in Wuhan in central China since the end of the nineteenth century.

But these early enterprises were few and isolated. When Jawaharlal Nehru received Indian independence from the British in 1947, Indian factories were producing only 6 per cent of the national income and employing less than 2 per cent of the working population. It was only in the 1950s that comprehensive industrialization schemes began to be pursued, and the serious story of industry in Asia (leaving aside Japan, which started earlier) is less than twenty years old.

In those two decades very long strides have been made. According to UN figures, industrial output in Asia expanded almost tenfold during those twenty years, and if only heavy industry is considered the development was even faster.[3] Average annual industrial growth in the developing countries of Asia during the 1960s has been about 8 per cent which means that industry has been expanding more than twice as fast as the other sectors of the economy.[4] Steel output stood at little more than 12 million tons at the beginning of the 1960s but has now reached some 20 million tons. (Japan's production in 1970 was 94 million tons, more than either Britain or Germany, and this is left out of the calculation.) India and China now supply a very large proportion of their own steel needs, with the exception of certain alloys and special products, and both have entered the steel export league.

Machinery manufacture has grown by leaps and bounds, and both India and China are now able to export complete industrial plants. The Chinese communists boast of having developed by their own techniques and without the aid of foreign advisers a 12,000-ton hydraulic free forging press, several 10,000-ton-class ocean-going ships, large electron microscopes, transistorized electronic computers and complete sets of automated metallurgical and chemical industrial plants. In the past two or three years India has sold her railway wagons to the Soviet Union, refrigerators to Hungary, machine tools to West Germany, steel pipe to New Zealand, telecommunications equipment to Africa and tyres to the United States.

India is more or less in the same industrial class as China, therefore, though her officials do not brag as much about it. But, unlike China, she has leant on foreign know-how and help. The two countries' differing experience in this matter reflects one of the greatest obstacles to Asian modernization, namely the difficulty of transmitting technology across national, linguistic, political, cultural and even psychological barriers. When the Chinese or the Indians wanted to launch large-scale modern industries, they had to seek the help of countries already advanced in this field. China was helped by Soviet and East European experts, India by a wider variety of East and West Europeans. The first giant steel mills to be put up in India under public ownership were largely the creation of their British, German and Russian designers, although subsequent ones are to be entirely Indian-designed and Indian-built.

The thousands of European technicians, engineers and foremen (not to mention their respective wives and children) who came for months or years to work on isolated sites in the Indian or Chinese countryside, totally unprepared for the unfamiliar manners and modes of a different civilization, found that some of their advice fell on deaf ears. There were instances of genuine friendship and sympathy, culminating in a completely smooth takeover of responsibility when the foreign expert returned home. There were also cases where the two sides quarrelled bitterly, distrusting and despising each other, with the result that the plant sometimes broke down for one reason or another soon after the home team had taken it over. Very often a rather homespun foreman from Europe was required to tutor a fresh young Indian or Chinese graduate, which is like an old-fashioned sergeant-major having to teach an aristocratic young officer half his age – with the worst kind of international misunderstandings and antipathies thrown in to bedevil the relationship.

A common defence mechanism on the European side was to insist on the letter of the book – what Bode Sperling (head of the German social centre at the Rourkela steelworks in India) calls in his fascinating account[5] of this extraordinary project 'exaggerated attachment to the craftsman ethic'. It is not, of course, rational, to insist that things in Bihar or Inner Mongolia should be done just as they had always been done in Sheffield or Kiev. The differences begin with the Asian super-abundance of labour and shortage of capital, and usually extend into matters of climate, social relationships, psychology and local raw materials as well. But the typical expert whose arm is twisted in London or

Moscow to do a stint in the Far East (and the best men in their professions or skills are usually unwilling to interrupt their lives and careers in this way) is not instructed in these complex matters. Mikhail Klochko, the Soviet chemist who defected to Canada after having served two terms as an adviser in China, wrote of his experience there: 'All too often the Soviet Union sent to China only middle-echelon specialists, especially when it came to matters of possible military application.'[6]

When a consortium of British firms handed over the steel mill whose erection they had supervised at Durgapur, it soon followed that many of the coke ovens were ruined by an attempt on the part of the Indian management to force up the pace of production in order to meet their government's production targets. The Soviet experts in China had many similar experiences, and when I visited the leading Chinese steel mill at Anshan four years after the Soviet technicians had left on their mass walk-out of 1960, the superintendent of the most modern blast furnace there admitted that he was still suffering from the troubles caused by the break.

The development of an indigenous technology and an indigenous corps of scientists and technicians is a time-consuming process. Where the Government deems it important enough fast progress can be made, as is clear from the nuclear programmes in India and China. The Chinese exploded an H-bomb seven years after their Soviet tutors had departed, and the Indians are now preparing to build a nuclear reactor near Madras entirely without foreign collaboration, having already built and operated for several years an extremely dangerous plutonium plant at Trombay without any technical aid from outside. But the Chinese communists wanted a nuclear arms programme as a political and diplomatic priority, while Nehru had personally steered India's programme for the development of nuclear power for civil development purposes past all opposition from doubters or critics.

It so happens that both India and China have scientists of world reputation in the nuclear and allied fields of study. But when it comes to steel technology, or petrochemical know-how, the story is different. Nineteenth-century Japan hired hundreds of European and American experts to supervise the creation of new industries and services, including her navy. To take one example, the NYK shipping line began operations in 1884 with 174 foreign employees. The number rose to 224 some ten years later but then gradually declined as more and more Japanese learned the science and business of navigation: by 1920 Japanese shipping was entirely home-manned. The presently developing countries of Asia are now going through this phase of borrowing, or buying, technological leadership from the already industrialized countries, including Japan herself. All are grappling with the dilemmas which this process poses, notably the need, not always rationally accepted by either the foreign expert or his eager pupil, for the alien technology to be married to local conditions.[7]

There is a vicious circle in this situation, since the very conditions that make the Asian developing country need so much foreign advice often mean also that its own tradition stresses the virtues of imitating the master and obeying the teacher rather than those of innovation and individual responsibility. So much so that the Chinese communists have made it an article of faith that too much foreign advice is harmful, because it inhibits the growth of the recipients' sense of self-reliance. The Chinese press is full of stories of factory workers, researchers and managers who have 'resolutely abandoned the road leading to blind worship of foreign technical "authorities" in whose wake they have to follow',[8] and who with consequently heightened self-confidence have proceeded to overcome their technical challenges. A typical report concerns the development by some Peking researchers of a new type of high-polymer chemical grout or mortar:

The chemical grout was developed by a group of young workers and technicians who had no previous experience on the job. Moreover they lacked technical data and reference material as a result of the blockade enforced by imperialism and modern revisionism. In the course of running tests, certain bourgeois technical 'authorities' tried to obstruct the work, pointing out that some foreign countries had studied the grout over a long period and had not been able to make significant progress, and suggesting that the young people could hardly hope to do better. However, the young workers were not in the least dismayed by such obstruction. On the contrary, they displayed increased confidence in their final success, in their ability to catch up with and surpass* advanced world levels ...⁹

This was after the Soviet Union abruptly cut short its technical and economic help in 1960, in retaliation for Mao Tse-tung's refusal to toe the Soviet line – but also as the culmination of innumerable minor quarrels over the proper role of the foreign experts.

The consequences of the new policy of self-reliance are hard to assess. In the short term the Chinese are denying themselves the many short-cuts which the more patient Indians are gaining from foreign collaboration, but in the long term their technicians will benefit from the necessity of going it alone. I was able to sense the contrast rather vividly in 1964 by visiting two chemical fertilizer factories, one in Shanghai and the other at Nangal in the Punjab, within the space of a few months. Each cost more than £8 million and employed over 2,400 people, but whereas at Nangal sixty foreign technicians had supervised the installation of the British, French, German and Italian machinery, the Chinese plant had been designed and built entirely by Chinese personnel and was run by a Long March veteran almost along guerrilla warfare lines. The Shanghai plant wore a homespun, almost amateurish look, but it did feel lived in. Nangal was by contrast elegant and efficient, all chrome plate and polished floors, but the Indian staff looked out of place and scared to touch their sophisticated surroundings.

In the early days of their post-war industrialization drives, most Asian countries emphasized the creation of heavy industry, importing 'machines to make machines' from which they could then build downwards to the final stage of consumer goods industries. It should be noted in passing that Japan does not provide an unequivocal precedent for this, since consumer goods received their fair share of attention in the early years of the Meiji era. Even as late as 1930, when Japan stood virtually ready to challenge the Western world, the entire complex of mining, metallurgy and machinery industries in Japan furnished a mere 8 per cent of the national product.¹⁰

*Internal Chinese propaganda for the national development campaign often appeals to the sense of nationalism, and a few years ago the common slogan was to 'catch up' with Britain's industrial output.

It was rather the Soviet example which both India and China followed in the 1950s, allocating more investment funds to the steel mills, power stations, chemical and heavy engineering factories than to either agriculture (which was more or less left to take care of itself) or light industry (which was felt to be of secondary importance, almost a luxury, catering chiefly for the consumer market and contributing little to the country's industrial potential).

By the end of the 1950s, however, the planners in both Peking and New Delhi were having second thoughts about these priorities. It was realized that light industry not only provided an important incentive for the farmer by producing the household goods which he needed, and would work hard to buy, but also constituted the main consumer for the products of heavy industry. There was little use producing steel if the domestic demand for it was limited.

Controversy continued to rage, however, about the relative merits of state and private enterprise in industry. Asian nationalism was suspicious of its native capitalists from the start, seeing them as symbols of an almost unpatriotic collaboration with Western or foreign interests. Indeed, Indians could look back to a famous indiscretion of a British viceroy, Lord Lawrence, who once exploded: 'I know what private enterprise means! It means robbing the Government.' The authoritarian tradition favoured state rather than private enterprise in all matters, and even Chiang Kai-shek, pillar of the Asian right wing, declared that China should control private capital 'in order to prevent the capitalistic control of the people's livelihood. ... National industries must be created.'[11]

The communists did not need to justify their ruthless reduction of private enterprise, although they have not been able completely to eliminate it. Private entrepreneurs continue to this day to hold shares in joint private-state enterprises in the small-scale sector of manufacturing and service industries of China, and even in the bigger factories (the Chungkiang Iron and Steel Works, for example[12]) some kind of reversion to private ownership was tried in the early 1960s – only to be criticized during the Cultural Revolution. At the end of 1967, when the Cultural Revolution was still in full swing, a Shanghai newspaper could attack the people who were 'speculating for greater profits, setting up unlicensed factories, and cornering badly-needed goods', and the resourcefulness and business acumen of Shanghai capitalists was proved when it was admitted that they were taking advantage of the state sector's failings by mass-producing and selling at good profit badges bearing the profile of Mao Tsetung.[13]

The Indian National Congress had voted very early in its career for the principle of public ownership of the defence and power industries as well as of many sectors of heavy industry in general. The airlines, insurance and banks have provided the only important cases of nationalization of existing private companies, however, and the controversy in India during the past twenty years has been over the restrictions on private entrepreneurs' entering new fields where the state wanted to exercise a monopoly. But the state has not been very successful in operating its own plant. The average profits of state-owned enterprises in the past seven years were only just over 2 per cent of capital employed, and with about £1,450 million tied up in them this represents a drag on national development. Hindustan Steel, which runs the three big steel mills, had lost a total of £62 million up to March 1968.[14] As one American scholar has commented: 'Such low money rates of return, which are approximately one-half the same rate in private industrial undertakings, ... indicate either misallocation of scarce capital and foreign exchange as well as other resources, poor management, an uneconomic pricing policy, or all three.'[15]

J. R. D. Tata, the present head of India's premier industrialist family, has complained that his Government:

armed with a formidable panoply of economic weapons in the shape of punitive taxation and monetary, price, distribution and other controls, ... successfully created a situation ... where not only had the capital market virtually ceased to exist, but any attempt to create or expand industries in the private sector involved a nightmarish process of long-drawn negotiations, discussions, applications, representations and reminders with, and to, a host of Ministries and Departments, more than sufficient to discourage the most enterprising and patriotic of Indian entrepreneurs not to speak of his foreign collaborators.[16]

Eventually, in 1962, the first serious breach was allowed to be made in Congress policy on industrial ownership. In the face of its own inability to take up the responsibility itself, the Nehru Government permitted private interests to put up an oil refinery, and since then the morale of the private sector has improved.

It was another matter to apply these more liberal attitudes towards foreign, as distinct from Indian, capitalists. The American Congress rebuffed President Kennedy in 1963 by refusing to authorize United States help for India's fourth giant steel mill at Bokaro on the ground that it ought to be a private rather than public sector scheme, with the result that the Russians gladly stepped in to fill the breach. Since then there has been a running battle between the Americans and the Indian Government over the establishment of private sector fertilizer plants with US participation. The Americans argued that since the Indian Government could not itself expand the chemical fertilizer industry fast enough to meet the needs of the new agricultural policy, it should open the field up to private enterprise. This was done, but only grudgingly and by many stages, and a number of American corporations initially interested in the idea dropped out as a result.

The debate goes on in New Delhi about the relationship between private and public industry, but there is a general feeling that the future is with the former rather than the latter. Thus both India and China have had to some extent to come to terms with the private entrepreneur. It might be noted that the Meiji Government in Japan did in its first fifteen years or so start modern railways, iron foundries, shipyards, machine shops, cement, glass and paper factories under its own management and ownership. But most of these ventures were sold off to private entrepreneurs from the 1880s onwards.[17] Whatever the motives at the time, the effect was to provide state initiative at a time when private initiative was lacking. India is coming round to a similar view now.

One important factor in this reassessment is the extent of the disappointments which all industries, whether Government or private, have encountered in these early years in Asia, and which have somewhat tempered Governments' appetite for this particular kind of responsibility. There are enough white elephants around to make officials think twice or thrice before taking on new and uncertain large ventures. The Insein Steel mill in Burma offers an example of a project too large for the available market and badly planned from the point of view of raw materials. Another case which has been well documented is the plywood factory at Dey Eth in Cambodia, erected in 1961 with Communist Chinese aid. This also was badly planned, and the products never became competitive with those imported from abroad: the factory was at one point utilized for an entirely different line of production.[18] Over-eager management can also misuse equipment.

Mismanagement at the earlier stages is often the cause of financial loss: the West Germans calculated that the delay of almost two years in commissioning the rolling facilities at the Rourkela steel-works cost the Indian Government as much as £60 million.[19] The rusting hulk of the Soviet-aided steel-mill at Tjiregon in Indonesia, left unfinished when the Sukarno regime was finally toppled, is an outstanding example of the waste that a large industrial project can cause. The Indian Government's two colossal plants for heavy engineering at Ranchi and heavy electrical machinery at Bhopal illustrate another temptation of pioneer industrializers, that of making things too big. In each case an extraordinarily wide range of manufacture is provided for under one roof, and the equipment is more than the demand calls for. A British industrial journalist described the latter as 'the most fabulous collection of metal-cutting and shaping equipment I have ever seen assembled in one place',[20] and the Indian writer B. G. Verghese calls the former 'a mistaken essay in giganticism'.[21]

Such mistakes should be seen against the background of frequent under-utilization of capacity, another important source of waste. At the end of the Sukarno period Indonesian industry was working at less than 20 per cent of capacity, and it took two or three years for the Suharto Government to bring it up to a more respectable tempo. Most of India's factories were in 1967 working at less than half capacity, so that the capital or savings which had been ploughed into them was half wasted. The reasons were the same: inadequate demand from the local market (stunned by inflation, war, food shortages etc.), combined with difficulty in getting raw materials and spare parts from within the country (for the same reasons) or abroad (because of the shortage of foreign exchange). It seems to have taken China seven or eight years fully to utilize the new industrial capacity so hastily and unthinkingly thrown up during the Great Leap Forward of 1958, and you can still see here and there from a Chinese railway train the skeleton of an unfinished factory extension. As P. H. M. Jones has sagely remarked, 'In the industrial West a factory is an end product of multiple economic and social forces, but the developing nation tends to see a factory as a device for calling these forces into existence.'[22]

Another headache is the provision of a good labour force. The technical difficulties are obvious enough, but there are also political problems posed by the premature expectation of the kind of role and authority which the industrial trade unions command in Europe and America. The Indian Government has consistently championed the status of unions, and the dignity and welfare of labour is enshrined in the Indian Constitution. It does not, however, give its industrial managers discretion to recognize what unions they please. In 1966 workers at the Durgapur steel-works belonging to unrecognized trade unions tried, under communist leadership, to blockade and physically detain the management by the tactic known as *gherao*. Two of them were killed in the subsequent clashes with the police, and the mill's blast furnaces were damaged as a result of the neglect caused by the fracas.[23] At the Anshan steel-works in China the Communist Party authorities during the Great Leap Forward of 1958 encouraged the workers to introduce their own technical methods and organization of work in defiance of the scientifically-qualified specialists,[24] and similar instructions were given towards the end of the Cultural Revolution in 1968. The South Vietnamese Constitution declares that 'workers have the right to choose representatives to participate in the management of business enterprises.'

The traditional deference towards authority in East Asian societies is the main explanation for the relative inefficacy of the trade unions in Japan and Hongkong, but the other side of this coin is the sense of security which workers have in a system where the enterprise is regarded as an extension of the family. The old-fashioned Chinese or Japanese factory manager often treats his workers as if they were kinsmen. It has been pointed out that people working in this environment can develop an 'exceptional innovation consciousness'[25] and feel no need to resist automation or other technical changes. It is almost unheard of for a manager to dismiss a worker for mere redundancy, and the Confucian tradition in both China and Japan would deal with the advance of automation by non-recruitment rather than dismissals.

The Japanese have proved that for this reason a conservative and hierarchical society can achieve fast economic growth. Unfortunately India has the worst of both worlds, with a caste system requiring a complex division of labour and costly over-manning of plant but without the intense group consciousness which would encourage a feeling of belonging among the members of an organization. And India probably suffers more than any of the other Asian countries from labour strife.

In spite of these difficulties, the industrial achievements of the past twenty years have been considerable, as the figures cited earlier show. It is impossible to go through the new industrial estates – Ohkla near Delhi, for example, or Jurong in Singapore, Tsuen Wan in Hongkong – without feeling the excitement, the sense of purpose and pride, the satisfaction which this new activity, when satisfactorily organized and managed, can engender. The same goes for the show-pieces, the big steel-mills, power stations and chemical plants.

In some of the smaller countries, especially those which have received more foreign aid per head of population and have a stronger educational base (and a better urban-rural balance) than, say, either India or China, the new industries have been so successful that they have become substantial exporters. This is particularly true of South Korea, Taiwan, Singapore and, for slightly different reasons, Hongkong.[26] Indeed these places have become used, initially by Americans but latterly by Japanese and Europeans as well, as overseas manufacturing bases for the home market. In the 1950s American textile merchants found that Japanese fabrics and clothing were cheaper than American and could be produced in the quantities required; imports of Japanese goods soon reached a level where the American textile lobby (comprising both manufacturing interests and trade unions) was able to persuade its Government to negotiate a ceiling with the Japanese. The American merchants promptly switched their new orders to Hongkong. Taiwan and Korea, and eventually the Japanese themselves began to play this game of international musical chairs, their wages having climbed sufficiently to make it worthwhile to invest in subsidiaries abroad and ship the finished goods in from Taiwan or Korea.

There are factories all over Asia now wholly or partly owned by Western interests and catering exclusively for a Western market, and the tendency for the Soviet Union and Eastern European countries to help put up new factories in Asia on the basis of their output's being exported back to the communist *bloc* shows that this is not merely a capitalist development. The loss to the Asian host country is the outflow of foreign exchange and profits, while its gain is a part of the value added which would otherwise have gone to the Northern country, plus the intangible but crucial asset of a growing body of workers and technicians initiated into these novel industrial and managerial techniques. So far textiles and electrical appliances (especially transistor radios) have been the mainstay of this kind of internationalized trade, but it is rapidly spreading into other fields.

The trend is accelerated by the initial privileges usually granted to new industrial investors, whether domestic or foreign, in many of the developing Asian countries. In Malaysia[27] and Singapore, for instance, there is legislation which gives new investors in certain named 'pioneer' industries (i.e. ones which the two countries want to acquire or do not yet have enough of) exemption from tax for at least five years, tariff protection[28] against competing imports and a number of other benefits calculated to attract businessmen. Similar schemes operate in Thailand and other countries.

The problem in countries so large and so predominantly rural as India and China is that the inroads of industry into the fabric of society as a whole are so relatively small.* The bulk

*Some statistics suggest how thin is the veneer of modernity in the developing countries of Asia, whose share of the value added in the world's mining and manufacturing industries was only 2 per cent a few years ago

of the population is untouched by the new ideas and attitudes and the spectacular techniques employed in the bright new factories of the towns. The problem of modernization in India and China is now seen primarily as a problem of developing rural rather than urban industry. One of the features of the People's Commune in China is its role as an organizer of local small-scale industry which in ideal conditions would render the Commune self-sufficient in such consumer goods as paper, household-ware, soap, clothing and even fertilizer and electricity. The story of the village backyard steel furnace which millions of Chinese peasants frenziedly constructed in 1958 only to find that most of them were useless[29] is well known, but the spread of more suitable village industries has not been inhibited by that costly blunder.

The emphasis is on the exploitation of local materials, and the production of tools and equipment which are suitable to local conditions – not, for instance, incorporating the labour-saving accretions which nowadays account for a large part of the cost of a machine produced in the industrialized West. This corresponds to the idea of developing 'intermediate technology', first proposed by E. F. Schumacher when he was advising the Indian Government several years ago on its rural development problems. In a British industry the cost of providing a work-place for each workman is around £2,000. In present-day India little more than £1 is spent on this, and the challenge is to provide equipment and tools that would start to close this extraordinary gulf, say to the value initially of about £50.

There are now institutions in India and elsewhere dedicated exclusively to the development, testing and promotion of low-cost equipment for rice-milling, sugar-refining, ceramics, cement

and is probably little more today, although they embrace half the world's inhabitants. (See *Proceedings of the Asian Conference on Industrialisation*, Manila, 1965). Their *per capita* energy consumption is one-tenth that of the Soviet Union, one-sixteenth that of Britain, one-twenty-fifth that of the United States. Their consumption of steel per head of population is about one-thirtieth that of the United States. At the last count their aggregate number of motor vehicles in use was less than a quarter of the number that ply the busy roads of the relatively small island of Britain, and they possess between them only one in fifty of the world's telephones. See Kirby, *Economic Development in East Asia*, Chapter 6 and p. 241.

manufacture and the like – equipment which in Europe and North America has long ago been discarded and forgotten.[30] What the newly industrializing small town in Pakistan or Indonesia needs is not the latest machine tools from Dusseldorf or Birmingham but crude, locally-made, single-purpose jigs and lathes which cost less and employ (and stimulate to innovational ways of thinking) more people. Industrialization must, as it were, begin at home, and must create more jobs to absorb the population growth.

Chapter Ten

The Population Problem

'I do not feel much encouraged to speak on family planning,' the late prime minister of India, Lal Bahadur Shastri, once remarked with humility unusual in a politician; 'I have six children of my own.'[1] But the population growth and the means of controlling it are now a familiar topic throughout Asia. Of the nearly three thousand million which is likely to be added to the world's population by the end of this century, Asia will be responsible for about 60 per cent. If this is a world problem, then Asia is its most important locale.

The background against which the Asian population problem must be seen is still not well enough known. It took about half a million years for the number of men and women on this planet to reach one thousand million, in about 1815. It took less than a century to add the next thousand million, by about 1920, and only forty years to reach three thousand million in 1960. Although this extraordinary acceleration in the rate of growth is expected by almost all demographers to reach a peak within the next two decades, and then to decline, it is virtually certain that the world population will reach between six thousand million and seven thousand million by the end of this century, and it could well reach fifteen thousand million before stabilizing about a hundred years from now. Our children today are therefore likely to see a world with four times the present population.

This is not because men and women have suddenly become more sexy, although, as a president of India once remarked of his own country, 'Sex is the only indoor sport open to us.'[2] The reason is to be found in the social and economic changes engendered by the industrial revolution. The rapid advances in medicine, transport, communications and technology which burst over Western Europe during the lifetime of Napoleon dramatically reduced the incidence of death, without simultaneously reducing the incidence of birth. In all countries which have undergone the process of modernization associated with the industrial revolution, the interval between the reduction of deaths and the reduction of births was anything from fifty to a hundred years, and this bulge in the population growth rate is capable of doubling or tripling a country's total population before it settles down again to a more modest and stable rate of increase.

ASIAN POPULATIONS
(United Nations figures in millions)

	Mid-1969 Estimate	1980 Projection	Annual Growth Rate 1963–69 (%)	Density per square km.
China	740	843	1.4	77
India	537	682	2.5	164
Indonesia	117	153	2.5	78
Pakistan	112	183	2.1	118
Japan	102	111	1.1	277
Philippines	37	56	3.5	124
Thailand	35	48	3.1	68
South Korea	31	43	2.5	316
Burma	27	35	2.2	40
North Vietnam	21	25	3.1	134
South Vietnam	18	21	2.6	103
Taiwan	14	17	2.8	384
North Korea	13	17	2.5	110
Ceylon	12	18	2.4	187
Malaysia	11	15	2.9	32
Nepal	11	14	1.8	77
Khmer Rep.	7	10	2.2	37
Hong Kong	4	4	2.2	3,859
Laos	3	3	2.4	12
Singapore	2	3	2.1	3,471
Mongolia	1	2	3.1	1

Source: *UN Demographic Yearbook* 1969 (UN, New York, 1970), pp. 107–110; and, for 1980 projections, *World Population Prospects as Assessed in* 1963 (UN, New York, 1966), pp. 140–1.

In the already developed countries about one in every hundred persons dies each year, but two are born, so that there is a net increase in population of about 1 per cent a year. In the developing countries, however, the death rate and birth rate are more than double those of the West, so that the net increase for them is about 2½ per cent a year. This is the position in Asia; to a population which is already approaching two thousand million, there are added every year some fifty million new mouths (the equivalent of the entire population of Britain) to feed. India, with a population today of about 550 million, is expected to exceed 900 million thirty years hence, and China is likely to move from 760 million to 1,250 million or so in the same period.[3]

The death rate in many Asian countries began to fall very sharply almost immediately after the end of the Second World War. One of the most dramatic international campaigns of the post-war period, reminiscent of wartime operations in its scale, was the drive against malaria. Regular spraying of DDT in areas containing malaria-bearing mosquitoes was undertaken throughout the tropics in the late 1940s. In Ceylon the death rate was slashed by 40 per cent in one year as a result of this campaign, and whereas the halving of the death rate had taken England at the time of its industrial revolution seventy years to achieve, it took only seven years in Ceylon. Hardly less dramatic examples could be adduced in other Asian countries, and the effect everywhere was a spurt in the rate of population increase. When the British left India, the average new-born Indian baby could expect to die at the age of thirty-two; today his expected life span exceeds fifty years. Asia was also able to utilize modern vaccines produced in the West at low cost, so that smallpox and many other traditional mass killers have become virtually things of the past.

The American demographer Irene Taeuber has remarked that the current rate of population growth in Asia 'is a measure of the greatest humanitarian achievement of all times',[4] but it must also be recognized that this sudden change, however well intentioned, has imposed an extraordinary and unprecedented strain on the countries concerned. Longer life spans in Asia are, as Carlo Cipolla, the Italian economic historian, puts it, 'the product of changes that matured elsewhere'.[5] In Britain and the other developed countries, population growth coincided with industrialization, whereas in Asia today it has preceded industrialization. The gift of longer life is thus proving a costly one, by virtue of producing rates of population growth and a level of ultimate population too fast and too high, respectively, for comfort. The instant availability of the accumulated foreign knowledge of two centuries brings new stresses as well as welcome relief, and the burden of bearing, in Cipolla's phrase, an 'agricultural' birth rate with an 'industrial' death rate[6] is a heavy one.

Whereas you can prevent someone dying by a timely application of medicine, you cannot so easily prevent a baby from

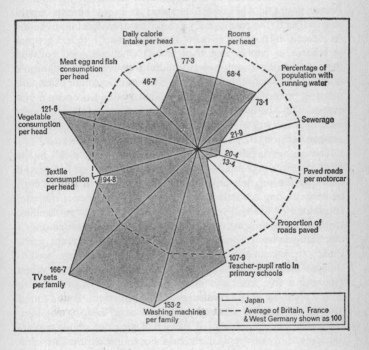

being born. A fall in the birth rate is the result of complex social changes which are likely to extend over at least one generation, if not two. It is a matter of changing attitudes and habits of mind. For millennia men and women have conceived children in the knowledge that very few of them were likely to live more than a few months. Queen Anne of England, some ten generations ago, bore no fewer than seventeen children, only one of whom survived the diseases of infancy – and he died at the age of eleven. In Asia, where the lineal family is a far stronger and more autonomous unit of society than it ever was in Stuart England, the tradition of married couples' desiring large families – and especially sons – dies hard. In Chinese villages the old proverbs about 'More Children, More Happiness' and 'Rear Children to Protect your Old Age' are still repeated, and some parents remain sceptical as to the permanency or validity of medical innovations so recently introduced. I once dined with two Filipino couples (a senator, a banker and their wives) who confessed between them to having twenty-seven children; and one of Sukarno's aunts bore twenty-three children. These are extreme examples, perhaps, but not so untypical as a modern young European might expect. The doctor whose version of the loop has been widely used in Asian has urged the Indian government to introduce an old-age pension to discourage the large families of the past.[7]

The change in attitude which led in Europe to a fall in the birth rate was accompanied by a rising standard of living, and although the relationship between the two is a matter of controversy among scholars it seems probable that better material conditions of life will reduce the desire to have large families. Unfortunately the vast majority of Asians have witnessed only a marginal improvement in their income per head in recent years. Finally there is an educational problem in addition to the need to change attitudes and improve material conditions. When Thailand a few years ago made a pilot survey of attitudes to family planning in the rural district of Photharam, it was found that 72 per cent of mothers wished to cease bearing children, but fewer than 1 per cent of them had any idea about contraception.[8] Many surveys in different Asian countries now show that a majority of Asian women would ideally like to have no more than three or four children, and ignorance of contraceptive techniques is probably a greater obstacle to population control than is lack of motivation.

It is worth noting that there is very little religious objection to artificial methods of birth control in Asia except in the Philippines, the only country with a large Catholic population, and the only one that ever makes serious reservations in what would otherwise be unanimous conclusions of Asian conferences on these problems. The Buddhist, Hindu, Islamic and Shinto faiths do not lay down for their adherents any rigid requirements of conduct in the matter of contraception.

It is nevertheless quite a new thing for these intimate matters to be discussed publicly. As a Shanghai newspaper explained a few years ago: 'Birth control is connected with sex, and for thousands of years no respectable man has spoken in public about sex. . . . Such feudal notions . . . still exert influence.'[9] It is extremely rare for Chinese to criticize their government in the presence of foreigners, and a Canadian correspondent who lived in China in 1959 and 1960 came across only one example of this: 'We all consider', he was told by this sole critic, 'that the State has no right to interfere in people's private lives. Raising a family is your personal affair, and has nothing to do with national progress.'[10] Similar sentiments are expressed in other countries. Some public leaders are reluctant to pursue birth control campaigns with the vigour that would be necessary for them to succeed, out of a kind of nationalism. Just as the prospect of devaluing the national currency stirs up irrational patriotic feelings, in Asia as in the West, so the possibility of a decline in the national numbers is usually viewed with horror. In some countries this is not without some justification. A Burmese minister of planning once declared that his countrymen, far from limiting their families, should strive to increase them so that the number of Burmese would double within about sixteen years: 'If present trends continue and there is no increase in the population,' he warned, 'the Burmese will disappear one day.'[11] The Burmese are indeed a rather small nation in a part of Asia which has in relatively modern times seen the virtual disappearance of some national groups through warfare and conquest.* But there is less excuse for the remark of an Indonesian member of parliament who, while supporting birth control, commented: 'We

*The Burmans proper form only a part of the total population of Burmese nationals and would like to increase their dominance in their own country: hence racial factors enter into this question as well. The Thai prime minister is opposed to a national birth control campaign because 'if we cut down Thai births and the aliens [i.e. the Chinese residents] keep on producing babies, we will one day become a minority race.' (*Bangkok Post*, 19 July 1966).

must be well prepared to prevent this family planning programme [giving rise to] the possibility of "population shortage" in Indonesia in the next twenty years.'[12]

Most Asian governments were hostile to family planning until very recently. It was forbidden to propagate birth control or to practise abortion not only in Meiji Japan but also in the Japan of Tojo and the Indonesia of Sukarno. When the new military government of Park Chung Hee took power in South Korea in 1961, it found on the statute books a law forbidding the import of contraceptives. Sukarno once explained: 'Our people are unspoiled and we don't want them spoiled. Birth control in the West has conduced to loose morals.'[13] Many Asians of the older generation are also afraid of the promiscuity which the spreading of contraceptive techniques can encourage (as indeed were their Western counterparts before it became too late to regret the new freedoms of the young). There is also at the back of many nationalist minds in Asia a suspicion that family planning is pressed upon them by Western advisers in order to reduce the eventual political importance of the nations of the coloured world. We shall return to this anxiety, but it is enough at this stage to underline the full complexity of the difficulties standing in the way of a political decision to bring the birth rate down to match the falling death rate. For the time being Asia (apart from Japan) is in the uncomfortable position of exercising death control without birth control.

It may be surprising that the full challenge of the Asian population increase (which, it may be noted in passing, can only by excessive journalistic license be called an 'explosion') took so long to be recognized. There are two reasons for this. The first is that firm information on the growth rate only became available when the results of the censuses of 1960 and 1961 had been published. The series of decennial censuses in Asia had been interrupted, naturally, by the Second World War, and in any case pre-war conditions in most Asian countries prevented the holding of a thorough count of heads. The 1950–1 censuses were, therefore, the first indications for many countries of the real size of their populations.

One must hasten to add that there are grave doubts about the complete validity of any of these censuses in view of the ingrained habit of not reporting births or deaths to the authorities: however, such difficulties exist even in the West, and so the post-war censuses in Asia at least offer a plausible starting point for estimating the total population. There were some surprises, notably the Chinese census of 1953 which recorded 583 million people living on the Chinese mainland – some 15 per cent more than most observers, including the Chinese communists themselves, had supposed.

But the absence of comparable figures for the previous decade made it impossible to use these census results for ascertaining the rate of growth, and it was not until the early 1960s that two successive decennial censuses could be compared. The results of this piece of homework proved quite alarming, especially in the southern half of Asia. India, Pakistan, the Philippines and Thailand all discovered that their populations were about 6 per cent or 7 per cent larger than they had expected, and that the rate of expansion was almost half as big again as they had estimated – $2\frac{1}{2}$ per cent a year instead of $1\frac{3}{4}$ per cent.

It was this new light on the population growth which led to the widespread acceptance among Asian leaders of the need to promote birth control as a very high priority. The first Asian Population Conference, convened in New Delhi at the end of 1963, agreed, in the opening words of its unanimously adopted final resolution, 'that the rapid growth of population in many countries of the ECAFE region is impeding their economic and social development and threatening the success of their efforts to reach satisfactory levels of living within a tolerable length of time . . .'[14]

But there was another difficulty which stood in the way of recognition of the problem, namely the opposition by the developed countries on both sides of the Iron Curtain to international discussion or action in the field of family planning. The Indian government had asked for the help of the United Nations World Health Organization in assessing and combating its population problem as early as 1952, only to be sent away with a flea in its ear. The Western countries which were predominantly Catholic or which contained large Catholic minorities refused to allow their funds to be used in promoting artificial methods of birth control. It was in any case a matter which many Westerners felt should not be elevated to the intergovernment level, whatever the religious sensibilities involved. President Eisenhower protested in 1959: 'I cannot imagine anything more emphatically a subject that is not a proper political or government activity or function or responsibility.'[15] Soon after this President Kennedy, though himself a Catholic, changed the official American attitude to one of constructive tolerance.

Meanwhile Sweden, which had been helping the family planning movement in Ceylon and Pakistan since the very early days of independence, had been taking the lead also in seeking UN recognition of the problem. But the hostility of the Catholics was matched by the distaste of the communists, who maintained a professional optimism about the capacity of science and technology to deal with the needs of a larger population. The Soviet Union and its allies attacked all talk of population control as a disgraceful resurgence of Malthusianism.* A Marxist is principally concerned to assert the conscious domination by man of his environment, and anxiety lest larger populations prove in future difficult to feed or employ is quite inconsistent with the spirit of Marxist-Leninism (although there were many wags in the UN corridors who passed the comment that in communist countries the production of everything is planned except the production of children).

When the Swedes at last gained a hearing for the population problem in the United Nations General Assembly in 1962, their resolution on Population Growth and Economic Development was adopted, but the crucial recommendation that the UN 'give technical assistance, as requested by governments, for national projects and programmes dealing with the problems of population' was rejected after a tied vote of 34–34, with 32 abstentions. Very broadly speaking the vote followed religious lines, the Protestant, Buddhist and Muslim countries voting for the recommendation, the Catholic nations against. Both the United States and the Soviet Union in the end abstained. In fact it was

---

*Malthus was the English philosopher whose *Essay on the Principles of Population* (1798) argued that population tended to grow geometrically whereas food production grew arithmetically, that population would always rise to exceed the limit of available food supplies, and that it could only be checked by the misfortunes of war, famine and pestilence.

doubted by UN officials whether the international organizations need any specific authority from the General Assembly to include family planning among their activities, and although the 1962 debate was formally inconclusive it proved to be the turning point. In 1965 India again requested United Nations advice for its family planning programme, and this time a team of experts was sent.

These days a compromise wording is commonly used at international conferences whereby family planning advice is authorized but only at the request of the government concerned and only as part of a wider context of organized health services. The factor which usually receives unanimous consideration is the need to protect the health of mothers obliged to endure unwanted pregnancies in the absence of family planning advice, and it is on this ground alone that some Asians justify the family planning programmes.

The methods of birth control used and propagated in Asia include the traditional contraceptive devices. But the relatively new panaceas – the pill and the loop – have a most important role to play. The contraceptive pill is still somewhat expensive for mass use in Asia, but the loop (Intra-Uterine Contraceptive Device or IUCD) can be manufactured for as little as two pence and is felt to be fairly effective. At Asian conferences on these matters the slogan is sometimes quoted: 'Loop before you Leap'.

But such is the gravity of the problem that the far more controversial practices of abortion and sterilization are also envisaged in some of the Asian schemes. Japan's success in halving her population growth rate from 2 per cent a year to 1 per cent during the 1950s is attributed more to abortions than to any other factor, and these operations were running at the level of about a million a year during the 1950s (the Japanese Diet passed the Eugenic Protection Law authorizing abortions in 1948).[16] Since about five years ago, contraception has replaced abortion as the main factor in holding the Japanese birth rate down, but it is recognized in the developing countries of Asia that the practice of abortion does exist, that it is difficult to stamp out, that it would be better and healthier to bring it into the open and that it does help to bring the birth rate down. Abortions are thus officially recognized, though not necessarily encouraged, in China, and the law prohibiting abortions is expected to be amended and liberalized shortly in India.

One Indian minister of family planning, Dr S. Chandrasekhar, proposed in 1967 that all Indian fathers be compulsorily sterilized after their third child.[17] He at least practises what he preaches, since he himself underwent vasectomy at the age of 38 after the birth of his third child. Sterilization in India is proceeding at the rate of more than a million a year, and cash rewards are given by State Governments in India to people volunteering for this operation. The Chinese prime minister, Chou En-lai, has also spoken in favour of parents undergoing sterilization

It should be added that the pressure on parents to limit their families is maintained in a number of ways, including such distinctives as fewer tax allowances and the withholding of extra rations[18] in India and China respectively, as well as the encouragement of later rather than early marriages. In one of the Indian State Assemblies a legislator has even tabled a private bill which would send the father of a fourth child to prison for six months, with the alternative of a £50 fine.[19]

The cost of sustained family planning campaigns across the whole of developing Asia is considerable. It is estimated that the prevention of one birth costs something in the order of £30. Richard Gardner calculates that the protection of the 170 million Asian women who he estimates are exposed to unwanted pregnancies would cost about £850 million a year: this would have the effect of bringing Asia's net population growth down to the level of 1 per cent a year.[20] In fact, of course, only a pitiful fraction of this is being spent: Pakistan expected to spend about £5 million a year on family planning programmes during the Third Five-Year Plan, and the Indian target is £14 million a year – little more than 3 pence per head. But this is nevertheless a vast improvement on the negligible sums that were being spent a decade ago, and there is ground for hope that this is one field at least in which technical and financial aid from abroad will rise substantially in the years to come. It is worth adding that population control, like the development of new hybrid cereals, is one of the areas in which the work of the Ford and Rockefeller Foundations has been an indispensable driving force right from the beginning. It is largely due to them, and to the bodies which they support, that the loop has become successfully popularized in Asia.

What, then, are the results so far discernible from these programmes of birth control in Asia? There is no sign yet of a downturn in the birth rate in any of the countries of South Asia, with the notable exception of Malaysia and Singapore. Although India was the first country in the world to adopt family planning as an integral part of its development policy, the really serious attack on the problem is too recent to be reflected in the vital statistics. The Government's aim is to reduce the birth rate from the present 4.1 per cent to 2.5 per cent by 1975. Family planning advice and equipment are made available in more than twenty-five thousand centres all over India, and by 1968 more than $4\frac{1}{2}$ million citizens had been sterilized, more than $2\frac{1}{2}$ million loops had been inserted and one hundred thousand women were taking the contraceptive pill under medical supervision. Dr Chandrasekhar claimed that these measures have so far prevented the birth of about 12 million Indian babies, and his Ministry argued that the tentative beginning of a decline in the birth rate could already be inferred from studies in selective areas.[21]

In Pakistan the family planning commissioner, Enver Adil, hoped to bring the birth rate down from its very high 5 per cent to 4 per cent during the Third Plan ending in 1970. Pakistan's birth rate is much higher than India's, and the authorities were slower in tackling it. It can be assumed that the attainment of a tolerable birth rate will take a long time in India and even longer in Pakistan. In Indonesia, as we have seen, the Sukarno era was unfavourable to family planning. It was only in 1969 that a concerted Indonesian birth control programme was envisaged as beginning. Burma, Thailand and the Philippines have not yet begun to take this problem seriously.

The picture is very different, however, in eastern Asia. Irene Taeuber was able to say as long ago as 1965 that 'birth rates are low or declining among all the Chinese or Chinese-related people along Asia's eastern periphery.'[22] Japan, of course, now enjoys not only the level of affluence and industrialization of Western countries, but also their relatively modest population growth – of about 1 per cent – and although Japanese planners are concerned at the prospect of their country's producing within a few decades a gigantic continuous ribbon of urbanization stretching almost the entire length of the island of Honshu, there is no serious anxiety over the possibility of sustaining the 122 million inhabitants which Japan expects by the end of this century. The Taiwan birth rate has been brought down by a third (from 5 per cent to 3½ per cent) over the past fifteen years, and the Hongkong birth rate has been reduced from 4 per cent to just under 3 per cent in the same period. Although the South Koreans did not come to grips with the problem until the 1960s, they have already brought the population growth rate down by about one tenth.

In China too the tide may have begun to turn. The communists began by rejecting the idea of population control, and there is a well-known dictum of Chairman Mao which was republished in 1961:

> It is a very good thing that China has a big population. Even if China's population multiplies many times, she is fully capable of finding a solution; the solution is production ... of all things in the world, people are the most precious. Under the leadership of the Communist Party, as long as there are people, every kind of miracle can be performed.[23]

But, as in the case of India, the initial optimism of the Chinese planners had to be tempered when the census results brought out the full gravity of the problem and food harvest failed to maintain a steady and substantial annual improvement. The Peking Government reverted to its pristine Maoist optimism during the period of the Great Leap Forward, but it is now carrying out a modest family planning programme which may have begun to show results, at least in the cities.

The urgency of the Asian population problem may not really lie in the question of feeding all the new mouths. It is true that Asian food production was either stagnant or else failing to keep pace with the increased population during the early 1960s. But its record was a good one in the 1950s, and in the last year or two there have been signs of a breakthrough with the use of new hybrid seeds and more chemical fertilizers. The evidence so far does not allow one to be optimistic, but it cannot justify pessimism either.

The population problem has perhaps more to do with employment than food supply. Because the spurt in the population growth rate is so recent, the Asian populations are heavily weighted by the young. Every other Asian is under twenty-one, and two in five are below the age of fifteen. The problems that this creates can be seen from the case of China: in the decade before the communists came to power 135 million Chinese children were born, but in the decade after they came to power the number of births was 207 million. How do you provide satisfactory employment for the sudden floods of school-leavers who are now entering the labour market? This proved to be one of the issues in the Cultural Revolution. Similarly, in India it is envisaged in the Fourth Plan that some twenty-three million prospective new workers will come on to the labour market, but only nineteen million new jobs will become available. The labour force in developing Asia is expected to swell by 56 per cent during the two decades between 1960 and 1980, creating a need for 336 million new jobs.[24] It is obvious from figures such as these that the promotion of rural public works, of the kind that have been rather successfully organized in the Chinese communes since 1958, will become more and more necessary throughout Asia.

The problem is aggravated, of course, by the reluctance of school-leavers to take up manual work, which the educated élite have always despised, in Asia even more than elsewhere. In Ceylon it has been found that unemployment actually increases with education, and one can therefore see the point of the Chinese communists' insistence on making desk-bound workers participate periodically in manual labour in order to destroy these long-nurtured prejudices.

The employment aspect of the population problem should not, however, be exaggerated. A new member of the population is not merely a number but a person, capable of producing as well as consuming, and possessing the potential talent and skill necessary to exploit the natural resources around him. Whether population growth places an unbearable strain on employment depends on the political and social organization of the country concerned and the extent of its untapped natural resources.

The real heart of the population problem is its tendency

to hinder national economic development. As Ohlin puts it in his masterly summary of the problem as it affects the world as a whole.

In the long run, the gravest prospect to be feared in the under-developed countries does not seem to be a failure to provide for continued support at present levels. One must face the more probable and equally far-reaching problem that excessive population growth will make the hopes of diminishing international inequalities futile.[25]

As things stand now, the average Asian country can hope to achieve economic growth of about 5 per cent a year, assuming reasonably normal weather and a modicum of good leadership, but half of this gain must be written off in order to provide for the new arrivals, and it thus takes twice as long to reach the development targets. To put it another way, if the Indian population had remained stable since independence in 1947, the gain in income per head would now be four times what has actually been achieved.

Furthermore, economists estimate that a country with a population growing by $2\frac{1}{2}$ per cent a year must invest $7\frac{1}{2}$ per cent of its total national income in order to maintain the same level of income per head in future years. President Johnson claimed in his speech for the twentieth birthday of the United Nations that 'five dollars invested in population control is worth a hundred dollars invested in economic growth.' Some economists argue that the return, in terms of higher incomes per head, on funds spent on population control is as much as sixty times greater than funds sunk into economic development programmes.[26]

These calculations can be disputed, but Dr Boerma, Director-General of the FAO, reflected the international consensus on the question when he declared in the summer of 1968 that, 'the threat of continued uncontrolled population expansion could make a mockery of all the benefits that technical progress holds out for mankind. To prevent this, family planning should become a built-in component of the vast infrastructure necessary for sustained economic development.'[27] As a recent Asian conference on problems of children and youth concluded: 'In effect, population growth is endangering the quality of mankind, as a large part of national resources must be devoted to simply maintaining existing levels of living, leaving few resources available for improving those levels.'[28]

There is a sentiment in Asia, all the same, that Westerners have over-dramatized the problem. As one Indian economist recently explained:

However, there is reason to believe that in many cases the agitation over population growth in Asia (and in developing countries generally) is politically inspired. The cry of alarm was first sounded in the industrialized countries; it represented a response not so much to an existing or potential demographic problem but rather to a political situation. Wearied by pleas from developing countries for greater economic assistance, the industrialized countries began to insist on the importance of population control, although it is evident that in many parts of Asia population pressure is only one of a number of factors responsible for the low rate of economic development. However, by singling out population control, industrialized countries have directed attention to an area in which developing countries must act first.[29]

It is perhaps inevitable that the motives of the outsiders who press advice on Asia are questioned. An extreme form of this can be quoted from a Burmese newspaper editorial of 1961:

Behind all the talk about population pressure and the need for control in Asia is the fear and bad conscience that one day soon enough masses of Asians will erupt and inundate with fire and sword the prosperous areas of the world in sole occupation by the European races...[30]

The additions now being made to the world population are principally in Asia and in the other parts of the developing world, but this follows an earlier period in which the Europeans not only enlarged their numbers in similar measure but also expanded into other continents by a process of exploration, colonization and imperialism. Are we now to redress the balance and revert to the pre-industrial-revolution pattern of racial distribution?

The accompanying table shows that the numerical relationship between Europe and Asia is not likely to change so dramatically, at least over the balance of the present century. Over the next thirty years the developed countries of the white world will continue to revert to their pre-industrial-revolution share of one fifth of mankind, but Europe's loss will be the gain, not of Asia but of Africa (which is only now beginning to make up for the depletions of the slave trade) and of Latin America (which has so much more space to fill). Indeed, Asia might, in this slightly absurd game of numbers, be said to have reason to feel aggrieved at only fractionally making up for her relative losses since the industrial revolution in Europe. Possibly the twenty-first century will see to it that the original balance between Asia and Europe is more nearly restored, but it is hard to justify the fears sometimes expressed in the West about the 'Asian hordes'.

CONTINENTAL BREAKDOWN OF
WORLD POPULATION (%)

	1650	1750	1850	1950	2000*
The North†	19	20	26	31	21
The South	81	80	74	69	79
Asia	61	66	64	55	56
South Asia				29	34
East Asia				27	22
Africa	18	13	8	8	13
Latin America	2	2	3	6	10

Indeed, the breakdown of the Asian projections into South Asia and East Asia shows that if there *is* a peril somewhere here, it is a brown one rather than yellow;[31] South Asia's share of world population is expected to rise in the next thirty years in the same measure as that of East Asia will decline. One should not make too much of this, because the projections are most fallible, especially for China (which alone of the major Asian countries has failed to publish the results of its second census in 1964).

The question of possible Asian expansionism across international frontiers worries many people. It is not justifiable to suppose, as some scholars have done,[32] that demographic pressures might of themselves lead such countries as China, India, Pakistan and Japan into the paths of aggression. These very large countries tend to be self-sufficient, or at least to strive for self-sufficiency, in all important materials and resources. Japan

*The U N medium-variant fertility projection. †Europe, North America, Australasia. Sources: Stamp, *Our Developing World*, p. 20, supplemented by *World Population Prospects As Assessed in 1963* (U N).

is the exception to this, and Japan was indeed an expansionist power in the 1930s. But this was to secure not so much *Lebens-raum* as sources of supply for the raw materials needed by Japanese industry. The humiliating defeat of 1945 had a traumatic effect on Japan, and she is unlikely to repeat that particular mistake, the more so since she has so successfully constructed over the past two decades a satisfactory network of world-wide trading relations that are purely commercial and peaceful in character.

One would also argue, I think, that China and India too can obtain from abroad more cheaply by commerce than by conquest the few materials which they cannot supply themselves in the amounts required. It should be emphasized that the population density in Asia is not much different from that in Europe – about 240 people per square mile in each case – and that in China the density is only three quarters of that. Furthermore, it is hard to imagine that any serious expansion (as distinct from such border conflicts as the Indo-Pakistan War of 1965 and the Sino-Indian War of 1962, such internal resumptions of sovereignty as the Chinese re-entry into Tibet in 1950 or such civil wars as those in Korea and Vietnam) could occur nowadays without fierce resistance on the part of those already in possession sufficient to ensure the intervention of far stronger forces from outside.

There is indeed some small part to be played by migration in the amelioration of the population problem, but this will be by international agreement (in the case of the Japanese emigrants to Brazil, for example, or the Indian and Pakistani emigrants to Britain) or purely internal. About 3 per cent of the annual increase in the population of Java is normally removed to the other less densely populated inslands of Indonesia under government direction, and the Chinese goverment operates similar relocation of population from the big cities on the eastern seaboard to the relatively underdeveloped regions of the western interior, in Sinkiang, Inner Mongolia, Tibet and elsewhere.

The real race is not against space, but against time. What is alarming about the Asian population increase is its speed. It allows so little time for the already overstrained political, social and economic organization of countries only recently entered in the modernization stakes to cope with a situation where numbers can double in little more than twenty years. This is the consideration which weighs most with those Asians who view this problem in its perspective.

Chapter Eleven

Economic Development

WHEN Gunnar Myrdal, the great Swedish economist, published in 1968 his long-awaited analysis of the reasons for the slow economic development of the countries of Asia, he called it *Asian Drama: An inquiry into the Poverty of Nations*. To compress into a few decades the turbulent and painful revolutions that have preoccupied the West over two or three centuries would be material for drama anywhere in the developing countries of 'the South', but there are reasons for it to be particularly intense in the Asia of our day.

The desire to banish poverty and to raise the standard of one's material life needs no explanation, at least for Western ears. Alberto Moravia extols what he detects as a cult of indigence in Maoist China,[1] and there are intellectuals and priests in Asia (not merely among the Buddhists and Hindus) who decry the Western quest for incessant material advance. But when poverty is dictated, not chosen, and when it is accompanied by ignorance, illiteracy and disease, it is generally accepted that development of the national economy is a good thing.

This is not, however, the only motivation for material progress in Asia. Its national leaders have been made to realize that their claims for equality in world politics have little chance of being heard without economic power to back them up. As Borodin, Sun Yat-sen's Soviet adviser, reported in the 1920s, Chinese intellectuals 'used to think that by reminding the world of China's long civilized history, they would get her a place in the family of nations. China has learned, since Versailles, that the family tolerates no poor relations, even with four thousand years of a respectable past.'[2] The slogan of Meiji Japan a century ago was *Fukoku Kyohei* – 'Rich Country, Strong Army'. There is thus a political driving force behind the quest for development, and prestige is as much a rallying cry as prosperity.

Japan, of course, is the only Asian country to have succeeded in attaining Western levels of economic development, and in terms of gross national product Japan now ranks third in the world after the two super powers, America and Russia. This has been accomplished in the space of the hundred years since the Meiji Revolution of 1868, under rather adverse conditions. Japan did not rely on foreign capital or foreign aid for her industrialization, and she was not allowed the privilege of tariff protection for her infant industries.[3] Some scholars now believe that the makings of an independent development of indigenous capitalism were already there in pre-Meiji Japan,[4] which would render Japan's case very different from any other Asian country's. These views are not widely publicized, for they must discourage other Asians striving to follow quickly in Japan's footsteps. Just as the Japanese defeat of Russia, a European power, in 1905 inspired nationalists all over Asia to dream of overthrowing European colonialism, so Japan's conquest of affluence is seen by Asian planners as proof that the West has no monopoly on economic development, and as an earnest of their own future. This does mean, of course, that Japan has become a part of the developed world, enjoying a level of income per head comparable with Italy's, and that the discussion which follows is about the still-developing part of the continent, Asia *minus* Japan.

Developing Asia is indeed the Cinderella of the South. Like Africa and Latin America, developing Asia is poor. According to the latest United Nations statistics for national income per head, the average for the world as a whole is £215.[5] The average Latin American income is £120, the average in the Middle East is £100, the average African's is $120 – but in East and South Asia (excluding Japan) the average is a derisory £35. As India's prime minister, Mrs Indira Gandhi, once explained, 'India has to work very hard just to wipe the tears from every eye.' East and South Asia hold half of the world's population, but only 15 per cent of its land area and 12 per cent of its current productive wealth.[6]

Also like Africa and Latin America, Asia is obliged to develop in a world dominated, materially and intellectually, by the already grown. There is physical and psychological pressure on the countries of South and East Asia to give health priority

over growth, to absorb unsuitable advanced technology and
social institutions, to pay salaries dictated by an inflated international market in scarce skills, to lose their primary product
exports at the hands of synthetic substitutes, and to follow
out-dated doctrines.[7] In the West and Japan, the trade unions,
democracy and public health came after the process of industrialization. India felt obliged to have these luxuries at a time when

A MEASURE OF POVERTY IN ASIA

United Nations Estimates of Gross National Product, 1968
in US $ millions

	Total	Per head
USA	880,774	4,379
USSR*	355,000	1,508
France	126,623	2,537
Britain	102,875	1,861
Canada	62,254	2,997
Australia	29,786	2,476
New Zealand	4,861	1,767
Japan	141,882	1,404
China*	68,000	89
India†	41,114	80
Pakistan	15,287	140
Indonesia	10,868	96
Philippines	10,814	301
South Korea	5,900	194
Thailand	5,588	166
Taiwan	4,199	312
South Vietnam	3,508	201
Malaysia‡	3,057	314
Burma	2,057	78
Ceylon	1,805	151
Hongkong§	1,550	442
Singapore	1,438	723
Khmer Rep.‡	920	147
Nepal	801	75
Laos§	168	67

*Unofficial author's estimates, not from UN.
†Figures for 1967.
‡Figures for 1966.
§Figures for 1963.
Source: *UN Yearbook of National Accounts Statistics 1969* (UN, New
York, 1970). But see note 5 to this Chapter.

she was still a backward agrarian economy. The Chinese communists, operating in a more authoritarian tradition, could dispense with independent trade unions and opposition parties, but they did opt for modern public health. Democracy and civil liberties make it difficult for a government to upset vested interests and initiate genuine change; welfare absorbs scarce resources which could otherwise be spent on development; while hygiene worsens the problem of population growth, as we have seen.

In all these respects the government of a developing country in present-day Asia is far worse placed than that of Japan or of the nations of the West at the time of their industrialization. Asia is trying to have it both ways, to have the fruits of industrialization without its horrors, and who can blame it for that? Japan's economic historian, William Lockwood, concludes that, 'Japanese capitalism displayed an all too callous disregard for the immediate well-being of the worker in the factory and the field. It perpetuated evils like child labour and tenant oppression long after the remedies were at hand.'[8] Is it really possible for the Indian or Chinese intellectuals of today to follow the same insensitive path, to sacrifice this generation of peasant and proletarian for the sake of the next, to tighten their belts and also stop their ears to the cries of the victims of the sudden changes they are imposing on their stagnant societies?

All these difficulties are shared by Asia with Africa and Latin America, but in one respect Asia is additionally burdened, over and above her lower starting point. Unlike Africa, Asia looks back to a golden age when her civilizations were the envy of the globe, and whereas the African turns relatively easily to new modes of production and behaviour, the Asian is paradoxically inhibited by the existence of a strong millennial social tradition which does not easily bow to foreign influence. In Latin America this difficulty is considerably reduced by the influence of the large body of European immigrants providing the initial dynamism for economic change. Asia thus seems doomed to be not only poorest of the poor, but also slowest of the slow, in the world economic development stakes.

There is nevertheless a satisfactory material basis for Asian development. The natural resources of South-East Asia – rubber, tin, oil, timber and crops, and minerals of all kinds – have been a magnet for European and Arab traders for many centuries. It was the gold and spices and silk of the Orient that first attracted the powers which ultimately conquered Asia. Asia is today the main producer of rice, cotton, jute, tea, oilseeds, rubber, tin and iron ore. It used to be thought that India and China were poorly endowed by nature, but the most recent results of soil analysis and geological prospecting indicate that neither of these two countries has much to fear in terms of attaining self-sufficiency in important materials, although India does seem short of non-ferrous metals. It is only in the past decade that thorough surveying and exploration has begun in the remote mountainous regions of northern India and western China, and there may yet be some surprises in store. Deposits in these areas will, of course, prove expensive and slow in yielding to commercial exploitation because of transport difficulties.

The two important shortages which do hinder Asian economic development programmes are those of capital and skills. The funds available for investment in development schemes are primarily dictated by the domestic savings and taxes of each country itself; given the low standard of living, the margin for capital accumulation is naturally small. Taxes raised by governments represent only about one-eighth of gross national product in developing Asia, compared with about one-third in the West.[9] Most Asian governments derive only about one-fifth of their revenues from income tax and other direct taxation. Unlike most Western governments, they depend much more on customs and excise duties, sales tax and other indirect taxation. The Meiji government in Japan obtained most of its funds for development and expansion overseas from the land tax even as late as the end of the nineteenth century.

But it is increasingly hard for the governments of the developing countries of Asia to cream off compulsory savings through taxation. The improvement in agricultural yields has primarily benefited the better-off farmer, who is more adept than the city-dweller at avoiding taxation. In India all forms of agricultural taxation are controlled by the State governments rather than the central government, and, at a time when the planners in New Delhi are desperately calling for more funds to be raised

UN and author's estimates of Gross National Product, 1966 (US dollar millions); the first figure indicates total GNP, the second *per capita* incomes.

from the land, the States refuse to tax farm incomes for local political reasons and some of them are actually abolishing or reducing their land revenue. Indonesia abolished the land tax in 1951 because it was associated with the colonial past, and today its economists regret the decision. Even in China, where

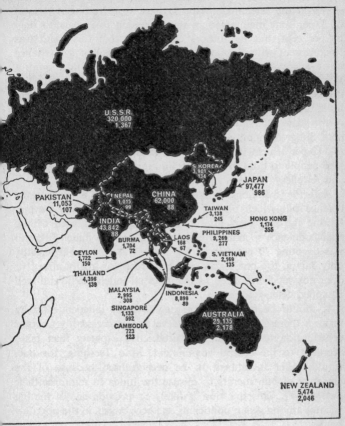

more authoritarian methods are used, the central government in Peking cannot get all the funds it wants from the localities, and one of the issues between the Maoists and the Liuists in the Cultural Revolution was the extent to which savings and investment should be exacted from the communes by the government.

As the political balance of power shifts away from the urban towards the rural élites in many parts of developing Asia, the prospect for centrally organized savings diminishes. The Indian economic development plan for the year 1967–8 envisaged a slump in the rate of domestic savings, from the average level of 9 per cent maintained in the preceding two years to only $6\frac{1}{2}$ per cent, but its authors commented that this trend was 'inconsistent with the accepted long-term goal of self-reliance at an adequate rate of growth. For this goal would require a saving rate of close to 20 per cent of national income.'[10] The problem is even tougher in a country such as Indonesia where inflation caused consumer prices to rise by 600 per cent in each of the years 1965 and 1966, and where the new regime of President Suharto found cause for satisfaction in bringing it down to 112 per cent in 1967. Such price rises discourage savings and lead people to hold their wealth in unproductive hoards of gold and jewellery.

A further additional burden on Asian savings is the sizeable defence bill which almost every government is now paying. During the five years after the 1962 border war with China, India's defence spending trebled, and Indonesia under Sukarno was devoting 70 per cent of her budget to defence. Ironically, only Japan, the one Asian country which can really afford it, does not yet feel obliged to maintain an independent and well equipped defence force.

It should be added that money invested independently by farmers themselves at the local level is not necessarily a worse contribution to the country's productive capacity than taxes accruing to the central government. Mao Tse-tung, for one, would prefer investment to be decentralized because of the tendency of bureaucrats to misuse the funds to reinforce their own power. This question is likely to provide one of the big debates among Asian politicians and economists in the next few years.

But domestic savings are only one part of the financial problem of a developing country in Asia. Money is also needed from abroad. One source of this is foreign aid and investment; these are discussed in detail in Chapter 23. Another source is export earnings, and since these are the only assured and dignified means of obtaining the foreign exchange to import the foodstuffs, fertilizer, capital equipment and other articles necessary for the country's economy, increasing attention is now being paid to this. China has dispensed with foreign aid, and normally exports slightly more than she imports. Her surplus earnings are used to pay for such invisible imports as shipping charges and insurance, diplomatic expenditure, and the modest Chinese foreign aid programme. But it is more common in the non-communist developing countries of Asia to run a substantial trade deficit, met by foreign aid. Thus India has been buying more from abroad than she has been selling to the tune of about £280 million a year in 1967, more than £400 million). It is, in a way, the difference between paying cash on the nail and buying foreign machinery on hire purchase, paying by instalments. India is getting more needed equipment than China but is mortgaging her future to do so.

Whichever method of purchasing foreign goods is employed it is obviously advantagous to earn as much as possible from exports. Unfortunately, exports by the developing countries of Asia have been increasing by only 4 per cent a year in the past fifteen years or so. The traditional primary commodities in which Asia is so rich are tending to fall in price, and there seems little likelihood of reversing this trend. High hopes are therefore placed on the export potential of Asia's new industries, beginning with the traditional light industries which are the easiest to launch – textiles, plastic-ware and light machinery including electrical appliances and radios. But another difficulty has been encountered here, namely that the rich industrialized countries which are the most attractive and natural markets for these goods are reluctant to allow unlimited entry of cheap manufactures. This is partly because of competition with domestic industry (a manufacturing lobby is less easy to ignore than a consumers' lobby, so that the argument of lower prices goes largely unconsidered), and partly out of defence considerations. If the US became totally dependent on Asia for all its garments and cloth, it would be disabled from clothing its armed forces in the event of war.

Nevertheless, following the footsteps of Japan, the most enterprising of the Asian developers – notably Hongkong, Taiwan, South Korea, Pakistan, India and the Philippines – have gained substantial shares of the American and West European markets in these items in spite of the latter's attempts to regulate them. In 1962 a long-term cotton textile export agreement was negotiated at Geneva between the main supplying countries and the main importing countries. It is still in force, and various lobbies in Washington, Lancashire and elsewhere would like to see it extended to synthetic fibres and wool. The effect of the Geneva pact was to freeze the market shares more or less where they stood in 1962, to the benefit of Hongkong and the few others which had pioneered the road, and to the disadvantage of the new entrants which would have liked to replace them in the 1970s.

So far the experiment of internationally controlling the import of low-cost manufacturers from Asia has been confined to textiles, although most advanced markets also impose unilateral quotas on household goods, toys, radios and the like when they come from low-wage countries in Asia and elsewhere. The potential sales of Asian manufactures in the West are thus limited by the unpopularity in the West of the attendant adjustment problems. When the British government faces clamour from men and women losing their jobs in Lancashire textile mills, its easiest response is to restrict low-cost imports and make it up for the poorer foreign countries concerned by a bigger hand-out of aid. But in the long term this is the wrong answer for everyone. Japan, incidentally, is now one of those countries which has to protect its own factories against low-cost imports from its Asian neighbours.

In the past three or four years many Asian countries have been able to expand their exports of manufactures on account of the war in Vietnam. American procurement orders for Korean steel, Taiwanese fertilizer and Thai cement, all destined for Vietnam, have been sizeable in the past few years. But this cannot be a permanent market, and there is bound to be some setback in the export earnings when the fighting stops.[11]

The other big obstacle to Asian development is the lack of skills. There is not enough experience – in new technology, in entrepreneurship, in economic decision making,[12] in almost every field in which change is being induced. It is now widely accepted that modernization is not simply a matter of passing a few laws and putting in new investments. The main burden of Myrdal's *Asian Drama* is the importance of changing the social structure, social attitudes and traditional values if a modern type of economic development is to take place. It is little use building atomic reactors in India, if beyond their fences you can still see peasants resisting new methods of cultivation, refusing to limit their families and faithfully observing the traditional Hindu taboos against the slaughter of useless cows. Educational reform is fundamental to everything else.

No more than 60 per cent of Asia's school-age children are currently attending school of some kind between the ages of five and fourteen.[13] Another 10 per cent of them are sent out to work and the rest stay at home to help informally at the household tasks. The Asian governments agreed at a UNESCO Conference in Karachi in 1960 that they would aim at seven years of compulsory free primary education for all by 1980. But even this modest programme is extremely costly and suffers from a shortage of trained teachers. The school-children in the Indian State of Orissa have more than quadrupled in the past ten years: one can imagine the strain thus placed on buildings, staff and teaching materials. Teachers are badly paid in most Asian countries, and in India it is even common for them to strike for salary increases. Asian ministers of education agreed at Tokyo in 1962 that they should spend between 4 per cent and 5 per cent of their countries' gross national product on education, but the actual performance falls short of this by about half. Average annual government spending is less than £1 a head, compared with £30 in Britain.

Illiteracy thus remains an important problem in Asia, where only one in three persons can read and write (in Nepal the ratio is only one in twenty). Illiteracy tends to be self-perpetuating in a society such as India where the education system discriminates against women: 80 per cent of Indian mothers are reckoned to be illiterate and thus unable to teach their children.

Changes in the traditional curriculum are also badly needed, especially in the interests of vocational relevancy and the acquisition of a more rational and scientific outlook. In Ceylon it was recently found that 85 per cent of school-children preferred arts to science, and that education actually increases unemployment because school-leavers refuse to take up manual work. The spectre of the 'educated unemployed', whom education has left unfitted for the social needs of the present day, is well known from Shangai to Bombay. Asia is not lacking in scientific talent, and has produced many Nobel Prize-winners in scientific subjects.[14] The Chinese nuclear programme is evidence of what can be done when it is considered important enough, and when political priorities are accorded to it. But the diffusion of science down to the schools leaves much to be desired.

Western scholars continue to argue about the degree of readiness of the Asian peasant to grasp new technology, new production methods, new opportunities for improving his life. One of the most imaginitive aid projects is the Indo-Norwegian fisheries scheme in Kerala, in South India, under which for many years Norwegian experts have been helping Indian fisher communities to modernize their operations. This is how one of the Norwegians puts the problem:

I think the main obstacle all along was the human mind. The technical things – they are never very difficult to get across. But when it came to the people, the local fishermen, it was always difficult. You see, economically these people had never in their lives had a spare *rupee* in their hand when they went to bed. Always, they used the money for the day. And they never set their targets higher than to live the following day. We tried to show them that if they changed their attitude, if they worked continuously and put effort and imagination in their work, then there might be money. They could use the money to build a house, to buy a small plot of land, and so on. We told them this over and over again, but they never believed us. The only thing they wanted was to earn money to buy enough food. And with the rest of the money they bought small gold things which they gave to their women.[15]

These, then, are the main problems besetting the modernization drive in Asia. How has the development strategy itself evolved over these past two decades or so? The concept of central planning is widely accepted. When India, China and Pakistan inaugurated their first Five-Year Plans in 1951, 1953 and 1955 respectively, Asia demonstrated its preference for planning. Only colonial Hongkong has maintained an unfashionable *laissez-faire* policy towards its economy, and with some success, but then its challenge was a small one by comparison with India's or China's. The plans have not run clear of trouble. China's second Plan was thrown out almost before it began, in favour of the ill-fated Great Leap Forward in 1958, and the Third Plan had to be delayed for three years because of the economic setbacks that followed. India's Fourth Plan was also delayed by three years because of the stagnation which crop failures and the 1965 war with Pakistan caused. It seems likely that both India and China are now working on annual rather than quinquennial plans because of the uncertainties that still surround their immediate economic future. In any case the validity of planning as a generator of change or development is now increasingly under question, especially since Myrdal's verdict on it in *Asian Drama*.

The *idea* of planning, however, dies hard on the Asian scene. Its content has altered as experience has gradually revealed the deficiences of the so-called Mahalanobis model (in India), or Soviet pattern (in China), both of which placed great stress on heavy industrialization requiring an extremely high rate of savings or else massive inflow of foreign aid. Both the Chinese and the Indians have now learned that there is a political limit to the forcing upwards of savings in a poor economy, that there is also a limit to aid handouts in a growingly sceptical world, and that balance between agriculture, heavy industry and light industry is an important condition of steady growth.

The Chinese, surprisingly, have shown themselves as the more temperamental developers. In 1958 they plunged with little preparation into an entirely new and extremely imaginative policy, the Great Leap Forward. By mobilizing manpower as never before, by decentralizing planning and by stirring the whole nation into a frenzy of hard work, they managed to double their growth rate from about 6 per cent to 12 per cent, but the tempo could not be maintained and the economy then went into a recession which lasted for several years. Tremendous resources were wasted, for example in the campaign to construct backyard steel furnaces in every village. Yet the Leap contained some features that made sense for Chinese conditions, and there was never any question of China's going back to the Soviet model again.[16] Similarly the stress on heavy industry in the Indian Plans changed during the Third Plan period.

The Indian Plans[17] have gained world-wide fame as models of a distinctively Indian reconciliation between three conflicting goals – a high rate of economic growth, greater social justice and democratic freedom. The text of the First Five-Year Plan is required reading for officials and economists throughout the third world. But a change is now discernible. After repeated pressure from the growing Indian business community and from external advisers (notably the American Government, source of most of India's foreign aid, and the World Bank) the Indian Government began after Nehru's death to liberalize the controls through which it had enforced planning in the past. Particularly from 1966 onwards the greater freedom extended to entrepreneurs and industrialists, together with the growing orientation towards the rural sector, meant that the central planners' control over the rate of saving was weakened. Some observers questioned whether India had not in effect rejected the bold long-term planning which had brought its economic development thus far,[18] while others rejoiced at the release of private energies to take up the torch from the bureaucracy.[19] Only time will tell which are right.

The case of India is worth dwelling on further, if only because it is both the largest and worst (i.e. the most difficult development challenge) in Asia, although it is far from representative of other Asian economies. The Indians hoped to double the *per capita* income of their people over a generation, or twenty-five years. This would entail an annual *per capita* income growth of about 3 per cent, which would in turn, given the increasing population, mean an overall economic growth rate of between 5 per cent and 5½ per cent. If this could have been maintained, by 1976, after five Five-Year Plans, the average Indian could hope to enjoy the far from princely annual income of £45. This modest goal has proved, however, over-ambitious. After three Plans costing an aggregate of £18,000 million in new investment, the *per capita* income has risen (at constant prices) by under 2 per cent a year. The average Indian income will fall short of the £45 target in the mid-seventies by a considerable margin. Most of the other developing countries of Asia have done a little better than India, but the Asian average is pulled down pretty close to the Indian performance because of the huge Indian population.

As for the so-called economic development 'race' between India and China, the two contenders for giant power status on the Asian mainland, conclusive comparisons are made impossible by the unreliability of our knowledge of the Chinese performance.[20] All that can safely be said is that the Indian tortoise does not in fact compare unfavourably with the Chinese hare, but that the revolutionary base for future modernization is probably better secured in China than in India. Outside observers used to deplore the internal excess of the Chinese communists, but it is now being realized that modernization does seem to require such drastic changes in social attitudes that a forceful overthrow of vested interests may perhaps be the most effective way of setting them firmly in train.

In Asia as a whole (always, of course, excepting Japan) the economic growth rate during the 1950s and the early part of the 1960s has been about 4 per cent a year. This covers a very uneven record, both in time and in space: income per head has actually fallen in some countries in some years, in Ceylon, for instance, in 1967, and in India between 1964 and 1967. One feature of the 1960s has been the relatively faster growth of the smaller countries of East and South-East Asia which started their serious planning later than India or China but from a higher base in terms of the then existing living standards and natural resources. The only countries in developing Asia to achieve a growth rate higher than 5 per cent a year during the 1960s were Malaysia, Singapore, Taiwan, South Korea, Thailand, the Philippines and Pakistan. Americans have been quick to point to the fact that these are, on the whole, the countries which have followed a more liberal policy towards private enterprise, both domestic and foreign, and have avoided unnecessary controls. The laggards until now have been Indonesia (rich in natural resources but slow to discipline itself to the long-term development tasks) and India (which has the most efficient and experienced planning mechanism, but working from the lowest possible base in terms of social immobility and economic backwardness).

The conclusion may seem a dismal one, in that Asia, already the poorest of the continents in *per capita* terms, is growing more slowly than the industrialized countries of 'the North' in spite of the very considerable efforts which have been put into development programmes: the economic gap between Asia and the rest of the world is thus growing wider instead of narrowing. Any attempt to project Asian development on the basis of the past two decades is also disheartening. U N economists have calculated that it will take developing Asia about 180 years, at her present rate of growth, to reach the living standard of present-day Americans – and by that time, of course, the Americans will be many times more prosperous than they are now.[21]

One ought nevertheless to draw attention to the three glimmers of hope in this gloomy picture. The first is that the economic situation in Asia today is unquestionably better than at any time in recent centuries. As the draft outline of India's Fourth Plan asserts, 'during the past fifteen years, a stagnant economy has been set stirring and moving, a traditional society is getting modern and mobile'.[22] This could also be said of China, of Pakistan and of most of the South-East Asian countries with the possible exception of Indonesia. Modern economic development has to have a start sometime: at least that start has been made in Asia, and this is more than could be said twenty years ago.

The second glimmer of hope lies in the inadequacy of the means by which we measure Asian growth and the north-south gap. Differences in standards of living are not really as great as the figures based on arbitrary money values and exchange rates would suggest,[23] and the slow growth in incomes in Asia disguises the substantial construction of new facilities which not only enrich life but also fulfill the preconditions for a faster improvement in living standards in the years ahead. In India, for example, the first fifteen years of planned development may have yielded an annual rise in income per head of less than 2 per cent, and yet they also saw a quadrupling of installed electric power capacity and very remarkable increases in roads, railways, schools and hospitals. We should not, therefore, become mesmerized by comparative national income figures.

Finally, to put Asia's current economic performance in another perspective, it is very much better than that of the already developed countries at the time of their own modernization. During the past century the average real growth (net of inflation) in gross national product per head in Britain, France and Germany was only $1\frac{1}{2}$ per cent.[24] During the crucial years of Japan's industrialization, from the late 1880s to 1920 or thereabouts, Japan's growth rate was nearer 3 per cent a year than 4 per cent. Even India is doing better than that, so there is some cause for pride and hope.

Chapter Twelve

The Appeal of Communism

WHEN an Asian prime minister[1] called communism 'an alternative to despair', he attributed to material poverty the appeal of Marxism for Asian minds. Westerners for whom communism has long been intellectually discredited tend to assume that only a society near the bread-line could take it seriously. But the attractions of Marxism in Asia go deeper than this. Intellectually it meets a need for cosmic explanations based on scientific reasoning. More than any other Western political philosophy it is a way of life, offering guidance in every department of a man's activities, with specific, ready-made solutions for almost every political problem. The certitude and comprehensiveness of Marxism is comforting to people suddenly disoriented by a runaway environment.

An American scholar concludes that, 'For the Japanese intellectual, Marxism has seemed the most useful key to the discovery of the essentials of Western civilization and of the long-range changes affecting the modern world.'[2] The Chinese civilization had always attached importance to doctrine, and the intellectual aspects of Marxism can come almost naturally to the Chinese, the Vietnamese and the Koreans (indeed, one British observer thus explains the fact that communists have come to power only in these particular countries of Asia).[3] Even the Hindu mind can profess to find familiar material in *Das Kapital*: 'Determinism is central to Marxist social thought and characteristic of Hindu cosmology: change is believed inevitable in both.'[4]

These comparisons are somewhat superficial, but Marxism also has specifically political attractions for Asia because it offers a programme of action for change, for reform, for revolution, for nation-building and for the development of a modern industrial economy. An intellectual conviction that revolt is necessary to improve life in a stagnant society, coupled with a psychological reluctance to take the first step, is a common personal predicament among Asian intellectuals, as Mao Tse-tung recognized in the saying which became the favourite of the Red Guards, 'In the last analysis, all the truths of Marxism can be summed up in one sentence: to rebel is justified.' Many a potential young Asian revolutionary must have inwardly thrilled to the formal 'Declaration of War on the Old World,' with which the Red Guards of the Peking Second Middle School announced China's Cultural Revolution in 1966. Above all it is the dynamism, the purposefulness, the address of the communists which draws such a response.

The poet Iqbal, the spiritual father of Pakistan, put it in a couplet:

> It comes to me, observing how our
> sovereign states proceed,
> That not without utility was Russia's
> headlong speed.[5]

In the end the sad lesson had to be learnt that speed can be counter-productive if each change is not firmly consolidated: the massacres of communists in Bali[6] and Java in 1965, and the fact that the Chinese economy has not after all grown faster than India's despite two decades of communist rule, provide two cautionary tales for the Asian iconoclasts and reformers of the 1970s.

Marxism appeals not only intellectually and politically but also emotionally, since its adherents are made to feel part of a vast and universal movement, flowing with the mainstream of history, informed with optimism and idealism. No other Western political philosophy or religion offers the Asian intellectual this escape from his nagging feelings of isolation and drift.

Westerners are increasingly alienated by the authoritarian nature of communism, but this does not disturb Asians, who have never experienced a libertarian society. It is true that Confucius, in what reads almost like an anticipation of the Maoist dilemma, warned that, 'like the boiling of a small fish, the government of a State should not be overdone.' But to obey the government and leave public affairs entirely in the hands of an educated élite are strong traditions throughout Asia. It has been argued that collectivism, too, fits better into the Asian context than the European.[7] Certainly the Chinese communes, which no European communist party would dare to imitate, appear so far to be minimally successful, though for how long is another matter. Most Asian rural communities are used to the idea of mutual aid in some form or another, but the failure of the co-operative movement in Indian agriculture proves that these traditions cannot necessarily be enlarged and built upon as a modern socialist would like.

Another factor which in Europe diminishes the interest of the bourgeoisie in communism is absent in Asia, namely the respect for private enterprise. Sun Yat-sen and Chiang Kai-shek both envisaged the development of China's heavy industry in public rather than private hands, and neither could be said to be a communist.[8] The Indian Congress Party strongly opposes communism, and yet the most conservative of its leaders, ex-Finance Minister Morarji Desai, told the visiting Soviet premier in 1968 that he was 'an ardent believer in the supremacy of the public sector in the Indian context'.[9] Private industry and commerce is associated in Asia both with foreign imperialism and indigenous greed: since the line is so blurred between responsible and public-spirited developers on the one hand and speculators, profiteers and blackmarketeers on the other, private business is seldom given the benefit of the doubt. The Marxist message does not therefore meet resistance on this count.

The particular appeal of Marxism has been reinforced in Asia by the sympathy which the Soviet Government has been able to evoke. When Deputy Foreign Minister Karakhan declared in 1919 that the Soviet Union was willing to abrogate the unequal treaties with China which it had inherited from the czarist regime, ripples of pleasure spread over an Asia chafing under the similar impositions of other European powers. The Russians never in the end withdrew from the greatest part of the Asian territory acquired by the Tsars, but the fact that they offered to, and were the first to climb down from the high pedestal from which the European powers had presided over their possessions in Asia made an almost indelible mark.

The Soviet encouragement of anti-colonial movements, Lenin's 'Theses on the National and Colonial Questions' and the work of the Comintern in assisting and coordinating the struggle against imperialism, all strengthened the good opinion which Asian intellectuals, whether Marxist or not, tended to hold of the communist idea. Ho Chi Minh was first attracted to Marxism by Lenin's anticolonial stand,[10] and even today students in South Vietnam will admit their admiration for Ho, not as a communist but as a national patriot who spearheaded the resistance to the successive imperialisms of France, Japan and America.[11] The fact that the Comintern, after the Baku Congress of the People of the East in 1920 and the Leningrad Congress of the Toilers of the Far East in 1922, persistently urged Asian communists to collaborate with bourgeois and nationalist elements in fighting Western imperialism also made it easier for Marxism to attain respectability among Asian intellectuals of all colours.

Indeed, it could be said that Stalin sacrificed the support of many convinced Asian communists in the interests of his grander strategy of striking at Western capitalism through its colonial life-lines. His insistence on maintaining a united front with the Asian middle classes merely because they hated the West led the Chinese communists into many Kuomintang ambushes, of which the worst was the Shanghai massacre of 1927, described in André Malraux's novel *La Condition Humaine*. M. N. Roy, the Bengali who was, after Mao Tse-tung, the most original of the Asian disciples of Marx, saw the contradiction from the start and opposed the strategy: 'Evidently landlords will flourish in the Republic of the *Panchayats*,' he wrote sarcastically in 1926 of the Indian National Congress' leadership of the independence movement. 'The lion and the lamb will eat out of the same pot in the land of Buddha. There is no end to bourgeois hypocrisy.'[12] In the end the most gifted Asian Marxists – Roy himself, the Indonesian Tan Malaka, and eventually Mao Tse-tung as well – parted company with Moscow.

The doctrinal rigidity of the communists sooner or later distressed the majority of the Asian intellectuals who, like Aung San of Burma and Nehru of India, were basically attracted by the Marxist idea. A small minority remained communist, but an overwhelming majority called themselves socialists. However conservative an Asian politician may be, whatever his vested interests in these inegalitarian societies, he will endeavour to lodge under the socialist umbrella. Sukarno saw a peasant working his field on the day that he crystallized his own political philosophy more than forty years ago: he asked the man about his work and his life, and he called his philosophy after the man's name, Marhaen. Marhaenism is 'a type of Marxism-Socialism adapted to the Indonesian community and spirit'.

Prince Sihanouk's political organization, the *Sangkum*, aimed to introduce in Cambodia a 'system in which the state takes over direction of the national economy, protects man from the exploitation of his labour by a privileged class, safeguards his livelihood and his dignity, and strives to give him the material means of finding happiness'. When Mrs Bandaranaike's left-wing Government was defeated in the 1965 elections by its more conservative opponents, their first action was to pledge that the socialist pattern of society would be maintained. The Congress Government in India continues the fiction of being socialist, includes socialists in the cabinet and vainly exhorts its citizens to behave more socialistically. One of the key passages in its Fourth Five-year Plan reads:

A decisive change that would shape and colour all our efforts is needed above all in the social and cultural climate. The inherited culture has in it strands of idealism and fellowship as also embedded privileges and discrimination practices. In daily life the latter choke the former. Socialism implies a radical change in the prevalent patterns of thought and behaviour. The ethos it seeks is of modernism and equality, of rationalism and humanity. The various programmes of production, education and welfare that constitute the Fourth Plan can partly help to create this new climate. But their impact could indeed be revolutionary if the social behaviour and administrative efforts bend themselves to establish equality and dignity of man. Without the application in daily life within the community of the values we profess, the motivations and incentives needed to accomplish the tasks that await will evade us. Sustained hard work and acceptance of the primacy of social needs over personal gains are the principal motive forces in the basic transformation we seek. Whether the tasks of development invite participation and satisfaction or lead to stresses and strains, depends upon the social ethos and the cultural climate. The test of earnestness about socialism lies in the critical effort made in imparting confidence to every citizen that he is at once the participant and the beneficiary of development which implies both sacrifices and rewards. Socialism is as much a national goal as a functional force. In the measure in which its functional role is enlarged and strengthened we shall come nearer the goal.

Politicians expend immense energy explaining that socialism is quite compatible with Buddhism, Islam, Hinduism and other religions. 'Marxist theory,' wrote U Ba Swe, Burma's first prime minister, 'is not antagonistic to Buddhist philosophy. The two are, frankly speaking, not merely similar: in fact they are identical.'[13] The poet Iqbal claimed, in a burst of that syncretism for which the Indian sub-continent is famous, that Islam almost equals 'Bolshevism plus God'.[14] It is very rare to meet a political leader in Asia who publicly disclaims socialism.

The parties which call themselves explicitly and exclusively socialist are not, however, successful. The domination of Burmese politics for two decades, a brief taste of power in Japan and Indonesia soon after the war, a few years in office in Colombo in the early 1960s – that is the sum of their achievements. The real burden of the Marxist mission is, of course, carried by the twenty-three million Asians who are card-carrying members of the communist parties. The figure sounds impressive, perhaps, but it includes the second and third largest parties in the world, the Chinese (with about eighteen million members) and the Indonesian (with perhaps two to three million still in spite of the 1966 massacres). North Korea and North Vietnam account for another two million or so, and the vast populations of India, Pakistan, Japan and the rest of South-East Asia accommodate a mere half million – a ratio of about one communist to every two thousand inhabitants.[15]

Some of the communist parties are almost half a century old, the Indonesian and Mongolian parties dating back to 1920, the Chinese and Japanese to 1921 and 1922 respectively. But only four of them have gained power, and in two cases (North Korea and Mongolia) their office is owed to the Soviet armies. The Vietnamese and Chinese parties made their own way to success, as Tito did in Europe, and this fact alone explains much about the Sino-Soviet ideological split.

Soon after the Second World War, at the time of the opening

salvoes in the cold war, the Soviet Union and its friends prepared for another push in Asia. Delegates at a conference in Calcutta in 1948 were initiated into the plan, which sparked the Malaysian emergency of 1948–60, the Hukbalahap rebellion in the Philippines, the Indian communist uprising in Telengana, the Madiun revolt in Indonesia, a left-wing rebellion in Burma and intensification of the inexorable advance of the communist cause in China (where Mao was already on the verge of victory over the Kuomintang) and Vietnam. But the plan was ill-coordinated and the revolutionaries ill-prepared. Chin Peng kept the British army held down in Malaya for more than a decade, but the other campaigns were either quickly snuffed out or lost credibility as serious threats to the governments.

Within a few years the Soviet Union and China were preaching the gospel of peaceful co-existence and idolizing Nehru, the hero of the Korean peace talks. After the Bandung Conference in 1955, when Chou threw his arms round Nehru and Sukarno, the Indian, Indonesian and other Asian communists were obliged to change step and concentrate on consolidating their strength within the parliamentary or other constitutional framework. The new policy was to build up the communists' prestige as the only solid, purposeful, disciplined, capable political force to which all citizens would turn in despair after all other possible solutions to their problems had failed. Instead of indulging in underground conspiracy and terrorism, the communists sought to demonstrate their power, skill and influence at all levels of public life.

But then came the Sino-Soviet split of 1960, when Khrushchev withdrew all the Russian technicians from China and abruptly terminated Soviet aid. The quarrel had many strands in it, including the Chinese feeling that Mao deserved recognition as the senior world communist after Stalin's death, disagreement over strategy and tactics in promoting world communism, Chinese resentment over the patronizing attitude of the Soviet advisers and national differences over the frontier and defence (China had wanted nuclear weapons and Soviet military help to regain Taiwan, but Krushchev refused).[16] Until 1960 the Asian communist parties had tended to see themselves as within the Chinese rather than the Soviet sphere of interest, but after the split they sought to assert their neutrality between the two communist giants. Mongolia could not escape the bear's hug, and North Korea's Kim Il-sung was at first obliged to behave like a Chinese satellite. But Kim eventually struck out on his own, and in a celebrated speech he extolled *Chuche*, the spirit of national identity:

> Only by firmly establishing *Chuche* can each country repudiate flunkeyism and dogmatism and creatively apply the universal truth of Marxism-Leninism and the experience of other countries to suit its historical conditions and national peculiarities, discard the spirit of relying on others and solve its own questions entirely for itself for its own responsibility by displaying a spirit of self-reliance.... For successful carrying out of revolution and construction it is necessary firmly to ensure the political independence of one's country, to create a solid, self-sustaining economy and to build up self-defensive capabilities in national defence ...[17]

Since this was precisely what both Russia and China had done in their own cases, they could hardly object to these stirrings of polycentrism.

Most of the communist parties in opposition in Asia proceeded to split into pro-Soviet and pro-Chinese factions. Moscow weaned Shiga Yoshio and his group from the pro-Peking Japanese Communist Party, and they set up a rival organization. The Indian party divided first into two and then into three after the originally pro-Peking faction itself broke up on the question of whether the Chinese were right to encourage the guerrilla activities of the so-called Naxalbarites[18] in Bengal. The main body of the so-called left communists, who had at first supported China against the USSR, resolved at Madurai in 1967 to disassociate themselves from both of the rival sources of foreign influence.

The Soviet Union has naturally been the largest financial provider and material helper of the Asian communists over the past half-century, but the Chinese now argue that this help is self-interested, and can be dangerous, even vitiating. In the words of Stuart Schram, his Western biographer, 'Mao does not have the slightest confidence in the willingness of the people or even of the proletariat either in the Soviet Union or in the advanced countries of Europe and America to risk their own

tranquillity in order to support the struggles of their less fortunate fellow men in Asia and Africa.'[19] Probably a majority of
Asian communists would now accept this appraisal, but without
Russian assistance their position would become even more difficult. The formal link with Moscow may be retained, but communism is becoming increasingly Asianized.

The basic Maoist formula for successful revolution is recognized as a tried and suitable model – a tough and disciplined
communist party leading a united front of other disaffected
elements, first in guerrilla and then in positional warfare, against
the existing government to victory, the establishment of a People's
Democracy and an effective communist dictatorship. The other
way, of trying to win power within the official 'bourgeois' framework, looks hopeless. But very few Asian communist leaders are
of the type to take readily to jungle warfare, and the temptations
of accepting a permanent niche as a small legal opposition party
prove overwhelming in some countries. The communists are in
any case as vulnerable as other Asian political organizations to
factionalism, which greatly reduces their effectiveness. In
Ceylon there is even a Trotskyite Party with more seats in the
legislature than the regular communist party.

In Japan the Communist Party reached a peak in its fortunes
at the elections of 1949, when it received almost 10 per cent of
the popular vote, but repressive measures by the right-wing
Government, combined with the Party's internal doctrinal
dissension, has led it to a position where it takes only 5 per
cent of the popular vote and wins 2 per cent of the Diet seats.
It is noteworthy that at the very moment when it seemed to be
on the crest of the wave, the Japanese Communist Party was
sharply attacked by the Cominform for attempting 'the naturaliza-
tion of Marxism-Leninism in Japanese conditions'.[20]

In India the communists gained office in the coalition governments of five states after the 1967 elections, having previously
succeeded in forming a government only in Kerala in the early
1960s. In the *Lok Sabha*, the central lower house, the two rival
communist parties won 8 per cent of the seats between them in
the 1967 elections. But their strength in the country as a whole is
uneven. In Kerala they can count on almost 40 per cent of
the vote, but Bengal and Andhra (where they draw support,

surprisingly enough, from landowning groups halfway up the social ladder) are the only other states where they consistently win more than 10 per cent of the votes. The opinion of most commentators is that the Congress Party has more to fear from its regional right-wing opponents than from the Marxist left. The Indian communists are also gravely embarrassed by their country's dispute with China. E. M. S. Namboodiripad, the communist chief minister of Kerala, put his finger on this central dilemma when he said: 'The main question before the Party after the Chinese aggression was how to integrate the patriotism of Indian Communists as Indians to their sense of proletarian internationalism as Communists.'[21]

In Indonesia the Party suffered a grave setback in 1965 when it apparently lent its name to a poorly-prepared *coup d'état* which sought to eliminate the leading right-wing generals in the army and confirm the left as the successor to Sukarno (whose health was at that time in question). Once again, as in 1948 after the abortive Madiun revolt, the Indonesian communists lost many of their leaders and followers and had to go underground. This time as many as half a million of their supporters may have been massacred, and it will obviously take many years for the Party to recover.

The European idea of a party based on a number of free individuals joining together to realize their common convictions does not easily take root in Asia, where the individual remains relatively unliberated and where group considerations weigh more than personal ones. A study of the communist guerrillas in Malaya in the 1950s showed that they tended to join the Party first, out of a variety of personal and emotional motives in which a detestation of British colonial rule played a big role, and to be indoctrinated into the communist ideology afterwards;[22] and the same probably applies in China, Vietnam, and a number of other Asian countries.[23] The fact that Marxism is fully understood only by those who have been substantially Westernized tends either to insulate the communist parties from the masses, or else to render them incapable of utilizing and harnessing to their ends the kind of strong indigenous political force which has thrown up the *Dravida Munnetra Kazakham* in Madras and the *Komeito* in Japan. In any case there are a growing number of sceptics who, like Eguchi Bokuro in Japan, question the appropriateness of the whole Marxist schema for contemporary developments in Asia.

The resistance which this most Western of all Western political philosophies is now beginning to meet is well illustrated in the exchange which took place in the Malaysian Parliament just before Singapore's secession. A minister in the conservative Alliance Government was warning the People's Action Party (the ruling party in Singapore, led by Lee Kuan Yew) not to introduce a foreign ideology into Malaysia, when he was interrupted:

Lee Kuan Yew: 'What foreign ideology?'
Inche Senu: 'Socialism ...' (laughter).[24]

In the sense that socialism is about dividing the cake, it is premature in Asia where the cake must be vastly enlarged before equal shares in it are of any significance. 'In India', wrote M. N. Roy, 'we still live in the age of the handloom and of primitive agriculture. Is it not premature to talk of the socialization of the means of production?'[25] Borodin, the Soviet adviser to Sun Yat-sen, made the same point when he observed: 'The only Communism possible in China today is the Communism of poverty, a lot of people eating rice out of an almost empty bowl. At present and for many years to come, communists and capitalists alike in China must have the same ideal of a prosperous and much more highly developed industrial China and a general rise in China's standards of living...'[26] Even today, forty years later, Mao is having to repudiate similar reasoning on the part of Liu Shao-chi and his faction within the Chinese Communist Party. Although in the 1950s it looked as if the Maoists had found a viable short-cut to economic progress, China's disappointing performance in the 1960s has weakened this particular attraction of communism.

In none of the Asian communist countries can economic progress be truthfully said to have been substantially better so far than in India or South-East Asia.

There will be many more revolutions in Asia, even, as the Cultural Revolution shows, within the communist states themselves. A rising threshold of economic expectation demands a political means of expression. The communists hoped that they would have a monopoly over this, but they have been disappointed. The closer one looks at the organized violent unrest in Asia – at the resurgent Hukbalahaps in the Philippines, for example[27] – the more one finds communists and communism a relatively minor factor in it. The Chinese have shown how almost unrecognizable Marxism can become when developed and implemented by a group of people firmly rooted in a non-European culture and not disorientated in the way that so many of the Western-educated communists of India, Japan and Indonesia are. The lesson seems to be that communism will be able to exploit the growing grievances of the people only if it becomes further Asianized, more polycentric and less internationally organized.

The Chinese seem well aware of this when they exhort their protégés in India and South-East Asia to be self-reliant, to build their revolutions from within and to be independent of foreign help.

Chapter Thirteen

The New Politics of Asia

JAWAHARLAL Nehru was once criticized in the Indian Parliament for making decisions without referring them to the cabinet, and for submitting to financial pressures. With a flash of anger, Nehru exclaimed: 'I am something more than Prime Minister – we are the children of the Indian revolution, and its fire still burns in our veins.'[1] The generation of leaders who ruled Asia in the period following the Second World War – when most of them first gained their independence from colonial rule – was an unusual, even an Olympian group. Independent Asian politics began with giants who were world figures in their own right, as Nehru, Chiang Kai-shek and Mao Tse-tung all were, or who at least possessed the authority and the mystique of having won the national struggle against more powerful foreign overlords. But this generation is passing, and Asian politics are becoming less easily comprehensible to Western minds.

There were several distinguishing features of this generation which coloured the institutions and the style of the early politics of independent Asia. For one thing, these men were driven by a hatred for colonialism and imperialism more intense than their successors'. Almost all of them carried the scars of European imperialism. Sukarno as a young student was humiliated by white boys and once asked a Dutchman for his daughter's hand, only to be ridiculed for imagining that 'a dirty native like you' would ever be allowed to approach a respectable white girl. In his autobiography, Sukarno comments: 'Do you not think such actions leave scars? Yes, I had an awareness as a child. My dedication of life started at sixteen.'[2] Mao Tse-tung complained of the China of the early 1920s that, 'If one of our foreign masters farts, it's a lovely perfume,' and when his school played football against pupils of an American-financed rival, he shouted from the touch-line, 'Beat the slaves of foreigners.'[3]

Atulya Ghosh, for many years the Congress Party boss in

West Bengal, lost an eye in an encounter with a British police baton, and personal insults and humiliations of this kind stimulated U Nu of Burma and many other nationalist leaders to enter politics. Having suffered vicariously and often personally from the inequalities and indignities meted out to their peoples for decades or even centuries, they identified themselves emotionally with their states.[4] This made them suspicious of the Western powers even after independence had been won. But they were involved in a love-hate relationship with the white world, from which they had learnt the means not only of establishing their independence but also of improving the life of their people. Most of these leaders had been profoundly influenced by the intellectual life and cultural values of European civilization, were fluent in European languages, and were cosmopolitan almost to the point of being rootless.

While they personally resented anything that recalled former dependence (the activities of Christian missionaries and schools, for example, or the need to rely on European experts and technicians), they plunged wholeheartedly into measures of modernization that derived entirely from this same foreign civilization, with little consideration of their inappropriateness for their own people. Mixed up with this generation of leaders were the representatives of the Asian 'old guard' – Sandhurst-trained officers like Ayub Khan; men who, like President Thieu and Vice-President Ky of South Vietnam, had served under foreign direction as part of the colonial apparatus;[5] and Oxbridge-educated aristocrats such as Tunku Abdul Rahman, the Malaysian prime minister, whose concern, as his Singaporean critic, Lee Kuan Yew, once remarked, was primarily to 'preserve the orchid from wilting'.[6]

In their place a new kind of leader is emerging, one who has less formal education, less wealth or polish or travel, but who is more strongly rooted in his own community and country. President Suharto never went to a university, and at the time he became president he had seen neither Europe nor America. The two men who succeeded Nehru as respectively prime minister and the most powerful figure in the Congress Party – Shastri and Kamaraj – had also never been abroad, and the latter speaks no English. The same kind of contrast can be observed between the

two strong men to have emerged in South Korea: Syngman Rhee
had lived in exile for much of his early life and was considerably
Westernized, whereas Park Chung Hee sprang directly from the
soil, so to speak, and operated in a far more subtle and successful
style.

In China the ranks of the survivors of the Long March of
1934–35, the élite of the communist party, are rapidly thinning
out, and the struggle will be now between the 'modernists',
Soviet-influenced and often Soviet-trained, who are more interested in the technical aspects of modernization, and the
'traditionalists' who appeal more to the conservative elements of
Chinese society and are shrewder judges of what is or is not
politically possible. Japan went through this cycle of foreign and
native political influences at a much earlier stage in her history,
but is witnessing an echo of it in the current transition from
leaders who speak English and co-operated with the American
occupation reforms (including most of the post-war prime
ministers) to a slightly different type or generation which is
less familiar with the West and better grounded in popular sympathy.

The change in personalities is accompanied by a transformation
of political style and methods. The anti-colonial freedom fighters
were also the constitution-makers, and they thrust on to their
countries the political institutions and ideas which they had
admired in the West – democracy, the rule of law, the separation
of powers, the party system and even Marxism. In many instances
these innovations were effective. When Mr Bandaranaike's
left-wing coalition took office after the Ceylonese elections in
1970, it was the fifth orderly transfer of power between political
opponents since the country's independence. The Philippines has
held regular presidential elections every four years, according to
its American-style constitution; only one president ever succeeded in being re-elected for a second term (which surely indicates that the people relish their moment of power at the ballot
box). The Philippine elections themselves are always violent,
however, the death roll reaching a hundred in the 1967 polls. In
India the world's largest single democratic election has been
faithfully and efficiently staged every five years, as the Constitution requires, and with a steadily rising level of turnout (45

per cent of the electorate voted in 1952, more than 60 per cent in 1967).

The scenes in some of the Asian legislatures are appalling. In the East Pakistan assembly in 1958 one party succeeded in having the Speaker formally declared insane, whereupon its rival threw chairs, lamps and microphones at the poor man's deputy and successor, who subsequently died of his injuries. In 1966 a Korean assembly-man, Kim Tu-Han, supported his charges of ministerial corruption by throwing a bag of shit at the Government front bench. Disorder and violence have descended on the Japanese Diet and on some of the Indian and other legislatures from time to time. But the tensions are caused by the underlying violent political forces, and it is difficult to argue that the violence would have been substantially less in a different kind of political institutional framework.

It is, however, arguable that the premises on which the system of parliamentary democracy is based, having evolved in London, Paris, the Hague and Washington, do not all obtain in Asia, and that the techniques of democracy may have to differ. The extreme case, that of the plebiscite which the United Nations wanted to hold in West Irian (where many of the primitive tribal inhabitants have not yet graduated from the Stone Age) is obviously un-representative. But even a citizen of sophisticated Singapore can claim that democracy of the Westminster type is irrelevant to him: 'If the choice is between an honest and efficient one-party government, or a highly corrupt administration with a free press, or a paternalistic government lacking a sense of urgency in its economic development programme, then for a Singaporean the choice is obvious.'[7] Ayub Khan justified his military dictatorship by criticizing the democracy which had prevailed in Pakistan in the 1950s:

The British parliamentary system which we inherited ... takes for granted too many prerequisites which do not really exist in a country like Pakistan. Our rate of literacy is appallingly low. Our means of communication are poor, even primitive. The rural population which constitutes over 80 per cent of the total is hardly touched by the world outside the villages ... An average villager with little or no education has no means of gaining personal knowledge about a candidate who is mixed up in a population of 100,000 or more, spread over a large area without any advanced means of communication and contact. Votes cast under these circumstances cannot but be vague, wanton and responsive to fear, coercion, temptation and other modes of misguidance.[8]

If the political institutions of a country have not grown naturally out of its own history and traditional culture, it is hardly surprising that they are not respected and utilized to the fullest extent by the population. The *Komeito*, Japan's new Buddhist party, complains that:

In Japan, the growth of a wholesome political sense is hindered by the people's inertia, egoism and indifference to politics stemming from pre-modern tradition ... Japan does not deserve to be called an advanced country. Her politics may well be called that of the eighteenth century ... We aim at enlightening the people politically to adapt the parliamentary politics of the United Kingdom to conditions in Japan.[9]

In the first place, the idea of a political party does not readily translate from Western Europe to Asia. In a society where the autonomy of the individual is not socially recognized and where pre-existing group loyalties predominate, the idea of individuals banding together to pursue concerted action merely on the basis of shared intellectual convictions seems strange and unnatural. It is often said of Pakistan that there are only two political parties, namely the army and the civil service. The same observation has been made about Thailand,[10] and the role of the bureaucracy in the old Chinese tradition ensures its continued importance even today in Japan (where the ruling Liberal-Democratic Party is increasingly dominated by former civil servants) and in Communist China (where Chairman Mao, in the struggle to free the Communist Party from bureaucratic domination, may have put it in fief to the army). When a political party does gain an important and sustained hold over an electorate in Asia, it is because it stands for an entire way of life, a distinct conglomeration of values and beliefs which makes the parties of Western democracy look anaemic by comparison.

But the more common pattern is for personal cliques and local factions to be the main force in politics. Neville Maxwell has said that, 'The faction indeed is the true unit of Indian political action, the parties are temporary and unstable coalitions of factions,'[11] while an Indian political scientist declares that, 'The Congress Party constitutes an elaborate party system by itself.'[12] The Indonesian parliament assembled after the elections in 1955 to find that it had twenty-nine parties represented, and when the Thais went to the polls in 1957 they had more than fifty parties to choose from. The natural means of political association is for a potential leader to acquire clients, usually on a personal, family or territorial basis: he then has a faction which may become allied with other factions but which will never lose its distinct identity and is always ready to withdraw from the alliance if it does not get what it regards as its fair share of power and privilege.

In Japan factionalism of this kind is actually encouraged by the electoral law which lays down multi-member constituencies. Because the Liberal Democratic Party – or the Socialist Party for that matter – does not have to agree beforehand on a single compromise candidate in a given constituency, faction rivalry becomes extreme and there are sometimes more candidates from a party than there are seats being contested (so that the electorate is invited to judge between factions of the same party).[13] There is however evidence that the emergence of policy-oriented parties is now on the way in Japan.[14]

Another problem relates to the role of the opposition in societies where the tradition is to obey and respect the government of the day. So unfamiliar is the concept of the 'loyal opposition' that it sometimes has to be artificially created in order to keep the democratic machinery (or its appearances) going. In Singapore the main opposition party, the *Barisan Sosialis*, recently went underground and boycotted elections, so that every seat in the parliament was won by the ruling party: a constitutional commission on minority rights recommended that an independent Council of State be appointed to offer informed criticism of the Government, 'especially where there is no responsible or effective 'opposition in parliament'.[15] The South Vietnamese Constitution of 1967 enshrines, in Article 101, a formal and institutionalized right of opposition, and Prince Sihanouk of Cambodia once experimented with a 'counter-government' which he appointed to keep the proper government on its toes.[16]

The two-party system which is regarded in the West as the ideal has not yet established itself in Asia. The Liberals and the *Nacionalistas* of the Philippines come nearest to it, but they have no ideological content at all and floor-crossing between them is endemic. India has what Brecher calls a 'one-party-plus' system of democracy in which none of the opposition parties has ever seriously challenged the Congress Party across the nation.[17] There is a trend discernible for two-party systems to be established within individual constituencies or districts, although the Indian system of the single ballot and the simple majority tends to disguise it.[18] The split in the Congress in 1969, between Mrs Gandhi's 'leftists' and Mr Desai's 'rightists', may lead to a new polarization at the centre. Japan, too, has been described as a 'one-and-one-half-party system', with the Liberal-Democrats likely to retain office for another decade or more after two decades of virtual monopoly.[19]

There is also a prejudice against parties on the ground that they inflame the existing divisions in society. The function of the government is to reconcile these divisions, and the encouragement of permanent political organizations which overtly seek votes on the basis of sectional appeals interferes with this. Vinoba Bhave and Jayaprakash Narayan, the Gandhians, criticize the Indian parliamentary system for exacerbating religious, ethnic and caste differences: a party tends to put forward a candidate who can appeal to a majority in a constituency on these grounds, and he then has to play up these loyalties and even compete with others who also seek to exploit them. Professor Tsuji Kiyoaki, the distinguished political scientist, has observed:

> The Japanese people have always had a vague but obstinate notion that, on the one hand, the government and the bureaucrats are impartial and neutral and that, on the other hand, partisan conflict and party politics are liable to upset the equilibrium of the established order.[20]

But it is important to draw the right conclusions from these disappointments of Western political models when transplanted into Asian soil. J. R. D. Tata, the Indian industrialist, declared in 1968 that, 'The British parliamentary system of government which we have enshrined in our Constitution is unsuited to the conditions in our country, to the temperament of our people and to our historical background.'[21]

Of these three factors, the first is transient while the second and third are longer-lasting. Several Western commentators have defended the trend towards authoritarianism in Asia on the ground that the need for strong government in the national interest must over-ride the niceties of free politics, just as they did in Western democracies during wartime. The simultaneous revolutions of nation-building and economic development which most Asian countries are desperately promoting might seem to call for a strong government untrammelled by constitutional opposition. 'Developing a country under democracy,' someone once remarked, 'is like trying to play poker without bluffing.'[22] But this is not self-evident, and the analogy with the wartime limitations on Western democracy is misleading.

It is not yet proven whether some kind of representative democracy is better or worse than some kind of authoritarianism at promoting faster economic growth or forging a sense of nationhood. Since one essential feature of economic growth is the release of individual initiative and enterprise, and since the forces that lie below the surface must come out and become fully engaged in nation-building, a relatively free political framework is probably better, though it may not be the most comfortable or pleasant. One must therefore reserve judgment on the tactics of democracy in Asia while still insisting that the strategy of aiming towards some kind of representative system is correct.

But the precise form of the political system and its institutions will certainly be progressively modified to suit – and express – the native genius. While this will obviously vary widely from country to country, three general areas of departure from Western modes can be distinguished.

The first is the rather obvious proposition that differences will appear from the growing strength and self-confidence of indigenous forces, whether these be of religion, of region or of cultural tradition. An observer of the Indian elections discerned in the 1967 poll results, 'A reaction against the Western-trained and Western-oriented leaders and groups who have determined the nature of the Indian state and have made the basic national and international decisions since independence, and ... the reversion towards traditionalism and distinctively Indian ways in reaction against the failures, real or fancied, of the efforts at modernisation.'[23] Much of the appeal of Sukarno lay in his insistence on 'returning to our own national personality', and the Cultural Revolution in China yielded the revival of many political habits and rituals from pre-republican days – the beating of gongs and cymbals to celebrate the downfall of opponents, the rash of 'big-character posters' on the walls of buildings, the humiliating procession of opponents through jeering crowds in the streets with weights on their necks and carrying enormous boards listing their crimes.

For the first fifteen years of independence Ceylon continued to install its heads of state in the traditional British uniform with scarlet sash, plumed helmet, sword and scabbard: only in 1962 was this changed to a simple white cloth and *banian*, the traditional lighting of oil lamps and blowing of conch shells, and a sermon from a Buddhist monk. This is an example of the external ways in which the forces of tradition are being invoked for the tasks of today. But the less obvious internal manifestation is the emergence of such religion-based political parties as the *Masjumi* in Indonesia, the *Jan Sangh* in Northern India and the *Komeito** in Japan, and such region-based organizations as the D M K in Madras and the *Shiv Sena* in Bombay.[24]

The second distinctive feature which seems to be visible in the new politics of Asia is a preference for the concept of hierarchy over that of equality, reflecting traditional values. Two scholars observe, of Thai rural society: 'It is difficult for an equal to give anything of value to an equal or to command his "respect". Indeed he stands as a potential competitor for favours. Group solidarity requires . . . framing unambiguously the relative rank of each.'[25] Thai leaders make no secret of their belief that a mild form of authoritarianism is consistent with Thai psychology and tradition and best for the country's current problems. The representative constitution-makers of South Vietnam in 1967 gave a dominant role to the presidency, and a scholar commented: 'There is a fundamental thrust in Vietnamese society towards

---

*Which declares that 'both the free competition system as well as communism neglect human beings; thus they are putting the cart before the horse'.

an authoritarian form of government in the desire for someone to create unity in the society in institutional terms, given what the people themselves recognize as a very divisive situation.'[26] Even in India, where representative institutions have taken some root, a survey has found that people do not necessarily feel more hostile to the idea of authoritarian rule as they become more educated.[27]

In Indonesia Sukarno developed the idea of 'guided democracy', which his successors continue under another name.[28] The explicitly authoritarian aspect of communism is one of the factors that has made it as widespread as it is in Asia, and European Marxists chide their Asian colleagues for allowing it more rein than would be acceptable in Europe. The Chinese communist leaders disobeyed their own constitution in such matters as the frequency of committee and National Congress meetings and regular election of officers, without feeling it necessary even to explain or justify these breaches, and the new constitution of 1969 vests extraordinary power in the virtually self-perpetuating inner élite.

Monarchies and aristocracies are taking advantage of the new opportunities offered by this rediscovery of the comforts of hierarchy. Prince Sihanouk of Cambodia (whose people used to call him *Samdech Euv* – 'Papa Prince') provided in his palmy days the best example of this, renouncing the throne in order to assume the direct political leadership of his country.*[29] King Mahendra has suspended party politics in Nepal and substituted a limited democracy under royal guidance, and in Thailand the young King Bhumiphol is regarded by some as a possible future force in Bangkok politics.

The Emperor Hirohito renounced his divine status only in 1945, and he is still something of a mystical figure in the national consciousness.[30] The story is often told of the American interviewer who asked a Japanese farmer during the occupation what he thought of General MacArthur, and who received the enthusiastic reply, 'The Emperor could not have chosen a better man.' A socialist leader wrote after the war that, 'The Emperor has always been regarded as head of the national family, and the

*Thus realizing the ambition of King Magnus in Shaw's *The Apple Cart*.

relation between the Emperor and the people has never been that of the conqueror and the conquered. From this point of view, Japanese monarchy and democracy are perfectly compatible with each other.'[31] Even the communist leader Nosaka Sanzo suggested that if his party came to power it would hold a plebiscite to decide whether the Emperor's office should be abolished.[32] The Chinese communists treated their prisoner Henry Pu-yi, the last emperor to sit on the Dragon's Throne, with consideration and generosity, allowing him finally to write his autobiography in peace and cultivate his hobby of gardening: some commentators suggested that they saw in him a useful trump card to play in internal politics in certain eventualities, with the implication that loyalty to the Manchu Dynasty is not quite dead even today.[33]

The maharajahs of India are enjoying a political comeback after their enforced democratization at the time of independence. In 1967 the Maharajah of Patna became the first former princely ruler to become chief minister of a state in independent India, having led the right-wing Swatantara Party to victory in the Orissa elections. The Maharanis of Jaipur and Gwalior have been elected to the Central Parliament and have already made their mark. Dinesh Singh, once foreign minister in Mrs Gandhi's cabinet, is a rajah. The Congress Party has steadily reduced the privy purses which were awarded to the princes at the time of independence, but they have now formed their own trade union to concert their defences. Almost the only political figure in Indonesia to have retained public respect throughout the many changes of the past quarter-century is Sultan Buwono Hamengku of Jogjakarta, the great royal innovator and reformer, fighter against Dutch rule and present minister for economic affairs.[34]

Even outside the traditional monarchies, the idea of dynasty has seen too many realizations in the Asia of today to be ignored. After his assassination Bandaranaike's government in Ceylon was continued by his widow, who still leads his party in government after defeating her predecessor in office, Dudley Senanayake, the son of Ceylon's first prime minister. Mrs Gandhi's claims to the prime ministership rested more on her status as Nehru's daughter than on her own abilities. Jinnah's elderly sister was brought out of the drawing-room at an advanced age to become the figurehead for the opposition to Ayub Khan in the 1965 elections. During the Cultural Revolution in China Mao's wife Chiang Ching (a former film star) became for a time an important political figure, and in Taiwan the line of succession from President Chiang Kai-shek to his son seems assured. The charisma of the leader is shared in some degree by his immediate relatives, and this is still a powerful political factor in Asia.

The cult of the father of the nation, which is carried to extremes in Asia, is a part of this heritage: Mao, Gandhi, Kim Il-Sung, Ho Chi Minh, even Nehru are literally worshipped in unsophisticated strata of their respective societies, as was Sukarno in his day.[35] A special flavour is added by the tradition of the people enjoying life vicariously through their king: the ruler finds it politically helpful to indulge (or at least to affect indulgence) in all the pleasures, including those of sex. The amours of Sukarno and Sarit, when they swayed it over Indonesia and Thailand respectively, were legendary, and even Sihanouk once rebutted a rumour that his politics were being influenced by a Chinese mistress, in the words:

Now I swear before the dear Venerables and the children that if I was truly in love with a Chinese girl, as alleged by Thanh, I would be condemned in hell for five hundred lives. . . . Being a nationalist, I prefer only girls of Khmer nationality. It is true that I had many Khmer girl friends. . . . When I was king, I was a good-looking boy. I was not pot-bellied as I am now. Because I was a handsome young king, I was loved and chased by girls who were also eager to take me as their lover. It is always the girls who wanted to make love to me, dear children. . . .[36]

The outstanding example of the authoritarian trend in recent Asian politics is the transition from parliamentary politics to army rule in no fewer than six countries – Indonesia, Burma, Pakistan, Thailand, South Korea and South Vietnam. In the old Confucian tradition the military was despised as the resort of untalented and desperate characters, so that one of the reasons for the inability of the present South Vietnamese Government to become a true focus for non-communist nationalism is the feeling that soldiers are basically 'ignorant people who have usurped leadership by virtue of their control of the means of violence, and that is not a basis for rule legitimation in Vietnamese society'.[37]

The Chinese communists did much to change that image by the discipline and restraint exhibited by the Red Army in the years of civil war, but even in Peking the official Maoist policy is that 'power comes out of the barrel of the gun', and that, 'Our principle is that the Party commands the gun, and the gun must never be allowed to command the Party.'[38]

The army possesses one huge advantage in a society which is traditionally hierarchic but is being pushed towards individualism and hates the interim: it does rest squarely on a strict sense of hierarchy. This is becoming increasingly embarrassing in egalitarian Western society, but in Asia is 'admirably fitted to the traditional modes of social organization', as David Wilson says of Thailand.[39] Furthermore, the army in many Asian countries is not merely a paid professional service, but a 'shareholder in the revolution', as General Nasution says of the Indonesian armed forces. In Burma, Indonesia, China and North Vietnam the soldiers were not differentiated from the civilian revolutionaries in the long fight against foreign rule and native capitalism: everyone was, almost literally, a soldier in these independence sagas. The generals and colonels of Rangoon and Djakarta thus observed the factional bickering and indecisiveness of the civilian politicians after independence with a feeling of betrayal and a sense of responsibility. The Burmese army actually returned power to the civilians after less than two years' caretaking in 1958–60, but soon found it necessary to intervene again, this time for an indefinite period in which it tried not merely to put the administration straight but to implement an ambitious policy of Burmanized socialism which has proved even more disastrous than the civilians' misrule.

The position is different in Pakistan and India, where the warrior had a high caste rating in antiquity and where army service is admired. But the British tradition of the non-political army took firm root: only the virtual breakdown of the country in the final stages of parliamentary rule brought the Pakistan army to stage a *coup d'état* in 1958, and, despite occasional murmurs of anxiety, an army take-over in India seems extremely unlikely.[40] Foreign military aid is another factor which buttresses the armed forces, reinforcing their ambitions and giving them the means to realize them. During the 1960s, the military budgets of at least five Asian countries (India, Pakistan, South Korea, Malaysia and Thailand) more than doubled,[41] and eight countries are now devoting more than 5 per cent of their gross national product to the economically unfruitful field of military spending (China, North Korea, North Vietnam, South Vietnam, Taiwan, Burma, Cambodia and Laos).[42] Only Japan, which suffered both domestic repression and international ignominy under its former militarist regime, seems determinedly and constitutionally pacifist, spending a smaller proportion of gross national product (1 per cent) on defence than any other Asian country.

But this account of Asian authoritarianism should not be misunderstood: the preference for a hierarchical structure is there, and Asian politics will be more hierarchical than European for a long time to come. This in itself is not the only criterion of good government, however, and the evidence from Japan, the traditional Asian society which is most advanced along the road to modernization with all the individualizing forces which that releases, is that the sense of hierarchy begins to crumble revealing an underlying sense of group-consciousness which survives it. Asia may eventually produce political institutions which cater for the feeling of group without the use of excessive authority.

So much for the preference for hierarchy over equality. The third generalization which could be made about the new Asian politics is that they spring from a thirst for consensus. 'Majoritarianism is a new theory for Japan,' declare Scalapino and Masumi in their study of Japanese politics, 'one of dubious validity and ethical worth. Decision making, Japanese style, is based on consensus.'[43] So Royama Masamichi, a leading political analyst, said of the Diet ratification of the Japan–United States Security Treaty in 1960 in the absence of the minority opposition members: 'Decision by majority under such conditions could not carry any moral authority.'[44] The Japanese socialists can exert considerable pressure on the Government by boycotting, or threatening to boycott, Diet sessions. In Indonesia the old custom of *musjawarah* – 'discuss and agree' – enabled decisions to be made without counting votes or imposing on the minority, although it needed imaginative leadership to work effectively.[45] The concept has been revived in present-day politics, not only in Indonesia but in the new Association of South-East Asian Nations (ASEAN) and in the Asia and Pacific Council (ASPAC). In India some State governments give grants to village *panchayats* (elected committees) which achieve unanimous voting.

The *panchayat*, or village parliament, was the central feature of the romanticized Nehruvian vision of an old Indian tradition brought up to date. But in practice this experiment in rural self-government has been disappointing. Both policy and its implementation are a state rather than central responsibility, and the picture therefore varies enormously across India. Only in three states do the *panchayats* at district level – the so-called *zila parishad* – possess any executive function, and in most places the political parties have treated the *panchayats* as legitimate arenas for their own competition. The villagers' apathy, the *panchayats*' failure to exploit their opportunities of raising funds, and the authorities' failure to spell out clearly the functions of the new bodies, combine to prevent success.[46] The draft Fourth Plan recommended that, 'All development and welfare schemes capable of execution at the district level should be transferred to *zila parishads* who should be responsible for both programme planning and programme implementation.'[47]

The *panchayats* are supposed to allow the village tradition to express itself in reaching decisions by consensus, but a study of the position in Nepal, where King Mahendra has taken a leaf out of the Indian book, concluded that the exposure of the *panchayats* to factional party politics could become even more disruptive than the parliamentary party system which the *panchayats*, in Nepal at least, were supposed to replace.[48]

In Pakistan the system of Basic Democracies was instituted by Ayub Khan as a means of insulating elections from rabble-rousers. But the result was to shore up the power of the rural élite, the better-off farmers who managed to dominate the elections of local councils. These naturally supported the government but tended to suppress the grievances of the rural poor, so that the system produced stagnation and resistance to change: by 1969 it had become so unpopular that it was swept away in the tide of revolt against Ayub.[49]

Every government in Asia has tried to create a satisfactory link with public opinion, especially in the countryside. The army-controlled Lanzin Party in Burma set up peasants' and workers' councils as the lowest tier of a new hierarchy of legislatures, but they continued to be dominated by the government party machine. The idea that you can criticize a particular policy of the government without being disloyal to the state, takes a long time to gain acceptance – as Mao Tse-tung found in the anarchism which was set loose in the Cultural Revolution out of similar motives. Prince Sihanouk held a National Congress twice a year in the grounds of his palace, an informal forum which peasants from all over the country attended to air their grievances and bask in their leader's presence. Under the prince's adept chairmanship this institution allowed the government to proliferate an awareness of the international and political problems of the country, while at the same time keeping its ears open to rural opinion. In Indonesia Sukarno revived the old village institution of *Gotong Royong*, or mutual co-operation, as a basis for his new ideology of the late 1950s. Consensus is a central feature of the Indonesian system.[50]

The Chinese also prefer to avoid the open confrontation of public voting. It is this factor which explains the apathy of Hongkong voters towards their Urban Council elections,[51] and in the long run it will prove to be one of the difficulties in persuading China to play a full role in the United Nations as it is presently constituted. In Hongkong the colonial government has sought to overcome this by promoting *kaifongs*, a form of street committee which can act as a channel of communication between the government and the people without resorting to alien institutions. Consensus is also an important concept in the People's Commune as well as in the new constitution of the Chinese Communist Party.

Much confusion about Asian politics arises from the syncretic *penchant* of Asian intellectuals. This is well known in the case of India, but it is also illustrated by the vision offered by Eda Saburo, the Japanese socialist leader, of a Japan which would combine the best elements of all systems — American living standards, Soviet social security, British parliamentary democracy and Japan's pacifist constitution. The socialism *à la Indonesia* of Sukarno, the socialist humanism of Nehru, the Buddhist socialism of Nu, the Basic Democracy of Ayub, the personalism of Diem – all these are 'portmanteau ideologies'[52] which draw freely from the ideas of Europe as well as Asia. At this stage of political activity in Asia they may be regarded as statements of long-range intent rather than as specific blueprints for action. When it comes to actually doing things on the ground, the only raw material available is the local tradition, which may have had its confidence shaken in the earlier days of confrontation with Western power and ideas, but which has now regained it.

The modes by which people organize their political actions are thus completely Asian in substance, even if sometimes Western-influenced in form. But the broad goals of freedom and of progress, provided they are pursued at a tempo which can be accommodated by most segments of society without too much shock or discomfort, are identical with those of Europe and, indeed, of the whole of mankind. The differences concern the means, not the ends.

Part Two: The Actors

Chapter Fourteen

The Chinese Dragon

CONSIDERATION now of individual countries of Asia must begin with China, not only because she is the largest in both area and population, but also because she has the strongest and richest indigenous tradition. Of all the Asian nations, China is usually found by outsiders the most difficult to understand. The Chinese of today has a traditional heart, a modern nationalist head and a communist face, and he has to be understood at all three levels.

The key to the distinctive Chinese personality lies in the fact that China developed a civilization broadly comparable in its achievements with those of the Western world but formed virtually in isolation from them. The early agricultural and urban civilization of the Near East and Mediterranean – even later, of Persia and India – had sufficient mutual connection to ensure a degree of intellectual cross-fertilization. But the comparable civilization that first grew up in the Yellow River basin had no sustained contact with its counterparts to the west.[1] The Chinese thus saw themselves not as one of a number of viable civilizations but as the very centre of world civilization itself. The name which they give to their country – *Chungkuo* – means middle kingdom or central state: it bears no racial meaning as do the names of the European nations.[2] This fact alone sheds light on the difficulties of the Chinese leaders even today in coming to terms with a polycultural world of equal sovereign states.

The history of China is the history of the spread of civilized social order from the Yellow River delta throughout the readily accessible and inhabitable areas all around, incorporating the entire Han race (which forms 95 per cent of China's present population) and spreading eventually to neighbouring races. But the sea put an effective limit on the spread of Chinese civilization to the east, and the mountains and deserts of central Asia placed another limit to the west. When European traders and missionaries first began to knock on China's doors four hundred years

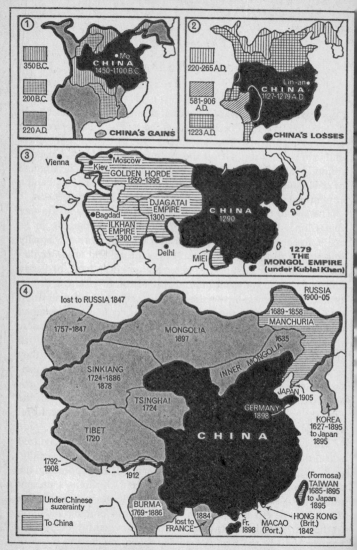

① 350 B.C. / 200 B.C. / 220 A.D.
CHINA 1450-1100 B.C. • Mo
CHINA'S GAINS

② 220-265 A.D. / 581-906 A.D. / 1223 A.D.
Lin-an • CHINA 1127-1279 A.D.
CHINA'S LOSSES

③ Vienna • Kiev • Moscow
GOLDEN HORDE 1250-1395
DJAGATAI EMPIRE 1300
• Bagdad
ILKHAN EMPIRE 1300
Delhi •
CHINA 1290
MIEI
1279 THE MONGOL EMPIRE (under Kublai Khan)

④ lost to RUSSIA 1847
1757-1847
MONGOLIA 1897
RUSSIA 1900-05
1689-1858 MANCHURIA
1635
INNER MONGOLIA
SINKIANG 1724-1886 1878
TSINGHAI 1724
JAPAN 1905
GERMANY 1898
TIBET 1720
CHINA
KOREA 1627-1895 to Japan 1895
1792-1908
1912
(Formosa) TAIWAN 1685-1895 to Japan 1895
Under Chinese suzerainty
To China
BURMA 1769-1886
1884
lost to FRANCE
Fr. 1898
MACAO (Port.) 1898
HONG KONG (Brit.) 1842

The expansion and contraction of China over the centuries.

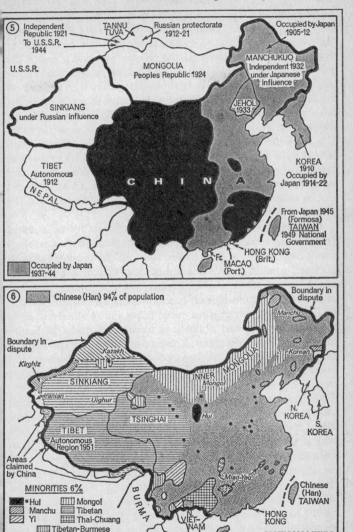

⑤ Independent Republic 1921 To U.S.S.R. 1944
TANNU TUVA
Russian protectorate 1912-21
Occupied by Japan 1905-12

U.S.S.R.

MONGOLIA Peoples Republic 1924

MANCHUKUO Independent 1932 under Japanese influence

SINKIANG under Russian influence

JEHOL 1933

TIBET Autonomous 1912

C H I N A

NEPAL

KOREA 1910 Occupied by Japan 1914-22

From Japan 1945 (Formosa) TAIWAN 1949 National Government

Occupied by Japan 1937-44

Fr. HONG KONG (Brit.)
MACAO (Port.)

⑥ Chinese (Han) 94% of population

Boundary in dispute

Manchu

Boundary in dispute

Kirghiz

Kazakh

Korean

INNER MONGOLIA

SINKIANG

Mongol

Iranian

Uighur

Hui

TSINGHAI

N. KOREA

S. KOREA

TIBET Autonomous Region 1951

Areas claimed by China

Miao-Yao

Chinese (Han) TAIWAN

BURMA

MINORITIES 6%

Hui   Mongol
Manchu   Tibetan
Yi   Thai-Chuang
Tibetan-Burmese

N. VIET-NAM

LAOS

HONG KONG

NATIONALITIES

or more ago, the Chinese saw themselves as the custodians of the only serious modern civilization known to mankind. To them the world stretched out from its Chinese centre in ever-widening circles, the nearest embracing the peoples who had accepted the gift of Chinese civilization (i.e. the Japanese, Koreans and Vietnamese), the next comprising those barbarians who insisted on retaining their own relatively primitive forms of social order but who were known to the Chinese and normally acknowledged the emperor in Peking as the symbol and fount of the world order (i.e. the South-East Asians, Indians, Tibetans and Mongols) and a final outer belt of those shadowy societies of which mysterious tales were occasionally retailed by travellers, and which on rare occasions even sent envoys and gifts to Peking but which could not be said to have been brought into 'the world system' (i.e. the Arabs, Europeans and Africans).[3]

It is hardly surprising, therefore, that the Chinese cultural tradition, after four millennia of continuous independent development, has become so deep-rooted and inspired its adherents with such self-confidence. We know this social system as Confucianism, after its most renowned teacher and philosopher. Its social and political relationships are based on the family: discipline within the family is strict, filial piety being the cardinal virtue in Chinese morality, and obligations to others outside the family are defined in similar terms. The emperor was thus the head of the whole human family, and obedience to local and central government officers was expected to be as complete as that to one's own father and grandfather.

Within this basically authoritarian society, great importance was attached to the dignity, if not to the autonomy, of the individual, and this is the root of the institution which Westerners tend to find most perplexing, that of 'face'. Face is the requirement that in any dealings between two or more people, proper respect for each person's feelings should be shown. Precisely because the individual has to repress so many of his own desires in order to fit into the Chinese social order, he clings most tenaciously to the psychological umbrella of face, which allows him to maintain his own self-respect even when he is at the losing end of an encounter. This is why the Chinese instinct in any conflict of interest is to bargain, to arrange reciprocal concessions, to compromise, to harmonize the contradictions.[4] Some of the behaviour of the Chinese Government in recent international affairs, from the border dispute with India to the unashamed holding of an innocent British newspaperman as hostage (both turning on the Chinese need for equal concessions to make a true bargain), can be explained in the light of this system.

The consequences of this strong cultural tradition is that the Chinese, unlike the citizens of almost any other developing country, glow with pride and self-respect, and exhibit no doubts at all about their own cultural identity. China is thus the only non-white nation to challenge whole-heartedly the Western assumption of world cultural leadership. Where we in the West, as a French observer notes, are trying 'to fit traditional worlds into democratic uniform of European type – too narrow or too loose', China is telling the nations of the *tiers monde* that 'in our present day they must re-invent themselves, or else disappear'.[5] The fact that the Chinese have always been the centre of their own world explains why, in Fairbank's phrase, 'the world's largest nation, with the longest tradition of ethnocentricity, is . . . the last to participate fully in the international order'.[6]

The trouble was that the traditional system proved increasingly inadequate to the needs of modern life: Confucius, as Dennis Bloodworth neatly observes, wanted gentlemen but produced players.[7] The near-impossibility of evolving a satisfactory modern political system and communications flow can be gauged from the explanation, given recently by an old teacher from Northern China, of the Chinese reluctance to discuss politics:

Because society today is very complicated, every person's thinking, point of view and opinions are not the same. If you discuss them you won't be able to reach a general conclusion. Possibly it will lead to some trouble. People will not understand your thinking: possibly they will think that it is not correct. They might pay special attention to your behaviour, or even lock you up.[8]

The lack of universality in traditional Chinese social relations proved in the end defeating. As Lin Yutang concluded in *My Country and My People*, 'seen in modern eyes, Confucianism omitted from the social relationships man's social obligations towards the stranger, and great and catastrophic was the omission. . . . In the end, as it worked out, the family became a walled castle outside which everything was legitimate loot.'⁹ Communism is being grown on good soil in China in the sense that individualism has not yet blossomed, so that it was possible for Lin Piao, the defence minister and Mao's chosen heir, to observe recently: 'Every person is affiliated with a certain class ... there is no such thing as abstract or independent individuals.'¹⁰ But a genuine sense of social responsibility and shared concern across family lines has yet to be established.

Confucianism is thus largely discredited as a practical system of social relations, even though, for many Chinese intellectuals, it remains 'treasured in the mind for its own sake after the society which had produced it and which needed it had begun to dissolve away'.¹¹ It continues to inform the instinctive behaviour of most Chinese, especially under stress, and its virtues remain admired: a communist newspaper declared as recently as in 1962: 'Marxism doesn't deny old moral concepts. ... Old virtues of the labouring people have a deep social foundation; they must be continued and further developed. Such a moral virtue is that of taking care of father and mother.'¹²

But the sociological basis of old-fashioned Confucianism is being steadily eroded, and the clear lines of authority have become disarranged. Lucian Pye, the American scholar, explains that as the traditional concept of authority in the Chinese political system has broken down over the past century, so the mechanism by which the Chinese personality handles its unconscious aggressions has been disrupted. The Chinese still expect too much of their rulers and have yet to find a way to genuine self-reliance and innovatory individualism.¹³

If this old China still lurks in the heart of the present-day Chinese, his head is all for modern progress on the basis of nationalism. The relative depth to which Chinese society sank in the nineteenth century, after its golden ages of the past, was seen by the Chinese not merely as a product of deficiencies within the system itself, but also as a direct consequence of foreign intervention and foreign control. Strictly speaking, China was never a colony of any European power, but this disguised the fact that (as Sun Yat-sen used to say) she was 'everyone's colony'. The Western powers ruled the so-called Treaty Ports, Shanghai and the rest, as if they were colonies, and the interior of China was so disordered, its administration so ineffective, that the Treaty Ports tended to set the pace in those activities leading towards modernization (including the harbouring of the nationalist and communist rebels of the day from a vengeful government: Ho Chi Minh, Sun Yat-sen and Mao Tse-tung all pursued some of their early political activity in these pockets of foreign rule).

It follows that the mood of Chinese nationalism today is anti-foreign, anti-imperialistic. It was necessary for China to throw off the soft, effeminate image which early Western visitors had formed of her. A Jesuit priest at the Chinese imperial court four hundred years ago observed: 'It appears to me the most difficult thing in the world to regard the Chinese as warriors ... they spend two hours every morning in combing and plaiting their hairs ...'[14] Today the queues are all cut off and Mao himself sets an example by swimming across the Yangtze River in spite of his old age.

It is also necessary to restore and maintain the unity of China as it was before foreign imperialism began to encroach. Hence the determination of the communists to take over Taiwan, hence their early action to assert control over Tibet, hence the official concern over their relations with the numerically small but strategically important minority nationalities in Sinkiang and in the south-west (whom Chiang Kai-shek regarded as branches of the Chinese racial family), hence the anxiety in South-East Asia over China's eventual intentions towards the distant areas and islands which she regarded in historical times as being in some loose way a part of the Chinese empire.

The possibility of Peking's control over the more distant provinces and regions becoming substantially weaker was a matter of grave concern during the Cultural Revolution. Probably the first two decades of communist rule represented a high point of central control over this vast and ill-linked country, and future Chinese governments will have to reconcile themselves to a considerable exercise of autonomy by the various provinces. Mao himself apparently thought that Chinese progress was more important than Chinese unity, and he was willing in 1967 to risk anarchy in the interests of revolution. But the minds of most of his colleagues and likely successors are less daring and more conventional, and this tension between the provinces and the centre could be one of the issues on which communism itself might eventually founder in China. Certainly it will become an increasing preoccupation of future Chinese governments.[15]

But the most important aspect of modern Chinese nationalism is its very real concern with the social modernization and economic progress of China herself. The concern shown by the Communist Government for education, health and other social reforms was popular among Marxists and non-Marxists alike. During the past twenty years the equality of women with men has been given a firm foundation, literacy has been brought up to a level of about 50 per cent, and public health and hygiene have been improved out of all recognition. The Communist Government has sought to destroy the stigma attached by the Confucianist tradition to manual work, and it has even declared war against face: in the official Party-inspired novels and films which are now being fed to the Chinese public, and which will mould the younger generation that knows no other literature, confrontations between members of society are depicted as direct, avoiding the use of go-betweens.

The Government of Mao Tse-tung has in these twenty years doubled China's gross national product, and although there has also been a 50 per cent increase in the population, this has still been enough to raise average living standards generally. The foundations of heavy industry and modern technology have been laid, and since 1960 this has been on the basis of self-reliance, i.e. without foreign aid. It may be observed here, however, that these two strands in Chinese nationalism – the modernizing and the anti-foreign – come into sharp collision over the problem of Hongkong, where acquiescence in the continued humiliation of European colonial rule over Chinese soil is a grudging product of China's need for foreign exchange (of which she obtains about £240 million a year, or half her total inflow from all sources, by selling food and consumer goods to Hong Kong).[16]

These internal advances were undertaken by a government sincerely motivated by the ideals of communism, and this provides the third and most recent level at which the Chinese *persona* needs to be understood. There is a great deal of argument among Western experts over the relative importance of nationalism and Marxism in the make-up of Mao Tse-tung and the other

Chinese leaders. The official Soviet view, shared by many communists throughout the world, was summed up in the jibe of Fidel Castro that the Chinese had made 'a laughing-stock of socialism': certainly European socialists and communists have found China under its present Government just as difficult to understand and to deal with as have European conservatives, liberals and capitalists.

But the Chinese communists, faced with the almost impossible task of introducing socialism to a society lacking the ideological basis for universal social concern, financially poor and economically stagnant, have certainly tried hard. During the Cultural Revolution the Maoists accused their chief opponents, the followers of Liu Shao-chi (Mao's heir-designate up to 1966), of losing sight of the ultimate goal of socialism in the effort to get a slothful society moving along the right road towards it. Perhaps the Liuists were ready, as the Maoists allege, to experiment with a mixture of public and private ownership in these early stages of the Chinese revolution. But all the factions in the Chinese Communist Party leadership, in the days before their differences came out in public in 1966, put their names and gave public support to very ambitious programmes of collectivization at which many a communist in another land would blench.

Chinese farming and modern industry were completely socialized during the 1950s, and the only official remnants of private enterprise are the private plots which each peasant family is allowed to maintain (and which probably account for 5 per cent of total agricultural land, 10 per cent of the total value of agricultural production), and the small factories, shops and service enterprises where the state usually has a controlling share. During the chaotic days of the Cultural Revolution in 1967 there was an upsurge of 'spontaneous capitalism', and in Shanghai private underground factories were reported to be making big profits out of the boom in metal Mao badges. But the official effort to keep enterprise in public rather than private hands cannot be denied. The People's Commune, first inaugurated with loud fanfares in 1958 as 'a new social organization' appearing 'fresh as the morning sun above the broad horizon of East Asia', is the Chinese communists' distinct contribution to the repertory of Marxist practice. Whatever its ups and downs in the past ten years, the commune remains a more plausible potential framework for socialist development in China's economic conditions than anything offered by communists elsewhere.

The fundamental contradiction in Chinese communism is that between ideology and organization, between doctrine and practice, between the red and the expert (those alternate heroes of the Chinese communist canon).[17] Mao is one of the great figures of the twentieth century: the precise attributes of his greatness will be debated forever, but not the greatness itself. He is a leader of unique charisma, and no one else could have maintained in harness all the turbulent and often antagonistic forces which were put in train by the communist capture of China in 1949. But Mao is no administrator, and he nurses what his biographer, Stuart Schram, calls an 'unquenchable desire to harmonize the two conflicting imperatives of "conscious action" by individuals and impeccable social discipline'.[18] Mao constantly sought the best of both worlds, to have both freedom and unity (a contradiction which inspired first the Hundred Flowers movement of 1957 and then the Cultural Revolution ten years later), both technical expertise and ideological purity (a contradiction which had certainly held back China's potential technological development).

But when Mao insisted on launching his last great campaign for socialist education and party reform in 1965–6 it was no longer possible to maintain surface harmony among the leadership. Liu Shao-chi was the organizing genius in the party, who had opposed many of Mao's policies during the period since 1949. Liu took the attitude that, while Mao was a brilliant guerrilla chieftain and a heroic focus for national loyalty, the task of actually governing and modernizing the country should be left to more skilled hands. Under the influence of Liu, the party had become, in Mao's eyes, bureaucratic and unresponsive to the peasants' needs. It had become an obstacle to further change, and its vested interest in power made it counter-revolutionary. Mao declared war on it by taking the lead of a new anti-party coalition comprising the army, the students and the government apparatus, all of which had a grudge against Liu and his party machine.

The army is more disciplined than the party and Lin Piao, the civil war hero who had become minister of defence in 1959, was chosen by Mao as his new heir-designate. It was Lin Piao who first produced the 'little red book' of selected sayings of Chairman Mao. The younger generation felt frustrated, not only by the rigidities of Party rule and the growing generation gap, but also by the continued promotion and success of the self-assured and sophisticated children of the bourgeois class against whom the communist revolution had been supposedly directed. Mao and Lin Piao were able to create the Red Guards as the shock troops of the new campaign against the conventional Party apparatus. But Mao was also careful to secure the support (or at least the sympathetic neutrality) of Chou En-lai and the 'technocrats' – the professionally-minded government administrators, including economists and scientists – who look up to Chou as their protector. With these formidable allies, and in spite of his numerically weak following within the Party itself, Mao was able to ensure the dismissal and disgrace of Liu Shao-chi and many other Party leaders unsympathetic towards his ideas. The climax came in the spring of 1969 when the Ninth Party Congress adopted a new constitution and a new leadership in line with Mao's ideas.

The Cultural Revolution of 1967–9 has best been described as 'really three things in one: an enigmatic multiple power struggle, wrapped in a crusade and superimposed on a scattering of more or less spontaneous, more or less politicized, student riots, strikes, peasant uprisings, mutinies, and palace coups.'[19] It is the first of these three-in-one struggles to which the Western press was most attentive, and in essence it is a contest for the succession to Mao, who is seventy-seven and not in the best of health. Liu Shao-chi's candidature has been stopped, but there are at least three other leading contenders for the mantle. Lin Piao was Mao's original choice, but his skills were organizational rather than charismatic and he lacked enough political talent to take full advantage of his preferment. Chou En-lai has improved his position during the Cultural Revolution, and he is the leader whom most Chinese intellectuals would probably choose, but he was slow in building the firm power base which the supremely successful Peking politician must command. Unlike the others he is himself from the mandarin class, and this in a proletarian party is a handicap.

Finally there is a small clique of ultra-radicals which includes Mao's wife, Chiang Ching, his former secretary, Chen Po-ta, and Kang Sheng. These enjoy special access to Mao, and they have rallied the younger generation to their cause. The only two young new faces to appear on the Politburo which was elected in the spring of 1969 – Yao Wen-yuan, reputedly Mao's son-in-law, and Chang Chun-chiao, Mao's acolyte from Shanghai, both still in their thirties – were sponsored by this radical faction. But its distaste for many of the senior army and government leaders is unconcealed – and reciprocated. These three groups are left by the Cultural Revolution in uneasy alliance, to the continuation of which the reconciling hand and authority of Mao seem indispensable. When Mao goes, Chou will take over with Lin Piao in turn disgraced. But Chou is over seventy, and the next strong man is probably waiting quietly unnoticed in the wings.

The contenders for the succession are not only jockeying for power; they also have principles and ideals, and the policy aspect of the struggle is probably, in the long run, more important than personalities. The policy differences between the Maoists and the Liuists extend over the whole field, from education to agriculture, defence to the arts, science to foreign policy. The essential difference is that between an optimistic and a pessimistic brand of communism. Mao is undeterred by the immediate and short-term difficulties which the communist programme faces in China, whereas the Liuists are daunted by the near-impossibility of achieving the conversion of 750 million hearts and minds.

Mao holds out for all or nothing of the communist programme, while Liu would settle for half, consolidating the progress already achieved and indefinitely postponing the next instalment of socialism. Mao puts all his faith in the emancipation of the poor peasant, Liu is more realistic in relying on the cooperation of the enterprising rich peasant who provides the natural leadership in the communes. Liu Shao-chi has been discredited, but his views are widely shared in the Party, as well as by many in the government and army leadership. Whatever the personalities, China is likely to adopt less ideologically-oriented policies, both at home and abroad, in the post-Mao era.

The third and final aspect of the Cultural Revolution is the general background of political frustration, anarchic tendencies and strivings for regional autonomy against which the struggles in Peking have to be played. 'To rebel is justified', was the most famous of Mao's slogans informing the Cultural Revolution. There are many forces ready to take advantage of the weakening of central control from Peking, and much of the strife and violence of the Cultural Revolution was both unintended and ungovernable by the leaders in Peking. The next generation of Chinese leaders will be facing an even greater challenge than the present one in merely governing China. It will also be even less familiar than they with the outside world.[20]

The Government of China is also as vociferously communist in its international politics as the Soviet Union or other communist states. Like the Russians, the Chinese leaders of all factions publicly look forward to a fully socialist world, and they are not scrupulous about the means which such an end would justify – only careful about the likelihood of their success. The particular contribution of the Chinese to this communist dream of world power is to marry it with the frustrations of the embourgeoisized proletariats of the industrialized world on the one hand, and with the newly articulate resentments of the economically exploited and under-developed coloured races on the other.

In 1965 Lin Piao published his notorious thesis entitled 'Long Live the Victory of People's War'.[21] This characterized the developing countries of Africa and Asia as the world's villages, the industrial nations of the West as the world's cities: it asserted that, just as Maoist communism had led China's peasants to victory in the Chinese revolution, so China would now take the lead in helping the developing countries to defeat their Western oppressors. The Chinese have supplied arms, military training, logistical provisions and diplomatic support to revolutionaries in many countries, especially in Africa, Asia and Latin America. But the volume of these activities is far less than similar efforts made by the Soviet Union and her European allies on the one hand or by the United States and the other Western powers on the other. In Vietnam, where the cause of world communism was most bloodily at stake, the Chinese never intervened with combat troops (although they supplied food and clothing, small arms and military engineers with service troop support), and in Korea, where again the frontiers of communism were specifically in question, China did not send in her 'volunteers' until General MacArthur's forces were almost on top of the Chinese frontier and in a mood to cross over it into China's industrial power-house of Manchuria.[22]

The clue to this apparent contradiction between words and deeds, so typical of the Chinese tradition but so misunderstood by communist friends and capitalist foes alike, was in fact spelled out in one passage of Lin Piao's thesis which the commentators often overlook:

In order to make a revolution and to fight a people's war and be victorious, it is imperative to adhere to the policy of self-reliance, rely on the strength of the masses in one's own country and prepare to carry on the fight independently even when all material aid from outside is cut off. If one does not operate by one's own efforts, does not independently ponder and solve the problems of the revolution in one's own country and does not rely on the strength of the masses, but leans wholly on foreign aid – even though this be aid from socialist countries which persist in revolution – no victory can be won, or be consolidated even if it is won.[23]

It is in this sense that the Chinese accept, as their foreign minister, the late Chen Yi often claimed, that revolution is 'not for export'. This does not mean that China will cease to give assistance to subversive movements throughout the world. The *People's Daily* once recalled that the Americans, in their War of Independence against the British king, had appealed for (and obtained) help from France, Holland, Spain and other continental European nations: 90 per cent of the arms used in the first eighteen months of the American War of Independence were imported from these latter countries.[24] What is wrong, the Chinese therefore ask, in helping in similar manner countries still fighting for their political and economic freedom? But if the Chinese did not realize it before, they have certainly had it rubbed into them now, that to extend a helping hand to an African revolutionary does not guarantee a leading place in either his affections or his formulation of future policy.

What, then, are the actual international objectives of China? They are really three, and they correspond to the three outer circles which seemed to surround China in the old days. The first of the three goals is to restore and maintain China's proper borders after the erosions of the European imperialists. This, as we have seen in an earlier chapter,[25] has now been largely consummated, with the exception only of the long Sino-Indian border (where there is nevertheless a *de facto* line which is *de facto* respected by both sides whatever their arguments) and the even longer Sino-Soviet frontier (where there are some areas whose final destiny seems doubtful).

The second of China's diplomatic goals is to protect the interests of the fifteen million overseas Chinese residents in South-East Asia and to re-establish China's influence over these one-time client states. This has never been explicitly stated by the Chinese, but it is an inference from their actions and speeches. They do not wish or intend to conquer South-East Asia by brute force, nor would they be likely to succeed in such a course. But they are responsive (as the developments in the Cultural Revolution showed) to the appeals of the overseas Chinese for material or psychological help in their running battle with local nationalists. This is not a simple matter for men like Mao Tse-tung or Chou En-lai to decide, since a purely ideological appraisal would identify most of the overseas Chinese as petty bourgeois and capitalist elements impeding the people's revolution of their adopted countries. The tangled question of citizenship of the Chinese residents in Indonesia came near to being settled in the 1950s by a degree of Chinese repudiation of their kith and kin abroad which must be credited to the international idealism of the Chinese communist leadership. But these policies did not stand the test of time, and Chinese diplomacy towards Burma, Cambodia, Nepal and Indonesia at the height of the Cultural Revolution in 1967, proved that a more chauvinistic sentiment lay just beneath the surface.

It is not only a question, however, of blood being stronger than water; the overseas Chinese happen to live in the only group of countries which have participated with any seriousness in the Chinese tributary system, only to turn face about from the time when the European arrived (and conquered them). If China has any desire to exert any real influence in the world, if she really intends to break out of the encirclement which the European powers have wrought on her, if she is to undo anything of the work of Western imperialism, it is only in South-East Asia that minimal possibilities exist. Unlike India or Pakistan, these are countries with which China has some experience and some long-standing connections. Unlike Japan, they are also countries which are either too small or too poor effectively to resist foreign influence. Finally, these are also the countries whose provision of military facilities and bases to Western powers makes China feel most vulnerable. By detaching them from their Western patronage and drawing them into a modern version of the former Chinese system of mutual trade and diplomacy, the Chinese Government would at the same time restore its self-respect, improve its own national security and morale, facilitate its external commercial needs and acquire more control over the fate of the overseas Chinese. It is scarcely conceivable that this is not an important long-term objective of any Chinese government.[26]

The third general goal of Chinese foreign policy relates to the outer circle of furthermost barbarians who have disconcertingly usurped the primacy in world affairs which China had thought to be hers. It is to assert herself as a world power and as a world culture. The question of power depends, of course, very intimately on the progress of China's own modernization and economic development. Even though the Chinese enjoy about the lowest living standards in the entire world, the Chinese Government is still able to dispose of an annual budget almost as large as those of the big Western European nations – France, Germany and Britain. China can thus 'afford' the H-bomb,[27] an African policy, and a world-wide diplomatic presence.

The quest for recognition as a great power was one of the factors behind the border war with India, the ideological quarrel with Moscow and the unprecedented Chinese penetration into Africa. It is surely implicit in the statement by Han Suyin* that, 'China, having completed her own revolution, is now consciously entering the arena as the vanguard and guide of all the revolutionary movements in the despised two-thirds of the world.'[28]

So powerful is this aspect of the modern Chinese drive that her

---

*Perhaps because of her Belgian ancestry on her mother's side, Han Suyin is almost the only Chinese alive who can speak persuasively, to a Westerner's ear, of China's dreams and nightmares, and her books are indispensable to an understanding of present-day China.

diplomats have been found using the expression 'we blacks' at Afro-Asian assemblies,[29] and some third world leaders (the more Westernized ones) are offended by what President Bourguiba of Tunisia once called China's 'inverted racism'.[30]

Indeed, this drive tends to become blunted precisely because it is directed at both political and cultural power status. To encourage anti-European feelings among Africans and Asians can be successful if it is intelligently conducted, but if the people doing it are simultaneously seeking to establish the equal validity of Chinese and European values and traditions[31] it is only to be expected that the Africans and Asians will suspect China of merely wanting to step into Europe's shoes. This is unfair to the Chinese, since they are not, after all, making commercial profits in Afro-Asia and their technicans adhere scrupulously to the local standards of living. But it is a reaction which is only human, and which many Africans and Asians have already experienced. The irony is that those Chinese diplomats who are most successful in making friends and influencing people in the *tiers monde* are the already Westernized ones, and that their patient work was in many cases undone by the positively non-Westernized Chinese who took over the foreign ministry at the height of the Cultural Revolution in 1967 and whose crude, blustering tactics made many enemies for China.[32]

But the Chinese will undoubtedly make efforts again to persuade others in the third world not to take Western cultural domination lying down. Since the Chinese by themselves constitute a quarter of mankind (and will soon be nearer one-third) it would be in the West's own interests, even if the Chinese fail to win support, to find some way of redressing the Chinese sense of injustice. Bertrand Russell argued thus many years ago:

I think that if we are to feel at home in the world ... we shall have to admit Asia to equality in our thoughts, not only politically but culturally. What changes this will bring about I do not know, but I am convinced that they will be profound and of the greatest importance.[33]

Law, diplomatic convention and international terminology are some of the fields in which accommodations between Western and Chinese culture could eventually be brought about. This is necessarily a long-term and somewhat speculative prospect. But we would mislead ourselves if we were to see the entry of China into world affairs as a purely political matter: it is also, as Geoffroy-Dechaume has said, 'a philosophical question'.[34]

The two small fringe states at the edge of the Chinese world can be considered more briefly. Taiwan, where the Nationalists under Chiang Kai-shek still rule and still officially dream of reconquering the mainland, is an enigma. Economically it is a showpiece for American-aided capitalist development, and in 1965 its economic take-off was so unequivocal that it ceased to qualify for American aid. Its land reform programme is a model of success. But politically Taiwan is a police state and the real wishes of its ten million indigenous Chinese inhabitants (whose ancestors sailed from the neighbouring mainland provinces at various times during the past five centuries) are impossible to ascertain. There is strong underlying tension between these native Taiwanese and the two million 'new' mainlanders who crossed the sea in 1949 to rule them.[35]

Taiwan is regarded by both the communists and the Nationalists as a Chinese province, and they protest equally indignantly at any suggestion that Taiwan could or should become fully independent in its own right.[36] As the only Chinese province to be separated from the others by sea, to have been ruled by the Japanese as a colony for fifty years up to 1945, and then since 1949 to have been retained under Nationalist control, Taiwan seems a border-line case which could opt either for independence or for re-integration into the mainland. For the time being it does not have to choose, but the passing of Chiang Kai-shek (who is now eight-five) would herald a new era of uncertainty. His successors might well come to terms with the communists,[37] especially if American interest in the Far East declines. But the native Taiwanese themselves would probably have the last say on the destiny of this richly endowed and prosperous community of free farmers.

Mongolia, unlike Tibet, succeeded in asserting its independence from Peking during the years of China's weakness in the first half of this century. Although the Nationalists in Taiwan remain unreconciled to this, the Chinese communists have grudgingly accepted it and have contributed generously to the development programmes of the Mongolian People's Republic.

When China quarrelled with the Soviet Union in 1960, however, Mongolia was obliged to take the Russian side and has since become to all intents and purposes a Soviet satellite. The position is complicated by the fact that only one million Mongols live in the Mongolian People's Republic, there being another million of them in the Inner Mongolian Autonomous Region of China and a few more in the USSR itself. It cannot be ruled out that Moscow might eventually return Mongolia to the Chinese sphere of influence in exchange for concessions or agreements with China over the disputed Sino-Soviet border.[38]

Finally, the two surviving pockets of European colonial rule on Chinese soil have acquired an unexpected importance since the communists came to power in Peking. Macao, the tiny Portuguese 'province' and centre of the world gold trade at the southern tip of the Pearl River estuary near Canton, was in early 1967 effectively taken over by a committee of local communists.[39] But Hong Kong, the British colony on the northern side of the estuary, goes from strength to strength in spite of a similar campaign by local communists, stimulated by the Cultural Revolution in China, during 1967.

Hong Kong is a city the size of Paris, 98 per cent Chinese by composition and sitting in a hinterland only half the size of Surrey. The city itself and the rest of Hong Kong Island were ceded to Britain in perpetuity under one of the 'unequal treaties' of the nineteenth century, while the so-called New Territories which run from Kowloon to the Chinese border and embrace all of Hong Kong's agriculture, half its industry and a large proportion of its water, are administered by Britain on a 99-year lease which expires in 1997 and is unlikely to be renewed.

Hong Kong in its present form can thus expect, at best, another quarter-century of life. There is a tacit understanding between London and Peking that Hong Kong will not be given its independence, and that British sovereignty will yield, if at all, only to Chinese sovereignty. The population in Hong Kong is so fluctuating, so transient and so little committed to the soil, with many refugees from communism hoping to return to their home towns when communism begins to 'thaw' in China, that to give them self-government would be rather like giving self-government to a railway station. But the Hong Kong Chinese are now acquiring a big stake in their political *status quo* in the sense that they have built the city into a manufacturing centre of considerable importance, producing about £600 million worth of goods annually, and exporting vast quantities of garments, fabrics, radios and other light industrial products to the USA, Britain, continental Europe and many other markets.

Hong Kong thus presents a baffling amalgam of roles, including that of the geographical and financial capital of the overseas Chinese sub-nation, an enforced museum-piece of Victorian colonialism as embarrassing to British liberals as to patriotic Chinese, a model for fast industrialization in the conditions of the under-developed world, the provider of half of Communist China's much-needed foreign exchange, and a window through which Chinese communism and the outside world can examine and assess each other.[40]

Chapter Fifteen

Japanese Balancing Act

RUDYARD KIPLING was not often at a loss to slot people into the crude pigeon-holes of Victorian imperialism, but the Japanese baffled him. 'The Chinaman's a native,' he wrote confidently after touring the Far East. 'That's the look on a native's face, but the Jap isn't a native, and he isn't a Sahib either. What is it?'[1] Today, in another century, Western observers are less arrogant but sometimes equally puzzled as they ponder the rising tide of Japan's cultural ambivalence.

By so many of the standards of the Western world Japan is an unquestioned success. She is the third richest producer in the entire world, after the United States and the USSR,[2] and the seventh most populous nation. Her constitution and political practice make her the third largest democracy in the world, after America and India, and the biggest constitutional monarchy with the oldest ruling house. Japan is the world's most prolific ship-builder (accounting for half of current world production) and manufacturer of motor cycles. She is the second largest maker of television sets and road vehicles, the second user of computers, the third steel-maker. She has produced the biggest tanker, the thinnest wrist-watch and the smallest television set, and her industrial inventions are copied in America, Germany, Britain and the Soviet Union.

In Kurosawa, Ozu and Mizoguchi, the world has recognized three of its finest film makers, to mention only one of the modern arts in which the Japanese excel. Japan belongs to all the best clubs – from that of countries which have provided chairmen of the UN Security Council and Nobel Prize-winners, to the OECD and that select group of banking powers which periodically bale Britain out of its sterling crises. She is a highly successful practitioner of the difficult art of modern capitalism and she could, as *The Economist* recently concluded,[3] become the third super-power if Western European unity continues to be elusive.

Hermann Kahn, America's scientific prognosticator, has even predicted that the Japanese will have a higher standard of living and produce more than either the Americans or the Russians by the end of this century.[4]

The basis for Japan's economic success is relatively clear. It may be summed up as good management of a work force which is disciplined, educated and savings-minded. Norman Macrae, deputy editor of *The Economist*, found the Japanese economy the 'most intelligently *dirigiste* system in the world today', and a leading business executive conveyed to him in one sentence the essential discipline underlying it: 'Although my main duty is to the interests of my company, I always remember that behind it must lie also the interests of the greater company of Japan.'[5] Seven out of every ten Japanese children stay at school till they are eighteen, against only four in Britain,[6] and the Japanese save between 35 per cent and 40 per cent of their gross national product, more than any Western nation.

The Japanese economy has recorded average real annual growth of 10 per cent over the past fifteen years – the fastest pace of all the industrialized countries. The late prime minister Hayato Ikeda's plan to double Japan's national income in ten years was realized in only seven and a half, and although the speed is likely to be reduced soon by the attainment of full employment, by the likely fall in the savings ratio, by the necessity of more investment in research and by the jump in defence spending,[7] Japanese economic growth is still likely to remain higher than that of Western countries for some time to come.

Japan now has a gross national product slightly larger than Britain's, but a population almost twice as numerous. Wages are thus about half of those prevailing in Britain, and the standard of living can best be compared with Italy's. But comparisons are odious, as the accompanying diagram shows. The circle represents average *per capita* standards in Britain, France and West Germany for a number of essentials in modern life. The anvil-shaped figure shows the Japanese performance, far worse in some respects but better in others. More than 95 per cent of urban houses in Japan have television, more than three-quarters have electric washing machines and two-thirds have refrigerators. But what the Japanese gains over his European rivals in these and other respects (including teacher-pupil ratios and vegetable consumption), he loses in highways, sewerage, meat and egg consumption and housing.

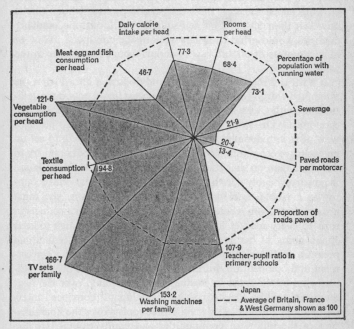

Japan's living standards compared with Western Europe. The circle represents average standards in Britain, France and West Germany expressed as 100. The shaded area represents Japanese standards expressed as a rate of 100. The Japanese are better off for T V, washing machines, teachers and vegetables but worse off for roads, sewers, housing, water and meat. Data relate approximately to 1967.

It goes without saying that Japan is now intensely urbanized and industrialized, with agriculture providing only 8 per cent of the national income and employing less than 20 per cent of the labour force (this latter proportion having halved over the past quarter-century). The Japanese are thus following the pattern of the West in becoming progressively uncompetitive in the simpler products of labour-intensive industry. Japan is now a net importer not only of silk but also of cotton goods, and provides a rich market for the plastic flowers of Hong Kong and the cheap shirts of Taiwan and Korea. But this helps to underline her growing dependence on the world economy as a whole. She is now less than 80 per cent self-sufficient in foodstuffs, and her factories would grind to a halt without the continued inflow of huge amounts of oil and raw materials from every corner of the globe.

It is for this reason that Japan could no longer afford what she attempted thirty years ago, namely an exclusive economic relationship with China and South-East Asia. As one of her leading economists, Dr Okita Saburo, has warned: 'From the point of view of raw material supply, it is unrealistic for Japan to set up an exclusive economic bloc with her Asian neighbours and try to develop Japan on that basis.'[8] Whether she likes it or not, Japan is now irrevocably tied to the fortunes of the international economy as a whole. Lacking raw materials of her own, she must import them from wherever she can and export their products in turn to every market in the world. Asia is not enough to keep Japan going at her present standards. Hence the international pressure on Japan to open her economy up to free foreign investment and competition, hitherto resisted on grounds of nationalism: one of the most interesting things to watch over the next few years will be the struggle between Japan's convinced internationalists and her less daring protectionists over the liberalization of the inflow of commodities and equity capital into the country. Only 2 per cent of equity capital quoted on the Japanese Stock Exchange is owned by foreigners.

It bears repeating that Japan's economic 'miracle' is not merely a consequence of following a Western model. The concerted drive of the Meiji Government in the half-century from 1867 to import not only Western technology right across the board but also Western political, legal and educational systems as a means of modernizing Japan quickly was, in Jawaharlal Nehru's words, 'remarkable and without parallel in history'.[9] But none of it would have succeeded so well if the pre-existing conditions had not been favourable. As William Lockwood insists, Japan's economic development 'was more than simply the absorption by the Japanese of the material drives and technology of the West. Its tempo reflected the release of indigenous forces long latent in Japan.'[10]

In this respect, as in many others, Japan differs from China. Although China furnished the biggest single influence on Japanese culture, the Japanese adapted Chinese art, the ideograms and Confucian principles of social relations and government to their own needs and their own genius. Anyone who doubts the fundamental distinctiveness of Japanese culture should read Hasegawa Nyozekan's classic collection of essays *The Japanese Character*. While the precise ethnic origins of the Japanese are still debated, the race is certainly a product of a very early mixture, including strains similar to the Chinese and Manchurians of the mainland and to the Malays of the islands of South-East Asia. This racial mix, as varied as that which went into the modern British nation, was given more than two thousand years of continuous stirring without any new ingredients being added.[11]

Japan has never in recorded history been conquered by foreign invaders. Kublai Khan, the Mongol emperor of China, attempted such an invasion in the thirteenth century but was foiled by the *Kamikaze* – 'divine winds' which saved the day for the Japanese defences. When later the European traders and missionaries began to arrive, the eventual Japanese response was to close their country to foreigners for more than two hundred years, from 1638 until the middle of the nineteenth century. This self-imposed isolation was breached by the 'black ships' of the American Commodore Perry in 1853, and within a few years a new set of rulers reversed Japanese policy, to usher in the era of Meiji reforms. One result of this unique history is the strong Japanese sense of homogeneity and continuity. They may share many of the political traditions and social customs of Confucianist China, but with the very important difference that they nurse a fierce loyalty to the nation as the 'biggest family'.

The contrasts with China are vividly seen not only in the economic field but also in politics. Japan has developed a democratic system of some stability as a result of the reforms imposed by the American occupation after the Second World War, which in turn built on the earlier foundations of parliamentary government that had been covered over by the fascist seizure of power in the 1930s. But the stability rests on the somewhat unsatis-factory pheomenon of what many commentators have called a one-and-a-half-party system. The conservative Liberal-Demo-cratic Party (LDP) has governed Japan virtually single-handed since the end of the war. In the last two elections it received just under half of the popular vote, enough to secure it some 56 per cent or 57 per cent of the seats. The real drama of Japanese polit-ics is thus to be found within the ruling party rather than in its relations with the opposition.

The LDP is a coalition of the personal followings of a number of generally right-wing professional politicians and bureaucrats. Its leaders share a healthy respect for the internal free-enterprise system and the external American alliance which between them have fathered the Japanese 'miracle'. Their electoral strength is chiefly among the rapidly diminishing rural population, over which they have strengthened their hold by reasserting central control over the local police and over local government (which now sees 70 per cent of its budget dependent on the goodwill of Tokyo), in both matters undoing American occupation reforms. The LDP is also supported by the business community, and its declared income of 1967 exceeded £5 million – more than twice that of the combined opposition parties.[12] If there were an honest redrawing of constituency boundaries to take account of the drift from the land to the cities of the past two decades, the LDP's position would undoubtedly suffer.

The big feature of Japanese politics, both in the LDP and among the opposition, is factionalism. Loyalty is built up to a local party boss or a faction leader rather than to the party as a whole. This is inherent in the Japanese social tradition, but it is also compounded by the prevailing system of multi-member constituencies, which encourages factions within the LDP to put up their own candidates in competition not with opposition party candidates but with those of rival LDP factions. Some of the LDP leaders, having found by experience that calls for the volun-tary liquidation of party factions never succeed, advocate a switch to the single-member constituency system followed by Britain. But so far vested interest has thwarted any fundamental reform in the electoral system.[13]

The LDP at present comprises twelve major factions and

numerous smaller ones. Out of the 410 seats which it holds in both the Upper and the Lower House of the Diet, the faction led by Sato Eisaku, the prime minister, numbers about 100. Those of Ohira Masayoshi and Miki Takeo, two possible contenders for Sato's mantle as prime minister, number about 62 and 47 respectively, while the others are smaller still. The Party leadership is constantly jockeying for power and patronage according to the varying sizes and electoral and financial fortunes of the factions: it is, in Professor Shinohara Hajime's phrase, 'a polyarchy of faction leaders'.[14] There are, of course, policy differences between the faction leaders. One of the important dividing lines is that between the professional politicians and the ex-bureaucrats who have furnished, in Yoshida Shigeru, Ikeda Hayato and Sato Eisaku, three of the outstanding post-war prime ministers. One of the conventions of the Japanese civil service encourages relatively early retirement, and increasing numbers of leading officials seek a second career in politics, so that nowadays this kind of L D P legislator out-numbers the professional politician.

It is also to be expected that such a large envelope as the L D P should contain a wide range of ideological viewpoints. The so-called 'old right' of the L D P with which Sato and his brother, ex-premier Kishi Nobusuke, are associated, takes a rather firm anti-communist line both internationally and domestically, but there is also a more liberal wing of the party (for which former foreign minister Fujiyama Aiichiro and Matsumura Kenzo usually speak) which is more sensitive to the nationalist feelings of other Asian countries and would prefer to come to terms now with Communist China. These ideological groupings are in the form of clubs whose membership cuts across factional lines: indeed, some observers see the glimmerings of a genuinely ideological two-party system in the fact that some of the Diet members' clubs which meet to discuss common policy objectives cut across not merely factional but also party lines.[15]

But none of the opposition parties has any early hope of challenging the L D P's domination of Japanese politics. The biggest of them, the Japan Socialist Party (J S P) won a little over a quarter of the votes (and the seats) in the last two elections. The remaining quarter of the Diet seats is occupied by members of the *Komeito* (Clean Government Party, sponsored by the *Soka*

Gakkai, a Buddhist sect), the Democratic Socialist Party (DSP) and the Japan Communist Party, and by independents.

The left wing is even more riven by factionalism than is the LDP. The socialists, having already lost the moderate group which has now become the separate party of the DSP, seem unable to make a clear choice between two rival sets of leaders, one under Sasaki Kozo which is uncompromising in its doctrinaire Marxism, and another under Eda Saburo which offers a more fabian approach to policy. The Eda group is currently on top, but only just. The JSP is the only left-wing party to adopt a sympathetic attitude to Peking, since the communists are closer to Moscow. The left wing as a whole (including the communists) usually manages to win about 40 per cent of the popular vote in elections, although it is now losing somewhat to the *Komeito*.

Socialism has thus failed at the Japanese ballot box, partly because of the bitter factionalism of its leaders (reinforced by the divisions created on the left by the Sino-Soviet split), and partly because of the continuous economic boom over which the LDP administrations have presided. In the most fundamental sense, as Robert Scalapino has said, Japan is a post-Marxist society.[16] The socialist opposition has had a little more influence on events than its electoral statistics might suggest. The famous *Zengakuren*, a student federation formed in 1948 which still attracts large numbers of angry young men and women, is dominated by the communist-controlled *Minseido*, and much of the political fruits of student demonstrations – whether against American bases or higher tuition fees – must be credited to the Communist Party's organization. The left-wing parties also secured the defeat of an important bill in 1957 designed to strengthen further the Government's control over the police, and although they were unable to prevent the ratification of the revised Security Treaty with the United States in 1960, they did force the Kishi Cabinet to resign over it.

The left-wing parties have been more concerned with European theories of Marxism than with the very formidable practical challenge of organizing political opposition in a Confucian society or with the real preoccupations of the ordinary Japanese. The *Komeito* is free from these weaknesses, owing nothing to foreign ideology and building its organization on traditional patterns (i.e. through the family and the social group). In the 1967 Lower House elections it won 5 per cent of the popular vote, and in the 1968 elections to the Upper House it received 10 per cent. The *Komeito* could well begin to challenge the J S P for the leadership of the opposition, although its vagueness in policy statements is a handicap and some observers feel that it may have reached its limit in terms of electoral appeal. The Buddhists are no more immune to factionalism than anyone else.

The questions which loom largest on the Japanese political horizon are the linked ones of defence, the United States Treaty and constitutional reform. Article 9 of Chapter 2 of the 1947 Constitution, produced by the Japanese to meet the requirements of the American occupation, renders Japan the first – and so far only – pacifist nation. It states that the Japanese people 'forever renounce war as a sovereign right of the nation and the threat or use of force as a means of settling international disputes', and, in order to accomplish this aim, 'land, sea, and air forces, as well as other war potential, will never be maintained'. After the martial rigours of the military regime and the war, Japan thus entered what the novelist Mishima Yukio called an 'effeminate and elegant period' of her history.[17] The horror of the atomic bombs which were dropped on the two cities of Hiroshima and Nagasaki, coming after the futile sacrifices of the Second World War, provoked among younger Japanese a profound revulsion against the military. This unusual collective pacifism will remain a factor in Japanese politics for a long time.

The Americans, faced with the new threat of communist expansion in the late 1940s, were soon urging Japan to rearm. Prime Minister Yoshida at first rejected these approaches on the ground that Japan could not afford it. The Korean War of 1950, however, made the Government realize how vulnerable Japan was, and gradually a new army, innocuously labelled a 'Self-Defence Corps', modestly equipped and avoiding publicity, was built up: it is currently a quarter of a million strong.[18] In 1951 a defence treaty was signed with the Americans. But when, free from foreign occupation again, the Japanese Government sought in 1960 to revise this treaty with a view to retaining American protection at less cost to Japanese pride and sovereignty Japan witnessed the worst rioting of the post-war period, culminating in the humiliating last-minute withdrawal of a Japanese Government invitation to President Eisenhower to visit Tokyo. The treaty was nevertheless passed, and the Americans still deploy about forty thousand of their servicemen in various bases on Japanese soil.

The treaty endured for ten years, after which it was to continue subject to termination by either side on one year's notice. Pressure therefore built up from the left wing (which wants to renounce the treaty, disband the Self-Defence Corps and throw Japan entirely into the lap of the United Nations for defence against any attack) to force the Government to change its policy in 1970. Meanwhile the right wing of the spectrum has been calling more and more loudly for a strengthening of the Self-Defence Corps, if necessary with nuclear weapons, and for a revision of Article 9 (which would require a two-thirds majority in the Diet, less than the LDP can muster on its own). The pressures from the right range from political extremists, typified by the *Kokuryu Kurabu* or Black Dragon Society, who seek to re-establish Japan's full independence and prestige in the world, to business interests resentful of the continuing American monopoly in the sophisticated areas of military technology (which always have profitable civilian uses as well). A minister of agriculture was forced to resign in 1968 because, commenting on an international incident involving Japanese fishing boats, he grumbled that if Japan did not have such a 'foolish' constitution which made her like a 'concubine', Japanese fishermen could be backed by atom bombs and a strong army, and could roam with impunity the seas where their rights permitted.[19] But he was only voicing openly what some people thought privately. A more subtle form of pressure comes from the United Nations itself, which would like to have Japanese forces to call upon in its peace-keeping activities.

The question of constitutional revision became acutely controversial in the period between 1956 and 1963. There is widespread agreement that on this matter, as on some others, the 1947 Constitution has proved too idealistic and impracticable. One of the most respected opinions is that of Dr Takayanagi Kenzo, the late constitutional expert, who saw in Article 9 'a rhetorical political manifesto trumpeting pacifism' rather than a specific legal provision.[20] Public opinion is reticent on this controversy. A poll taken in 1968 showed that 36 per cent interpreted the Article as prohibiting all arms, 38 per cent as allowing arms for self-defence. Only 31 per cent voted for a revision of the Constitution.[21] Another poll in the same year revealed that less than one in ten Japanese wanted their country to have an independent defence capacity.[22]

The Government has recently begun a long-term campaign to educate public opinion into the responsibilities of independent nationhood. The fear of many Japanese is that once the military genie is let out of the box, it will take over:[23] it is mistrust of the underlying strength of their own democratic institutions, more than starry-eyed idealism about international relations, which underlines their fear. It should be emphasized again, however, that, in the words of Professor Kawai Kazuo:

> The present movement for the revision of the new Constitution and for the modification of many of the political reforms of the Occupation period does not represent a trend toward complete repudiation of democracy and reversion to traditionalism.[24]

It would be wrong to deduce from all this that the Japanese experiment in democracy has failed, or that it is fatally vulnerable to what Professor Seki Yoshihiko calls the 'latent authoritarianism'[25] of the Japanese people. An outsider should not judge Japanese institutions by his own standards. Japanese democracy will have to negotiate the Security Treaty issue in 1970, the emergence of the *Komeito*, the question of electoral reform and several other crises before it can be said to have come of age. The Japanese are nevertheless governed by a system which is more responsive to public opinion, more tolerant and more conducive to non-violent changes of government and shifts in leadership than any which they have enjoyed before.

What of the underlying structure of Japanese society itself? How much has this changed, how fast is it still changing? The pioneering work of Ruth Benedict, who in *The Chrysanthemum and the Sword* attempted an analysis of Japanese society from the distance of the other side of the Pacific battlefield, has encouraged Westerners to think of Japan as a prime example of a society basing its internal sanctions on the sense of shame (which depends on others' attitudes) rather than, as in the West, on the sense of guilt (which depends on oneself). More recent sociological study, notably by the British scholar R. P. Dore,[26] suggests that guilt also has a place in Japanese society, though it is built on social experience rather than religious or ethical teaching, and that the difference between Japan and the West is not one of shame replacing guilt but of being differently applied in social situations.

Japan is nevertheless a society in which there is a fundamental tension between the sense of group identity cultivated by its own tradition, and the sense of individualism encouraged by modern Westernization, especially among younger people. As in China, so in Japan, 'The family was a despotism', in the words of Lafcadio Hearn.[27] The Japanese is unable by his upbringing to see himself as a completely autonomous human being; rather he is taught to feel himself, more modestly, as a 'debtor to the ages and the world', as Benedict puts it.[28] He lives in a society where there are sixteen forms of the word 'you', each appropriate to a different context. He lives in a world of particular rather than universal obligations: hence the cruelty in unusual situations noted by so many Allied soldiers in the war and contrasting with the almost unnatural politeness and courtesy of the Japanese at home. Hence, incidentally, the warning by a Japanese sociologist that 'We need to examine even more closely the spirit of dependence which seeks refuge and security in a socialistic order while avoiding the baptism of liberalism and individualism – while, that is to say, skipping over the process of individual reformation in the field of consciousness. In a typically Japanese way, the necessary revolution in individual attitudes – a revolution which is only possible through the self-awareness and effort of each individual – is being omitted.'[29] The new slogan for Japanese young women is the ideal match '*Ie-tsuki, Car-tsuki, Baba-nuki*' – 'with house, with car, but without mother-in-law'. The modern way of life of the salaried man and his small family in the Japanese suburbs conduces to the growth of individualism but the conflict between two quite different concepts of human relations – between that codifying duty by status and that respecting the unique personality of the individual – remains. It is within each person, and it promises to deepen as time passes.[30]

In fact the conflict has provoked surprisingly little disruption in Japanese society by the standards of the West during its industrialization or of China today. The suicide rate, for example, is lower than that of France or Sweden.[31] The question is whether the superficially satisfactory mix of traditional and modern in present-day Japanese life is a stable adaptation to modern conditions,[32] or whether the survival of traditional elements merely identifies areas where modernization is lagging behind but will ultimately take over.[33] This is one of the issues which is now fascinating sociologists, both Japanese and foreign. There is a good deal of evidence to show that change is rather slow in fundamental areas of social relationships. One of the earliest post-war studies of Japanese youth showed it as still very dependent and needing to lean on others, conservative in action if radical in thought or speech.[34] The romantic love-match may be the explicit ideal of Japanese youth, but in practice they still prove unready for it.

The arranged marriage, the *kimono* (male and female), even the emperor himself,[35] are having something of a revival. As the Japanese learn more about other countries, and as their economic success feeds their self-confidence, they retreat – or advance, depending on one's viewpoint – into those elements of the Japanese tradition which do not directly hinder material progress. Mishima Yukio's dramatic hara-kiri in 1970 was an extreme example. Even the inevitable dropouts in the modernization rat-race, the failures and the frustrated, find refuge in revivals of traditional institutions: the so-called new religions of which the *Soka Gakkai*, with its cells, its rituals, its oaths, its mass meetings and prayers, is but one example. The new religions provide 'a refuge, a basis for hope, and a bridge to a new life for many millions of people in various states of dis-privilege and frustration'.[36] The result is a very distinctively Japanese reconciliation between the contradictory drives of individualism and association. Scalapino and Masumi write of Japan as 'an open society made up of closed components',[37] and this is a good summing up. It looks as if Japan will absorb Westernization today just as expertly as she absorbed Chinese civilization – and retained her own personality – in ancient times.

What does this mean for the outside world? What are Japan's

eventual international aims likely to be? The Meiji reformers tried to get Japan accepted into the Western club by merit, by imitation and good conduct. But the experience after Versailles soured her. The Europeans refused to insert into the Covenant of the League of Nations the clause proposed by Japan proclaiming the equality of races. The annulment by Britain of the Anglo-Japanese Alliance in 1921 'was viewed', in Churchill's words, 'as the spurning of an Asiatic power by the Western world',[38] and the growing restrictiveness of American immigration laws at that time confirmed many intelligent Japanese in their feeling of rejection by the West in spite of having fought for the Allied side in the First World War. It was against this background that the group of right-wing militarists led Japan not only to conquer the whole of East Asia but even to take on the wealthiest world powers in the Second World War. This gross underestimation of the resources of the Anglo-Saxon world is recalled with horror by the executives and politicians of today.

'In those days,' a Japanese businessman once told me, 'our view of the world was limited, like a frog's from the bottom of a well. Now you see us trying quietly to learn the truth about the world and to make friends with it – like a long-eared rabbit, timid but attuned to every noise.' There are also, of course, economic reasons for Japan's 'low posture' diplomacy, which reminds Europeans of the shopkeeper diplomacy associated at unkind moments with Britain. President de Gaulle once spoke privately of a visiting Japanese prime minister as a travelling salesman of transistor radios. But the motives of 'The Country that Doesn't Want a Front Seat', as the *Economist* headline once put it,[39] in pursuing a passive role in foreign affairs go much deeper than the need to loosen the restrictions placed by the West on Japanese exports.

This phase of rabbit-like foreign policy is now drawing to a close as economic growth becomes established, as the Japanese – a generation after Hiroshima – recover their confidence, and as the Western powers, less and less able to contribute to the maintenance of stability in Asia themselves, press Japan to take up the burden. The first turning point was perhaps the Olympic Games in Tokyo in 1964, which finally convinced Japan that she was back on the international scene again: another was the

EXPO '70, the international exhibition staged in Osaka. But there is still an inhibition which prevents the Japanese from taking a fully independent international stand.

Up to now the American alliance has been her sheet anchor. Japan's wartime foreign minister predicted in 1941 that Japan, if defeated by America and submitted to a cruel peace treaty, 'would break off such fetters or bonds within thirty years'.[40] We are now twenty-five years on from the end of the war, and one detects the beginnings of resentment at an alliance in which Japan is condemned perpetually to sit in the back seat. 'To count on another country for vital national defence,' wrote a former Tokyo police chief in 1965, 'is nothing but abject colonialism',[41] and it is easy to whip up a sense of outrage at the continued presence of American bases in Japan. Furthermore the credibility of the American nuclear guarantee diminishes as China develops her own nuclear capacity capable of striking across the Pacific.

Paradoxically the withdrawal of American bases would further reduce the credibility of the American guarantee, since there is nothing like the involvement of your own national troops to overcome any doubts you may have about threatening to use your nuclear capacity on behalf of an attacked ally. A notable plea for Japan's acquisition of nuclear weapons and an independent deterrent was made by Doi Akio, a former army officer, in a magazine article in 1966.[42] But the opinion polls show no consensus on this: one in 1966 showed 18 per cent in favour of reliance on American arms, 16 per cent in favour of expelling American bases and declaring Japanese neutrality, 12 per cent in favour of Japan's building up her own independent defence force, 6 per cent in favour of throwing the responsibility out of American hands and into the UN's, and 48 per cent not knowing which course would be best.[43] Small wonder that the politicians are still groping in the dark.

There is latent anti-Western sentiment in Japan. The novelist Hayashi Fusao has written recently about the Second World War as the culmination of a Japanese mission:

For the last 100 years Japan single-handedly played the role of equalizing the coloured races and the white race. Neither China nor India would do it. That's why we had to rush into that tragedy ... The West and Japan came to a showdown for the first time (in the Pacific

War) and Japan lost in the end, but not until after proving that both the coloured races and the white race could be on an equal footing and that unless the coloured races are given an equal footing, there would be another war.[44]

There was irritation with the United States over the long retention of Okinawa in American hands (reciprocated, be it added, by American annoyance with Japan's inability to propose alternatives to the nuclear base at Okinawa, regarded in Washington as still playing a key role in Pacific strategy). But this should not be exaggerated. The Americans did not after all impose a 'cruel' treaty on Japan, and their occupation is remembered with gratitude by very large numbers of Japanese. In spite of the irritants thrown up by the conflicting commercial interests of the two countries, there is little reason to doubt that friendship with America will continue to be a basic feature of Japanese policy.

America is only one of the three powers with which Japan has to juggle, the others being China and the Soviet Union. Before the war China accounted for one third of Japan's foreign trade, but today the United States has assumed that position, and trade with China now represents only 3 per cent of Japan's total foreign commerce. The Japanese, as will be argued in another chapter,[45] will probably come to terms with China as soon as they can gracefully do so. Their association with the American diplomatic boycott of Peking was uncomfortable and unnatural. China, North Vietnam and North Korea are the only remaining countries with which Japan has not yet restored normal relations, and such restoration will remain a high priority. The Japanese are unlikely at the one extreme to become involved in another war against China, but they are even less likely at the other to forge a close alliance with China (presumably directed against Western, Soviet and other Asian interests).

Japan will rather seek a mutually useful working relationship with China of the kind which would not jeopardize her other relationships. It might be possible to play Russia off against China, although this would call for a very high standard of diplomacy. The Japanese are still in dispute with the USSR over the Northern Islands retained by the Russians, and the diplomatic agreement reached with Moscow in 1956 has not yet been replaced by a full-scale peace treaty. But the Russians are keen to have Japanese investment and technical assistance in developing the enormous mineral and timber resources of Eastern Siberia. It might take some time for the two sides to build up enough trust and goodwill to implement this, but it probably will eventually be realized.[46]

Finally, Japan sees her world role also as that of a guide and model for the developing countries of Asia. The thinking behind this is well expressed by Yanaga Chitoshi:

By virtue of her experience of more than a century, Japan is in an advantageous position to function as a purveyor of Western ideas and particularly Western techniques of production which have gone through a process of screening, modification, and adaption, if not Asianization. After being subjected to such a process of selection, adaption, and assimilation by Japan, ideas and techniques of the West would appear much less alien and far less repugnant to those Asian peoples who are still strongly anti-Western in their orientation.

Since Japan is the only country in Asia which voluntarily embarked upon a carefully and deliberately planned programme of Westernization and modernization in the nineteenth century, and adopted and adapted to her special needs Western techniques of production, finance, and government administration as well as Western educational and national defence systems, her experiences provide invaluable lessons to other Asian nations which are at present undergoing the difficult process of adjustment. It is generally recognized that in Japan both Eastern and Western cultures have met and merged to a greater extent than anywhere else in the world. This qualifies Japan peculiarly for the role of an intermediary in the harmonization of the elements of the East and West.[47]

It is on this basis that Japan is extending foreign aid and investment to developing countries, mostly in Asia, to the tune of over £400 million a year.[48] In the summer of 1968 a Ceylonese water engineer was feted in Tokyo as the 10,000th trainee from the developing countries to undergo technical studies in Japan at the expense of the Japanese Government since the end of the war. Japan even has her own version of the Peace Corps in the Japan Overseas Cooperation Volunteers, of whom 325 had been sent to serve in eight countries of Africa and Asia by the middle of 1968.

These multifarious world roles tax Japan's diplomatic capacity enormously; she has in fact rather few specialists of her own conversant, shall we say, with Indian or Vietnamese affairs. An Indian journalist, perhaps able to speak the more plainly because he is half Japanese himself, commented after a recent international conference where the Japanese had sought to persuade the South-East Asian countries to retain their own ideas about the region's economic development:

> The Japanese are poor communicators, astonishingly introverted for so active a people; inept in diplomacy and often tactless despite a politeness that has nothing hypocritical about it. They are incompetent linguists, socially rather withdrawn, with a preference for being 'proper' rather than friendly. Add to this their success, the background of the Pacific war, their frightening economic virility, and their limitless energy and enterprise. Small wonder that the developing Asian countries are not easily reassured.[49]

But there is no real possibility of a return to the pre-war style of nationalism. In the present world of diffused economic development and political power it is impossible for Japan to retrieve, economically or militarily, the same international strength and prestige which she built up in the pre-war period. Nor is it likely that any substantial number of Japanese could once again conceive of Japan's mission as that of spreading Japanese values throughout the world by force. The return to some of the old traditions, even Mishima's new version of the emperor cult, are inward- rather than outward-looking.

In a persuasive study by Japan's most brilliant political scientist, Maruyama Masao, this conclusion is carefully spelled out. 'Even if,' he observes, 'there is a systematic effort to recentralize the dispersed and amorphous national sentiments of today, it does not seem likely that sufficient strength can be mobilized for the resultant nationalism to be an independent political force. In all likelihood the new creation from old fabric will be joined to a higher political force, perhaps to an international power. It will then be permitted to exist only in so far as it serves to further the latter's set political goals.'[50]

What will these goals be? Can the Japanese go on enjoying 'a non-purposive society in the midst of economic prosperity', as Professor Seki describes their present condition?[51] There is one school of thought, best expressed by Sakamoto Yoshikazu, which would assert Japanese leadership in the post-national stage

of world development, with Japan as a neutral pacifist state ident-
ifying her future security with the United Nations and encouraging other countries to follow suit. But this pioneering role seems
too dangerous and unlikely to succeed for other thinkers, like
Kosaka Seigyo, who would settle for a continuation of Japan's
alliance with the United States as the best available, if far from
ideal, course open to her: at least there is some constructive
content in such an alliance in helping to diffuse successful capitalist economic development and the beginnings of democracy in
the rest of Asia, as well as in seeking to wean the West out of its
sense of cultural, as distinct from technological monopoly in the
world.

These are goals big enough for any idealist. But if they sound
too grandiose and too distant, perhaps the last word should lie
with the *Yomiuri Shimbun*, which sells eight million copies a day
and whose editorial for the Meiji Centenary celebrations in 1968
ended with the sentence: 'What is required at the Meiji Centen-
nial is that Japan should bring about its independent culture and
a creative technology, and render economic aid to the developing
Asian countries as their friends.'[52]

China and Japan thus present very different pictures today, in
spite of their superficial similarities. Sandwiched between them is
Korea, also a recipient of Chinese culture, independent enough
to retain, like Japan, its distinctive national personality, but too
weak to resist Japanese imperialism in the earlier part of this
century. Since the end of the Second World War, when the Japanese surrendered to the Russians in the north and to the Americans in the south, the Koreans have been divided. The rivalry of
the northern communist and southern capitalist regimes for the
honour of reuniting the country made Korea a flash-point in 1950,
and could do so again in the 1970s.

The ambitious Kim Il-Sung, leader of the communists, sees now
his last chance to become the great unifier – with the Sino-Soviet
split reducing the restraint which either or both of his two big
brothers can lay upon him,[53] with the Americans demoralized by
the Vietnam war, with the Japanese still militarily powerless and
with the southern regime only precariously poised on the threshold of economic take-off. North Korea has been rather successful in its industrialization, but at the cost of political stagnation.

The cult of Kim appears to go beyond the worst excesses of Stalin and Mao.

By contrast, the south has only recently begun serious economic development, but it has absorbed many political lessons. After the long dictatorship of the formidable Syngman Rhee and the unhappy successive experiments of the liberal politicians and the army, a rather stable amalgam emerged in the 1960s under President Park Chung Hee, the soldier-turned-politician whose strong rule but expert feel for public opinion seemed to provide the best of both worlds.[54] Park has now been in power for ten years, and was confirmed in office in the 1971 elections. A constitutional restriction would have prevented Park from serving a third term as president, but this was amended by referendum in 1969 and the democratic facade of his regime is wearing very thin.[55]

The Government of Seoul is helped by the strong wind of economic boom which has been blowing for the past six or seven years, with annual increases in gross national product averaging 8 per cent net in inflation. The £1,800 million of American and Japanese aid which was poured in from the mid-fifties on is now producing its harvest. The development of petrochemical and steel industries has seriously begun, and South Korea has become a most attractive site for foreign investment.[56]

But the raids by North Korean communist agents in 1968, coupled with the northern regime's seizure of the American intelligence ship *Pueblo*, considerably increased the political tension and South Korean morale has been lowered by the apparent intention of the United States to withdraw from Vietnam. After Vietnam, South Korea becomes the most vulnerable of the non-communist states in the Far East, and its relations with its closest plausible protector – Japan – remain clouded.

United, Korea would play an important role in East Asia with a population almost as big as that of France, displaying all the energy of the Japanese and Chinese but with none of their deference, and with a potentially viable economy. The Koreans are a tough-minded people who will not opt out of the world. But divided Korea remains vulnerable and unstable, a cockpit for the quadrilateral of big powers which decide the destinies of East Asia – China, Japan, Russia and the United States.

Chapter Sixteen

The Indian Sub-continent

A MODERN Indian poet has referred to his countrymen as 'locked in a dream of death'.[1] There is in Indian life a dream-like quality which has baffled or repelled, and occasionally overwhelmed, outsiders: what Nehru himself characterized as 'a vagueness of outlook, a divorce from life as it is, a credulity, a woolliness of the mind where fact was concerned'.[2] There is a long list of books by distinguished and intelligent foreign visitors to India which convey the shock, horror and dismay that almost invariably attend the non-Indian's first exposure to this huge country, from Katherine Mayo's famous *Mother India*[3] of forty years ago to the more recent Ronald Segal's *The Crisis of India* and V. S. Naipaul's *An Area of Darkness*.

Even those who overcome the initial shock and come to terms with some of the basic unfamiliarities, to the point perhaps of beginning to appreciate the many beguiling attractions of India, often sense a kind of despair at the lack of urgency and paucity of action over the country's pressing challenges, from famine and poverty to religious intolerance and military vulnerability. As a Canadian commentator recently put it: 'Nowhere in the world is the ratio of problems to those able to solve them so high.'[4]

This poor image which India projects to the rest of the world is partly a product of the very openness which Westerners admire in their own countries and whose absence they bemoan in such nations as China and Japan. India has never been insulated from the outside world, and is herself an extremely heterogeneous society with a long tradition of the free expression of opinion. The dirty linen which in China and Japan is tucked carefully away into cupboards where foreigners cannot pry is in India flaunted in the visitor's face. There is no feeling of solidarity *vis-à-vis* the foreigner, and no visitor has any difficulty in getting an Indian friend to tell him all about the misdeeds of other Indians.

As the recipient of both cultural and demographic invasions

throughout history, India goes more than half way to meet the outside world. One legacy of her absorption of foreign products is the status of English as the *lingua franca*, and this again means that most foreign visitors have an immediate channel of communication maximizing their access to information about Indian life. But, being human, they usually expect too much from it, and the ultimate disappointment when fundamental conflicts of culture appear is all the greater for their being expressed in the foreigner's mother tongue.

These are some of the ways in which India's *malaise* becomes exaggerated in the minds of outside observers. There is nevertheless a *malaise*, and one which may conveniently be discussed under the five headings of unity, political direction, public morality, economic development and security. These are the outstanding problems of modern India.

There is almost no single criterion by which the 550 million inhabitants of India enjoy homogeneity save that of their common citizenship. The official *Gazetteer of India* lists many physical types and ethnic elements in the racial make-up of the population, which includes people whom the Western layman would classify loosely as white, yellow, brown and black – or as Caucasian, Mongoloid, Dravidian, Arab and Negroid. The variety of physical appearance is matched by differences in dress, hairstyle, adornment and cosmetics, as a glance around any second-class railway carriage would show. More than 80 per cent of the population is Hindu, but there are also 60 million Muslims, 12 million Christians, 10 million Sikhs and 4 million Buddhists, and these various religions are scattered throughout the country. The Hindu population is in turn divided into many hundreds of castes, and the *Gazetteer* refers to several hundred languages, of which a score or so are spoken by very large numbers and boast rich literatures. It is small wonder that pessimists and sceptics speak of the frail unity of India, or that her political leaders and patriots should spend so much time proclaiming its strength.

The Hindu caste system provides the natural social units through which group interests of various kinds are pursued. The system is not as immobile, inflexible or resistant to modernization as might be supposed,[5] nor is there a consensus among scholars that it plays a preponderantly divisive role in either political or social affairs. Apart from the ex-Untouchables, who number about eighty million and whose continuing disprivilegement provides a constant source of tension, there seems no need for pessimism about the capacity of the caste system to shake off the undesirable accretions of the centuries and meet the challenge of modernization.[6]

On the language question[7] one cannot be so confident. Left to itself, without legislative or administrative interference, it would slowly approach a natural resolution as English declines and as the non-Hindi-speaking states to the east and south gradually adopt Hindi as their second language in place of English. But the zeal of the petty nationalisms of the states and regions, especially in the Hindi heartland that spreads from New Delhi across the northern plain, may not allow of such a long drawn-out solution. Unfortunately, northern demands to accelerate the switch from English to Hindi as the official national language are invariably followed by a southern reaction against Hindi.

The speedy elimination of English appears in Banaras or Agra as a natural consummation of India's independence from British rule, but the same goal appears in Trivandrum or Madras as a means of discriminating against southerners (and Bengalis too) in the all-India services and professions.[8] It would be all too easy for the smaller nationalisms to precipitate a crisis, even a breakup of India, on the language question unless good leadership and common sense can restrain them. But this is the only issue on which the development of state patriotism seems really dangerous. In all other matters it is obviously a consideration of selfinterest to remain within the larger Indian federal framework, as the new anti-Congress state governments in the south recognized in 1967.

Thus far one could confidently echo the opinion of India's leading social scientist, Professor M. N. Srinivas, that 'There is no need ... to be unduly frightened by the existence of "divisions" in the country. It is true that a person does feel that he is a member of a particular caste, village, region, state and religion but these loyalties can represent a hierarchy of values and are not necessarily inconsistent with being a citizen of the Indian Republic.'[9] But a far tougher problem emerges when one looks at the northern and north-eastern fringes of India where people of

Mongoloid stock, insignificant in numbers but more or less disenchanted with Indian rule, occupy militarily strategic hilly or
mountainous areas. Indian forces have been fighting rebels
among the Naga tribes for fifteen years, and the neighbouring
Mizos began armed resistance to the Indian Government in the
early 1960s. The Nagas are themselves divided, and some of them
are loyal to New Delhi. But one group has taken the lead almost
from the beginning in holding out for a completely independent
Nagaland.[10] Since the Nagas bestride the Indo-Burmese frontier,
this raises international issues, and the Indian and Burmese
governments now cooperate in their military and administrative
operations in the jungle terrain which they share at this point on
the map. At one time, although there are little more than half a
million Nagas in India, the Indian army had forty thousand
troops pitted against the rebels.

Nehru ultimately agreed to give the Nagas a state of their own,
and this was formally inaugurated in 1963. A cease-fire was
arranged shortly afterwards and there have been protracted
negotiations ever since.[11] But fighting broke out again in 1968,
and it seems that the Nagas are now coordinating their resistance
with the Mizos and Lushais, who also straddle the Indian border,
not only that with Burma (the Mizos have affinities with the
Chins of Burma) but also that with Bangla Desh.[12] There is a
religious element in this tangled dispute, since 80 per cent of the
Mizos and 60 per cent of the Nagas are Christian converts:
British missionaries have been most active among the hill tribes,
and have tended to become involved with them politically as well.
This does not make it easier for New Delhi with its increasingly
aggressive Hindu lobby. A new element is the hand of China.
Since 1967 several thousand Indian tribesmen have been trained
in guerrilla camps in Yunnan Province, and Chinese arms are
being used by the Nagas, who have to cross Burmese territory for
these purposes.[13]

In 1968 the Indian Government announced plans to form a
new autonomous hill state of Meghalaya within Assam to cater
for the special needs of the Garo, Khasi and other tribal peoples.
But the 'balkanization' of Assam is naturally resisted by the
plains Assamese themselves, and since the whole area is so important for India's defences along two hostile borders (with Paki-

stan and China) there is bound to be further difficulty ahead. The tribal peoples of the North-East Frontier Agency (NEFA) are also beginning to savour the taste of university education, modernization and nationalism, and will probably give New Delhi more cause for concern over the next few decades. India handled these north-eastern minorities clumsily during the first two decades of her independence, but there is evidence that some lessons have been learnt from the mistakes, and that there is now more awareness of their complexity.

The second criticism commonly levelled against India is her failure to decide firmly what political direction she should take. In the first two decades of independence the Congress Party, which had launched and led the independence movement, movement, naturally dominated Indian politics. In the first three general elections (in 1952, 1957 and 1962) the Congress secured 45–48 per cent of the popular vote and three-quarters of the seats in the *Lok Sabha* (the Lower House of Parliament). In the 1967 elections, however, its popular vote fell to 41 per cent and it lost control of half of the state governments: its majority in the *Lok Sabha* fell to 55 per cent.[14] The electorate was then suffering from grave food shortages, industry was in recession and the entire economy had been badly hit by the Kashmir war and the consequent interruptions in American aid. The Congress Party went to the polls for the first time without Nehru, and its leadership was in open disarray.

The rivalry between Morarji Desai, the last of the old guard of independence leaders, and the so-called 'syndicate' of state party bosses (Kamaraj of Madras, S. K. Patil of Bombay, Atulya Ghosh of Calcutta and Sanjiva Reddy of Andhra) had come right out into the open after the death of Nehru's successor, the universally respected Lal Bahadur Shastri. The fact that Mrs Gandhi, Nehru's daughter and the new prime minister, supported by a younger group of 'technocrats' in the cabinet, had differences with both Desai and the syndicate did not make things any easier.[15] Finally, Congress paid the penalty of neglecting youth. Half of the Indian electorate is under thirty-five, with little memory of Gandhi or the struggle against the British Raj. Yet Congress fielded only six candidates below the age of thirty, and two-thirds of its candidates were over forty-five.

As the organization which fought for independence, Congress naturally embraced a very wide spectrum of political and ideological viewpoints, ranging before 1947 from communists to fascists. It subsequently lost the communists and some of the more extreme right-wingers, but still contained a left and a right wing increasingly at odds over social and economic policy. These differences, combined with personality clashes, led to the division of the Congress Party in 1969, when Mrs Gandhi challenged both Desai and the 'syndicate' on a platform of bank nationalization and other socialist measures. She then went on in 1971 to win a convincing victory over all her opponents in surprise elections.

The opposition parties do not yet threaten to topple Congress in the country as a whole, but they have recently begun to prove their capacity to rule in some of the states. One of the Congress bosses used to say that, 'The alternative to Congress is "mobocracy"',[16] but after the 1967 elections reasonably effective non-Congress governments took office in Madras, Kerala and Orissa under the leadership of the *Dravida Munnetra Kazakham* (D M K), the Communist Party and the Swatantra Party respectively.

The Marxist left-wing opposition parties seem less plausible at the moment than the others. Between them they won only 17 per cent of the *Lok Sabha* seats in the 1967 elections, and they suffer from multiple fragmentation. The socialists have been separate from the communists all along, but had the wind taken out of their sails by Nehru's protestations of socialism during his premiership. Many socialists remained within the Congress fold, and some who left it after independence eventually returned – to the cabinet, in the case of Ashok Mehta. The Indian Communist Party attained a membership of only 150,000 before being split down the middle by the Sino-Soviet rift in the early 1960s, compounded by the Sino Indian war in 1962. The pro-Soviet wing remained the stronger of the two, although it was the pro-Chinese wing which was victorious in the Kerala elections in 1967.

Since then the leftist communists have in turn divided over the question of armed revolt, as advocated by Peking and pursued with some initial local success in the Naxalbari area of West

Bengal, where a parallel 'government' under the revolutionary faction of the leftist communist party has redistributed land to the peasants over an area of about thirty square miles. But these tactics have little chance of permanent or widespread success, and they are denounced by the majority of Indian communists. The fact that there are now in effect three rival communist parties and as many socialist parties diminishes the appeal of the Indian left as a whole at a ballot box.

The non-Marxist opposition, by contrast, has developed remarkably in strength and maturity over the past three or four years, though it is even less united than the Marxists. There are now three important such parties participating in state governments; the Swatantra Party, which represents what one might call the economic right wing, and the D M K and the *Jan Sangh*, which represents what one might call the 'Hindu right wing'.* Swatantra was founded a decade ago by dissident Congressmen under C. Rajagopalachari, the first Indian Head of State. It claims to be the party of 'property, liberty and democracy', but it chiefly attracts businessmen and former princes, and it cannot yet be said to have decided its essential character.[17] The *Jan Sangh* and D M K are explicitly popular parties, and both feed on the sense of Hindu revival, on the growing self-confidence and ambitions of the lower castes, and the localist loyalties which the Congress Party has had to suppress in its own ranks. In all these respects the two parties are similar, and yet they are potential antagonists because one represents northern and the other southern interests.

The *Jan Sangh* (the name means 'people's party') was founded in 1951 as the political arm of the extreme, almost fanatical Hindu religious organization associated with the assassination of Gandhi (whose life-long dedication to reconciling the Hindus and the Muslims made him anathema to the conservatives on both sides). But the *Jan Sangh* has grown in stature since its religious origins and now admits Muslims as members[18] on the basis that, 'every Indian, whatever his religion, is a Hindu'. It would like to make Sanskrit the national language, and naturally supports

---

*One could equally well call them the 'non-socialist left', since they are populist, anti-state and anti-privilege. The European labels really do not fit.

Hindi against English: indeed the persona which it exhibits most strongly is that of rescuer of India from the dangers of Westernization. But if its leaders take a more realistic and less fanatical policy line than its original parent body, they can nevertheless rely on the latter's three million members during election campaigns.

The D M K similarly began as an idealistic and backward-looking organization, but has since been transformed into a party representing specific local interests and accepting democratic parliamentary values and practices.[19] It would be misleading to think of either the *Jan Sangh* or the D M K as composed of fascists, but their potential appeal is thus expressed by an Indian journalist: 'A nation of 500 million people, poor, bitter and humiliated, are all too ready for the doctrines of chauvinistic nationalism, of anti-Western, or even anti-white, revanchism. They are eager to obliterate their feelings of misery and inferiority through self-glorification based on historic myths.'[20]

On the eve of the 1967 elections *The Times*' correspondent in India wrote a series of articles under the title 'India's Disintegrating Democracy',[21] in which he argued that the parliamentary system accentuated the country's social and religious differences, and that he was probably witnessing the last general elections in India. 'Maintenance of an ordered structure of society,' he predicted, 'is going to slip out of reach of civil government and the army will be the only alternative source of authority and order.'[22] Jayaprakash Narayan, the most prestigious figure in the ranks of the opposition to Congress, has urged a coalition government in the centre in order to avert military rule.[23] But these fears seem exaggerated. India is the world's largest democracy, and its political system has functioned rather effectively in these past two decades as a process by which the public can express its opinions of its government, its parties and their leaders. When Kamaraj, Ghosh and Patil were all personally vanquished by opposition candidates in their own constituences in the 1967 elections, Indian democracy scored a victory, not a defeat. Since then the economy has recovered, Congress has rallied again and the opposition parties have shown more responsibility. In any case, regional and personal rivalries within the army render a military initiative extremely unlikely.[24]

Reinforcing the anxieties about the Indian political process is a related concern about corruption, the weak sense of public service or patriotism, and the general immaturity of public morality. Nepotism, time-serving, parliamentary floor-crossing, bribery, abuse of office and the elevation of personal or family considerations above those of community or country are very widespread in India. An Indian journalist was horrified recently to find bitter caste hostility and disillusion even in the village of Sewagram which Gandhi had made his headquarters.[25] Collective activity does not come easily to the Indian: not only has communism failed to evoke a response, but even the 'cooperative joint farming', which the Congress Party decided in 1959 should be the basis of the new rural India, has never struck root and shows no sign of being widely followed. Considerable disappointment has also been felt over the village *panchayats*, which were meant to provide a forum for rural leadership and progress, but which tended in many cases to be ineffective or to become dominated by local vested interests because of the apathy of the villagers themselves. Kusum Nair's remarkable book, *Blossoms in the Dust*, paints a sad picture of the stagnation of rural society in many parts of India.

This line of thinking invariably leads Indians into self-analysis on the score of their national character. There are very few serious studies of this,[26] but one Indian scholar argues that India's conquest, first by the Mughals and then by the British, has generated a collective sense of inferiority. He adds: 'There seems to be an inner compartmentalism that prevents the free flow of implications from one area of life to another', and this tends to slow down the processes of modernization.[27] But the best conclusion would seem to be that of Raghavan Iyer, that, 'If the Indian personality seems to be effervescent and volatile, tossed between abstract idealism and concrete cynicism, this is because it has still to gain the confidence that comes from experience in a new environment.'[28]

The very openness of India to the new influences first of Islam and then of Europe, and the very eagerness with which Indian intellectuals have grasped this multiple legacy and made themselves world citizens in far greater measure than those of any other non-European country, have prolonged the sense of inferiority of indigenous values and institutions. Nehru's leadership ironically did little to heal these wounds: as an atheist, heavily influenced by Marx and more interested in the affairs of the West than those of the Indian villages, he could do little to restore a genuine sense of pride and self-respect. But now the creation of linguistic states, the growth of state nationalisms, the decline of English, the release of caste from the stigma of foreign disapproval, the gradual entry into the corridors of power by the relatively un-Westernized and previously suppressed or ignored elements of Indian society, the steady development of the economy, the advances in science and technology, and the belated emergence of a realistic national foreign policy – all these combine to revivify the Indian personality.[29] This in turn is bound to raise the standards of public morality and inculcate a sense of public duty.

For there is no doubt that the economy is on the move.[30] India is the tenth country in the world ranked by wealth and production, with a gross national product of £16,450 million in 1969. But the enormous population means that India ranks almost at the bottom of the world league in income per head. This poverty was inherited from British stewardship, and the past twenty years have seen one of the earliest and best-organized economic development programmes to be found in the entire *tiers monde*. The goal of India's Five-Year Plans (the fourth of which is now in operation) is to double income per head within a generation, or twenty-five years.

The first two Plans were reasonably successful, but the third proved disappointing, partly because of the wars with China and Pakistan which diverted funds into defence spending, partly because of unusually bad weather which caused a minor famine in 1966–7, and partly because of the suspension of American aid. The average annual rate of economic growth during the first three Plans (1951–66) fell just short of 4 per cent: since the population was growing at a little over 2 per cent a year, the increase in *per capita* income was about 1¾ per cent. This understates the achievement, however, because many services have been provided which do not immediately or directly produce more income but which do provide the infra-structure for future growth. Income per head rose by only 30 per cent during the first three Plans, but installed electric power, to take only one example, was quadrupled.

The Fourth Plan had to be postponed for three years but is now under way, and the development of high-yielding hybrid strains of rice and wheat, together with the bigger public investment in fertilizers and other agricultural aids, assures India of avoiding large-scale famine in future. Much depends in the longer term on the success of the family planning campaign, for unless the population growth rate can be steadily reduced the gains of economic development will be partly lost. Probably the biggest hurdle which the economy must face is the unexpected decline of foreign aid, coupled with the growing difficulty of squeezing tax revenues out of the farmers.[31] But only a partisan observer would deny the ferment of economic progress which thousands of urban and rural entrepreneurs are now spreading throughout the land.

The final question-mark that hangs over India concerns her security and defence. The problem begins with the mutual hostility between India and Pakistan. To some extent this was dictated by the history and circumstances of the struggle for independence from British rule, but it has been exacerbated by the problem of Kashmir, whose Hindu Maharajah acceded to India only after his throne was threatened by his Muslim subjects, aided and encouraged by Muslim tribesmen from Pakistan.[32] This led to the first Kashmir war of 1947–8 and a *de facto* division of the state between India and Pakistan along a cease-fire line.

India's case on Kashmir has since been damaged by her inability to maintain the parliamentary freedoms in her part of the state. In the words of an Indian journalist, Kashmir 'has remained a police state within democratic India for twenty years'.[33] Sheikh Abdullah, till now the 'Lion of Kashmir' and its unchallenged spokesman, has been in and out of Indian jails during most of this period, and now that Mrs Gandhi's government has released him, his authority is under challenge from younger and more militant leaders even less sympathetic with India. There was a possibility at the end of Nehru's premiership of a settlement of the Kashmir problem on the basis of a loose federal structure in which India, Pakistan and Kashmir would be equal sovereign participants.[34] Kashmiris would certainly welcome some form of independence or autonomy, but only a strong Indian Government willing to brave the protests of its chauvinistic lobbies could move in this direction.

The twenty-two-day war in 1965 was the result of Pakistani desperation, since seventeen years' diplomatic activity at the United Nations had failed to bring about the plebiscite which Nehru had originally promised and which would almost certainly result in a Kashmiri verdict against India. It began, as the earlier war had, with a revolt on the Indian side helped by infiltrators from the Pakistani side, and it led to a military stalemate, to costly losses and the suspension of foreign aid to both sides, and to the Soviet mediation at Tashkent. As before, India could not quite win the war but was able to win the peace, securing at Tashkent a Pakistani commitment not to use force again in Kashmir, without making any concessions in return. Relations have since deteriorated to their former state.[35]

There have been many proposals for the agreed partition of Kashmir,[36] and Sheikh Abdullah has proposed a temporary UN administration over the particularly difficult area of the Kashmir valley itself. But a solution will depend on the basic relations between the two countries. These are not unrelievedly bad: in 1959 the World Bank was able to get their agreement to a mutually beneficial division of the waters of the River Indus,[37] and there is more contact and traffic between the two countries than the outsider might suspect. Some of their leaders are related by blood: in 1969 the Foreign Minister of Pakistan and the Indian Secretary of Foreign Affairs, for instance, were not only first cousins, but colleagues in the pre-independence civil service. But this generation is passing and the forces of nationalism are becoming stronger, and only an incurable optimist could hope for Indo-Pakistan amity in the near future.

India also faces a hostile China across a very long and mountainous frontier. In some of these Himalayan or sub-Himalayan regions India is in trouble with tribal people on her own side of the frontier, as we have seen. There are also three independent or semi-independent states strung along the Sino Indian border.[39] The largest of these is the independent kingdom of Nepal, home of the Gurkhas. Nehru had helped the Congress Party politicians in Nepal to overthrow the reactionary Rana regime in the early

1950s, and to introduce democratic elections thereafter. But the politicians could not take a firm hand of the country, and in 1960 King Mahendra threw them out and took over the government himself. He has fared a little better, though not much better, in prosecuting the gradual modernization of the country and building up a sense of national unity. Nepal has taken a neutral stand as between India and China, although her relations with China tend to be merely correct where those with India are fairly friendly. It seems to be an open question whether Nepal's uneasy independence of her two giant neighbours can be maintained, although it probably suits both the Indians and the Chinese to have what is in effect a buffer zone between their territories.

To the east of Nepal lie the even tinier states of Sikkim, which has an American queen and a defence treaty with India, and Bhutan, which is gradually weaning itself from Indian tutelage and proclaimed its independence, with reluctant Indian blessings, in 1971.[40] It should be noted that the smaller peoples who find themselves sandwiched between India and China are increasing their links with one another, and that there has been a proposal for a confederation of Himalayan or Inner Asian States, possibly embracing not only Nepal, Bhutan and Sikkim but even Tibet, Kashmir, Nagaland and N E F A.[41] But this is looking very far ahead, and no one can really say what course Himalayan politics will take, except that since the Sino-Indian war of 1962 there is a *de facto* border which is now strongly defended on both sides and which even shows signs of growing stability. Another international war over this border seems improbable, although the tension will continue and minor clashes are inevitable. The real battle between India and China will be for genuine political influence over the tribal peoples whom they share.

Nehru's policy of non-alignment in world affairs paid handsome dividends, but they accrued to the West and to the Soviet *bloc* more than to India herself. Nehru's role in thawing the cold war between America and Russia, and in bringing the Korean war to an end, was probably crucial. India has also been one of the sturdiest pillars of the United Nations, physically participating in the United Nations interventions in Korea and the Congo. But in the end the thanks which India gained for this sophisticated, universalist and trusting policy were unaccompanied by any material advantages or enhancement of her own security. Since Nehru's death a more realistic and calculating note has crept into Indian foreign policy. She criticizes the American intervention in Vietnam, but her leaders indicate privately that an American presence in Asia is welcome.[42] It is now common knowledge that Nehru requested massive American air support during the border war with China at the end of 1962,[43] although the Indian Government still opposes the creation of new Western naval-air bases in the Indian Ocean and defied Washington in the 1971 Bangla Desh crisis.

A debate is now opening on the question whether India should follow China in acquiring a nuclear armoury. A group of middle-of-the-road scholars has called on India to abstain from the nuclear non-proliferation treaty and to retain the option of building up her own nuclear deterrent.[44] There are indications that a substantial number of Indian politicans would favour joining the nuclear club,[45] although the economic implications of this would make the Government pause even if it did come round to that view.

Broadly speaking, India seemed to have four choices in her future foreign policy. The first was a revised version of non-alignment under which she would settle her differences with both Pakistan and China and thus feel able to devote her attention to internal problems. This was a view which found support from Jayaprakash Narayan and Namboobiripad, the Kerala communist leader, among others, but it was perhaps too passive and conciliatory to square with the rising nationalism of the country. The next two possibilities were to patch up the quarrel with Pakistan and form a joint front against China, or, conversely, to come to terms with China and then bring Pakistan down to size. Both of these courses have been advocated in the press and political circles.[46]

The final possibility was to find an ally to support India's confrontation against both Pakistan and China:[47] the Soviet Union seems to be the only likely candidate for such a role, and the Indians wrote a formal treaty of alliance with the Russians in 1971 before embarking on their intervention in the Bangla Desh rebellion and cutting Pakistan into half. India is thus caught in a quadrilateral power system in which she, Pakistan, China and

Russia tug constantly against each other and make only temporary and limited common cause with one or two of the others against the rest. For the moment it looks like an Indo-Russian front against a possible Sino-American 'undersanding'.

An examination of India's engagement with these five fundamental problems of unity, politics, morality, development and security, should modify the common preconception of India as a failure. There is no convincing evidence that India has in all important respects been doing any less well than China or other Asian countries (always excepting Japan) during these past two decades, although the disappointments and the delays in India's modernization are far better known than the successes.

In many basic respects Pakistan resembles India. They were, after all, administered more or less together until 1947, and the twenty-five-years-old international frontier separates societies which for millennia had lived and mixed, so to speak, under the same roof. Even the religious difference must be measured against the survival of twelve million Hindus in Pakistan and sixty million Muslims in India. But politics have taken a very divergent course in Pakistan, which inherited a negligible middle class and a grave shortage of administrators. Politics quickly deteriorated after the successive deaths of Jinnah, the founder, and Liaquat Ali Khan, his only outstanding colleague, and in 1958 the army stepped in to end the undignified antics of the politicians. But Ayub Khan, who quickly emerged as the strong man in the so-called Martial Law Administration of 1958–62, found that reform by painless doses from above was impossible.[48]

Since Pakistan, like Israel, was founded explicitly on the basis of religion, the *mullahs* and *maulanas* expected to dictate state policy. When Ayub in a new constitution removed the adjective from the name of the country ('Islamic Republic of Pakistan'), they obliged him to restore it, and he had eventually to arrest some of the religious leaders who opposed his liberal attitude to family reform and birth control.[49] Ayub introduced the system of Basic Democracies, somewhat modelled on the Indian *panchayats*, which threw up 'kulak' village leaders happy to cooperate with the Government and its business allies.[50] Ayub then 'went civilian' and became president of the Pakistan Muslim League, as whose candidate he was duly elected president of the nation in

1965, defeating the combined opposition candidate, Jinnah's elderly sister, by almost two to one in an electorate of 80,000 Basic Democrats.[51]

But Ayub's success rested on a constant personal manipulation of the country's antagonistic political forces, and on a constant personal restraining of the greed and ambition of his own relatives and cronies. The failure of the 1965 war with India and the diplomatic disappointments of the Tashkent agreement in early 1966 tarnished his image, and also caused the economic development programme to run into difficulties through interruptions in foreign aid. There was a gradual increase in the scale and overtness of corruption and inequality. Ayub's own son, for example, quietly built himself up into an extremely rich and powerful political figure in Karachi city, trading on his father's name and prestige.

When in these circumstances Ayub fell ill in 1968 and had to loosen his grip on the government for several weeks, resentment against his administration intensified and he never again brought his friends and colleagues back into control again. The highly personal nature of his rule was exposed. The defection of Zulfikar Ali Bhutto, his fiery and fiercely anti-Indian young foreign minister, combined with the return of some of the older politicians to active public life after the period of retirement which Ayub had enforced upon them when he first took power, provided a new leadership for this growing opposition.

The end came when Ayub was abandoned by two of his most trusted military colleagues, each well respected in the nation at large, Generals Asghar Khan and Azam Khan. Early in 1969 Ayub was forced first to jettison his cosy system of Basic Democracies and re-instate the Westminster-style party politics which he had originally vowed to prevent, and then to give way to the popular upsurge and resign, yielding the presidency to General Yahya Khan.

The army knew it could not keep the political situation under control for long without severe repression, and it therefore opted for another parliamentary experiment. Bhutto in the West and Sheikh Mujibur in the East were the victors in the 1971 elections, but Yahya could not reconcile them on Mujib's autonomy demands, and civil war broke out in the East in March after

Mujib's arrest. Indian forces eventually entered and put the Bangla Desh leaders into power in a new sovereign state of 75 million people. Meanwhile Bhutto succeeded Yahya Khan as President of the stump West Pakistan, released Mujibur and tried vainly to retain some links with Bangla Desh – whose viability was initially suspect as dependent on Indian arms. Nor was the Awami League Party of Mujib free from the factionalism which has always cursed Bengali politics.

Pakistan's economic development had furnished up to then one of the third world's success stories.[53] After a shaky start, the Government moved much earlier than India to rely more on the mechanism of the market and less on bureaucratic controls: the mistake of investing too much initially in heavy industry was also avoided. The growth rate in the Second Five-Year Plan (1960–5) exceeded 5 per cent, and this was maintained during the early part of the Third Plan in spite of the 1965 war and the cuts in aid. But in the Second Plan no less than 40 per cent of gross investment came from foreign aid, and Pakistan was therefore badly hit by the fall in external assistance. Industrial development had been particularly good, and in the 1960s a rather successful rural works programme was operated under the aegis of the Basic Democracies – one of the reasons why they voted for Ayub in 1965.

But relatively fast growth had been purchased at the cost of concentrating wealth in few hands. As Ayub himself once observed, 'An archaic type of feudalism ... had vested the entire political, economic and social might of the country into a limited group of families.'[54] About two-thirds of the country's industry and four-fifths of its commercial bank assets are owned by twenty families and, in the words of one Pakistani official, there is 'a wide uneasiness lest the Pakistan Government in its justified and successful pursuit of economic growth, may not be perpetuating a degree of social inequality that contains grave risks for future stability'.[55]

Foreign policy had been dominated by the feud with India, in the course of which the Government had moved from an overtly pro-Western stance (Pakistan was a founder member of Mr Dulles' CENTO and SEATO) to the other extreme, an alliance with Peking. Pakistanis are divided as to their best interests:

Ayub, perhaps representing the older generation which remembers the undivided British Raj, was more exercised by 'the danger from the north' and probably himself personally favoured joint defence arrangements with India: while Bhutto, more in tune with the rising nationalism of the younger generation, and open critic of Ayub's concessions at Tashkent, is identified with the need for 'a confrontation against India'.[56]

The unity of the East and West wings of Pakistan is far less assured than that of India, and indeed it can be said that Pakistan's national cohesiveness today is more a product of the external 'threat' of India than of positive forces within the country. Now that the aid ingredient in Pakistan's economic development formula is going off the market, and now that the pendulum has swung back to party politics again, it may be surmised that Pakistan's problems will grow bigger rather than smaller.

Ceylon, nestling at the foot of the sub-continent, has been slower than either India or Pakistan in its development. It has been through three distinct stages since independence. The first decade was dominated by a Westernized urban elite who simply stepped into British shoes and hardly changed anything. In 1956 the rural Buddhists rebelled and brought the leftist Bandaranaike Government into power on a wave of Sinhalese nationalism. But this administration proved too Marxist for the liking of the Buddhists, and Bandaranaike was assassinated by a monk in 1959. His policies were continued by his widow; in 1965 the electorate swung back again to the urban-conservative leadership of the Senanayake family, but Mrs Bandaranaike regained power in the 1970 elections. Ironically she was plagued in 1971 by anarchist-Communist armed rebels. The difficulty is that in placating the demands of the Buddhist Sinhalese, the Government inevitably offends the very large Tamil or south Indian community which originally came in to work the British plantations and is most unwilling to return to India.[57]

But the political problems of Ceylon should not allow the fact to be forgotten that it is the only Asian country except the Philippines where the opposition has been allowed on several occasions to take power from a ruling party after parliamentary elections and without undue bloodshed. Ceylon indeed has become the outstanding example of the 'Westminster model'. This is helped by Ceylon's being small, being an island, and being relatively slow to change its social set-up. The skill of Sir Ivor Jennings, the British constitutional lawyer, in drawing up the constitution of Ceylon also played its part, and it is sometimes forgotten that the country had a very early introduction to democratic institutions. The first Sinhalese was elected to the Legislative Council before the First World War, and he was the first non-European to be elected to any British colonial legislature.[58]

For its first decade or so of independence Ceylon was content to rely on its tea, rubber and coconut plantations, and only in the 1960s did a real effort to industrialize and diversify the economy begin. Ceylon forfeited American aid for three years in the middle of the 1960s as a punishment for nationalizing American oil companies with inadequate compensation. But by the end of the 1960s a general improvement was discernible in both agriculture and industry, and indeed in the Government's management of the economy, although these gains began to be lost by Mrs Bandaranaike in 1971–2.[59]

Chapter Seventeen

South-East Asia

NEWCOMERS to the continent are often invited to regard
South-East Asia as a kind of Balkans. Like most Asian analogies
with Europe, this can be highly misleading: if South-East Asia
were superimposed on the map of Europe it would stretch from
Ireland to the Caspian Sea, and it encloses a population even less
homogeneous and more than three times bigger than the Balkans'. It is nevertheless true that South-East Asia is a collective
label for the numerous countries in this corner of the continent,
countries which are small by comparison with India or Pakistan,
China or Japan, and countries which contain an extraordinary
mixture of races, religions, languages and cultures. As a label, it
is variously defined, but it is here used to denote the sub-continent
of Burma, Thailand, the three successor states to the old French
Indochina (Vietnam, Cambodia and Laos), Malaysia, Singapore,
the Philippines and Indonesia.

The potential giant here is Indonesia, which accounts for about
40 per cent of the sub-continent's population and area, and is
feared for its underlying aspirations more than for its present
power. The late Muhammad Yamin, the philosopher of extreme
Indonesian nationalism, argued that Indonesia was the rightful
heir to all the former territories of Nusantara, the prehistoric fore-
runner of the present Republic. This 'Greater Indonesia' would
include not only the whole of Malaysia and Singapore but even
parts of southern Thailand, and Yamin predicted that Indonesia
would one day 'develop again to become the sovereignty of
Nusantara, covering the Austronesian people....'[1] This expansionist element in Indonesian nationalism seemed to come to the
surface during the successive campaigns in the 1960s first to
secure West Irian and then to dismember Malaysia. Indonesia is
the only country in South-East Asia which sees itself as potentially
a world power.

Unlike China and Japan, which were never colonized, or India and Pakistan, which won their independence by bloodless negotiation, Indonesia had to fight for her freedom.[2] Only in 1949 was her independence from Dutch rule assured, and much of her sense of bitterness against the outside world springs from this unfortunate experience. The liberal parliamentary system which Indonesia operated during her first decade of independence was not successful. Four principal parties contended for power, but none of them was strong enough to govern by itself, and mistrust brought successive coalition administrations tumbling.[3] These four parties were the PNI nationalists, the *Masjumi* (progressive Muslims), the Nahdatul Ulama (NU, Muslim Teacher's Party, representing the more conservative and orthodox body of Muslims) and the PKI (communists). The first general election in 1955 showed that these four parties were fairly equal in their appeal, gaining respectively 22 per cent, 21 per cent, 18 per cent and 16 per cent of the total popular vote.

At its peak in 1965 the PNI claimed $4\frac{1}{2}$ million members and another 7 million active supporters. The *Masjumi* was banned in 1960, leaving the NU as the main orthodox spokesman for the religion which claims some 85 per cent of the population. The NU claims to have more than 6 million members and 20 million active supporters, chiefly from more backward rural areas. On the eve of its sudden decimation in 1965, the PKI claimed 3 million members and 19 million active sympathizers: if elections had been held then, it expected to win one-third of the popular vote. But the turmoil of 1965–6 showed that this mass support rested on weak foundations. Many PKI officers and members are uneducated and ignorant of the real aims and premises of the party: the fact that it derives its funds mainly from the Indonesian Chinese community also renders it vulnerable to the charge of being run by a hostile foreign power.[4] All of the parties are uncomfortably aware of the 350,000-strong army looking over their shoulders and nursing political and administrative ambitions of its own.

In 1959, after a succession of weak administrations and cabinet crises, President Sukarno suspended the parliamentary experiment and took over the government himself, with the support of the army. For seven years he conducted what he called a guided democracy with the participation of the three pillars of Indonesian society, namely nationalism, religion and communism (NASAKOM*). In practice this formula became a means by which Sukarno enforced an uneasy co-existence between the two principal antagonists at his court, the communists and the army.

The army, which had its origins in the violent struggle for independence, became progressively disenchanted with the politicians and acquired a growing vested interest in regional government as well as in various sectors of the economy. Both the generals and the communists recognize in each other their only serious threat, but the brilliantly imaginative political manoeuvring of Sukarno succeeded in containing this tension until 1965.

Strictly speaking the army does not represent any particular economic or class interest. In eastern Java, for example, the principal drama is acted out between the depressed and landless peasants (supported by the communists) on the one hand, and the landlords, associated with the leading Muslims, on the other. The land reform law, which contained an unfortunate loophole in the provision that religious foundations are exempt from land redistribution, was blatantly evaded in this part of the country, and the PKI encouraged landless peasants to occupy some of the extensive estates owned by the Mosques. At first the army commanders in the region tended to be neutral and to act as a buffer between left and right.[5]

But many generals were increasingly alarmed by the rising influence of Aidit, the PKI leader, by Sukarno's alliance with Peking against the West, and by the more and more vociferous demand of the PKI for President Sukarno to permit the arming of a worker-peasant militia which would destroy the army's monopoly of organized force. In the autumn of 1965, in the so-called *Gestapu* incident, a group of PKI sympathizers murdered six right-wing generals and provoked an army counter-*coup* which ultimately led to the downfall of Sukarno, the slaughter of hundreds of thousands of communists and the imposition of army rule under General Suharto, who succeeded Sukarno as president in 1968.[6]

*From the Indonesian words *Nasionalism*, *Agama* and *Komunism*.

The assassination of their senior colleagues put an end to the army's neutrality in domestic politics, and in the months that followed between 300,000 and 500,000 people (mostly communists) were killed in an orgy of collective revenge and resentment led by Muslim organizations under military encouragement or even direction. The scores which had accumulated over the years were settled in a blood-bath which astonished and appalled the outside world.[7]

Suharto gradually eased Sukarno's followers out of their positions of influence, replacing them by reliable politicians, expert civil servants and army officers. He offered the country a middle-of-the-road leadership characterized by a lack of rigidity on all issues save that of suppressing the Indonesian communists. But he is in the awkward position of having to satisfy both the civilian politicians and the armed forces. The 1971 elections gave his Sekber Golkar 'party' of soldiers, civil servants, union leaders, businessmen and some moderate politicians a surprisingly large majority. The military already provide over half of the provincial governors, nearly half of the heads of government departments and ambassadors abroad, as well as a small number of cabinet ministers, and there is growing anxiety among the civilians on this score. There is further tension within the armed services, particularly between the army on the one hand and the navy and air force on the other. The latter are heavily involved in illegal smuggling and are less hostile to the P K I and the Sukarnoites, incurring Suharto's displeasure on both counts.

The students and youth groups played a very significant role in the downfall of Sukarno and the rise of Suharto, whom they trust as personally sincere and incorrupt. But many observers find the intellectual calibre and political grasp of the leaders of the younger generation disappointing. The complaint of Sjahrir, the late socialist leader, almost a quarter of a century ago, is still echoed today:

Our young people do not as yet have a true understanding of the struggle in which they must lead our nation. They have learned to march, and upon a command to attack and to die the hero's death, but they do not know how to give proper leadership to the people ... Their mental condition is disappointing. Our youth glows with enthusiasm but wanders aimlessly in the dark.[8]

The unity of the regions is also a continuing problem,[9] as is the position of the three million or so Indonesian Chinese, resented for their control of the country's internal economy but for the time being indispensable for its day-to-day operation.[10] The Chinese suffered after the *Gestapu* affair because of the involvement of the Peking government and many in their own community with the P K I. The upheaval in the entire administration which followed the *Gestapu* affair has weakened the central government's control over the outer islands and intensified the regional and ethnic rivalries within the country. To oversimplify, there co-exist within Indonesia pagan tribal peoples in the mountains, Hindu-ized farmers in the plains and valleys, Islamic communities around the coasts – and the Chinese minority as well. Overlapping all this is the tension between the mystically-inclined Javanese and the outer islanders.[11]

In their foreign policy, the instinct of Indonesia's nationalists was to follow the path of non-alignment pioneered by Nehru, whom they admired and who was of considerable help in their fight against the Dutch. Indonesia was thus host to the assembled Afro-Asian states at the Bandung Conference in 1955. But the personal rule of Sukarno after 1959 led gradually to a Djakarta-Peking axis directed against the West. This began with the campaign to take over West Irian, the western half of New Guinea which had been part of the Netherlands East Indies but which the Dutch had retained after Indonesian independence. Sukarno made this a burning issue for Indonesian national pride, and his diplomatic efforts, backed by a remarkable military build-up with Soviet equipment and military credits,[12] finally succeeded. In 1963 the United Nations placed West Irian under Indonesian administration. Meanwhile Sukarno had developed his thesis that the principal confrontation was that between the old established forces of imperialism and economic privilege on the one hand, and the new emerging forces of socialism and Afro-Asian resurgence on the other (O L D E F O S and N E F O S).[13]

The Irian campaign was quickly followed by the military confrontation with Malaysia over the question of the inclusion of Sabah and Sarawak, on the northern coast of Borneo, in the enlarged Malaysian Federation. It was on this issue that Sukarno took Indonesia out of the United Nations, engaged in guerrilla warfare against British, Australian and Malaysian troops, and incurred the hostility of many Western and Afro-Asian governments, including India. Under Suharto Indonesia has returned to the United Nations, joined the Association of South-East Asian Nations (ASEAN) and reverted to the Nehruvian style of nonalignment, although there are strong voices in the senior army leadership for an overtly anti-Peking foreign policy.

Indonesia is extremely rich in natural resources but weak in her capacity to exploit them, and income per head is estimated at only £40 a year. Her rubber, oil, tin, tea, tobacco, copra and other primary commodities find ready markets abroad, but her economy has tended to stagnate since the Dutch left, and living standards are increasingly threatened by the growth of population: the island of Java, which contained merely 2½ million people in 1800, must today contain 80 million.

There was moderate economic growth in the first seven or eight years of independence, but these gains were dissipated in the final decade of Sukarno-ism. Ambitious development plans were adopted, but the political leadership of the country showed a marked reluctance to attack the fundamental social and economic roots of the development problem, preferring to rely on external help and superficial slogans and substitutes for sacrifice. Rubber and coconut trees were not replanted, ports silted up, irrigation canals dried out, bridges and roads were not renewed. Sukarno made no pretence of understanding economics, which he dismissed as boring and demeaning, and there was one year in which the draft budget was inexplicably lost in the Secretariat.[14] The diplomatic campaigns against the Dutch and British were accompanied by the nationalization of foreign estates and enterprises, and the Chinese traders and moneylenders were also required to cease their activities in the rural areas. Since there were insufficient Indonesians with the skill and experience to take over these enterprises, their efficiency was diminished.

Suharto thus inherited in 1966 foreign debts of more than £1,120 million (representing six years' normal foreign exchange earnings) owed in roughly equal proportion to the West and to the Soviet *bloc*. But export earnings had declined to a mere £180 million a year (less than half their value in the early years of independence), while the minimum import requirement for the economy was calculated at £250 million.[15] Even rice, the staple foodstuff, was having to be imported[16] at a cost of £40 million a year, and any resumption of the economic development programme must inevitably entail higher imports of capital goods. Such is the vicious circle in which the Indonesian economy is trapped today. The foreign debts have been re-scheduled, but it will be many years before the ground that was lost through the neglect of the Sukarno decade can be recovered.

The Government's options in economic policy are limited by the fact that it has to sustain a pay-roll of more than four million employees in the civil service, armed forces and state-owned enterprises. Inflation is so acute that prices rose by 4,000 times during the decade 1957–67. This affects only a minority of the population, since many of the rural areas operate on a barter system without recourse to cash: the Government admits that more than 40 per cent of the money in circulation is in the capital city of Djarkarta itself. This explains the resilience of the rural economy, but it does not help development. The Government cannot afford to protect its employees against inflation, and low wages and salaries lead to institutionalized corruption and smuggling (the latter alone is officially admitted to cause the loss of £100 million a year to the treasury). What little industry there is has been running at less than 30 per cent of capacity in recent years,[17] and a number of new projects, including the first modern steel-mill, which the Russians have been helping to erect, have been scrapped. Indonesia is not self-sufficient even in such simple manufactures as cotton cloth.[18]

The Suharno administration has made a start in cleaning this Augean stable. Foreign companies have returned to their owners, the budget has been balanced, inflation reduced. The country's leading economists have been admitted to the highest levels of decision-making. New attractions have been offered to prospective foreign investors,[19] and the World Bank has become a willing ally in the effort to rehabilitate this ailing economy and start the development process going again. But it will be a very long haul indeed.[20]

Only time will accord Sukarno the judgment he deserves. He found Indonesia an unformed, disparate, unwieldly state: he handed it over to his successors as almost a nation, with a remarkable level of national consciousness. This is a precious asset on which the next generation can build. Sukarno constructed the ideology of Indonesian nationalism,[21] but it is now for others to exploit this as an instrument for modernization.

*

The Philippines is the only Asian country to have a Christian majority, a product of Spanish rule. Spain was succeeded by the Americans, whose well-planned and peaceful grant of independence in 1946 endowed the country with an early start in democratic politics but a continuing sense of dependence on Uncle Sam.[22] 'We are the only country wherein a constitutional proviso allows for alien sovereignty rights within our jurisdiction,' President Marcos was able to complain as recently as 1966.[23] Since then the expiry of the 99-year agreement to permit U S military bases, signed at the time of independence, has been brought forward to 1991. But only in the past year or two have the first cautious commercial and cultural exchanges with the communist countries of Europe been allowed, and the Philippines will probably be the last nation on earth to recognize Peking.

It needed the suggestion of an American withdrawal from Asia in 1968 to shock thinking Filipinos into debating the need eventually to come to terms with the two nearby powers, Japan and China.[24] A treaty of commerce and navigation was negotiated with Japan a decade ago but remains unratified by the Philippine Senate, so that the position of the Japanese in this country remains abnormal a quarter of a century after the end of the war. The difficulty is the insistence of Senators that more restrictions should be imposed on Japanese businesses operating in the Philippines to prevent their dominating the country. The concern over foreign economic control may be judged from the following representative passage from the Philippine press:

The nationalist traits of the revolutionary period ... have all but vanished in this materialist and highly Americanised society of ours. With the connivance of colonial-minded Filipinos, we have become the tool of foreign interests rather than the wheel of our own destiny. The Filipino has become the visitor in his own house ... Filipinos, supposed owners of the national resources, are nothing but the marionettes in the hands of aliens.... The economic dominance of the Chinese and the

Americans, both the colonial Americans who have outlived their use-fulness and the newcomers who take out of the country more than they bring in, must be reduced to a level that will not jeopardise the domain of the Filipinos.... There are more things to discover than what the Americans have taught us. After all, the Americans are only motivated by self-interest.[25]

Under the so-called Laurel-Langley agreement, Americans are allowed to operate in the Philippine economy as if they were nationals, while Philippine products enjoy preference in the American market. These mutual favours expire in 1974: Philip-pine nationalism would like to discontinue them, but about one-third of the country's exports would be affected by the loss of preference and so the nation's diplomacy on this matter is far from single-minded.

Philippine politics bear a superficial similarity to American, in that two parties, the *Nacionalista* and the Liberal, contend for power in a presidential system, but with little or no difference between their ideologies. Even at the highest level of leadership party loyalty is extremely weak.[26] The communist party is sup-pressed, and the left-wing in general has very little strength.[27] But the Philippines was in the early 1950s the scene of a communist-led uprising by the Hukbalahap, a band of guerrillas who first took arms against Japanese occupation and then challenged the independent Philippine government.

At their peak the Huks' ten-thousand-strong army controlled much of the central part of Luzon Island, feeding on the peasant grievances of these areas, where share-cropping is widespread. Half of the land in the Philippines is owned by less than 1 per cent of the population (the Church being an important landholder) and the number of landless peasants has been swelling gradually over recent decades. The Huks' rebellion was crushed in 1953 by the immensely popular President Magsaysay,[28] but they began to cause trouble again in the mid-1960s. This was linked with the inadequate implementation of the Land Reform Law which was belatedly passed in 1964,[29] but most commentators now minimize the ideological element in the Huks' leadership.[30]

Some of Magsaysay's followers are still trying to inject into Philippine politics a more serious concern with social and econ-omic reform. The former Senator Manglapus, after first failing to convert one of the two traditional parties to a reform platform, and then unsuccessfully trying for the presidency at the head of a new party, has now launched a 'Christian Social Movement' which rejects both capitalism and communism in favour of 'communitarianism'.

*

Malaysia has been called 'an Asian Switzerland',[31] in that its Malay citizens (42 per cent of the population) sometimes identify with the glamorous nationalism of their more numerous cousins in Indonesia, while the Chinese inhabitants (40 per cent of the total) tend to look to China, and the Indian minority to India, for cultural inspiration. The Malays resent the economic domination of the Chinese and regard them as relative newcomers, to which Lee Kuan Yew, the Singaporean prime minister, once replied that, 'Malays began to migrate to Malaysia in noticeable numbers only about seven hundred years ago.'[32] But the Malays' sentiment is that they, 'as the sons of the soil made the great sacrifice of agreeing to share their birthright with other communities . . .'[33]

The older generation of Malay, typified by the first prime minister, Tunku Abdul Rahman, is content to leave the country's business to the Chinese in return for Malay political supremacy.[34] But this formula on which Malaysia has depended since independence in 1957 was unlikely to last. Vulnerable to the Indonesian jibe of Malaysia's being 'a marriage between feudalism and Chinese capitalism', it is more and more questioned by younger elements in the Malay leadership. Yet the leisurely pace of the Malay awakening, and the persistence of the stereotype of the Malay as a pre-industrial child of nature (so tenderly drawn in Henri Fauconnier's novel *The Soul of Malaya*) is demonstrated by the fact that less than a quarter of the degrees and diplomas awarded by the University of Malaya in 1966 went to Malays – and most of those were in arts rather than sciences.[35]

The ruling party in Kuala Lumpur[36] is an alliance between three racial organizations representing respectively the Malays, the Chinese and the Indians, presided over by Tun Abdul Razak. The 1969 elections, in which the Alliance lost some ground but remained in power, were followed by ugly racial riots, after which democracy was suspended. New urban unemployment provided the economic force in the clashes, and the generation gap played its part. Rahman's government seemed unable to control the Malay extremists.[37] There was a return to restricted parliamentary rule in 1971. As the world's biggest and most efficient producer of both rubber and tin, Malaysia was enjoying annual economic growth of 6 per cent until the price of rubber dropped in the mid-sixties.

Malaysia has fought two wars and won them with British military help. The first was the rebellion of communist-led Chinese under Chin Peng, who had won an OBE for his exploits against the Japanese, in the late 1940s and 1950s. His movement was virtually extinguished by a long-drawn-out campaign of counter-insurgency, and when Malaysian independence was declared he retired with a few survivors across the Thai border where his harassments have recently begun to revive anxiety in both Bangkok and Kuala Lumpur. The second war was the *Konfrontasi* by Indonesia following the inclusion of Singapore, Sabah and Sarawak in an enlarged Malaysian Federation in 1963. This dispute was discussed in an earlier chapter.[38] Its resolution in 1965 left the Malaysian Government with the challenge of reconciling the two Bornean states* to its rule and defending Sabah from the resuscitated Philippine claim.

*

But Singapore has provided the worst headache for Rahman since the Indonesian attacks ceased. When Singapore graduated in 1963 from British colonial rule into membership in the Malaysian Federation, it was expected that it would become the 'New York' of the Federation, with a population that was three-quarters Chinese (and only 14 per cent Malay) and an average income per head 70 per cent bigger than peninsular Malaya's. But this role was too restrictive for Lee Kuan Yew and his ambitious and able colleagues in the People's Action Party (PAP), which has dominated Singapore politics for the past decade. They first contested elections in Malaya itself, and then launched a platform for a 'truly Malaysian Malaysia', i.e. a multi-racial federation in which the Malays would not monopol-

*There is a third – Brunei, a feudal sultanate under British protection and allied with Western oil interests, which survived the abortive Azahari rebellion in 1962.

ize political power. This was so upsetting to the delicate balance of racial politics in the Federation that Singapore was forced to secede in 1965.[39]

The Singapore Government is undoubtedly the most efficient and progressive in South-East Asia, though it depends on the physical suppression of its communist opponents (the communists also have some influence in the *Barisan Sosialis*, a party which won over 30 per cent of the votes in 1963 but which boycotted the 1968 elections to allow the PAP to occupy every single seat in parliament). The Government's record on housing, on industrialization and on developing the economy in general has been excellent. But its international situation is problematic, as the following warning by the Indonesian writer Mochtar Lubis illustrates:

The Singapore Chinese entrepreneurs would do well, for their own future, to learn to do good business with Indonesian and Malay business people, dealing with them on an equal footing as they had been doing in the past with their own Chinese friends or relatives in these countries. And at the same time Singapore must be stopped from remaining an island of prosperity for itself, siphoning riches and fortunes off all the countries around her.[40]

An independent Singapore is feared by its neighbours as a potential 'third China', or as a South-East Asian 'Israel' or 'Cuba'. But these dangers are recognized by the PAP leaders, who have taken care to play down Singapore's Chinese image by such means as enforcing Malay as the official language. Lee once threatened to offer Singapore as a naval base to the USSR,[41] but this was not seriously intended. Despite the break with Malaysia, which was followed by the separation of currencies and the building of a tariff wall between the two, there is still some collaboration across the Causeway, and the relationship with Malaysia remains different in quality from that with other neighbouring countries.[42]

*

Thailand is distinguished by its successful resistance to Western colonialism, and lacks the sense of inferiority *vis-à-vis* the West so prevalent elsewhere in Asia. A strong and farsighted monarchy in the nineteenth century ensured for Thailand a very early start in modernization from the top downwards, *à la Meiji*. In particular a relatively efficient professional bureaucracy was created,[43] whose products have more or less monopolized political power in recent decades, its military and civilian champions in the post-war period being Pibul Songgram and Pridi Phanomyong respectively. In 1957 power was seized by another military commander, Sarit Thanarat, who was succeeded on his death in 1963 by his deputy, Thanom Kittikachorn. In these two latter hands the government has displayed an 'imaginative and adaptive authoritarianism'.[44]

In 1968, after many years of drafting, a new parliamentary constitution was promulgated. Party politicians are not as free as they had been in earlier periods, and indeed martial law continued to be enforced during the elections which were held in 1969. As expected, the Thanom Government was confirmed in power by the elections under its new label of the United Thai People's Party. The principal opposition was provided in the new parliament by the Democratic Party, under former premier Seni Pramoj, which won all of the seats in the capital city of Bangkok. The electoral turn-out was a low one, attesting to Thai apathy towards the parliamentary process. The Communist Party is illegal and very small in numbers, and the only other important figure on the political scene is King Bhumiphol, the popular incumbent of a traditionally popular royal house, who is bound to grow in stature and authority in the coming decades (he is in his early forties).

The chief tension in Thai politics is within the ruling party. Thanom's deputy premier and minister of interior, General Prapas Charusathien, is the nation's strong man who has so far been willing to take second place in the political hierarchy. But he had his own group of supporters in the new parliament, some of them sitting as independents, and it was always possible that a struggle for the leadership could surge up. Prapas would be a ruler in the old style, and the intellectuals would greet his promotion with some anxiety. Thanom represents a less colourful but more dignified, more modern and more sophisticated form of government.[45]

The parliament had a strong right-wing bias and will not give the Government real trouble. And Thanom has the secret of combining firm administration with economic prosperity but without obvious repression, and any attempt to unseat him would be ill-received in the country. Nevertheless he suspended parliament in 1971 and reverted to open dictatorship, partly because of impatience with the delays of the parliamentary process.

The Thais are blessed with rich crops and mineral resources, and by accepting the economic role of the Chinese immigrants and opting firmly for a basic reliance on the forces of the free market, the country enjoyed an average economic growth rate of 5½ per cent in the 1950s and over 7 per cent in the 1960s.

The difficult problems have come from the areas inhabited by ethnic minorities where resistance to Thai rule has been encouraged and assisted by the Vietnamese and Chinese communists. The worst case of this is the north-east, where poor soil and lack of water dictate unusual poverty among people who feel themselves closer to the Laotians across the border than to the Government in distant Bangkok.[46] It is here that foreign-trained Thai guerrillas have obliged the Government to introduce, with massive American aid, an Accelerated Rural Development Programme, since 1967 under direct army control.

Although the Mekong River, the frontier in this area, is vulnerable to agents from communist-controlled parts of Laos, the threat of subversion has been exaggerated. The Chinese foreign minister reportedly named Thailand in 1965 as the 'next target for liberation', but supplies from China and Vietnam have so far been limited to small arms.[47] Although the northeast farmers are poor, the vast majority of them own their own land, as is the case throughout Thailand, and it would be surprising if the Government, despite its aloofness from rural problems, proved unable to retain control. There is also trouble in the southernmost provinces abutting on Malaysia, where Muslim separatism has joined cause with the surviving Chinese communist guerrillas expelled from Malaysia,[48] and also among the various hill tribes on the northern borders.

*

Burma affords a contrast to Thailand in many respects. It was absorbed into the British empire and resumed independence in 1948 on a very weak political foundation. It opted for the socialism and non-alignment of Nehru rather than the pro-Western private enterprise of the Thais. The partiamentary system became gradually discredited in spite of the charisma of U Nu, and in 1958, the army seized power temporarily in order to arrest the decline. It returned the reins of government to civilian politicians, only to feel it necessary to take them back again in 1962 when Nu was about to concede more autonomy to the ethnic minorities than the generals felt was safe for the country's unity and security. The Burmese army is one of the few that has never laid down arms since the Japanese war. Ever since independence the Government has fought armed revolt both from ethnic minorities (Shans, Chins, Karens etc.) and from rival communist bands, and in the last year or two Peking has begun to give active help to these guerrillas.

The socialist sentiments of Burma's nationalist leaders were reinforced by a determination to end the economic control exerted by immigrant Indian and Chinese traders and money-lenders. The 'Burmese Way to Socialism' propounded by the military Government under General Ne Win involved thorough-going nationalization of almost all private (and especially foreign) enterprise, and it is officially claimed that more than 170,000 aliens have left the country in recent years. But the Burmese themselves, for all the sincerity and good intentions of many army officers, were unable to fill the gaps so suddenly created, and the Burmese economy is admitted to have declined disastrously during the 1960s.[49]

Ne Win chose to support the leftists in the army high command (represented by Brigadier Tin Pe) rather than the moderates led by Brigadier Aung Gyi, and at one point during the military administration most of the leading civilian politicians and journal-ists, together with Aung Gyi and other dissenting senior officers, were in jail. They were eventually released, and U Nu proclaimed revolt from his exile in Thailand in 1969, but there is no group able to challenge the army and Burma's prospects are far from bright.

*

In Indochina one comes to the most complicated – and most tragic – area of South-East Asia. Though dominated by the Vietnamese, it contains numerous nationalities and is currently divided into three separate nations, each of which contains numerous ethnic minorities. It has provided the historical frontier between Indian and Chinese cultural expansion, and many parts of it have been engaged in continuous warfare for the past two or three decades.

Vietnam itself is stretched out along the coast of the South China Sea in the shape of the letter 'S', and many of its difficulties derive from the extraordinary fact that the ethnically Vietnamese population extends over a strip of 1,500 miles of territory which in places is barely two miles wide. Tonkin in the north has often been separated from Annam and Cochinchina in the south, but under French rule the country was united and the present division between the communist regime in the north and the anti-communist in the south is officially a temporary one pending reunification.

The communist regime established itself in North Vietnam at the end of the Second World War by virtue of taking the lead in resisting both the Japanese occupation and the French colonial return, thus acquiring the support of nationalist and anti-foreign feeling within the country. Ho Chi Minh's Government has not been particularly successful in its domestic policies, which have followed the conventional communist path of collectivization, mass mobilization and austerity. But its energies have been distracted by the lengthy campaign to win the south for the communist cause, initially through the encouragement of southern rebels and ultimately with regular northern troops engaging the Americans in the central highlands.

The French fought bitterly against Ho Chi Minh and endeavoured to establish a rival indigenous government under the emperor Bao Dai. But in the mid-fifties the French had to acknowledge military defeat at the famous battle of Dienbienphu, and the North Vietnamese agreed to the international settlement negotiated in Geneva in 1954 whereby the fighting stopped, the French left and elections in both halves of the country were to lead to peaceful reunification. But the government of South Vietnam then passed into the hands of Ngo Dinh Diem and his family, who were determined to resist communist influence. The presence in the south of large numbers of Catholics, of active Buddhists and of refugees from the rigours of the communist regime in the north, supported Diem's ambitions and ensured

American underpinning. Soon the Geneva ceasefire was drowned in a sea of mutual recrimination and mounting violence. Only in 1968, after power had passed to a group of young army leaders in Saigon, and the Americans began to despair of either winning the war or getting a sound Saigon government to back, did peace talks in Paris begin to hold out the prospect of an end to the fighting.

*

Cambodia and Laos were incorporated in French Indochina and have been conquered by the Vietnamese earlier in their history. But both emerged from the 1954 Geneva Accords with their sovereign independence recognized. Cambodia is the home of Khmers whose civilization once extended beyond the country's present borders and who built the most famous and beautiful of South-East Asia's historical ancient monuments, the complex of temples at Angkor.[50] Cambodia's brilliant prince Norodom Sihanouk abdicated the throne in 1955 in order to assume the active political leadership of his vulnerable state, threatened by both Thai and Vietnamese irredentism.

Sihanouk, one of Asia's most engaging and original figures, was occasionally troubled by Thai-supported rebels (the *Khmer Serei*) and by the few Cambodian communists, whom he derided as 'valets of North Vietnam'. But he maintained his own popularity through his *Sangkum* (People's Socialist Community) and through frequent radio broadcasts. Like Burma and Indonesia, he followed a neutralist policy abroad and a quasi-socialist policy at home. He built up cordial relations with China, in spite of occasional friction over the role of the Chinese residents in the country, and these survived the tensions of the Cultural Revolution in 1967.[51] In 1963 Sihanouk renounced American aid 'because it breeds dishonesty',[52] yet a satisfactory development of industry, communications and public services was achieved with the assistance of many foreign countries. Everything was subordinated to escaping the fate of a South-East Asian 'Poland', partitioned between her two larger and more dynamic neighbours.[53] But the formal spillover of the Vietnam war into Cambodia in 1970, when American and South Vietnamese troops openly entered the country, and the deposition of Sihanouk by a more overtly anti-communist group, made this fear very much more real. Under the successor regime of Lon Nol the country was renamed the Khmer Republic.

*

'Laos,' says Richard Harris of *The Times*, 'has never been a country; it was a patchwork of kingdoms overlaid by a short period of French influence.'[54] It is still a kingdom, guaranteed and neutralized under the subsequent Geneva Agreement of 1962, but effectively split into a communist-controlled north-east and a non-communist south-west, led respectively by the two princes Souphanouvong and Souvanna Phouma, who are half-brothers. Sporadic fighting still goes on between Souphanouvong's Pathet Lao and the royalist troops based on Vientiane, the former under increasingly overt control of North Vietnam, the latter enjoying the full support of the Americans and the Thai armed forces.[55] The so-called 'Ho Chi Minh trail', along which the rebels in South Vietnam are supplied and reinforced from the north, runs through the mountainous jungles of eastern Laos, ensuring the maintenance of tension in a country supposedly neutralized by international agreement.

The eventual fate of Laos and Cambodia will not be known until the war in Vietnam has ended. Sihanouk convened an Indo-chinese People's Conference in 1965 which set up a permanent secretariat to settle disputes and discuss common interests,[56] and he proposed that the three countries eventually come together in a federation of some kind.[57]

*

Despite their heterogeneity, most of the countries of South-East Asia do have three important common features not shared by either India, China or Japan. The first of these is the over-lapping heritage of both Chinese and Indian influence. So deep is the imprint of these larger civilizations on South-East Asia that George Coedès, the *doyen* of its prehistorians, has declared that, 'From prehistoric times, all of these peoples seem to have shared the same lack of inventiveness and to have been receptive rather than creative when brought into contact with foreign civilizations.'[58] But the forms which Indian and Chinese influence took were rather different. As Duncanson puts it, 'Most of the lands of South-East Asia once belonged to the cultural orbit of India, but from the earliest times they belonged to the political orbit of China . . .'[59]

Harris has argued that Asia can be divided into a Chinese-influenced East and an Indian-influenced South,* and that the line may actually be drawn along the frontier between Vietnam on the one hand and Laos and Cambodia on the other. He explains some of the complexities of present-day Indochinese politics by the fact that in French Indochina, 'Western imperialism unwittingly flung itself astride the border dividing East Asia from South Asia'.[60]

Linked with this shared ambiguity of historical links with India and China is the presence throughout South-East Asia of the overseas Chinese, whose circumstances have been discussed in an earlier chapter.[61] Their entrenched position in the economy, taken in conjunction with China's assumed ambitions in the area, lead some observers to accept the view of an American scholar that, 'Historical indications point to the ultimate engulfment of South-East Asia within the . . . Chinese cultural fold.'[62] The South-East Asian governments are in the dilemma that if they want fast economic growth they must encourage overseas Chinese enterprise,[63] but if they place a higher priority on national resurgence and the acquisition by their people of a true self-confidence, they must restrain or even destroy the overseas Chinese business network. Thailand represents the first, Burma and Indonesia the second extreme.

In fact it looks as if the overseas Chinese are becoming 'South-East-Asianized', as distinct from their cousins at home as the Australians or the Americans are from their European ancestors, and the eventual personality of the sub-continent will be an amalgam of indigenous and overseas Chinese elements.

This in turn leads to the third common feature of the South-East Asians, namely their sense of insecurity as a quarrelsome collection of small states which are politically, economically and

---

*Harris's notion of the 'hard' and 'soft' cultures of East and South Asia respectively (the former characterized by 'dedication, tirelessness, intellectual endeavour', the latter passive, open and non-authoritarian) has been adopted by Myrdal in *Asian Drama* to explain South Asian reluctance to use compulsion in economic development or social reform.

militarily vulnerable not merely to the powers outside Asia (America, Britain and Russia) but increasingly also to the Asian competitors in the power game, China, Japan and, to a much lesser extent, India.

Chapter Eighteen

Political Cooperation

THE Thai defence minister, General Praphas, once compared Prince Sihanouk, the Cambodian head of state, to 'a toad who sits in a coconut then dreams of immense deeds',[1] and the foreign minister of Pakistan referred to his opponents as 'Indian dogs' in a speech to the United Nations General Assembly during the 1965 Kashmir War. Asia differs little from Europe in the rivalry of nations and the chauvinism of national leaders – unless it be in the use of a wider and more homely range of epithets. The Chinese communist delegate who insisted, at the time when Indian opinion was denouncing Peking's suppression of the Tibetan rising of 1959, that the people of China would 'never allow foul hogs to poke their snouts into our beautiful garden',[2] was not untypical of the quick and colourful responses which Asians tend to make to any kind of supposed slight. The limitations on political cooperation among the countries of Asia are self-evident.

There are nevertheless some features of the political scene in East and South Asia over the past two decades which are favourable to collaboration across frontiers. Most of these factors owe their origins to the common inheritance of anti-colonialism which inspired the new nationalist heroes of the post-war era. Men like Nehru, Hatta and Ho Chi Minh, though leaders of otherwise unconnected national independence movements, met and collaborated in the international anti-colonial movements and conferences in Moscow, Brussels, Paris and London in the 1920s and 1930s. Though they never used any Asian language when speaking to one another, this small band of men felt themselves to be fighters in one cause.

They rationalized their community of interest by looking back into an imagined Asian unity of the past and idealized it by looking forward to an equally imaginary united Asia of the future. Nehru saw the period of European domination in Asia as one of unusual isolation between the Asian countries. Once that domination was ended, as he told the historic first pan-Asian conference in New Delhi in 1947, 'the walls that surrounded us fall down and we look at one another again and meet as old friends long parted'.[3] This is doubtful history, but it was good psychology. The sentiment of having shared the indignities of European exploitation, and of having jointly succeeded in throwing it off, was a very real force in that generation of nationalist leaders.

The Asian Relations Conference in New Delhi in the spring of 1947 was the first step on the road that led to Bandung. The idea for it came from the few Asians attending the early meetings of the United Nations in San Francisco in 1945. Fearing that the United Nations was likely to become little more than a White Man's Club, they suggested that Nehru should summon a conference in Asia which could more dramatically express Asian viewpoints on the political structure of the post-war world. In fact Nehru was profoundly disappointed by the conference. The Chinese delegates lobbied strenuously to prevent the pan-Asian idea from coming under Indian leadership, and they had little difficulty in stirring up the suspicions of the smaller countries of South-East Asia about Indian motives. All the tensions of post-war Asia were apparent to the percipient observer at the New Delhi Conference of 1947.

A further meeting of Asian leaders was held in New Delhi in 1949, but this was largely concerned with ways and means of assisting Indonesia's armed struggle against the Dutch. The same leaders came together again in Colombo in 1954 to consider the peace settlement in Indochina, and it was almost as an afterthought that they accepted an Indonesian suggestion for a full-scale Afro-Asian conference in Bandung.

The Bandung Conference of 1955 was the high point of pan-Asian solidarity. The two rival leaders, Nehru and Chou En-lai, were both on foreign ground, and neither succeeded in capturing the conference. There was very severe tension on the ideological plane, between the conservative and pro-Western leaders (notably Kotelawala of Ceylon, Romulo of the Philippines and Mohammed Ali of Pakistan), on the one hand, and the communists and their defenders on the other.[4] Nehru and U Nu led the effort to conciliate these opposing viewpoints, and surface harmony was maintained with the agreement on ten principles of international behaviour, offered as a guide for world peace and cooperation. The most important of these were: (a) respect for human rights and the UN Charter, (b) respect for other nations' sovereignty and territorial integrity, (c) equality of races and nations, (d) non-intervention and non-interference in other countries' affairs, (e) the right of self-defence, singly or collectively, and (f) peaceful settlement of disputes.

A shorter selection of these principles had been first listed in the 1954 Trade Agreement between India and China concerning Tibet, and a few weeks afterwards the Indian and Chinese prime ministers had jointly offered these Five Principles as a panacea for world peace.[5] Later in the same year the Indonesian prime minister had visited New Delhi and referred in a speech to the Five Principles (*Pantja Sila*) propounded by Sukarno in 1945 as the philosophical bases of the state of Indonesia, namely nationalism, humanism, freedom, social justice and faith in God. This had struck a chord among his Indian hearers, to whom the phrase *Panchsheel* recalled the first five commandments of Buddha, 2,500 years ago. Nehru had immediately given the name *Panchsheel* to the Five Principles of peaceful co-existence launched by himself and Chou En-lai and they in turn became the basis for the Bandung declaration.

But the formula was inadequate for Asia, let alone the wider world: ten years later, when the attempt was made to hold a second African-Asian Conference in Algiers, the leading figures involved could not agree even on the ground rules and the scheme was abandoned.[6] There was open jockeying for national advantage, and by then the tension between India and China (with Indonesia at that time supporting Peking) had become too strong to be contained in a conference of this kind. In any case, the Africans had their own divisions, and by 1965 the Afro-Asian honeymoon was over. Two small permanent secretariats, the Afro-Asian Economic Committee (AFRASEC) and the Afro-Asian People's Solidarity Committee (AAPSC) survive in Cairo, but are rendered ineffectual by these internal divisions.

One of the strands in the Bandung Conference was the principle of non-alignment in international affairs, of which Nehru was such an eloquent advocate. In essence this means a determination to exercise an independent judgment on questions of foreign policy, but in the context of the cold war which was then raging it also meant a studied neutrality in the disagreements between the West and the Soviet Union. On the Asian scene itself this was an unreal policy, since China was at that time an open follower of the Soviet camp and yet was treated by Nehru and Nu as almost a potential neutral in the ideological struggle. Many of the smaller nations of South-East Asia were unwilling to renounce their Western protectors, and this enabled Dulles to form an overtly anti-communist defence pact for the region. The South-East Asia Treaty Organisation (SEATO), launched in Manila in 1954, included Pakistan, the Philippines, and Thailand as well as Australia, New Zealand, Britain, France and the United States. An Asian People's Anti-Communist League (APACL) was formed at the same time in Seoul: although an unofficial organization, it is actively supported by the South Korean, Taiwanese and South Vietnamese governments. Malaysia retained her defence treaty with Britain, but took a slightly less committed position in Asian politics.

Apart from the four communist states of China, Mongolia, North Korea and North Vietnam, whose international policies followed broadly the same line, this left only Indonesia, Burma, Cambodia, Laos, Nepal and Ceylon as potential supporters of Nehru's non-alignment. The most substantial of these, Indonesia, became a doubtful ally in the early 1960s as Sukarno drifted more and more towards the Chinese standpoint in international affairs. Nehru's interest gradually shifted from the 'Bandung' line of Afro-Asian Conferences to the 'Belgrade' series of non-aligned summit meetings, as he found Nasser and Tito more congenial allies in the fight to reconcile Moscow with the West. It is no accident that India, the UAR and Yugoslavia have taken the most constructive lead, in and out of UNCTAD, in seeking to redress the economic balance between north and south.

In the end, for all Nehru's earlier hopes, India and China squarely faced each other as rivals for power in their continent: a confrontation symbolized by the Himalayan border war of 1962 and the inability of six 'neutral' states (including Burma, Cambodia, Ceylon and Indonesia) to conciliate it. There is no possibility of a political grouping in Asia which would include both India and China and it is inevitable that they vie for influence in South-East Asia. Avuncularly pressed by the three big Asian powers (India, China and Japan), South-East Asia does understandably provide a possible case for political cooperation. The underlying feeling was well expressed by the father of Burmese independence, Aung San, when he declared in 1947 that, 'while India should be one entity, and China another, South-East Asia should form an entity on its own; and then finally we should come together in a bigger union'.[7] But it was only after the Geneva Accords of 1954 that conditions became sufficiently settled in South-East Asia for action to be taken in this direction.

The man who first launched the diplomacy which led to the Association of South-East Asian Nations (A S E A N) was Tunku Abdul Rahman, the prime minister of Malaysia (which became independent only in 1957). An idealist who was well aware of the vulnerability of a nation such as Malaysia (with fewer than ten million inhabitants), Rahman made soundings in 1958–9, first in Ceylon and then in the Philippines, for a proposed treaty of friendship and economic cooperation. Burma, Indonesia, Thailand and the Indochina countries were envisaged as joining. But the fact that the initiative came from two staunchly pro-Western nations (Malaysia and the Philippines) aroused the suspicion of the neutralists, and Rahman's proposal met with little response.[8] In 1961, however, the Association of South-East Asia (A S A) was formed by Malaysia, the Philippines and Thailand. The three pioneers were careful to emphasize the positive objectives of their Association, notably in the economic field, rather than the negative anti-communist feelings which all three undoubtedly shared. They spoke of the Nordic Council as a model for their grouping, and explained that the most important goal was 'to acquire the habit of sitting down together'.[9]

Indonesia remained aloof from all this because of her non-alignment policy, and in 1962 she quarrelled with Malaysia over the inclusion in the enlarged Malaysian Federation of the two northern Borneo states of Sabah and Sarawak – a quarrel which provoked the 1963–6 military confrontation. It was during the

Philippine efforts to mediate this conflict that the new concept of Maphilindo, overlapping with A S A, was launched – in the Manila Declaration by the three Heads of Government (Rahman, Sukarno and Macapagal) on 5 August 1963. Macapagal referred to the three countries as 'triplets who, after birth, were placed under the care of three different foster-parents'. The Maphilindo Declaration foresaw an eventual confederation 'to restore and strengthen the historic unity and common heritage of the Malay peoples'. Some intellectuals in each country had dreamed of a return to the great Malay empires of prehistory, supposedly extending from Malagasy in the west to Easter Island in the east.[10]

Later, Rahman explained that Maphilindo had been 'stillborn because it was a concept based on a racial idea, and on the supremacy of the larger elements dominating smaller ones....'[11] There are in each of the three countries considerable minorities which cannot seriously be claimed as members of the Malay family – the Negritos of the southern Philippines, for instance, the Papuans of New Guinea and the Dyaks of Borneo. Indeed the Malays themselves are in a numerical minority in Malaysia. But the real difficulty about the Maphilindo concept concerns the several millions of people of Chinese descent who are now resident in these three countries, many of them possessing local nationality. Anti-Chinese feelings are probably at the root of the popularity of the movement to extol the ancient virtues and achievements of the Malay race, and the Manila Declaration of 1963 was taken by some ardent nationalists as a declaration of war against the 'slit-eyes' whose command of the economy is so widely resented in South-East Asia.

In the end, after the confrontation between Indonesia and Malaysia had ceased, Indonesia was brought into the A S A club. This was the effect of the creation, in August 1967, of A S E A N (comprising Indonesia, Malaysia, the Philippines, Singapore and Thailand) and of the subsequent merger of the old A S A into the new organization. The Bangkok Declaration of 8 August 1967 made an important concession to Indonesia's surviving neutralism by insisting that foreign military bases (i.e. the British in Malaysia and Singapore, and the American in the Philippines and Thailand) were 'temporary and remain only with the expressed concurrence of the countries concerned, and are not intended to be used directly or indirectly to subvert the national independence and freedom of states in the area or prejudice the orderly processes of their national development'.

This did not prevent the Peking press from declaring that 'a new anti-China anti-Communist alliance was knocked together on the orders of United States imperialism in Bangkok yesterday . . .'[12] Since the independent government of Singapore is a full member of A S E A N, the latter cannot be described as anti-Chinese in the broadest sense. But each of its members does actively suppress communism within its own borders, and there are signs that the initial reluctance to adopt a collective standpoint overtly inimical to Peking in particular, or to the communist world at large, is beginning to disappear. A S E A N may well acquire a defence content as the British and Americans reduce their military presence in the area.

One's expectations from A S E A N should nevertheless be modest. The fighting between Malaysian and Indonesian troops in the jungles of Sarawak is still fresh in the memory, the Philippines-Malaysia dispute over Sabah has now become a major storm, Malaysia and Singapore are at daggers drawn on a number of important issues, and there is potential trouble over Malay irredentism in South Thailand. A S E A N is likely, all the same, to survive these stresses in the long run. It corresponds with the idea voiced by Aung San, that South-East Asians should cooperate to protect their interests, not merely *vis-à-vis* the great world powers – Europe, America and the Soviet Union – but also against the big three in Asia itself. Some A S E A N members would like to have Burma, Cambodia and Ceylon in the club – but there is a consensus against inviting Japan, India (and therefore Pakistan) or China (and therefore Taiwan). The eligibility of Vietnam and Laos will depend on the outcome of the peace settlement in Vietnam. As long as A S E A N remains a trade union for the smaller countries of the region it will provide a needed framework for the politics of the area.

The growing interest of the A S E A N quintet in mutual defence arrangements coincided with the declining prestige of S E A T O, weakened first by the advent of de Gaulle and his overtures to Peking, and then by the Sino-Pakistan honeymoon of the 1960s.

But in 1965 the South Koreans, who had always hankered after some kind of 'North-East Asian Treaty Organisation', began a campaign for a new Far East grouping of more or less explicitly anti-communist powers. At a conference in Seoul in 1966 nine nations (Australia, Japan, Malaysia, the Philippines, New Zealand, South Korea, South Vietnam, Taiwan and Thailand) agreed to form the Asian-Pacific Council (ASPAC), and this has continued to hold annual conferences and to pursue discussions through a standing committee in Bangkok.

But ASPAC has not really settled down to agree on its true *raison-d'être*. The hard-liners (i.e. the Koreans, Vietnamese and Nationalist Chinese) would like the organisation to be openly anti-communist, whereas the Japanese, the Malaysians and the Australians are opposed to this. The group of nine is in any case too heterogeneous and too dispersed to act as a cohesive unit. It seems that ASPAC's real function is to provide a continuing forum at which the non-communist countries of eastern Asia and Australasia can keep in touch with each other, discuss their political and diplomatic dilemmas at a time of great uncertainty and fluidity in the region's affairs – and, when opportune, present a collective viewpoint which might carry more weight with the Americans, the Russians, and even the Chinese. But its origin in a Korean initiative inevitably renders it suspect as a possibly American-influenced organization.

If ASEAN is the organization likely to deal most effectively with the 'power vacuum' left in South-East Asia by the withdrawal of the British from Malaysia and Singapore and the failure of the American intervention in Vietnam, there is no such framework for the cooperation of the non-communist powers across Asia as a whole. Some Western strategists talk of a coming India-Japan or India-Indonesia-Japan or India-Japan-Australia axis to contain Chinese communism in the post-Vietnam war Asia. Alastair Buchan, former Director of the Institute for Strategic Studies in London, has argued that a 'treaty of mutual cooperation between India, Australia and Japan' would provide the best core of 'an indigenous system of countervailing power in Asia' to reduce China's opportunities for creating instability in the area.[13] But the connections between India and Japan are still very slight indeed, and it is hard to envisage any meaningful political alliance between them in the foreseeable future. The Japanese tend to think of India as a somewhat hopeless swamp of poverty and inertia, and prefer to deal, both politically and economically, with the more familiar ground of East and South-East Asia. A conference in Canberra in 1967 found that the potential for a real Indo-Japanese-Australian alliance was doubtful, since each of the trio differed economically, culturally and in their assessments of the Chinese threat.[14] Indonesia is still licking her wounds from the days of Sukarno and is not yet in a position to pursue a very active Asian diplomacy. Indonesians of all political colours (even Sukarno himself, in his day) identify China as their principal potential enemy, at least in the long-term, but one is prompted to comment that it would take a war with China to make the Indonesians willing allies of either India or Japan. 'All in all,' an Australian scholar concludes, 'one must concede that, unaided, the Asian powers must look like a rope of sand in relation to China for the next decade or so.'[15]

In the absence of anti-Chinese or anti-communist leadership from either India or Indonesia, the future intentions of Japan assume unusual importance. The Japanese are obviously unhappy with the American policy of boycotting China, and, in almost every way short of actual diplomatic recognition, Japan maintains a more active relationship with China than any other non-communist nation, including Britain. The excesses of the Cultural Revolution weakened China's image in Japan. But the Japanese are conscious of their cultural debt to China (far stronger than that which Byron felt towards Greece) and are aware of a certain guilt at having invaded China so wantonly in the 1930s. The 'Okuma Doctrine' of the end of the nineteenth century, by which Japan was to repay her old cultural debt by restoring China to a place of honour in an East Asia free from Western domination, still finds a response in some Japanese minds, although China's acquisition of nuclear bombs has removed some of the grounds for this.[16]

For all these reasons there is a very strong underlying sentiment in Japan which looks forward to the restoration of normal links with China, and is profoundly sceptical of the possibility of China's ever launching an unprovoked attack of Japan.[17] The Japanese are therefore likely to seek to come to terms with China as soon as possible, although they are handicapped by their treaty with the Nationalists, by their sentimental associations with Taiwan dating from the days when it was a Japanese colony, and by their important economic links with the island (whose trade with Japan is still more valuable than Communist China's).

There is one school of thought in the West which believes that Japan will in the end collaborate with China.[18] The two of them together could ultimately achieve what Japan tried to do alone thirty years ago and what some Chinese would perhaps like to do today. They would make a very formidable team. But Japan's mood is still very hostile towards any kind of external adventurism, and her economy is now intricately linked with the entire world trading system. China's mood and economic interests are quite different.

It is well on the cards that Japan and China could eventually establish a *modus vivendi* under which China's quest for political influence over the smaller nations around her might be respected by Japan, in return for Chinese acceptance of Japan's need for an important commercial stake in the same countries. Japan's and China's likely political and economic demands on their smaller neighbours would not really conflict. China would probably seek informal recognition as the great nuclear power of the region, an end to non-Asian military bases or alliances, and a market for her light industrial products; Japan would have no political demands at all, but would need a market for her heavy industrial goods, stable sources of supply of industrial raw materials and sites for low-cost manufacture by Japanese subsidiaries abroad. But such an alliance, if it could deserve the term, would remain informal (Japan's economic need for good political relations with the West and the Soviet Union would ensure that), and would be concerned only with a mutual accommodation of interests within eastern Asia. It could not last if it sought to extend its operation to other parts of the world.

Let it be added that one is here trying to anticipate the most likely outcome of the application of common sense and rational assessments of national interest to the conduct of foreign policy. It is possible that either Japan or China (or both) could at some future time come under the control of fervid expansionists with dangerous dreams of world conquest, in which case the smaller nations of the area would have cause to tremble. But such a possibility seems far slighter than that of the limited *modus vivendi* which I have outlined.[19]

In any event this is all far in the future. For the time being the Japanese are preoccupied with ensuring that they are not excluded from any free trade arrangements which the Western nations might make among themselves, and that their special trading links with the rest of East and South-East Asia are not harmed. Hence the official interest in the various schemes for a Pacific Free Trade Area (PAFTA) or Pacific Economic Community (PECOM), the hard core of which would be the three Pacific states most hard hit by any further steps towards economic integration in the European-Atlantic area – namely Australia, Japan and New Zealand.[20] As a nation logistically vulnerable to interruptions in foreign trade and shipping, Japan is obliged to place economic considerations far above the political. But the political climate for moves towards closer links with Australia and New Zealand is improving in all three countries.

The prospects for political cooperation in Asia are thus obscure, perhaps because the continent is too vast, diffuse and culturally divided. Some Westerners believe that nationalism will play itself out more quickly in Asia than it did in Europe: 'Regionalism,' said Professor Walt W. Rostow recently, 'is something that will replace nationalism' in the area.[25] But the hard fact is that the solitary regional organization which can unequivocally be called the product of purely local initiative – ASEAN – is itself uncertain of survival. There are two other groupings which are genuinely indigenous, but they each contain only one of the countries of South and East Asia: Pakistan is linked with Iran and Turkey in the rather successful, though modest, Regional Cooperation for Development (RCD), while India is a member (with Yugoslavia and the UAR) of the tripartite Council of Economic Ministers of the Non-Aligned Nations, which is pioneering the road of tariff cuts among the developing countries themselves. The verdict of the veteran

Japanese correspondent, Maruyama Shizuo, who has represented the *Asahi Shimbun* in many Asian capitals, is deserved: it is, he says, 'incorrect to regard regionalism in Asia as anything more than an embryonic movement, a groping in the dark'.[22]

Chapter Nineteen

Economic Cooperation

'A STEEL mill, a chemical plant, some technical advice, these things we can get anytime; from the Russians, from the Americans, from the Germans. But to develop national identity, that takes years, and even in Indonesia we have only begun to accomplish that now.'[1]

So the former Indonesian foreign minister, Dr Subandrio, speaking in 1963. Asia's political leaders in the 1950s and early 1960s were more concerned with the very basic political goals of independence and nation-building than with development of their economies. Given the fact that their political cooperation with each other is somewhat limited, it can be deduced that the climate for economic cooperation within Asia is also far from good. The economic links between the countries of South and East Asia had been artificially enfeebled through the experience of Western colonialism. Twenty years ago India's trade and industry was geared largely to the British market, Indonesia's to the Dutch, the Philippines' to the American, Vietnam's to the French. These distortions were not easy to correct since they had created powerful vested interests, not merely in business but even in foreign language skills. Even today it is easier for an Indian exporter to negotiate with a British buyer than to effect entry into the less distant Cambodian or Indonesian markets. After twenty years of independent economic management, the developing countries of South and East Asia (excluding China) still conduct only two-fifths of their foreign trade with each other, three-fifths with the developed countries of Europe, North America and Japan.

A rational approach to development in Asia would include the promotion of more trade within the area, and also a degree of regional cooperation in reproduction. Unfortunately, the political will necessary for this is largely lacking. India badly needs more chemical fertilizer factories but lacks the indigenous raw materials. Several commercial interests, both Indian and foreign, have proposed the construction of plants in India which would utilize the surplus natural gas of Iran. This makes economic sense, but the prospect of dependence on a country whose religious associations are more with Pakistan than with India, and which might be vulnerable to pressure to cut off supplies in the event of an Indo-Pakistan war, proved difficult for the Indian policy makers to accept – particularly since the gas might be brought in through a pipe-line across Pakistani soil.

India is perhaps a special case: she is so large that her progress towards economic autarchy seems inevitable. No Indian industrialist need be anxious about the adequacy of his domestic market. India professes sympathy with the natural rubber growers of Malaysia and Indonesia, but she has also started a synthetic rubber industry of her own; her national interest must prevail over her international sentiments. The same goes for China.

But it is otherwise with the smaller countries of Asia, most of whom are endeavouring to industrialize independently on the basis of very small domestic markets of only ten, twenty or thirty million inhabitants. These new industries can take root only behind a protective wall of tariffs or restrictions on competing imports, and competitiveness in export markets is therefore minimal. It would obviously make much better sense to agree to specialize in industrial production and to move towards some kind of customs union or free trade area which would enable industrial products to secure a larger regional market among neighbouring countries.[2] A team of Japanese metallurgical experts has recommended that the Philippines and Taiwan, for example, could profitably cooperate in steel production, the former making cold-rolled sheets from the latter's hot-coil.[3]

But a moment's consideration of the political relationships in the area over the past two decades is enough to render recommendations of this kind theoretical in the extreme. Now that Malaysia and Singapore have deliberately, and as recently as 1965, thrown up a tariff wall between them which did not exist before, it is hard to think of any two countries in South and East Asia with sufficient trust in each other to accept any degree of mutual dependence in economic matters. India and Pakistan were eventually persuaded by the World Bank (i.e. by Western pressure) to cooperate over the disposition and development of the River Indus waters, to the material benefit of both sides. But in every other respect India and Pakistan have emerged as determined competitors in all forms of production.

If international cooperation in the economic sphere has a future at all, it ought to be in South-East Asia where the need is greatest. The regional groupings described in the previous chapter each envisage economic cooperation, but none has pursued it with real vigour. In 1967 ASA had belatedly reached the point of drafting a list of products of the three countries concerned – Malaysia, the Philippines and Thailand – suitable for tariff-free entry into the other two countries. But only twenty-one products could be named, and even this inadequate list could only be agreed to with numerous reservations.[4] ASA was then merged into the larger ASEAN, at the foundation of which there was no mention of tariff changes but only the usual generalities about collaboration in industry, agriculture, transport, etc. When ASEAN did hold its first economic conference in Manila towards the end of 1968, a Philippines proposal for limited free trade arrangements had to be shelved because neither Malaysia nor Singapore was ready to discuss it.

The economic content of ASEAN is thus meagre, although its potential remains large.[5] All that has been done in the ten years since Tunku Abdul Rahman first launched the idea of a South-East Asian regional organization is window-dressing – some co-ordination of tourism promotion, some progress in radio and telecommunications, some exchanges of technical personnel. None of the ASEAN countries has been able to envisage the merger of its small national airline into a stronger collective fleet. It is a sad comment on ASEAN's relative lack of economic consciousness that one of the most important developments affecting its members' common commercial interests took place outside the ASEAN framework when, at a Bangkok conference sponsored by the United Nations in 1968, preliminary agreement was reached on an Asian Coconut Community. This is to comprise Ceylon and India as well as the ASEAN quintet, and, since these seven countries between them account for 80 per cent of world production, they are in a strong position to strengthen the market in this commodity. As for ASPAC, the South Korean-sponsored larger forum for East Asia and Australasia, there has been no important agreement or action on economic cooperation, although Taiwan has proposed the establishment of commodity banks to serve the region (rice, wheat, fertilizer and cement being suggested as suitable candidates).

One of the best-known organizations concerned with economic development in Asia is the Colombo Plan, child of the first meeting of Commonwealth foreign ministers ever to be held on Asian soil. When Bevin, Nehru, Spender, Pearson, Senanayake and Ghulam Mohammed met in Colombo in 1950, they were inspired by the Marshall Plan and President Truman's Point Four Programme to propose a Commonwealth programme for technical assistance to South and South-East Asia. At subsequent meetings this initiative was developed further, and the Asian countries concerned were invited to present six-year development programmes (beginning from mid-1951) as a framework within which both capital and technical assistance could be facilitated. These programmes, which represented the first essays in planning in India, Pakistan, Ceylon, Malaysia and Singapore, were considered at a meeting in London at the end of 1950.

This meeting produced a 100-page report which constituted the original 'Colombo Plan'. It analyzed the national programmes, observed that the main limitations on their size and speed were the shortages of capital and of trained men, estimated what would be needed from outside in these respects and set these as targets for the richer industrialized members of the Commonwealth to meet. The report based these recommendations on three arguments. The first was that economic development is a precondition of the social and political stability in Asia which future world peace demands. The second premise was that the 'restoration of the area to its key position in world trade' was vital, not only for the Asian countries themselves but also for the growth of 'an expanding world economy based upon multilateral trade'. The third premise was that the remarkable innate cultural resources of Asia must be unlocked, through economic advance, to allow them to contribute fully to the lives of peoples everywhere. To this day a better statement of the Western stake in Asian development has not been produced.

What the Colombo Plan amounts to now is an informal but highly valued framework for the negotiation and co-ordination of economic aid, and also a clearing house (in the form of the Colombo Plan Bureau, which occupies a small house in the suburbs of the Ceylonese capital) for technical assistance, both the training of Asian technicians and the provision of Western experts. It is no longer a Commonwealth monopoly, since the members now include Thailand, Nepal, Bhutan, Burma, Cambodia, Indonesia, Laos, the Philippines, South Korea and South Vietnam among the 'recipients', and the United States and Japan among the 'donors'. All these countries meet in a different city every year at the ministerial level to review the progress of economic development in the region, to identify and consider the emerging problems and obstacles and – behind the scenes – to have an orgy of bilateral haggling over the details of the individual aid contracts which are the main business of the Colombo Plan. Unlike United Nations meetings, the Colombo Plan conferences are informal, exclude newspaper reporters and rely on consensus rather than majority voting: it is these characteristics associated with the Commonwealth image which have enabled the Colombo Plan to become so popular.[6] It has certainly helped to lay the foundation for the intra-Asian trust and familiarity upon which genuine economic cooperation can come to be built in future generations, but its very informality removes it from areas of decision-making.

If the Colombo Plan is mainly an influence on Asian economic cooperation, ECAFE – the United Nations Regional Economic Commission for Asia and the Far East – offers itself explicitly as a decision-making forum at which representatives of governments commit themselves in formal voting on resolutions. ECAFE is in many respects one of the oddities of the United Nations family.[7] Its very name perpetuates the muddled thinking of the early post-war years when Asia was so disorganized. When it first met in Shanghai in 1947 the colonial powers were still strong in Asia, and to this day ECAFE is weakened as a spokesman for Asian interests by the presence of Britain, France, Holland, the Soviet Union and the United States as full members.

This kind of situation was avoided altogether in ECAFE's African counterpart, and is evaded in Latin America by the custom of holding exclusively regional conferences as well as full membership conferences, the difference being the presence or absence of the United States. ECAFE was further impoverished by its exclusion of three communist states – China (the largest country in the region, whose absence contributed heavily to the artificiality of ECAFE's proceedings), North Korea and North Vietnam. Only in 1972 did Peking begin to participate in ECAFE's work.

Finally, ECAFE is the least homogeneous, most widely scattered and most heavily populated of all the United Nations Commission regions. It is just possible to bully the Africans and Latin Americans, respectively, into cooperating on economic matters of common interest, because their geographical and cultural links are not insubstantial, and because they are mostly states of comparable size and importance. But the area which ECAFE covers extends from the Muslim states of Iran, Afghanistan and Pakistan in the west, through Hinduistic India and the small Buddhist nations of South-East Asia, to Confucianist Japan, the Catholic Philippines and Anglo-Saxon Australia and New Zealand to the east. Not only are these countries very different from each other in language, cultural tradition, religion, and racial origin, but they are also of very different sizes and enjoy very weak connections with one another.

At any ECAFE meeting there are two inescapable tensions, namely the determination of the Asian members not to be pushed around by the Europeans and Americans present, and the equally strong determination on the part of the smaller states not to be bullied or patronized by India, Japan or – since 1972, after Peking entered the UN – China. The energy expended in these two competing confrontations leaves little over for the real problems of economic cooperation. The first two executive secretaries of ECAFE were Indians, appointed in the days when Indian leadership in Asian matters was taken for granted and when India was almost the only country to have suitable men available for such posts. But for the past decade the ECAFE secretariat in Bangkok has been headed by the Burmese U Nyun, who has carried even further than his predecessors a disposition to prize harmony above action. Many of the efforts of the six hundred international civil servants who sit in the rambling old palace in Bangkok called *Sala Santitham* (Hall of Peace) are thus directed to reconciling the viewpoints of delegations whose interests are so different that the only result can be a lowest common denominator of little real significance. What one critic calls these 'policies of appeasement'[8] have allowed ECAFE so contribute to political understanding within Asia, but have prevented a real progress across the board on economic matters.

In its role as Asia's 'economic parliament', ECAFE has nevertheless become Asia's most important forum for discussing economic development problems – at its annual ministerial-level conferences, at its numerous committees and sub-committees, and in its increasingly sophisticated research work. On trade matters the ECAFE secretariat has not been able to persuade the governments of the region to give each other tariff preferences, India in particular having reservations about the effects of this on its balance of payments. Some kind of payments union would perhaps be necessary for this method of boosting intra-Asian trade, and the region is not nearly ready for that.

This question of intra-regional trade is important because it is one way of reducing Asia's dependence on outside manufactured goods, of keeping the cost of imports down, of expanding exports of Asian manufacturers (which tend to be restricted in the markets of the West) and increasing their competitiveness generally. Yet not until 1966 was ECAFE successful in staging, in Bangkok, the first International Asian Trade Fair – earlier efforts to hold it in Karachi having been abortive because Pakistan would not in the end give facilities for Israel to participate, a risk which ECAFE officials had apparently underestimated.[9] Latterly the ECAFE economists have been pushing much more strongly the idea of industrial specialization and the co-ordination of Asia's industrialization, under the influence especially of Professor Hiroshi Kitamura. The first success in this endeavour is yet to be seen.

In defending its record, ECAFE can point to four particular projects which have been rather successful. The list begins with the Mekong River Scheme, which aims at utilizing the hitherto untapped resources of the 1,500-mile Lower Mekong and its many tributaries for power generation, irrigation, flood control, drainage, navigation and water supply.[10] This scheme benefits (and is controlled by) the four riparian states of Cambodia, Laos, South Vietnam and Thailand, and since these countries are not the best of friends, to put it mildly, the survival of ECAFE's Mekong Committee on which they all sit is something of a miracle. It is to be explained firstly by the fact that twenty-three countries outside the Mekong Basin, together with thirteen United Nations agencies, are supporting the scheme and have pledged more than £50 million in funds towards it, and secondly by the sustained and skilful diplomacy of U Thant (who has taken a personal interest in the scheme), U Nyun and its brilliant American director up to 1969, Dr C. Hart Schaaf. Already two large dams have been completed in Thailand and four others are under way in Laos and Cambodia. In 1965 Thailand and Laos signed the first convention for the exchange of electric power under the Mekong Scheme, and over the next few years we are likely to see a gradual economic revolution in the basin as tens of thousands of farmers begin to win a little more freedom from floods and drought, and to have electric power placed at their disposal. The United Nations regards the Mekong Scheme as one of its showpieces, and with every justification.

The Asian Highway, another brain-child of ECAFE which has received considerable publicity, is less important in its effects. It envisages the linking up and improvement to uniform standards of some 36,000 miles of roads, to form a system linking one end of Asia to the other. The so-called A-1 Highway runs from Bargazan on the Turkish-Iranian frontier to Saigon, while the A-2 Highway begins at Ghasr-i-Shirin on the Iraq-Iran border, and proceeds via Singapore and through Java to Denpasar on Bali Island. But about a quarter of the mileage along the Asian Highway remains neither asphalted nor concreted, and there are portions of it, notably on the Burmese borders, which remain impassable. The Asian Highway is an imaginative scheme, but its contribution is more psychological than practical and ECAFE has not yet got to the point of producing an integrated transport policy or programme for Asia.

The latest offshoots of ECAFE are the Asian Institute for

Economic Development and Planning founded in 1964 and responsible during its first five years for training more than 750 budding officials and planners from the region, and the Asian Development Bank. The idea of a regional bank had gained acceptance in ECAFE circles at least as early as 1963, but it was not until President Johnson waved his cheque book in its direction in 1965 that the idea began really to take shape.[11] It opened for business at the end of 1966 with a Japanese president, a headquarters in Manila and capital resources of some $1,250 million. Two-thirds of the capital and 70 per cent of the directors came from within Asia itself, and the two biggest subscribers (Japan and the United States) each control only 16 per cent or 17 per cent of the votes. There is nevertheless a feeling on the left wing that the Bank is an agent of Western interests; the Russians did not in the end subscribe to it after attending one of the preparatory meetings, Cambodia resigned from the Bank, and the Chinese have attacked it savagely.

The fact that the Bank has followed the World Bank and the Americans in placing great emphasis on agriculture rather than on industrialization, and in adopting conventional banking orthodoxy and in caution in lending, has not endeared the Bank to all its customers. Nor have the efforts of Japan to tie her contributions towards the Bank's Special Fund for Agriculture to South-East Asia helped to allay fears of the Bank's becoming an instrument of Japanese economic expansionism... It is true, as a Malaysian minister has said, that the Bank's loans would be 'a drop in the ocean'[12] if they were shared by India and Pakistan, and since the initial lending resources of the Bank in its early years do not exceed £30 million a year there is bound to be either jealousy or disappointment over the size and distribution of the Bank's loans. The Bank thus reflects the underlying contradictions of ECAFE itself, and one is tempted to predict that at some point it will become a South-East Asian Development Bank.[13]

For Japan, taking the lead in launching the Asian Development Bank was the culmination of a number of efforts to give financial and technical help to the developing countries of Asia. As the only developed country in the entire continent, Japan is envied and admired by other Asians, but as the only power in recent history to have conquered large parts of Asia by force, Japan is also distrusted. It will probably take the passing of another generation, say twenty years, before the Japanese are fully accepted again in the countries of South-East Asia which they ruled in the early 1940s.[14] Yet Japanese assistance to the rest of Asia is now second in importance only to American, and its relative significance is bound to grow as US aid falls away in future. The dilemma which the Japanese face in their Asian diplomacy is thus a troublesome one.

The Japanese aid story began with the comprehensive war reparations agreements under which the Japanese Government is paying some £600 million over a twenty-two-year period (beginning in 1955 and ending in 1976) to eight of the countries which suffered damage as a result of the Japanese invasions.[15] Japan was then admitted to the Colombo Plan as a donor member and began a regular scheme of foreign aid over and above the war reparations payments. In 1970 Japanese Government aid, including credits on special terms, reached £200 million, while private investment funds and credits to developing countries brought the total outflow from Japan to £650 million.[16]

Some 80 per cent of these funds are directed to the countries of South and East Asia, and Japan now accepts, in donor circles, a special responsibility for this area. As a former director of the Japanese Foreign Ministry's Economic Cooperation Bureau explained a few years ago:

It is ... natural that we, as a close neighbour, are concerned with the economic, political and social stability and progress of the countries in the (South and East Asian) region, which depend very much upon the successful achievement of their development objectives. We are much concerned, for it is in this region of the world where the widest gap exists between the peoples' pressing desire for higher standards of living and the hard conditions that actually surround them. If our experiences and resources are of any use for accelerating the economic development of the region, it would be in the interest of Japan as well as the countries in the region. We cannot live alone; we must live happily with our neighbours. It is for this reason that we have been keenly interested in development assistance to our neighbouring countries and have been doing our utmost to expand such assistance. In short, our economic cooperation with South Asian countries is inspired and strengthened by our fundamental recognition that we belong to Asia and are associated with our Asian neighbours by a solid bondage of sympathy, friendship and mutual interest.[17]

Indeed, it is fair to say that South Korea, Taiwan and the Philippines represent an 'inner ring' of clients for Japanese aid, the South-East Asian countries representing a second area of special interest. Japan is a member of the Aid-India Club, but is unlikely to increase its contributions to a country of which it has no experience, and which many Japanese regard as lacking in determination to change. In 1966 Mr Sato, the Japanese prime minister, convened the first annual ministerial conference on the Economic Development of South-East Asia, and this has since become a regular framework for Japanese aid to the area – serving for Japan the purpose which the Colombo Plan fulfilled for Britain and the other Anglo-Saxon Commonwealth countries.[18] These meetings are not always harmonious; the Japanese foreign minister had to endure at one of them a lecture by President Marcos of the Philippines on the evils of economic colonialism in Asia, and the *Manila Daily Bulletin* headline after the second of these Japanese-sponsored ministerial conferences in 1967, was: 'BANZAI! Japan Rules the SEA'. Nasty memories of the Greater East Asia Co-Prosperity Sphere of the 1940s are quickly recalled, although its defect lay not in the idea of co-prosperity as such, only in its imposition by force against the others' will. But in the long run these economic relations between Japan and South-East Asia are likely to grow.

Less than one quarter of Japan's foreign trade is conducted with the developing countries of South and East Asia, however, and the single market of the United States is thus more important to her. Japan is unfortunate in being the only leading industrial nation so geographically remote from the others, and Japanese businessmen begin to tremble at the least wind of protectionism (or regional integrationism) in North America and Europe. Professor Kojima Kiyoshi, the Hitotsubashi University economist, has proposed a Pacific Free Trade Area (PAFTA) to embrace Canada, the United States, Japan, Australia and New Zealand.[19] Such a grouping would greatly increase trade and production within its ranks, and its advocates talk of securing for the developing countries of South-East Asia some kind of associate status encouraging them to sell more of their raw materials and simple manufactures to the five advanced Pacific nations in return for heavy manufactures. Tariff preferences and special aid arrangements are envisaged.

A five-nation conference of interested academic, official and business leaders is now organized every year by the advocates of this line of thinking, and the Japanese Government (especially under the foreign ministership of Miki Takeo) has committed itself to promoting the concept of an 'Asian-Pacific region'.[20] But these are only the preliminary moves in a development which may take decades to materialize. The globalism of American trade policy makes PAFTA an unlikely candidate for United States' support, and even within the smaller trio (Japan, Australia and New Zealand) the agricultural protectionism of the former and the industrial protectionism of the latter two render PAFTA a hard row to hoe.[21] It has been suggested that two preliminary organizations be established: one for Pacific trade and development (to be a counterpart of the OECD in Paris), and a Pacific bank of settlement to reduce the pressure on the dollar in the Pacific area, again in imitation of Europe. Even if they are premature, the foundations are being laid for collaboration along these lines. In 1967 private businessmen from Japan, Canada, Australia, New Zealand and the United States formed a Pacific Basin Economic Cooperation Committee; though primarily interested in investment (and especially in joint development schemes for New Guinea and Nauru) this formal organization is a sign of the permanency of the closer links which are only now beginning to be forged.

The formation of international groupings within South and East Asia is thus progressing slowly, if at all. But the developing countries of the region (i.e. excluding Japan) do have a common interest, along with Africa and Latin America, in bringing pressure on the industrialized countries (of the West as well as in communist Europe) to improve the international climate for their own economic development. The force behind this is the passionate sense of grievance which most Asian leaders feel towards the West, and which has been put most articulately by the prime minister of Singapore, Lee Kuan Yew:

Africans and Asians have been exploited for more than three centuries as economic serfs to produce the raw materials that freed the industries of Europe and America and as captive markets for the manufactured products of these industries. Without Asia and Africa, the West would never have accumulated the wealth and capital it has used to create its rich, industrial societies. Must we, the dispossessed, the under-developed, unite to extract compensation for all the exploitation and indignities that we have suffered in the last 400 years; must we have to compel the rich nations to repay the debt they owe the non-white people for their present wealth ?[22]

Many Westerners would feel that this is an exaggerated statement, and yet an objective examination of the facts of our international economic system reveals enough to invest Lee Kuan Yew's analysis with some justice. Pierre Jalée, in his book *The Pillage of the Third World*, has outlined the way in which the international capitalist system works inevitably to the benefit of its rich and powerful members: political imperialism may have had its day, but economic imperialism (what Sukarno used to call neo-colonialism) continues. Indeed, Western imperialism is now seen not as a form of political domination which can be ended by creating new nationalist governments, but rather as a deeply-etched pattern of economic relations which requires a combination of lengthy social revolution and complex universal international agreement to alter.

Such complaints by the developing countries of Asia, voiced in ECAFE and other forums, reinforced the similar demands from the Latin American and African countries and helped lead to the first United Nations Conference on Trade and Development in Geneva in 1964. With considerable reluctance the Western nations there agreed to cooperate in a new United Nations organization, now known as UNCTAD, to deal with these problems: UNCTAD has become in one sense the trade union of the South, in another sense the forum for the North-South debate about the development gap and world economic reform.

The principal theme of the first two UNCTAD conferences (the second was held in New Delhi in 1968) was the so-called Prebisch thesis. Dr Raul Prebisch, a distinguished Argentinian economist who had been U Nyun's opposite number in the United Nations' Economic Commission for Latin America, was appointed the first Secretary-General of UNCTAD, and, in collaboration with a team of economists from the South – including Asia – he propounded a basis for the debate which has raged ever since. He calculated that if (as the United Nations had already agreed when it hopefully declared that the 1960s would be a 'Development Decade') economic growth in the South were to be maintained at 5 per cent a year, then the need for the import of capital goods from the North would create, in the light of existing export trends in the South, a trade gap between North and South which by 1970 would reach about £8,000 million. To meet this gap, Prebisch proposed three concurrent courses of action: to raise the world price of the primary commodities which the South sells to the North, to increase the sale of simple manufactured goods from the South to the North, and to augment the North's aid to the South to reach the level of 1 per cent of the North's income.[23]

Each of these three programmes is of immense importance to Asia. There are some commodities – notably tin, rubber, copra, tea, jute and rice – of which Asia is by far the largest producer. But the developed world of the North is divided among those (notably the 'Anglo-Saxons') who seek to maintain a large element of free trade in commodities, and those (France and the Soviet Bloc) who would prefer a deliberate planned organization of markets for them. Until this question is resolved, effective action on world commodities is impossible. Prebisch hoped to secure international price-fixing and production-controlling agreements between consumers and producers of the principal tropical commodities, to prevail on the North to extend the subsidies by which it protects its own farmers to the benefit of producers of temperate primary commodities in the South as well, and to squeeze from the North some kind of compensatory financial contribution if neither of these schemes succeeded in improving the South's terms of trade.[24] There is now a Sugar Agreement and a draft Cocoa Agreement (of more interest to Africa and Latin America than to Asia), but this part of Prebisch's programme has failed to gain overall approval. Meanwhile Asian governments are themselves beginning to take the initiative more and more to form the initial producers' cartel which is the starting point for an international agreement on minimum prices (rubber and copra being two such candidates).

In the case of manufacturers, the Prebisch argument is that since these are going to provide the South with its fastest-growing source of the means with which to pay for Northern machinery, the North ought to give them privileged entry into its domestic markets. All of the North, in fact, ought to give tariff preferences on manufactured goods to all of the South, without demanding reciprocal concessions which would defeat their purpose. Since the West hopes gradually to reduce the general level of its tariffs, through such negotiations as the recent 'Kennedy Round' in the GATT (General Agreement on Trade and Tariffs), the value of tariff preferences would tend to diminish, and American officials have calulated that the system proposed by Prebisch would yield to the South additional exports of manufactures to the extent of only £250 million a year, representing a 15 per cent increase over present levels (and the equivalent in effect merely to a 10 per cent increase in North-South aid).[25] It is nevertheless now accepted in principle, since the New Delhi UNCTAD Conference, and was formally instituted by the North in 1971–2.[26] The South hopes that its new preferences would induce more Northern manufacturers to invest funds and know-how in Southern industry.

One important consideration in the preference-and-commodity-debates in UNCTAD is the threat of contagion of exclusive regional preference systems. The privileged entry of African producers into the European Economic Community market has goaded Latin Americans into seeking compensatory favoured access to the United States' market, and this would perhaps lead the world into sterile 'vertical' compartmentalization (in which Asia, with only the Soviet Union and Japan to look to as potential patrons, would come off worst). In fact, Asia has more to gain from manufactures preferences than the other two Southern continents, since it includes the most successful exporters of manufactured goods: Hong Kong (responsible for one fifth of the South's total), India (10 per cent), the Philippines, Pakistan, South Korea and Taiwan (each $2\frac{1}{2}$ to 5 per cent).[27] A corollary to preferences in the Prebisch proposals for increasing Southern exports of manufactures is the programme to boost industrial production and exports in the South on a regional basis, along the lines discussed in ECAFE. But this is taking longer to realize.[28]

The third part of the Prebisch remedial programme is the least controversial of all, since the North finds it easier to fork out money than to adjust its sensitive and complex economics to changes in the trading system. It was agreed at New Delhi that the North would work towards the target of 1 per cent of gross national product (which would mean swelling the present level of aid by some 50 per cent) but without any target date. 1968 was after all a bad year in which to talk about increases in the level of aid.

Ministers of the developing countries in Asia met in Bangkok in 1967 to prepare their contribution to the meeting of all developing countries at Algiers on the eve of the second UNCTAD Conference in New Delhi. The so-called Algiers Charter, which set out the demands of the South, was something of a compromise between the Asian and the other points of view. Each individual country in the South has a slightly different package of economic self-interest, and it is perhaps natural that the only basis on which they can agree is the maximum for everybody. For the South to be fully successful in UNCTAD requires a degree of co-ordination in leadership and in bargaining strategy which it has not yet been able to manifest.

In the early days of UNCTAD the initiative from the South was very much in the hands of India (whose brilliant but disdainful scholar-bureaucrat K. B. Lall could be said for a time to have operated as the acknowledged ambassador in Europe of the entire South) and a trio of the larger Latin American states. But as the Prebisch debate got into its stride, and as each country in the South became aware of its particular interests as they would be affected by the Prebisch proposals, the assumption that India could speak for the South, or even for Asia, became progressively more dangerous. There were times at the New Delhi UNCTAD Conference when the capitalists and communists of the white North were able to sit back and observe while the Asians, Africans and Latins strove to maintain their fragile united front. Unexpectedly, one of Asia's additional burdens in economic cooperation is the strain of leading this awkward coalition of the South.

Part Three: The Spectators

Chapter Twenty

The Vietnam War

THE relations between Asia and the outside world, including both the West and the Soviet Union, have become progressively dominated and distorted by the war in Vietnam, which must rank as the bloodiest and costliest ever to be waged within one small country. Most of the issues discussed in this book can be found at work in the succession of accidents, errors and mis-understandings which brought this conflict to its final pitch of horror, since Vietnam has more than its share of indigenous discord on grounds of race, religion, language, ideology, borders, culture, class and poverty. To all this has been added foreign involvement, not only by the bigger Asian powers in the area, China and Japan, but also by the leading nations of the white world – France, Britain, the Soviet Union and the United States.

At least four separate wars have thus coalesced in this un-fortunate country: a civil war among the Vietnamese themselves, a war of independence by the Vietnamese against foreign armies, an international ideological war between communism and capital-ism, and an international war to decide the balance of power between China and the United States in the Asian continent as a whole during the rest of this century. This list omits a number of smaller scores which are being settled amidst the general con-fusion. The war has become a nightmarish compound of the pre-modern, medieval brutality of some of the indigenous participants (symbolized in the almost ritual disembowelling and severing of the genitals before death, of which the authenticated cases are legion) with the science-fiction atrocities made possible by the chemical and electronic products of the great American corporations (symbolized in the extravagant use of napalm and defoliatory poisons on a larger scale). Over three-quarters of a million lives have been lost in all the fighting that has beset Vietnam during the past two decades.[1]

The cost of the war to the American tax-payer is generally

estimated at almost £12,000 million a year, or £32 million a day: almost equivalent to the combined budgets, both current and capital account, of the governments of China, India and Japan with more than 1,350 million citizens to care for. Another calculation puts the financial drain of the war at $3\frac{1}{2}$ per cent of the American gross national product. It costs £100,000 to kill one communist guerrilla fighter, the Americans find, in a country where the average *per capita* income is no more than £30 a year. Such are the paradoxes and the entangled agonies of a war which has stood between Asian-European understanding for one whole generation and has poisoned the atmosphere for the next.

The first strand in the story is the struggle of the Vietnamese to establish their independent nationhood and protect it from divisions within and from Chinese expansionism without. The three parts of Vietnam – Annam, Tonkin and Cochinchina – are sufficiently different in character to find their unity fragile when left to themselves, but at the same time they are sufficiently alike to keep the ideal of that unity a vital factor in Vietnamese politics. French imperial rule brought them together (though it did not integrate them administratively) and succeeded by its repressive nature in facilitating the Vietnamese communists' leadership of the independence movement.*

In the 1940s the struggle against French colonialism merged into the less seriously waged resistance movement against Japanese occupation, in which the communists again took the lead: the Vietminh was founded for this purpose in 1941. Luckily for Ho and his colleagues, the honour of receiving the surrender of the Japanese army in North Vietnam was awarded by the Allies to Nationalist China, whose dislike for French imperialism on its frontiers overrode its distaste for communism. The Chinese Nationalists were in any case officially collaborating then with the Chinese communists, the Soviet Union and the various guerrilla forces in South-East Asia against the Japanese foe. The communist-dominated resistance movement consolidated itself in the north and proclaimed the Democratic Republic of Vietnam in September 1945.

But the southern half of the country was delivered by the

*Ho Chi Minh was a founder member of the French Communist Party in 1920 as well as the Indochina Party in 1930.

Japanese to a British general, who, on instructions from London but contrary to the wishes of some of the American leaders, allowed the French back – and the French had no intention of losing to the communists what they had just, through their stronger Western allies, won back from the Japanese. The resistance against Japan thus merged almost without interruption into another phase of armed resistance to French rule, a phase which formed the setting of Graham Green's novel *The Quiet American*. The French tried to discard the colonialist label by setting up a puppet state in the South under the emperor Bao Dai, but they were too unpopular to make much headway against the Vietminh even with the American military aid which they began to receive in 1950 as the universal cold war opened. In May 1954 General Giap inflicted the humiliating defeat of Dienbienphu on the French army and the French decided to quit.

To save French face and gain time the Western powers used the international Geneva Conference on Korea, already in session, to negotiate a cease-fire and a political settlement. Ho Chi Minh was in full cry after the enemy and saw no reason to halt on the threshold of victory. But the Russians and the Chinese, then acting in concert in a bid to re-establish their *bona fides* on the world stage after the damage done by the Korean War, brought immense pressure to bear on the Vietnamese communists to accept a cease-fire: otherwise, they argued, the Americans would certainly intervene. Probably against his better judgment, Ho gave in, and the Geneva Accords of July 1954 brought into existence the present *de facto* border between North and South Vietnam along the 17th parallel. The two sides were to regroup on either side of this line, the French were then to leave in good order and the indigenous authorities in North and South were to hold elections within two years leading to reunification under one Vietnamese government.[2]

But this formula was very much a British-Soviet-Chinese creation, and it was not a genuine product of the agreement of the parties actually involved in the battlefield: moreover the Americans refused to sign it, foreseeing a communist victory in the elections, and the French were in no position to enforce it. From that moment things began to turn against the Vietminh. The trek of almost a million refugees, many of them Catholic, from the north side of the parallel reminded both the Southern Vietnamese and the outside world that the North was not the land of milk and honey which communist propaganda described. The unexpected breathing-space provided by Geneva was exploited by the remarkable Ngo Dinh Diem, a Catholic aristocrat who had been made prime minister by Bao Dai on the eve of Dienbienphu, and who fifteen months later deposed the ineffectual emperor to assume the presidency himself. Diem's resolution provided the non-communist Vietnamese in the South with a rallying point, and the Americans quickly came to his help with military supplies.

But Diem proved in the end inadequate as a standard-bearer for the nationalist, non-communist forces in Vietnam. His first error was to refuse the Vietminh's request to normalize trade and communications between the two halves of the country (as the Geneva Accords had specified). Suspicious of communist intentions, Diem made the parallel into an iron curtain behind which Vietminh frustrations had no outlet save in a more and more cramping dependance upon Soviet and Chinese assistance. Diem then took advantage of the communists' own troubles. In 1956 the leaders in the north had to admit openly their 'errors' in imposing collectivization too hastily and ruthlessly on the Vietnamese farmers, and a minor peasant revolt against Ho's administration at Nghe An had to be militarily crushed. This was grist to the anti-communists' mill, but Diem and his family went to even further extremes in seeking out and liquidating not merely communists but also liberals of various persuasions who for one reason or another disliked the Diem policies. As Philippe Devillers, the French scholar on Vietnam, observes of this period:

> It was thus by its *home* policy that the government of the South finally destroyed the confidence of the population, which it had won during the early years, and practically drove them into revolt and desperation.[3]

The communists naturally fought back, though at first they were probably pressed from Hanoi not to resume the guerrilla fighting: Chinese and Soviet pressure was still at work in the Northern capital, partly because the two wanted the Vietnam situation subordinated to the wider needs (at this time for peaceful co-existence) of the world communist movement, partly perhaps because they recognized the incipient rebelliousness and expansionism of the Vietnamese and welcomed any delay in the country's reunification. But Ho could not remain the hero of Vietnamese nationalism and continue to ignore the plight of his ideological supporters still living in the south. At the end of 1960 the National Liberation Front of South Vietnam was formed, and began organized rebellion against the Diem regime on some scale, carrying a certain amount of 'liberal', non-communist opinion with it but relying on the organizational skills of the communists and the material assistance of the Northern government. By now China had quarrelled with the Soviet Union and was retreating from the 'peaceful co-existence' policy line. The Chinese threw their weight behind the NLF, certainly as a means of checking Ho Chi Minh's empire-building (Ho and Mao did not hit it off together, and Sino-Vietnamese hostility is a matter of history).

The war thus began again, and the Geneva Accords were recognized as abandoned by both sides. Gradually the number of American military, first advisers and then troops of the line, stationed in Vietnam to support Diem grew and grew. There was a notable escalation in the early part of President Kennedy's administration. But Diem was a difficult ally and he did not like the Americans. His domestic policies, for example on land reform and village resettlement, proved less and less effective, and he needlessly antagonized many of the non-communist elements whose support he should have courted. His powerful sister-in-law, Mrs Ngo Dinh Nhu, was openly contemptuous of the Buddhists and told the American reporter David Halberstam, 'It is embarrassing to see people so uncultured claiming to be leaders.'[4] When the Buddhists rebelled against Diem in 1963 they were suppressed unmercifully, and soon afterwards Diem was assassinated: the Americans evidently had a hand in his deposition.

Since then the south has been governed by a *junta* of generals by no means united among themselves and unwilling to give civilian politicians more than a token share of power. Meanwhile the Viet Cong (the guerrillas of the NLF) steadily extended their control over large parts of the South Vietnamese countryside to the point where they probably held three-quarters of it. There were villages which they controlled by night but had to yield to the

Southern forces in the daytime, and they never succeeded in winning any of the large towns or cities.

The leadership in Hanoi, conscious of its previous mistake in failing to follow through its early victories, then resolved on the strategy of throwing in regular units of its army to fight the Americans in positional (as distinct from guerrilla) fighting. Peking advised against this, but in vain, and the result was a further reinforcement of the American forces and the escalation of the war into North Vietnam by American bombing. This intensified the risk of Chinese involvement in the war, but the Chinese and the Americans apparently agreed at one of their regular meetings in Warsaw that the threshold of Chinese military intervention would not be reached until the Americans sent land forces into North Vietnam or bombed either China itself or certain facilities on the China-Vietnam border.

It then began to dawn on the American decision-makers in Washington that they were not going to win the war militarily: their vastly superior equipment remained virtually useless in rural guerrilla warfare, and, unlike the British army in Malaya in the 1950s, the Americans were never really willing to fight at this level. Nor did they dedicate themselves sufficiently to the task of capturing 'hearts and minds', by gaining civilian support from the general population against the Viet Cong. As aliens in culture, race and language, they stood little chance of boosting morale among the non-communist Vietnamese, and the Diem Government and its successors did not do much better. The realization of this began in 1966, when the Americans began to try to secure as graceful a winding-up of the war as possible, and crystallized after the communists' Têt (New Year) offensive in 1968. One attempt to negotiate at the end of 1966 was sabotaged by a combination of American bungling and Vietminh suspiciousness: a later one led to the Paris peace talks. But the Americans were trapped by their own logic and had to deal with an enemy who had sniffed the loss of morale and was tempted to make the most of it.

The result of any cease-fire and political settlement must almost inevitably be the gradual extension of communist control over South Vietnam, since no political leader or group in the south can begin to match the communists for organization, hard work, sense of purpose and concern for the underdog. The mistake of the Americans was to suppose that anything in their power could change this. It is perfectly true, as Dean Rusk and President Johnson never tired of saying, that the Viet Cong and the NLF are not positively supported by more than a minority of the ordinary people of South Vietnam. Organizational control is not the same as popular support. But to start a crusade against the unpopularity of governments is to take on the impossible. As the *Guardian* once put it in a leader, 'A country of 15 million people that needs a million and a quarter troops to maintain its internal security cannot be accepted as a viable political proposition . . .'[5]

No one is going to be able to achieve any lasting progress or reform or development of any kind in Vietnam except the Vietnamese themselves. As bad luck (from the Western viewpoint) would have it, the communists in Vietnam are, for specific reasons of history which have been explained, the best organized political force in the country. There is little that outsiders can do, therefore, but leave it to them to make a success or a mess of it as they will, and to leave the Vietnamese people to effect their own rescue if it *is* a mess. This is what the West has done in the four other countries where a communist administration has come to power without the aid of foreign troops, namely Russia, China, Yugoslavia and Cuba. This is what the Americans must in the end do in Vietnam.

The official American defence of the intervention is threefold. First it is claimed that 'North Vietnam has attacked the independent nation of South Vietnam', in the words of President Johnson. But this is a dubious reading of history, a distortion of the Geneva Accords and an underestimation of the still-surviving force both sides of the parallel of pan-Vietnamese nationalism. The Vietnamese may or may not choose eventually to reunite, and this vision has dimmed over the past decade, but it is still rash to presume that their decision has already been made.[6]

The second claim is that, again in Johnson's phrase, 'Americans and Asians are dying for a world where each people may choose its own path to change.' But thus to oversimplify the extraordinarily complex factors standing between the desires of the individual Vietnamese and their materialization is to invite being laughed out of court. There is no need to defend the Vietminh record, which has its share of incompetence, cruelty and sheer blind insensitivity, to rebut this argument. Devillers has put the matter in a fair perspective:

The fact is that the people of Vietnam have always been caught between Communism and a form of anti-Communism which they could not accept. In the days of the French, they had to choose between Communism and a hated colonial regime; today the Americans give them a choice between Communism and dictatorship of a type which is at one and the same time Fascist and mediaeval.[7]

The so-called elections which the generals of Saigon arranged in 1967 were hardly more genuine an expression of political choice than the elections held in communist countries, and they were staged only in order to prevent the loss of American support. A world in which every people is free to choose its own road would be a fine world to live in, but it is not the world of reality: all an outsider can do is to seek to minimize the external constraints to which every small country is prey. To some extent this American view is coloured by an unduly defensive assessment of communist strength: to assume that the Vietnamese communists would have an easy time running their country as they wish is both to overestimate their capacities and to underrate the Vietnamese people.

The third stage of the American argument is that, whatever the situation in Vietnam itself, the United States is fighting to to save South-East Asia, and even the *tiers monde* as a whole, from both communist and Chinese expansionism. In fact, of course, these are two separate points. The theory is that a communist success in South Vietnam makes it inevitable that the communists will go on to take the neighbouring South-East Asian countries in turn: the 'domino theory'. But one must consider each case in its own light. A Viet Cong victory in South Vietnam would certainly jeopardize the right-wing governments in both Laos and Cambodia. This is because both countries are extremely vulnerable to infiltration and subversion from Vietnam, especially a united and internally peaceful Vietnam enabled to resume its old dreams of hegemony over the whole of the former French Indochina. Even the north-eastern provinces of Thailand, which in some ways are closer to Laos than to the Bangkok delta, would come under strong pressure.

It is possible that Vietnamese expansionism might succeed, in the absence of superior indigenous non-communist forces in either place, in installing communist or pro-communist governments in Vientiane and Phnom-penh. (Whether they would be dutifully obedient satellites of Hanoi, given the triangular stresses and strains between the Vietminh, the NLF and the Chinese,[8] not to mention the Russians, is another matter.) But the question whether communist subversion would then succeed in the main body of Thailand, in Burma, in Malaysia and Singapore (to mention only the peninsular countries most vulnerable to frontier infiltration) is very different. Burma is susceptible, but to Chinese rather than Vietnamese expansionism, and one cannot see that the Vietnam war has really reduced the chances of Chinese interference in Burma. The others are not so vulnerable: they enjoy relatively effective indigenous governments, with some tradition behind them and, in the case of Malaysia and Singapore, with recent experience of communist insurgency that has hardened public opinion against it. Land tenure is not a serious problem in those countries, and they are enjoying something of an economic boom – a boom that disproportionately benefits the already well-off, it is true, but that does give the ordinary farmer and urban dweller *some* stake in the *status quo*. It is extremely unlikely that these three countries will cross the iron curtain merely as a result of the Viet Cong winning in Saigon.[9]

Certainly China and the Vietnamese communists will not abandon their ambitions to extend their influence in South-East Asia at the West's expense. But the effort expended in the hopeless attempt to 'save' South Vietnam would have been better applied to promoting development in countries where there is already a viable political system capable of resisting communist pressure.

The application of Vietnam to the question of communist subversion not merely in South-East Asia but in the entire developing world is usually based by the Americans on the so-called Lin Piao thesis, which in this view is seen as a blueprint for worldwide revolt in the *tiers monde* as a preliminary to a communist

attack on the industrialized centres of capitalism in Western
Europe and North America.[10] But this interpretation is not
self-evident, and it is more natural to regard this long article by
Lin Piao as a cautionary exhortation, expressed in the flamboyant
style of the Chinese communists, against starting a revolution
before its groundwork has been properly completed.[11] It seems
unnecessarily diffident to suppose that the *tiers monde* is so frail
that it timidly waits for the next gust of communist wind to fall
down.

More recently the Americans have been better able to find
justification for their intervention in Vietnam in the belated
expressions of support from the non-communist states. Most of
these are horrified by the Americans' use of a steam-hammer to
crack such a tiny nut, and they resent many aspects of the
American presence in Asia. Ambassador Reischauer told the
Senate Foreign Relations Committee in 1967 that the Japanese had
'an instinctive revulsion at seeing what is essentially a Caucasian
nation with superior weapons fighting Asian people without those
weapons'.[12] But they are also aware that America is their last
available source of external help in the event of any future
communist *putsch*. The American thwarting of communist plans
in Vietnam has indeed 'bought time' for them to consolidate
themselves without the distraction of external threats. The
Indian, Burmese, Singaporean, Malaysian, Thai, Philippine and
Cambodian governments have all made this clear, in private if
not in public, to Washington.

But to some extent they are the victims of the Americans'
own propaganda in this: it was the Americans who elevated the
Vietnamese conflict to such strategic importance for the 'free
world', and it is not surprising that some Asian politicians,
engrossed in their own domestic affairs and relatively ignorant
of the real state of play in Vietnam or its neighbours (as are the
American leaders too), are vaguely worried at the prospect of an
American withdrawal. If it were a question of a retreat into
Fortress America, a return to the isolationism of the 1920s, then
these fears would have substance. But the American involvement
in Asia is now too great and too diffuse to be capable of sudden
voluntary abandonment.

Indeed, the very opposite argument has been advanced by

Prime Minister Lee Kuan Yew of Singapore, that the present balance of power in Asia is 'too directly dependent on an American intervention on so prodigious a scale that it cannot go on indefinitely'.[13] In other words, the Americans have played their highest trump card too early, and risk losing not only the game but the rubber as well. The view is gaining ground among Asian scholars that the American analysis of the Vietnam problem was a fundamental misapprehension. Violence is unavoidable at the pre-nation-state stage of political development which Vietnam, in common with the rest of South-East Asia, has reached.[14] The paradox is well put by the Japanese writer Sakamoto Yoshikazu, that the Americans are 'attempting the systematic destruction of a traditional society in Vietnam as a means of countering the destruction of that society by the indigenous forces of revolution'.[15]

Chapter Twenty-One

The Western Burden

> Watch out for English and Americans,
> The enemy of all nations.
> They commit the most heinous crimes
> Against the Asian people....
> Smash them to pieces!

THE lyric could easily be a Chinese communist chant: in fact it is a song which the Japanese popularized in South-East Asia during the Second World War, and which was revived in Indonesia during the *konfrontasi* of 1964–5. Distrust of the West is widespread in Asia, and not merely among communists or those who have had to fight against Western power. A Philippine Congressman opened a recent conference of the Asian Parliamentarians' Union with a speech in which he belaboured the West for pretending to decolonize while in fact keeping Asian countries dependent on it economically and even politically: citing the conflicts over Vietnam, Korea, Taiwan, Kashmir and Sabah, he thundered that, 'The West, one way or the other, contributed greatly to the aggravation of all these strifes'.[1]

But Congressman Mercado is an extremist in this respect. The Singapore foreign minister, S. Rajaratnam, spoke for a more dispassionate view which is now gaining ground among reflective Asians when he declared that, 'Today Asians live in fear not of Western imperialism, but of one another's imperialism.'[2] Many Europeans still feel embarrassed, even guilty about their colonial past, and Arnold Toynbee has expressed the opinion that the West must expect to account for some at least of its misdeeds: 'I have a foreboding that our twentieth-century Western world may be required to pay reparations at compound interest for the sins against China that the nineteenth-century Western world committed'.[3]

But Asian thinkers are themselves looking at the historical record with less emotion, and the considered judgment of Burma's first prime minister, Ba Maw, is representative of the change of climate:

> We are in a position now to take a complete view of colonialism or imperialism, to see the brutal truth that colonialism was historically right and progressive in certain regions under certain conditions, but by the working of the same historical laws it has now become in every instance an ultimate crime against humanity. So the British coming to Burma a hundred years or so ago was a historical necessity to pull us out of the ruts in which we had long lost our way, and their leaving also was a historical necessity; and the Burmese revolt against them also was such a necessity.[4]

There are a few tiny outposts of Western colonialism left in Asia. Hong Kong is the most important of these, but everyone knows that it remains under British administration only because the Peking Government is not yet ready to do without the economic gains which accrue to it through this remarkably successful free market and financial centre. Macao, Hong Kong's pale shadow on the further side of the Pearl River estuary, has already been taken over by its communist elements, although the superficialities of Portuguese sovereignty are preserved for similar reasons (Macao makes a fortune out of the gold trade). The Portuguese flag is also flying still in Timor, where Indonesia shares an island with Portugal and has refrained as yet from imitating India's march on Goa.[5] All these anomalous survivals from the European empires have this in common, that they would not stand for a single day if China or Indonesia were once determined to end them. The tension between Japan on the one hand and America and Russia on the other, over the latters' continued occupation of Okinawa and some northern islands, is not because the basic sovereignty of these places is questioned, and President Nixon has agreed to return Okinawa in 1972. Nor has the American or British position in some of the smaller islands and chains in the Pacific and Indian Oceans (the new colony called the British Indian Ocean Territory,[6] for instance, or Wake in the central Pacific) seriously troubled Asian opinion as yet. The colonial page of history has been turned, and a different agenda is now engaging Asian politicians.

Indeed, there has been a long enough interval since the formal withdrawal of the colonial powers for a certain *rap-*

prochement to have taken place. Now that the West Irian dispute
is out of the way, the Dutch are welcomed in Indonesia – as
advisers, investors and patrons – more than other Western
nationals, since they do, after all, have more in common with
the Indonesians. The continued French links with Indochina and
the British connection with India, Pakistan, Ceylon and Malaysia
are even stronger, particularly in the form of military aid,
language training, commerce and investment and in intellectual
life in general. The Commonwealth has not proved a very
successful institution in Asia, whatever its achievements in
Africa: Nehru made the multi-racial Commonwealth possible
in the first place by agreeing, against some opposition within the
Congress Party, to join it after independence, but it was never
able to contain the fierce enmity between India and Pakistan, and
the refusal of Burma to follow Nehru's lead left the association
of the former British possessions without formal expression.
More recently the Commonwealth link proved too weak to
prevent a diplomatic rupture between Malaysia and Pakistan
or the parting of the ways by Singapore and Malaysia. The
sterling devaluation of 1967 caused some irritation in the Asian
Commonwealth, and the tariff preferences are exploited more
effectively by the colony of Hong Kong than by any of the
independent members. When Harold Wilson criticized India's
part in the Kashmir War of 1965, Frank Moraes, the Westernized
editor of the *Times of India*, declared that the Commonwealth
had 'lost its validity and relevance', being 'as anachronistic and
as out of date as aspidistras and antimacassars'.[7] The Asian
prime ministers will still attend the Commonwealth Conferences,
but are unlikely to take any lead in them, regarding them merely
as convenient occasions for *ad hoc* diplomacy.

The Commonwealth does retain an important significance,
however, in Australia and New Zealand, those outposts of the
Western world on the edge of Asia. The Australians are sometimes
liked in Asia in a way that Europeans or Americans are not. Their
genuine sense of egalitarianism, their good humour and lack of
patronizing stuffed-shirt airs endear them. Prince Sihanouk
specifically exempted them from his periodic outbursts against
the Anglo-Saxon powers, and even chose Australia to represent
Cambodia's interests in Saigon when its diplomatic links with

that country were broken – an unusual gesture of confidence by an Asian state in a white nation.[8] In the United Nations Economic Commission for Asia and the Far East, Asia's economic parliament, Australia and New Zealand have been designated 'regional members' and are thus allowed to participate in the inner-circle discussions from which Britain, the United States, the Soviet Union and the other Western powers are excluded. The *Bangkok Post* even ran an editorial under the headline 'Australia is Asian'.[9]

The Australian Government dispenses a foreign aid programme worth about £70 million a year, and although 60 per cent of this is channelled into Papua and New Guinea, the eastern half of the island which Indonesia recently acquired from Holland, and which Canberra is grooming for eventual independence, the rest goes mainly to Asia, and Australian and New Zealand aid is welcomed more readily than others'. Australia also earned gratitude in Asia for being the first advanced country to grant non-reciprocal tariff preferences for imports of certain manufactured goods from the developing countries, anticipating the UNCTAD agreement. Economically Australia and New Zealand are increasingly drawn into Asia, with Japan now their second most important trading partner after the United States (but before Britain) and with China already a major buyer of wheat and other products. New Zealand is more closely tied to the British market than Australia, but it is recognized that the eventual shape of things in their region will almost certainly be some form of free trade among the developed Pacific countries (Japan, Australia and New Zealand, possibly with North America as well) involving special relations with the developing countries of South-East Asia.[10]

All this has its cultural implications, raising the question, 'whether the end of European domination in Asia might mean eventually the end of Europe in Australia', as a Canberra professor puts it.[11] The one blot on Australia's copy-book as far as Asians are concerned is, of course, the 'White Australia' policy under which, until quite recently, only white immigrants were admitted. Now there are some 40,000–50,000 non-European Australians (mostly Chinese), and about a thousand new Asian immigrants arrive each year.[12] The city of Darwin has elected a

Chinese mayor, and there is considerable pressure among liberals and intellectuals for a relaxation of these restrictions. In the long run the requirements of labour (and skill and capital) for economic development may force a change,[13] but meanwhile trade union and political circles ensure that no sudden influx is permitted.

The traditional Australian policy regarding its security interests in Asia was that of 'forward defence', meaning the despatch of Australian troops to fight in Korea, Malaysia and Vietnam, but only on the basis of 'powerful friends' (i.e. America and Britain) bearing the main burden of defending South-East Asia from communism. Now that the British are withdrawing their bases from South-East Asia, and the credibility of an American land involvement in the future is diminished by the low cost-effectiveness of the Vietnam intervention, the Australians are puzzled what to do. Their anchor is the ANZUS Treaty of 1951, which was extracted from a reluctant Dulles as the price of an Australian signature to the Japanese Peace Treaty and a guarantee against a resurgence of Japanese nationalism.[14] Now it has become a guarantee against Chinese expansionism (Indonesian expansionism being no longer as seriously feared as in the days of Sukarno). Australia and New Zealand are too small to do more than marginally reinforce whatever Asian governments themselves decide to do about their own defence: probably they will continue to support Malaysia and Singapore with token forces, but more for their psychological value than for any real use, as is the case with the British garrison in Hong Kong. Otherwise it will be left to the United States (supported by Britain), operating from island bases and staging posts, to do whatever it can to prevent the Asian mainland from becoming hostile to the Australasian interest. In the very, *very* long run the only way of ensuring this may be for Australasia to become progressively Asianized, to burgeon into something like a British version of Hawaii – though Britain's unhappy experience with multi-racial immigration has made this less likely in Australia.

The American image in Asia is far bigger than the European or Australian, and is therefore less clearly focussed. The respect which Americans can attract may be judged from the gesture of Prince Sihanouk, who did not often miss opportunities to castigate them, in naming a street in the new port of Sihanoukville 'Avenue J. F. Kennedy'. But anti-American sentiments lurk close to the surface, leading the respected Siamese writer Kukrit Pramoj to declare not long ago, at a time when thousands of United States troops were supposedly helping defend Thai independence, that 'Americans are enemies of the Thai people'.[15] Lee Kuan Yew spoke for many when he offered the opinion that Americans were less understanding and less wise than Britons, adding that if the United States had been the colonial power in Singapore and Malaysia instead of Britain, 'I would have been in jail, probably tortured and dead'.[16]

But the multi-faceted nature of the American personality is recognized. A Filipino, Alfredo Roces, writes of 'the ambiguous double personality of the bungling do-gooder and the efficient exploiter'.[17] The latter aspect of the American presence is, of course, well publicized in Peking's propaganda, and even an independent thinker such as Nirad Chaudhuri can speak of 'an American East India Company presided over by Mr Governor Galbraith.[18]* But the American capacity for self-critisicm comes to the rescue of the image: it was, after all, two American authors who wrote that damning exposure of United States aid and diplomacy in Asia, *The Ugly American*. But the age of satellites and camp-followers is past. Never again will an Asian head of government say, as Ayub Khan said in 1960 of Pakistan, that his country 'has openly and unequivocally cast its lot with the West'.[19]

Asia, in short, is for the Asians, at least in the eyes of a growing number of Western leaders. When Enoch Powell argued his case for withdrawing the British military presence from east of Suez, he explained that:

In Asia ... the eventual limits of Russian and Chinese advance ... will be fixed by a balance of forces which is itself Asiatic ... Every advance or threat of advance ... calls into existence countervailing forces, sometimes nationalist in character, sometimes expansionist, which will ultimately check it ... The ultimate attainment of this equilibrium of forces may at some point be delayed rather than hastened by a Western military presence.[20]

*Kenneth Galbraith, the Harvard economist, was President Kennedy's Ambassador to India.

An American scholar cites Kuomintang China in the 1940s and South Vietnam in the 1960s as examples of how 'a dominant American presence can effectively demoralize indigenous defense forces and disintegrate the political discipline of local élites'.[21]

But the fact remains that most of the smaller nations in Asia, especially those that are divided as Vietnam and Korea are, feel vulnerable to the pressures of their larger neighbours. The Singapore head of state, Inche Yusof bin Ishak, put it clearly in a speech to parliament a few years ago: 'So many of our neighbours and we ourselves would not have had a separate existence if purely Asian forces were to settle the shape of decolonized Asia.'[22] He was referring in Singapore's case to Indonesian interference, but that threat has now receded again and the real difficulty is with two nations whose natural dynamism is now reinforced by communist ideology, namely North Vietnam and China. These are the prospective villains of the piece, at least, in the estimation of many in South-East Asia.

If a Western power is asked by a *bona fide* Asian government, one that is as popular and effective as can reasonably be expected of any government in a modernizing society, to protect it from direct overt aggression or from the violent rebellion of an armed minority encouraged from without, the instinctive reaction of most Western leaders would be sympathetic. But too intimate a Western involvement in the defensive apparatus designed to deter such aggression or subversion defeats the purpose. Ultimately China and her neighbours have to establish their own balance of power, their own equilibrium, based on their particular circumstances and conditions, just as the European powers did in earlier centuries. A Western presence can prevent this organic relationship from developing. It can also lead to a stifling control of local forces, of the kind that provokes this kind of reaction from a sensitive Asian, the Ceylonese Christian, Richard Hensman:

For people in the West it is naturally most difficult to enter sympathetically into the sense of hopelessness, of aimless drifting, of dull resentment, of a loss of identity, of shame, which the most sensitive Asians feel. It is also difficult for them to recognize the fact of Western domination.

In this context 'the West' does not mean democracy, or science, or the music of Mozart, or the Gospel of Jesus Christ, or civilization, or even ordinary men, women and children in Europe and North America. It means contemporary Europe and North America, in so far as they intrude into, destroy and 'asphyxiate' the rest of the world with their power, wealth, their social structure, their objectives and their operative values.

No one doubts that Western civilization is one of the very great civilizations the world has ever known. It is unlikely that its greatness or power of survival is increased by the imposition of Europe and North America on the rest of the world. For such great things as Europe and North America in their creative phases have contributed to the progress and welfare of mankind tribute will undoubtedly be paid to them by the people who will take these things and use them and even develop them. The confining of the power and rule of Europe and America within Europe and America is not going to impoverish the world. Why does the West, as represented by Dean Rusk or Harold Wilson, feel threatened by the democratic spirit in the Third World?[23]

One could argue that this is, in a sense, a racialist view: for a European to defend another European from attack is acceptable, but for him to defend an Asian is unacceptable merely because of the ethnic or cultural difference. President Johnson was always particularly insistent that Americans would sacrifice their lives for any race that was threatened, whether white, yellow, brown or black, and he saw the United States role in Vietnam as superlatively noble in this respect. Why should Asians be left to bully each other on the ground that how they run their continent is their affair? Does not this line of thinking rob us of any possibility of universalism, of the ultimate triumph of ideas over emotions, of the chances of the United Nations slowly growing into the world government which we all need?

The same point is made in a different way by Dr Coral Bell, who remarks that: 'The assumption that the appropriate balance *vis-à-vis* China is a regional balance made up of exclusively Asian powers is based on an unconscious premise that China is, and is likely to remain, just a regional power with primarily Asian interests.'[24] In fact China does not see herself as a merely Asian power – far from it. She is conducting a worldwide battle with the Soviet Union for the allegiance of the Marxist multitudes, she has entered the nuclear club and staked her claim to be the third super-power of the 1980s or 1990s, she is building railways in Africa and organizing revolutions in Latin America. Japan has twice taken on European or American adversaries in modern war; Indonesia once endeavoured to establish a forum for the new emerging forces of the entire world, including Europe and America, as a rival to that Anglo-American creature, the United Nations; and India is bound, in her slower and calmer way, to assume ambitions that are not bounded by the cartographers' label of Asia. The West should not discourage the universalist claims of Asia, but neither should it withdraw completely into its own backyard. Only in an open world can we build the kind of international society we all dream of.

The temptation for the West to become too closely involved has luckily diminished in recent years as we have rid ourselves of the myth of communist superiority. In Reischauer's words, 'Monolithic conspiracy has little future in the soil of Asia's diversity.'[25] A leader in *The Times* recently elaborated the point under the heading, 'Asia Goes Its Own Way', arguing that Asia is not a collection of pieces of blank paper ready to receive any imprint from outside but a series of complex organisms resistant to change except in their own terms, and that Asia is turning away from a horizontal awareness to a vertical one.[26] This analysis can lead to scepticism, as in the remark of an American journalist that, 'Thailand's good fortune appears to be that its Communist guerrillas are no more competent in waging an insurgency campaign than is its government in fighting them'.[27] But it is nearer the truth than the old monolith-conspiracy concept.

As for China, there is little that the West can do to persuade the Maoist regime to a less combative outlook.[28] It is easy to pinpoint the mistakes of the past: the excessive American commitment to the Kuomintang, the over-hasty resumption of United States naval patrols in the Taiwan Straits in 1950, the dog-in-the-manger attitudes of Dulles.[29] But these merely buttressed what was already a conditioning on the Chinese communist side to be suspicious of the West, and they cannot be undone. The Nixon administration's policy is to wait until a less didactic leadership comes to the fore in Peking and to be ready then to do business with it.

The debate in America about how to respond to subversion in the non-communist Asian countries is a more difficult one. In 1962 Nehru asked the American naval and air forces to stand by to help if China launched a full-scale attack, and the same request was made in 1965.[30] The Truman Doctrine of 1947 still stands, that: 'It must be the policy of the United States to support free peoples who are resisting attempted subjugation by armed minorities or by outside pressure.' But as Senator Fulbright has observed, the United States, under President Johnson at least, was 'taking on the role of policeman and provider for all of non-communist Asia',[31] and this is simply beyond the means even of a super-power. Walter Lippmann has called it 'preposterous to think that we can regulate and determine the course of the revolutionary upheaval through which the people of Asia are fated to pass. Our task is to co-exist peaceably and helpfully with them while they find their way.'[32] As Han Suyin loves to remind American audiences, 'after all, it was *you* who started all these wars of national liberation when you fought for *your* independence in 1776.'

The Nixonian riposte to that would be that no one directed the American War of Independence from outside, and that what has to be faced in Asia today is what Robert Scalapino, chief academic supporter of American intervention in Vietnam, calls 'neo-aggression in the form of sponsored national liberation movements'.[33] This question of sponsoring is a matter of fact that could theoretically be tested, but the plain truth is that the relations between native revolutionaries and their foreign supporters are necessarily secretive and ambiguous, and that to judge them one would have not only to be fluent in the relevant languages (Chinese, Russian and Vietnamese, in the case of Vietnam) but also gain access to information which all the governments concerned would dearly like to possess but which would jeopardize the whole rebellion if it became generally known. One is reduced to making the best possible guess, and this is inevitably highly coloured by one's own fundamental ideas about society and how it works. The best view would seem to be that mainly sponsored movements have little chance of success, while mainly indigenous ones are more likely to win. The Viet Cong does not seem to be merely a creation of the Chinese, and that is why the Americans cannot defeat it.[34]

Indeed, if the West tried to oppose every 'national liberation movement' or armed rebellion under whatever name in Asia, it would fall into the trap described by Senator Edward Kennedy, of making Asia 'safe for the mandarins and landlords',[35] which is neither its business nor in its interest. And in the last resort, a piece of plain speaking by the British Labour MP, R. T. Paget contains more common sense than might at first appear: if, he said, there are Asian countries incapable of defending themselves, then 'they do not deserve independence, and I see no reason to believe that a Chinese empire in this part of the world would hurt us'.[36]

There are three possible strategies open to the Americans in Asia: to continue to seek to 'contain' China (without necessarily isolating her, although the one tends to induce the other), to withdraw to off-shore defence positions in the Pacific islands, and Australasia (and in the Philippines and Taiwan as long as they are willing), or a middle course of holding a 'redoubt' on the Asian mainland comprising, perhaps, Malaysia and Thailand.[37] It must be questioned whether the Americans can 'hold' Laos or Cambodia if they cannot defeat the Viet Cong. But they could make a stand against reinforced subversion in Thailand. The risk would be to freeze the socio-political revolution in Thailand and unleash the very forces that it is sought to keep down. This is the continuing debate among the policy-makers of the only Western power which can afford the luxury of an effective Asian policy at all. For the other Western nations the possibilities of influencing Asia one way or the other are minimal, save in the spheres of intellectual and economic life – especially trade, investment and aid.

Chapter Twenty-Two

The Soviet Image

THE interest in Asia of the Soviet Union and its European communist allies has recently quickened. Unlike the West, the USSR is permanently and physically involved with Asia, for not only does it march with China and Mongolia for more than 5,000 miles, but it includes within its own frontiers almost eight million square miles of Asian soil.

The Asian Republics within the Soviet Union – Turkmenistan, Uzbekistan, Tadzhikstan, Kirgizia, Kazakhstan, Siberia and the Soviet Far East – enjoy a rather special significance, for Asia as well as for the Russians. They are at once a fully authentic test-case of the Soviet development model and a Russian window onto the countries of South and East Asia which are the subject of this book. Khrushchev once told an audience in Kirgizia: 'You live in the very centre of Asia. The Soviet Republics of Central Asia are a beacon to all the peoples of the East showing them how to build life in a new way on a Communist basis.'[1]

The achievements have indeed been spectacular, and any visitor to the land of Tamerlaine comes away impressed. The development of industry, the modernization of agriculture and the diffusion of education, public health and welfare are obvious to the eye. The average Soviet Asian is better off than the average Turk, Greek or Spaniard,[2] let alone his fellow-Muslim of Iran or Afghanistan, and an American scholar concludes from a study of various non-monetary indicators of development (industrial production, literacy, infant mortality, newspaper circulation, energy consumption and the like) that whereas these people forty years ago enjoyed standards slightly lower than those prevailing in India and Pakistan today, now they stand at a level comparable to Italy or Japan.[3] The Soviet communists did not vacate the territorial aggression of the Czars, in spite of the promise to do so by Deputy Foreign Minister Karakhan in 1919, nor did they 'repatriate' the Russian

settlers who had gone out to develop these economically backward regions.[4] But they did implement a thorough programme of
economic and social modernization, partly at their own expense,
and they have secured a narrowing of the gap in wealth and living
standards between the Asian and the European parts of the
USSR.

The Russians made their mistakes in Central Asia, and the
model is not a flawless one. The loss of livestock in Kazakhstan
and the ruthless reduction of the nomadic populations in the
course of collectivization in the 1930s must be put on the other
side of the ledger. As Professor Alec Nove remarks in his study
of the Soviet economy:

> To follow the Soviet models of collectivization, to launch a struggle
> with the property-owning peasantry, might have fatal results for Asia
> ... The Soviet industrializing ideology in fact tends to strengthen
> those elements which have contempt for peasants and are all too ready
> to neglect agriculture.[5]

Furthermore the emphasis laid on industrialization is reaching a
point where Russian interests must be sacrificed or else the sense
of local ethnic grievance inflamed. 'Years of industrializing ideology,' a British observer writes, 'are producing dragons' teeth
which could cause considerable embarrassment to the Moscow
ideologues of today. If the Uzbeks and Tadzhiks succeeded, for
example, in pressing home their pleas for a share of the cotton
industry proportional to their raw cotton production the effect
could be serious for the large group of highly skilled Russian
workers in the heavy concentration of the Soviet cotton textile
industry in the "Russian Manchester", i.e. Moscow and Ivanovo
oblasts.'[6] There are stresses and strains behind the Soviet Asian
success story, and other Asians will want to be selective in following its pattern.

But the main price which has to be paid for this material
progress is political. The vital decisions that affect the pace of
modernization in Soviet Asia are made in Moscow by Europeans.
In the Asian Republics themselves the *indigènes* are, to be sure,
encouraged and given high office. The First Secretary is invariably
a local. But the Second Secretary is invariably a European. The
Asians are still not able to fill all the technical and higher admini-

strative and professional posts, and Russian remains the key language for a public career, especially in science and technology, just as English does in India. The element of European Russian control of the modern sectors of Central Asian life would not matter so much, perhaps, and might be accepted as a temporary crutch, were it not for the fact that Asians are excluded from the higher echelons of both Communist Party and Central Government leadership in Moscow, the final seat of power. The Party leadership is, if anything, becoming more Russified than ever before: since the fall of Mukhitdinov there is no Asian voice in the inner circle of the Kremlin.[7]

Nor are the Asians exhibited to the world as full open members of the decision-making Soviet élite: at international conferences, at ECAFE and other United Nations forums, the Soviet delegation is almost always a white European one, and the Soviet Embassies in Asian and other capitals usually lack a representative of the forty million Soviet Asians. Even Russia's claims to participate in the Afro-Asian conferences (grounded in her status as the biggest single Asian landholder, supported by India but almost hysterically opposed by China) are not promoted, as one would have expected, by the choice of Asians to represent the USSR at such gatherings. This is noticed, and a reservation is usually entered on the score-card of the Soviet Asian model. Looked at in another way, the relation between Moscow and the Asian Republics could be represented as almost a colonial, or neo-colonial one. But the Asians have certainly gained economically from Soviet rule, and their relative political powerlessness stems as much from their own recent backwardness as from Russian desire to hold the reins. Two British Sovietologists conclude: 'If we do not call the present relationship colonialism, we ought to invent a new name to describe something which represents subordination and yet is genuinely different from the imperialism of the past.'[8]

In fact the Asian Republics are not seriously involved by the Kremlin in matters of foreign policy in Asia, which seems to be dictated exclusively by considerations of the Russian national interest. It has fluctuated in the past two decades from the relative neglect of the Stalinist era (when relations with Western Europe and America almost monopolized Moscow's attention) to

Nikita Khrushchev's 'discovery' of the third world and the Asian neutralists in the mid-1950s, from the subsequent mild disenchantment to a new recognition of the realities of Asia's development problems and the importance of reducing China's influence in Asia.

The central issue in Russian policy toward Asia is, inevitably, the intentions of China. The Russians have nursed vague fears of the yellow races ever since they were conquered by the 'Golden Hordes' of the Mongols (and they are, after all, the only European power to have suffered defeat at the hands of a 'yellow' power – the Russo-Japanese war of 1905). This underlying hostility came to the surface in the nineteenth century as Tsarist Russia expanded relentlessly eastwards through Central Asia and Siberia to the shores of the Pacific Ocean, mostly at the expense of the titular claims of Chinese sovereignty. Since the Russians never absorbed territory actually inhabited by members of the Chinese race, but only the homelands of the smaller minority nationalities such as the Mongols, the Uighurs and the Siberian Eskimos, these Chinese claims must remain shadowy. But the Russian march to the east brought the two countries for the first time into direct physical contact along the longest land border in the world.

When the Bolsheviks came to power, China was in a state of extraordinary ineffectiveness at the early stages of the republican regime, and the first intentions of some of the communist leaders to hand back the gains of Czarist plunder were quickly engulfed in the twin tides of Russian nationalism in its new guise and the sense of modernizing mission towards the backward societies in these regions. Stalin encouraged the Chinese communists, but was abysmally ignorant of their true circumstances and often dispensed disastrous advice. He was sceptical to the end about the chances of Mao Tse-tung's guerrilla forces succeeding, and he assumed that the communist revolution in China would come from a proletarian rather than a peasant movement. His position *vis-à-vis* the Chinese communists and the Kuomintang remained equivocal throughout their long struggle for the government of China.*

*In 1968 a Soviet journalist, Victor Louis, visited Taiwan and talked to Defence Minister Chiang Ching-kuo (the Gerenalissimo's Moscow-trained son and heir, who has a Russian wife), and Chiang senior has talked of a

When Mao emerged victorious, Stalin came to terms with him, but somewhat grudgingly: the economic aid which the Kremlin offered to its new ally was far less than the Chinese had expected, and some of the last vestiges of the former Czarist encroachments on Chinese sovereignty had to wait until the Khrushchev era before being given up.[9] During the 1950s there was a false honeymoon between the Soviet and the Chinese Communist Party, but they never really cooperated and they never really understood each other or worked off the old underlying tensions bequeathed by history. Disagreements soon emerged over the strategy to be employed in spreading universal communism, and it became obvious that the Chinese, with less to lose, were prepared to take more risks and indulge in more nuclear brinkmanship than the Russians, who found that they had acquired a stake in world stability.

The two parties also quarrelled over the economic policies to be applied to China's own development, and eventually Mao challenged Russia's claim to be the principal custodian of the Marxist message. Purely nationalist conflicts of interest came to the surface in the course of the ideological dispute, and the world was reminded that the sovereignty of vast areas of potentially important border lands was still unsettled. All those issues were openly debated in what the Chinese called 'the Great Polemic of the General Line of the International Communist Movement', taking the form of argumentative correspondence between the two parties – the Chinese published it, while the Russians tried to keep it quiet.[10]

The charges and counter-charges were bitter and abusive (the *People's Daily* of Peking called Khrushchev 'a Bible-reading and psalm-singing buffoon').[11] It is inconceivable that the two countries could patch up their quarrel as long as Mao is at the helm in China. But there is still some trade between them, and there is a school of thought in the Chinese Communist Party as well as in the Chinese army that China's interests would be better served by playing down the ideological rift and seeking a resumption of Soviet technical aid. There are circumstances in which a post-Maoist leadership in Peking might seek a limited and partial *détente* with the Soviet Union, but in the long run

joint campaign with the Russians against Mao (see Stanley Karnow's despatch in the *Washington Post*, 4 November 1968).

the two countries are bound to compete for power and influence in Asia.[12]

The immediate arenas for this rivalry are in Mongolia (where the Russians have consolidated their influence at China's expense), and in North Korea and North Vietnam, the two small communist states which border on China. But the Sino-Soviet dispute has been used by these two states and by other communist parties elsewhere as an opportunity to assert their own independence from both Russian and Chinese tutelage.[13] China has only one proven ally, and that is the tiny and isolated outpost of the communist world, Albania.

Japan is another country where Moscow and Peking vie for influence over the small and divided left wing, but the Russians have the advantage of official diplomatic representation in Tokyo. The dispute over the Northern Islands which the USSR occupied at the end of the Second World War, and still rules, presents an emotional territorial issue arousing memories of the ignominious defeat of 1905. This question still stands in the way of a formal peace treaty between Japan and the USSR, but it has not prevented active economic and diplomatic relations. Both sides seem gradually to be working towards a formula for the joint exploitation of some of the untapped mineral and forest resources of the Soviet Far East and Siberia, with Japanese firms supplying both capital and technical skills in return for a proportion of the raw materials which would be produced – especially oil and copper.

As for the developing countries of Asia beyond the Communist *bloc*, the Soviet interest was minimal until the mid-1950s: the story is often retold of Stalin's revealing to Dr Radhakrishnan (who subsequently became President of India) that he believed Ceylon to be a part of India. Khrushchev changed all that, and one of the straws that broke the camel's back in Sino-Soviet relations was his agreement to give massive aid to India, China's rival in Asia. Nehru welcomed this new Russian interest, and the Soviet position in India has now become far more important than either the British or the American.

Indeed, when the Western powers asserted their neutrality in the Rann of Kutch frontier dispute between India and Pakistan in the spring of 1965, Frank Moraes, the influential and pro-

Western editor of the *Times of India*, urged his Government to abandon its policy of non-alignment and to collaborate with the USSR, because the latter's greater involvement in Asia made it more reliable than either Britain or the United States. Subsequently Prime Minister Kosygin presided over the Tashkent conference which endeavoured to conciliate India and Pakistan after their war over Kashmir in 1965. The Russians proved that they were in a better position than anyone else to perform this kind of service, although they were not in the end able to bridge the gulf of hostility and mistrust between India and Pakistan.[14] Since then Moscow openly aided India in helping Bangla Desh to win independence, against strong Chinese criticism.[15]

There are now about forty giant industrial projects which have been put into operation or are under construction in India with Soviet financial and technological assistance, including the Bhilai steel-works, the heavy engineering complex at Ranchi, the oil refineries at Barauni and Koyala and the Bokaro steel project (which the Russians underwrote after the Americans had backed down, as had happened with the Aswan Dam in Egypt). The Russians have made unusual efforts to buy more goods from India to enable her to pay for these projects. To begin with it seemed that the Russians were turning to the Indian cotton mills as an alternative source of low-cost textiles after the Sino-Soviet dispute had interrupted the flow of these from China. But the Soviet Union is now importing more and more complex manufacturers from India, including – if recent negotiations succeed – a very big order of Indian railway wagons. The two Governments have even agreed to co-ordinate these developments by trying to dove-tail their respective five-year plans.[16]

There was some disillusion in India in 1968 when the Russians, following the logic of their situation (as the British and Americans had to before them), began to extend military aid to Pakistan as well as to India in order to avoid being identified with one side or the other in this dispute. Even the commercial relations encounter snags, such as the decision by India on technical grounds not to buy the latest Soviet jet aircraft. The Russians were also annoyed at being refused refueling and supply facilities for their navy in Indian ports, after their substantial provision of military equipment (including missiles, Migs and submarines) to the

Indian armed forces. Yet the Russian stake in India has the look of permanency about it, in spite of the potential embarrassment of the Indian Communist Party's opposition to the Congress Government with which the Russians are dealing and collaborating in all these projects.

It could be said that the main focus of Soviet interest in the developing countries of South and South-East Asia is on India and Pakistan which, together with Iran and Afghanistan, now receive the lion's share of Soviet foreign aid. This is modest, compared with the West's, running at an average of only £50 million or so a year during the past fifteen years, from Russia and Eastern Europe to South and South-East Asia.[17] The Russians have always been interested in the Middle East because they share both frontiers and ethnic and religious communities with that region. Now that China has become a rival and a rebel instead of a client, India must appear as the next best partner for the kinds of commercial exchanges which are of mutual interest to a developed and a developing country. Indian seaports could also give the Soviet Union an outlet by proxy into the Indian Ocean, where the Russians' Pacific fleet of 750 ships and submarines would like to wave the flag, and in any case the interests of Soviet security could not allow India, Pakistan or Bangla Desh to fall under Chinese control.

In South-East Asia the Russians are late arrivals, except in Indonesia where they have had long-standing connections with the communist movement. When President Sukarno wanted in 1960 to build up the country's military strength in order to win West Irian from Dutch rule, the Kremlin decided to take advantage of the Americans' rebuff, and it supplied on credit the Indonesian armed services with sophisticated weapons, planes, warships and military equipment worth about $700 million. When this subsequently helped the Indonesian army to suppress the local communists and seize power on a markedly less radical platform than Sukarno's, the Russians had mixed feelings: they were angry at the setback to progressive forces in the country, but pleased at the fall from grace of China. Since the Indonesians were unable to meet their bills for the military equipment, the Russians have been extremely unforthcoming in meeting requests for further aid.

Here, as in India and Pakistan, the Soviet position approximates more and more closely to the American in seeking a modicum of stability, an emphasis on economic development rather than military adventures, and at all costs the barring of the gates to the Chinese. The cooperation even assumes an overt form, for example at the Haldia oil refinery in West Bengal which is being put up under a tripartite formula with French, Rumanian and Indian interests all involved.[18] (The East European countries follow broadly the Asian politics of the Soviet Union, with minor variations, but they often act at kite-flyers or pioneers in ventures of this kind, which the Russians might later copy if they turn out well.)

There is another forum at which the identity of Soviet and Western interest has become apparent, namely the United Nations Conference on Trade and Development (UNCTAD). Russia supported UNCTAD at a time when the Western powers were opposing it, precisely because it seemed a way of embarrassing them and proving to the Afro-Asian countries that the Soviet Union was more sympathetic to their economic ambitions. But once the organization was launched after the Geneva Conference in 1964, the Russians found themselves put in the dock alongside the West on a number of counts, including the use of state control over internal prices to discourage the expansion of their own market for products of the developing countries, the resale of such products to Western markets at prices which undercut the original producer's, and refusing to commit themselves to the aid target of 1 per cent of gross national product which was ultimately accepted by the West at the second UNCTAD conference in New Delhi in 1968. The Soviet Government has consistently taken the attitude that the present economic backwardness of Asia and Africa is the direct result of Western European imperial exploitation in the past, and that it is the West alone which should pay for the damage – an argument which does not endear it to the Asians. Recently Russian economists have begun to come round to the grave view of the Asian population growth which the West has long urged.[19]

In recent years the Russians have been able to ride a wave of goodwill largely because their aid and trade activities in the area are so new; since they started from such a low base, they are able to show annual improvements far in excess of anything that a Western country can produce. This is now being seen in the smaller countries of South-East Asia where the Soviet Union has until very recently been excluded (in Malaysia, Singapore and the Philippines, for example)[20] or inhibited in exploiting its opportunities (in Thailand, for example, where it has been diplomatically represented for many years but relatively inactive).

Now that the Sino-Soviet split has revealed the Russians as genuine enemies of China, and now that the thaw in the Soviet-Western cold war has begun to be accepted in the outer fringes of Western client states, the Russians are at last being welcomed where previously they were feared. Once more they are delighting new Asian countries with their linguistic finesse and their respectful interest in local traditional culture, two areas of diplomacy in which the Americans do not excel. Bangkok was charmed when the Soviet Embassy produced not merely a pretty Russian girl to interpret in Thai and Russian, but one whose Thai, learnt in Moscow, was more fluent and idiomatic than any Western diplomat's. There are commercial factors involved: Russia has been the biggest single customer for Malaysian rubber for the past seven or eight years.

But soon the Soviet Union's aid and trade activities in these countries will approach their natural ceiling, and then the pressure on it will increase and its political dividends from the investment will tumble. It seems likely in any case that the current Soviet foray into South-East Asia is designed more to help delay the emergence of China as a power in Asia than to lay the foundation of permanent Russian interests or ambitions.[21]

The Russians are still officially anticipating and encouraging the conversion of what its theoreticians now call the 'national democracies' of South and South-East Asia into 'people's democracies'. India and Pakistan, in the analysis of Professor Ulyanovsky of the International Department of the Soviet Central Committee, are countries which have been liberated from imperialism and are friendly towards the Soviet camp, but are still ruled by 'the national bourgeoisie as a whole or else in alliance with the semi-feudal ... land-owners'.[22] The Professor admits that the public sector of Indian and Pakistani industry, to which all Soviet aid is directed, stands as an earnest of potential transformation to a genuinely socialist economy, but in Pakistan it is being 'gradually converted into a means of speeding up the development of privately-owned industrial capitalism', and even in India such tendencies have made themselves felt. Only Burma, in this analysis, receives the accolade of being in the 'vanguard of the forces of national and social liberation for the peoples of Asia . . . as a direct ally of the world socialist system'. But the speeding up of the progress to socialism in this area, whose complexity is at last being recognized in Moscow, does not, in the current Soviet policy line, involve guerrilla warfare or subversion, and Soviet pressure on the Vietnamese comrades has erred on the side of restraint more than of adventurism.

The Russians enjoy certain advantages over Westerners in the image which they project to Asia. In spite of their being the only Europeans to have retained the territorial acquisitions of imperialism, their reputation is one of fiercely opposing colonialism. In spite of their agricultural failures and the narrow range of their industrial successes (by comparison with the West) they are associated still with the dramatic momentum of the earlier years of communist development. Unlike the anarchic individualism of the West, the spirit displayed by Russians abroad is usually one of discipline and purpose, and this strikes a favourable chord in Asia. Above all, the Russians stand for the idea that the exclusive coterie of Western nations is not destined to monopolize the wealth and power of the entire world: if a country on the fringe of Europe, dismissed often enough in the past as barbarian by those in the citadels of Western civilization, can thus challenge that supremacy, and from such a modest base, then there is hope for those even further removed, in Asia.

Yet the wheel is beginning to turn. Now that the Russians have forced their way into the citadel, they are tending to forget the others still waiting outside. More and more they are behaving like new members of the Western club, interested in stability and gradual adjustment more than in revolution. And by tacitly claiming parity with the West they incur the same standards of judgment. Most educated Asians are now aware that, while the Soviet Union is more egalitarian than the West and cares more for the material condition of its people, the West is still richer,

freer, more cosmopolitan, more open, more varied, more
sensitive. Adam Malik, the Indonesian foreign minister, wrote
a book in the early 1950s, *Soviet Russia As I Saw It*. He described
the Russians' sense of inferiority, their suspiciousness of foreigners, their reluctance to discuss things frankly, their ignorance
about the outer world. Russia has changed since then, but these
features are still there, more than in the West. They muddy the
Soviet image, and only the native goodwill of the Russian, the
palpable idealism that his new form of society has released in him,
enable it to hold its own in Asia.

Chapter Twenty-Three

Foreign Aid

FOREIGN aid, says the cynic, is a process by which financial resources are transferred from the poor inhabitants of the rich countries to the rich inhabitants of the poor countries. But almost all economists agree that a sizeable proportion of the £1,250 million or so* of official aid that is poured every year into South and East Asia by the governments of the rich countries of the North (including the West, Japan and the Soviet *bloc*) does help Asian economic development. Internationally co-ordinated aid to Asian development is now an accepted part of the world order.

Indeed, until very recently Asia basked in the limelight of the aid drama. Since the end of the Second World War the South and East Asian countries have received about £17,000 million worth of official aid, or roughly one-third of all that has been dispensed throughout the globe. In the early post-war years the principal concern of United States aid was, of course, the Marshall Plan for Europe and the rehabilitation of defeated Japan. But in the 1950s the emphasis shifted away from the rehabilitation

---

*Aid is notoriously difficult to measure, and the lay reader must expect to be confronted with seemingly contradictory figures from different sources. Good records were not kept in the early aid years, and it is a matter of choice where one draws the line between gifts, interest-free or low-interest loans, and loans bearing normal commercial rates of interest. Some aggregate figures include military as well as economic aid, while the latter sometimes embraces all net financial flows including private investment and businessmen's long-term export credits. Further confusion is caused by the difference between amounts of aid budgeted for, pledged and actually disbursed, and between gross disbursements, disbursements net of amortization and disbursements net of interest. Figures for aid by the Soviet countries are ill-documented. The figures used in this chapter do not, unless so specified, include private investment or private credits but only official disbursements, by governments or through such international agencies as the World Bank, to developing countries for economic development purposes.

of the industrialized countries from wartime destruction or neglect to the quite different target of helping the non-industrialized countries to get into the modern development league. The developing countries of South and East Asia have been getting between 40 per cent and 45 per cent of total world aid during the 1960s, far more than either Africa or Latin America.[1] It was the Indian case which started in 1958 the formal international institutionalization of aid in the shape of a consortium of nations aiding India (familiarly known as the Aid-India Club) organized by the World Bank. The club meets regularly to review Indian development and utilization of aid, and for members to pledge their annual contributions. In 1960 Pakistan acquired a consortium and now a number of other developing countries, not all in Asia, are following suit.[2] Nevertheless, in aid per head of population, Asia does rather worse than the other developing continents – an annual £1·50 per head from the West during the three years 1964–6, against £2·35 for Africa and £1·75 for Latin America, according to OECD calculations.[3]

The precise character of foreign aid has never been agreed. Some Asians argue that it is the repayment of an historical debt, because European industrialization and modernization in the nineteenth century was partly built on the exploitation of Asian resources.* This is a theme which the Russians encourage, since it fits in with Marxist-Leninist theory and also reduces their embarrassment at providing aid on a much smaller scale than the West's (since they can say that Eastern Europe played virtually no part in colonial expansion). But most Westerners reject this argument, believing that the economic balance-sheet of colonialism is a much more complex calculation which would have to include the boost to modernization which the colonial experience brought with it. This is also the view of many thoughtful Asians. It is nevertheless easier to arouse feelings of guilt than those of generosity, and the advocates of more aid on both sides of the North-South curtain often play on these. There is a more sophisticated version of the argument, already alluded to in the discussion

---

*A character in a Rabindranath Tagore novel exclaims: 'Let us first fill our country's coffers with stolen goods and then take centuries, like these other countries, to answer for them if we must' (Sandip in *The Home and the World – Ghaire-Baire* – Tauchnitz, Leipzig, 1921, p. 41).

of population problems, which says that the developing countries of today, unlike the pioneers of the nineteenth century, have to live side by side with the already developed and are morally stimulated to adopt their medical and welfare advances as well as physically affected by their medical progress. This makes their dilemma graver than that of the European countries and Japan in the nineteenth century, and in this light the Westerner who argues that every nation has to make its own development sacrifices and should not depend on outside assistance (citing Britain as an example) must appear somewhat callous.

WESTERN AID TO ASIA*
Eight Years 1960–67, Total Official Bilateral Flows in US $ million

Donors		Recipients	
USA	14,103	India	7,347
Japan	1,261	Pakistan	3,084
West Germany	1,076	South Vietnam	2,286
Britain	924	South Korea	1,826
Canada	579	Indonesia	889
Holland	146	Taiwan	616
France	128	Philippines	439
Others†	239	Laos	404
Total	18,456	Thailand	330
		Afghanistan	279

In addition to this bilateral aid the Asian countries mentioned received $1,550 million of aid multilaterally from the UN, World Bank etc., bringing their total aid from the Western world to $20,006 million.

Burma	188
Malaysia	148
Ceylon	145
Cambodia	137
Nepal	103
Ryukyu Is.	97
Hong Kong	26
Singapore	11
Others‡	101
Total	18,456

*The figures given in this table do not include private credits or investment, or military aid.

†i.e., Austria, Denmark, Italy, Norway, Portugal, Sweden, Switzerland and (from 1965 only) Australia.

‡Including aid shared by more than one recipient.

Source: *Geographical Distribution of Financial Flows to Less Developed Countries, 1960–64, 1965 and 1966–67*, Organization for Economic Co-operation and Development, Paris, 1966, 1967 and 1969.

Another argument common among benevolent Westerners is to appeal to the sense of charity, and it is in this context that the Christian churches throughout the Western world are usually in the front of public opinion, urging it to give more for the needy of poorer lands. But there is distaste for this approach, both among Northerners who feel that the development challenge of the *tiers monde* is far too serious to be left to amateurs and church collection boxes, and also among Asians who resent being cast in the role of supplicant.

An object-lesson in the shortcomings of this approach was provided by the Indian famine of 1966–7. Up to February of 1966 the warnings of the experts, both Indian and foreign, about imminent deaths from starvation were taken seriously in the West, and particularly among churchmen and such voluntary organizations as Oxfam. *Pro India* posters appeared in Catholic churches, collecting-boxes were sent round and high-level appeals for charity were made by U Thant and the Pope, among others. But once the tide of additional American Government food shipments had turned, the Indian authorities began to deprecate the scaremongers and the exaggerated predictions – so that well-intentioned leaders at the distance of Europe and America were made to feel that their help was not wanted. It is never easy to give charity tactfully, nor to accept it with grace. As the conservative Indian newspaper, the *Statesman*, commented at the time: 'There is enough waste and gluttony in our own lives to make acceptance of gifts from the children of other countries a dishonourable act.'[4]

Guilt and generosity have in any case proved inadequate motives for aid, and so the appeal of the Western aid lobby is increasingly made to self-interest. Just as the English Victorian élite saw that its own safety and continued prosperity would be better secured if the flagrant injustices and inequalities of early industrial society were removed (thus preventing violent revolution), so, according to this argument, the rich North of tóday's world, which is no bigger than the Britain of 1800 in terms of communications facilities, would be wise to insure against the rebellion of the poor by giving them ground for hope within the existing system. This is the theme of U Thant and of most of the experienced figures in the various aid organizations and lobbies. It is sometimes embellished with racial overtones, since the North (with the important exception of Japan) happens to be white-skinned and the South is not. This argument is a long-term one, but there is a short-term version of it which explains that giving aid is good for the donor nation's current business. About two-thirds of all foreign aid is 'tied' to the goods and services of the donor, and harassed donor government officials frequently deflect domestic criticism of the annual aid hand-out by citing the procurement orders which it yields to manufacturers at home, and the export footholds which it gains in Southern markets.[5] The trouble is that this kind of analysis robs the aid concept of its altruistic and development aspects. One commentator even dismisses aid as 'little more than a means within developed countries of redistributing income towards exporters'.[6] This is far too extreme. There *is* an element of genuine economic sacrifice in foreign aid, but donors who wrap up gifts, loans and private investment all in the same aid package to make it sound bigger have only themselves to blame if they thereby muddy the message.

Meanwhile the self-interest appeal is noted in Asia, and interpreted as evidence of insincerity – whether capitalist or communist. Chinese representatives often warn their fellow-Asians against Soviet and Eastern European aid, attacking the European communists for

lacking a sincere desire to help Asian and African countries develop their independent national economies. They demand that some of these countries become their suppliers of raw materials and even control the economy of other countries; they do not trade at reasonable and mutually beneficial prices ... they sometimes provide the machinery while holding back the key machine units and parts; sometimes they provide equipment while holding back the techniques, trying all they can to make the Asian and African countries economically dependent on them.[7]

In point of fact every aid effort derives from a mixture of these motives, and it would be absurd to dogmatize about them. A potentially more important debate is the effectiveness of aid. There are Westerners like Lord Cromer, ex-Governor of the Bank of England, who regard aid programmes as primarily matters of 'overseas financial patronage',[8] helpful for diplomacy but marginal for development. Enoch Powell, the British Conservative politician, has publicly stated[9] that aid does more harm than good, involving an arrogant imposition of the donor's ideas, values and experience on countries where their appropriateness is questionable. There is an academic school which argues, in the words of Professor P. T. Bauer of the London School of Economics, that foreign aid has led India 'from poverty to pauperism'.[10] All these views coalesce with that already mentioned, namely that development, like revolution, cannot be exported and that, if you want to modernize, then you must gird your own loins and get down to a few decades of hard work, just as Britain, the United States, Japan and the other now industrialized countries had to. The aid debate thus becomes, as the *Economist* once remarked, a '*dialogue de sourds* between the poor, who parrot the need for aid, and the rich, who parrot the need for efficiency'.[11]

This is not merely a Western or Soviet view. There are Asians who doubt the efficacy of aid, and the Chinese communists, of course, have explicitly renounced it since 1960, when Khrushchev recalled all the Soviet experts and abruptly curtailed Russian assistance towards the Chinese Five-Year Plan. Making a virtue of necessity, Mao Tse-Tung has since elaborated the policy of self-reliance of which we have seen examples in earlier chapters. Self-reliance does not explicitly exclude foreign aid, otherwise the Chinese could not, after all, justify the modest but politically effective £10 million-a-year aid programme which they themselves operate for selected developing countries.*

'The policy of self-reliance,' a Chinese communist writer declares, 'is, of course, not a policy that calls for isolation and rejection of foreign aid. . . . However, such economic cooperation must be founded upon the principle of complete equality,

---

*India also runs an aid programme, though on an even more modest scale than China's, and less well organized. She virtually underwrites Bhutanese development, competes in the aid game with China for influence in Nepal, and has extended credits to Indonesia, Ceylon, Burma and some African countries. Pakistan has also extended credits to Indonesia, and Taiwan operates a successful technical assistance programme in Africa designed to sway UN votes on the controversial China seat question. The appeal of the Asian Development Bank stems partly from the fact that each borrower is also a subscriber of capital, so he does not feel entirely at the mercy of others' charity.

mutual benefit and comradely mutual assistance. . . . The correct relationship between self-reliance and foreign aid must place primary emphasis on self-reliance and secondary emphasis on foreign aid. . . . The people must not look outward, extend their hands and depend upon others. . . .'[12] As we have seen earlier, the encouragement of initiative, independence and enterprise is a prime ingredient in the recipe for economic development, and the habit of relying upon foreign resources can be an obstacle to this. As Maurice Zinkin has neatly put it, 'The bootstraps of others are liable to break in the hand.'[13]

Nirad Chaudhuri, the controversial Indian author who recommends his countrymen to give up foreign aid, is scathing about their lack of self-confidence: 'There is nothing which frightens the present Indian ruling class more than the idea of doing anything without the advice and help of white experts.'[14] And now that the full cost and future unreliability of foreign aid has been brought home to Indian opinion, Chaudhuri is no longer preaching in the wilderness. In any event the official Congress Government programme is to become fully self-reliant in the sense of dispensing with aid by the end of the Fifth Plan, in 1979.

Nevertheless the most common attitude prevailing in Asia today, at least outside China, is that aid is helpful if it is given and received in the right manner. A leading Asian communist, Prime Minister Yumzhagin Tsedenbal of Mongolia, has put it in this way:

If one has the power to carry only 70 kilograms, but wishes to carry 120 kilograms, then one carries his maximum 70 and asks others to help carry the reamaining 50. By doing that, it becomes possible to carry more in the same amount of time. It is also possible to save time.[15]

Mao Tse-tung and Enoch Powell would both no doubt retort that the recipient, being human, tends to relax his own efforts by the side of such helpers (and thus increase his own dependence on them), while the donors, being also human, tend to begin to give orders about how the whole operation is to be conducted. But most Asian leaders appear willing to ride this particular tiger, at least for moderate distances. A representative statement of Asian attitudes on this matter was contained in a recent speech by President Suharto of Indonesia:

The largest requirement of our foreign policy in relation to our economic stabilisation programme is to invite foreign capital into the country, both in the form of investments and as loans and other kinds of assistance. I would like to stress here that, by inviting foreign capital, we do not wish to sell ourselves to any foreign country or to any foreign interests. Our long-term strategy for national development remains the exploitation and marshalling of our own national potentials. Our economic growth would be unsound if it were always to depend on foreign assistance. For this reason, foreign capital investments in this country will function only as an instrument to generate our own economic ability. We welcome economic aid, from whatever country it comes, provided such aid is in line with our needs, with conditions we can meet and without political strings harmful to our sovereignty and our dignity as an independent nation.[16]

The vexed question of strings used to preoccupy Asians considerably in the 1950s, and Burma provided an extreme case of a nation so apprehensive about foreign interference that it deliberately refused foreign aid. But it is not easy to draw a strict line between legitimate and improper advice by foreign donors, as Nehru himself acknowledged in an early policy statement in the *Lok Sabha*:

We shall continue to accept help provided there are no strings attached to it and provided our policy is perfectly clear and above board and is not affected by the help we accept. I realize – I frankly admit – that there are always certain risks involved. There may be no apparent risk but our sense of obligation might affect our policy without our knowing it. All I can say is that we should remain wide awake and try to pursue our policy consistently and honestly.

There have been times when one word from us would have brought us many of the good things of life. We preferred not to give that word ... If at any time help from abroad depends upon a variation, howsoever slight, in our policy, we shall relinquish that help completely and prefer starvation and privation to taking such help ...[17]

These fine thoughts were put to the literal test in 1966–7 when the Americans, whose relief wheat shipments were saving thousands of Indians from starvation, felt compelled to place conditions on their economic aid: not political conditions, be it noted, in the sense of abandoning non-alignment or anything like that, but economic policy conditions. The Indian Government was obliged to promise to give private enterprise a freer entry into the fertilizer industry, in view of its own inability to expand the public sector adequately to the agricultural need. Since a donor is obviously entitled to select the programmes which he offers to help financially, there is an element of pressure involved in any aid operation. This has become recognized now, and grudgingly accepted. There is, of course, the possibility of aid having consequences not necessarily intended by either donor or recipient. Since political power usually depends on the control of funds, aid always tends to strengthen the power of the government of the day in the aided country, including its power to resist internal criticism. A Pakistani political scientist has argued, for example, that American aid encouraged the emergence of military dictatorships in Pakistan, Thailand, Korea and Vietnam.[18]

It is not hard to find examples of aid which obstructs rather than promotes developments. Most donor governments prefer to direct their efforts towards specific projects identifiable with their national prestige or towards planned development objectives, rather than simply supply whatever goods or materials the recipient government asks for, and this is a constant drag on aid effectiveness. Thus, under West German project aid India imports German cables for the German steel-mill project, and the same goes for the British, Soviet, French and other foreign-assisted industrial projects. Yet it would be more rational and economic from India's point of view to save the money spent on expensive foreign cables, allocate part of it to importing copper and other cable materials not available domestically and then develop her own cable industry to supply the steel mills etc. 'In other words,' says one commentator, 'aid as now disbursed inhibits self-reliance instead of accelerating it.'[19] Even technical assistance can be both wasteful and harmful for the recipient country if unsuitable techniques are indifferently taught.[20] Hence the growing recognition of Dr Schumacher's 'intermediate technology', or the need for less dramatically advanced new equipment and techniques to be first introduced.

But when all is said and done the area of conflict between aid and self-reliance is rather small. In India, to take the country most often cited in this connection, foreign aid at its height represented only four cents per week per head and it is hard to see this as fatally corrupting the Indian will to self-improvement. A good round estimate of the ratio of aid to total investment in Asian development would be 10 per cent at the most* (it should be remembered that some aid finances consumption rather than investment). To put it another way, foreign aid could very broadly be said so far to have enabled the developing economies of Asia to add another 1 per cent to their annual growth, boosting it, say, from a 'natural' 3 per cent to an actual 4 per cent. Aid is very much less important, therefore, than population growth when it comes to the measurable effect on development. It does nevertheless make up in quality, at least when it is effectively extended, what it lacks in quantity. As a former president of the World Bank put it, aid is 'the all-important leaven for the loaf'.[21]

Unfortunately the aid effort appears to have reached a plateau in the past two or three years, and there is serious doubt whether it can be prevented from declining in future. Three factors have combined to render the West's aid lobby increasingly ineffectual since the mid-fifties. The first is the cease-fire in the Soviet-American cold war. As long as Western politicians could persuade themselves that their aid was preventing India from falling under the influence of the Soviet camp, there was little difficulty in raising domestic support for the expenditure. But now the apparently friendly co-existence of both Soviet and American aid projects in India symbolizes the waning competitiveness of the two super-powers for exclusive influence in Asia. Each one is willing to underwrite to a considerable extent the small client states in which its dominant influence is unchallenged and which are important for its military defence strategy (Mongolia and Thailand, for instance), but flinches from a full commitment to the economic development of the really large nations who refuse to join either of their camps (India, China and Indonesia, for instance).

In any case, what competitive instincts might still survive on Capitol Hill are increasingly suppressed by the knowledge that the tussle is incredibly unequal. Western aid to the South as a whole is running at almost *twenty times* the level of Soviet bloc

*This figure hides a very wide difference between individual countries: 2 per cent for Communist China, about 20 per cent for India and even more for such small favourites of Uncle Sam as Taiwan.

aid – £2,650 million a year against £145 million – and this ratio holds good for Asia. The United Nations calculation is that Soviet bloc aid to developing Asia in the fourteen years 1954–67 amounted to some £1,450 million in terms of commitments[22] (and Western analysts say that only about a third of these commitments actually materialized in disbursement form during that period). By contrast, $3,640 million is what Western bloc aid donors disburse at current levels in fourteen *months*. The 'competition' was thus unreal at the best of times.

The second factor now weighing against aid is the frequency with which aided nations fight wars against each other. In Asia the Indo-Pakistan fighting of 1965, following the Indonesia-Malaysia confrontation of 1963–5, convinced some Americans and Europeans that their charity was merely escalating the level at which (and machinery by which) Asians could kill each other. You can prevent your economic aid from being spent directly on armaments, but if you refuse to sell arms to an aided government on strictly commercial terms (which it is more easily able to meet because your aid is relieving the pressure on its overall budget) then you are accused of tying political strings to your aid.

The third millstone around the aid lobby's neck is the growing awareness of the element of sheer waste and extravagance in aided development. The official charges against Marshal Sarit, the relatively popular and efficient dictator of Thailand from 1958 to 1963, of embezzling over £12 million of state funds during his reign, provided one of the most dramatic pieces of evidence for this, but there is no dearth of it elsewhere. Sukarno's minister in charge of Central Bank affairs openly boasted at his trial in 1968 that he had six wives and twenty-six mistresses, and that he used to pay out millions of dollars to young actresses on presentation of notes signed by Sukarno. But the tradition of making gifts to government officials is a very old one. François Bernier, the French doctor who toured India three hundred years ago, began one of his subsequent reports to the French Court:

In Asia the great are never approached empty-handed. When I had the honour to kiss the garment of the great Mogul Aureng-Zebe, I presented him with eight *roupies* [equivalent to £1 in those days] as a mark of respect; and I offered a knife-case, a fork and a penknife mounted in amber to the illustrious Fazel-Kan, a Minister . . . on whose decision depended the amount of my salary as physician. Though I presume not, My Lord, to introduce new customs into France, yet I cannot be expected, so soon after my return from Hindoustan, to lose all remembrance of the practice just mentioned, and hope I shall be pardoned for hesitating to appear in the presence of a King who inspires me with very different feelings than did Aureng-Zebe . . . without some small offering . . .[23]

In no Asian country today would it cause much surprise for an official to be offered small gifts in the course of his duty, or for a politician to make no distinction between the public and private funds that pass between his hands, or for men in public life to use their office to enrich their familites. Standards are changing, and these practices are becoming less common and less open than before, but it will be decades, even generations, before a public morality of the Scandinavian type could become established in Asia.

Here again our Western criticism is historically ungenerous. Like democracy, incorrupt administration is a relatively new acquisition for the West. Queen Elizabeth I's ministers made personal fortunes out of the public purse: Walpole paid his mistresses with Government money and left office with about as much plunder, in terms of contemporary spending power, as Marshal Sarit of Thailand.[24] Indeed, scholars who have studied various Asian societies and how they work now argue that bureaucratic corruption plays a useful role in countries whose resources do not allow of adequate salaries for civil servants.[25] One should not blindly seek to translate the values of one's own society into another's. Seen in their actual social context, graft and corruption appear less emotive, less obviously harmful. But the US congressman or European legislator who is asked to vote funds for foreign aid programmes is not usually a student of Asian sociology, and the more he reads of bribery and embezzlement in Asia the less he is inclined to be generous with his constituent taxpayers' money.

The same response occurs to waste, even by personally incorrupt Asian officials. When aid money is spent on prestige projects, from steel mills to nuclear reactors, jet airliners to automated factories, the American congressman's sense of duty towards the poor, struggling South is diminished. Paradoxically, the recent recognition of the importance of intermediate technology in developing Asia has the effect of stiffening the same congressman's resistance to large financial handouts destined for application to these more glamorous projects, of which his own district or constituency is also probably short. The governments of the North face growing pressure on their financial resources as the appetites and aspirations of their citizens are aroused. 'Becoming more prosperous,' as Andrew Shonfield has put it, 'does not of itself make countries more generous,'[26] especially when the proposed beneficiaries are so distant. The British public spends more on pet food than it does on foreign aid.

So the yearly struggle between the American President and the American Congress over the amount of the Foreign Aid Bill has now effectively halved the United States contribution to this international effort, from its peak of a few years ago. British aid will be lucky to remain on its current plateau, and will more likely decline as the balance-of-payments saga goes on. Japan and the Continental European nations, less troubled by foreign exchange difficulties, are indeed increasing their aid contributions, but this is not enough to prevent an overall decline in the coming years. Even the Russians are jibbing at higher aid demands. Asia is especially vulnerable to this kind of squeeze, since Europe and North America feel more involved with Africa and Latin America, respectively, than with more distant Asia, and the first victims of the cuts are in India, Pakistan and South-East Asia. Even the World Bank under its new president, former United States Defence Secretary Robert McNamara, has felt obliged to pay relatively less attention to India and Pakistan, more to Africa and South America.[27] Only Japan feels physically involved with developing Asia, and Japan's foreign aid is now virtually fully directed towards Asia, especially South Korea, Taiwan and South-East Asia. But the Japanese *Okurasho** can never replace the United States Treasury as a provider for the development plans of such vast populations.

One response to the dilemma of shrinking aid funds is to concentrate them more ruthlessly on those countries best able to

*Ministry of Finance.

use them. Andrew Shonfield argued some years ago: 'in economic development we must frankly accept the principle of unfair shares'.[28] With only limited funds to offer, it may be better to get the most promising horses past the post of self-generating growth (after which they will in turn be able to join the ranks of the donors) before turning to the more sickly starters: by sharing aid out 'fairly' among all candidates one would be merely dissipating its effect. Already there are success stories to support the strategy of concentration. Taiwan 'graduated' from the United States aid academy on 1 July 1965, when official American handouts ceased. Taiwan is now able to command the development funds it needs from abroad on its own standing, through the normal commercial channels which anyone in the world can use to borrow money if his credit-worthiness is good enough.[29] Other countries in Asia are also chalking up excellent annual economic growth rates, partly as a consequence of large inputs of Western aid, notably South Korea and Thailand. The tragedy is that because the Indian development challenge is so much greater than any other, India's claims for aid priority are ill-received.

Debt servicing has recently become a key issue in the complex aid relationship. Loans extended in the earlier days of aid are now coming up for repayment, and the aggregate volume of them is such that the interest payments have become a heavy burden on the average Asian exchequer. Like a snake eating its own tail, aid could even begin to disappear as the 'reverse flow' of interest and amortization payments approaches the level of new aid disbursements.

By 1968 this reverse flow from the South had passed the £2,750-million-a-year mark, and represented one-fifth of the entire export earnings of all the developing countries put together. By March of 1968 the Government of India's public debt owed overseas stood at Rs 54,000 million (or £2,900 million),[30] or nearly two years' of its entire budgeted revenue from all sources. India's annual overseas debt servicing payments have now reached almost £120 million a year, or a third of its annual non-food aid from abroad. She pays one pound back, as it were, for every three she receives.

Already Indonesia and India have been obliged to seek the

rescheduling or refinancing of debt servicing and their creditors have had to give them more time in which to pay. The need for rescheduling is going to increase, since Western aid has gradually come to include a higher and higher proportion of loans (as distinct from grants or gifts). In the past two or three years Western donors have begun to liberalize the terms of their loans, and Britain and the United States have followed the Chinese example of lending free of interest. But for the next decade or two the atmosphere surrounding the foreign aid operation is likely to be soured somewhat by unwilling defaults.

When the chief spokesman for British industry referred recently to the foreign aid operation as a 'terrible failure' and an 'absolute busted flush',[31] he excepted from his criticisms the activities of private foreign investors in the developing countries, since they had a direct personal stake in success and knew how to run enterprises. Foreign investment is indeed keenly sought after by almost all the Asian governments.

This is not because Asians prefer their factories, mines or plantations to be owned and run by foreigners – far from it. The sentiment of economic nationalism is strong everywhere, from the Philippines where successive administrations have applied the so-called 'Filipino-First' policy designed to winkle foreigners out of their positions of dominance in the economy, to India where for many years foreign interests were prohibited from having a majority holding in new industrial ventures. Japan, it should be noted here, has provided an example in this matter, and has been astonishingly successful in retaining industrial ownership in the hands of her own citizens despite all the blandishments of foreign governments and the giant international corporations.

The ideal of every Asian politician and businessman is to drive out foreign ownership and foreign control of their own national resources. But this is a long-term goal, and meanwhile foreign investment provides three valuable aids to Asian development in the form of capital, technology and managerial and marketing skills. At the end of 1966 the accumulated foreign private investment in developing East and South Asia was estimated at about £1,800 million (less, be it noted, than in either Africa or Latin America). Half of this was British, another third American, with Japan and Germany furnishing the next largest amounts. About one third of the total investment was in manufacturing industry, another quarter in oil: 5 per cent was in mining and the rest in plantations, services, commerce, etc.

Some of this £1,800 million was money that had been invested in colonial days, in tea and rubber estates, for example, and which some of the newly independent governments in the late 1940s and early 1950s would have liked to nationalize. But state take-overs would have offended the former metropolitan powers which remained the chief markets for these products and the chief providers of aid for Asian economic development. In the case of the Philippines the Americans retained special privileges relating to investment and ownership which still prevail, so that they enjoy the same status as Filipino citizens *vis-à-vis* other foreigners.

Most of the new governments had too many other problems on their hands to regard expropriation of foreign assets as a high priority, and in any case they grudged the funds necessary to buy them out. (If they had nationalized without compensation, as Sukarno did with Dutch firms in Indonesia in 1957, then they would have forfeited the sympathy and cooperation of the West as a whole, and virtually closed the door to further new foreign investment: Indonesia did in the end negotiate compensation for these expropriations, and in other cases handed enterprises back to their original foreign owners.) One satisfactory way out would have been for the foreign interests to have been persuaded to sell to indigenous private interests, but the incipient capitalist class in developing Asia has little money to play with and prefers to sink it in enterprises likely to be more profitable and prestigious than agricultural estates.

In any event the fate of the existing investments at the time of independence was largely determined in the end by Asia's need to attract new capital from the same sources, not so much in estates as in mining and industry. These are fields in which local expertise is weak, and there are only two ways of overcoming this obstacle; by retaining ownership and hiring the experts from abroad, or by offering foreign interests ownership and thus giving them an incentive to introduce the expertise and profit from it.

The former course often leads to disappointments because all the risk is on the inexperienced Asian side. The latter is more successful in getting the expertise transmitted, but aggravates the different problem of foreign ownership and control in the Asian economy.

The sophisticated expectation of the advocates of the second course is that the intangible benefits of the transmission cannot be prevented from spreading generally in the host country, and that one just has to be patient. A British firm investing in a synthetic fibre factory in Ceylon will seek to keep its technical secrets to itself. But nowadays almost every foreign investor seeks a local partner to share the risk and help jump the administrative and political hurdles which Asian governments put in the way of new enterprises. Such partners cannot be permanently suppressed, nor can indigenous employees be permanently retained. Sooner or later the Ceylonese shareholders will use their experience gained in this venture to start other concerns, perhaps on their own, and Ceylonese foremen or technicians may eventually resign and go to other, fully Ceylonese-owned, enterprises or even launch their own modest ventures with capital support from friends and family. In the end everyone is satisfied: the Briton gets a reasonable return on his investment, while expertise is brought into Ceylon and spread about.

This view of the foreign investment question is particularly valid when there is a marketing angle as well: if the synthetic fibres are to be shipped to Britain or Australia to meet the demand there for goods formerly supplied by the British factory then this is the best way for Ceylon to get a foothold in a new export market – at first under British patronage but eventually, by the process described above, on its own. Foreign investment can be a piggy-back into foreign markets.

Indeed, one of the motives behind the South's demand in UNCTAD for preferential access to Western markets for its manufactured goods, is to accelerate Western investment in the South to take advantage of lower labour costs. The hope is that if toys made in Britain come to compete in the British market equally with toys made in developing Asia (because both are exempt from import duty, unlike toys coming in from such other developed countries as Germany, Japan or the United States), the British manufacturers will increasingly see the advantage of making their toys in an Indian or a Thai factory where low labour and running costs might ensure a landed cost in Britain less than the British-made product's even with freight charges added. Japanese manufacturers are already extremely active in establishing subsidiaries in this way in Korea, Taiwan and South-East Asia, and so are the Americans.

Most of the Asian governments thus offer attractive terms to new foreign investors, as has been seen in the discussion of industrialization in Chapter 9 above: it is common for them to gain exemption from tax and duties for an initial period as well as protection from competing imports and so forth.

But the same problem of repayments bedevils foreign investment as it does foreign aid. The return of the typical British or Western investment in developing Asia is around 10 per cent on the capital put in, after local tax. Some of this is ploughed back into the enterprise or re-invested elsewhere in the host country. But the foreign investor will want a decent slice of his profit remitted to him in his own hard currency, so that the host government faces an annual claim on its usually limited foreign exchange resources. And if eventually the foreign investor decides to pull out and sell his enterprise to local buyers, he will expect to have his capital repatriated in foreign exchange. These claims on foreign exchange can be extremely serious.

In India's case it has been calculated that foreign investors (whose stake is now about £1,000 million, and who are estimated by Michael Kidron to own a quarter of the modern sector of the Indian economy[32]) drained India of almost £250 million of foreign exchange during the fourteen years 1948–61, their provision of new foreign exchange being only one-third of what they caused to be paid out in profits, royalties, repatriation of capital, etc.[33] This is a heavy price to pay for the inflow of expertise, and it must cause no surprise that the Indian government has rejected foreign investment as a general source of capital. Nevertheless the draft Fourth Plan envisages some £25 million a year of new private investment into India from abroad, and every non-communist country in developing Asia seeks its share of private foreign investment (even the communists seek capital investment from Eastern Europe).

The Indonesians have experimented with a production-sharing formula, by which the profits on foreign investment are taken in the form of an agreed proportion of the products of the enterprise (say nickel or copra). This relieves the Indonesian government of the burden of providing foreign exchange, but it also entails the risk of letting products go out of the country at prices less than the prevailing world market would offer.[34] The formula by which Shell constructed an oil refinery in Thailand, on the basis of running it and sharing the profit for ten years, after which it has to be surrendered to Thai Government ownership, has created much interest in the *tiers monde*.[35] There is no perfect mechanism for balancing the conflicting interests of host country and guest investor. But the degree of overlapping mutual advantage is sufficient to ensure a future for this kind of relationship, one which promotes the interdependence of Asia and the rest of the world, works against the forces of isolationism and narrow nationalism on both sides, and is thus supported by Western governments.

But the annual flow of private investment capital and private export credits to Asia remains far smaller than the annual provision of official economic aid, and it is aid policy which dominates the purely financial aspect of the economic relationship between Asia and the West (and between Asia and the industrialized nations of communist Europe). The aid lobby in Western capitals is now formed by an uncomfortable three-way coalition between liberal idealists who believe, as Robert McNamara declared in his first public speech as President of the World Bank, that 'aid does work, it is not money wasted, it is a sound investment';[36] the near-chauvinistic flag-wavers who see the aid programme as an extension of their foreign ministry budget and a means of twisting Southern arms; and those business interests which have fattened on the aid programme and might not survive without it. Standing against these ill-assorted allies are the growing number of sceptics who doubt the efficacy of aid and want the money spent on more parochial needs including, at one point in 1971, the US Congress.

One can only hope that the coalition will survive, and that this instrument for accelerating world-wide development and modernization, for maintaining the capital flow necessary to that purpose, will not be discarded merely because it has proved disappointing or unsuccessful in a small number of cases. The contribution of aid should not be exaggerated, but neither should it be denied. The report of the Pearson Commission on International Development, recently published under the title *Partners in Development*, should provide encouragement and ammunition to the aid lobby.

Part Four: The Future Programme

Conclusion

ASIA is the least homogeneous of the continents, although we in the West, accustomed to the viewpoint formed when our real encounter began, sometimes fail to recognize it. That encounter happened to be at a time of both cultural and material decline in Asia: hence the whole cycle of imperialism and independence which we have just completed. Only now are we able to resume the relationship in its free natural state after several centuries of distortion. The dicta of Asian intellectuals about the unity of Asia during the period of the Western embrace should not weaken our acknowledgement of this diversity.

When Okakura Kakuzo, the Japanese writer, asserted at the beginning of the century that 'Asia is one ... not even the snowy barriers can interrupt for one moment the broad expanse of love for the Infinite and Universal which is the common thought-inheritance of every Asian race, enabling them to produce all the great religions of the world, and distinguishing them from the maritime peoples of the Mediterranean and Baltic who love to dwell on the particular and to search out the means, not the ends, of life,'[1] he was pushing Western and Asian philosophy into too narrow compartments. Asia differs from Europe most obviously in space (i.e. climate and terrain, and their consequences), and in time (i.e. the historical stage of development, especially in social and economic life), but in all essentials of human thought and life the contrasts are ones of small degree. 'Personally,' said Nehru once, 'I do not believe that any profound difference exists between the Orient and the Occident. Such differences as can be accounted for by history, tradition and geography, exist even among the Asian countries and, in fact, even within the same country.'[2] An editorial in the *Bangkok Post* recently conceded that: 'Historically, Asia – that convenient geopolitical term formed first in Western thinking – has been a loose hodgepodge of isolated, introverted, insular and often xenophobic nation-states ...'[3]

But the Asian countries do at least have this in common, that (with the significant exception of Japan) they are all beginning the painful process of modernization, of transforming the material, technological, social, intellectual and organizational base of their societies. This involves them necessarily in turbulence. No community can undergo such an experience without flashes of violence, without sharp fluctuations in policy and direction. It is not the case, as some Europeans believe, that sound economic growth is an antidote to this instability. Myron Weiner, the pioneer in probing the connections between economic and political revolution in the Asia of our day, observes in *The Politics of Scarcity* that, 'Growth by itself is not only not stabilizing, but often politically unstabilizing.'[4] Society does not change its fabric without a struggle: if there is no struggle, that is a sign that there is no change either. Asians themselves have not fallen into the trap of assuming that material advance is the key. India chose from the beginning to pay a price for the maintenance of a relatively free and open society in a slower rate of economic growth than, say, the Chinese were earlier attaining under communism. But the Cultural Revolution has shown in turn that China too is aiming not merely at more production but more (and more intelligent) producers, which is a different and more difficult goal.

All this means that the nation-states of Asia are far from crystallized: we do not yet know whether the year 2001 will bring one China or twenty-five Chinas, one India or fifteen, nor whether a new state, or a series of states, or a group of a new kind of sub-state unknown to the Western system, will have arrived on the map in those mountainous regions where China, India and South-East Asia meet.

This in turn means that the Asian balance of power is uncertain. Some Asians believe that the 1970s will see the opening of a new 'Asian century' or 'Pacific era' in which a nuclear balance between the three Pacific powers (America, Russia and China – two super-powers and the most convincing candidate till now for the third seat at that table in another few decades) will be the principal pillar of world peace and security. Europe will opt out of the game of world crisis management, the United States will be obliged gradually to disengage from the western shores of the Pacific because of China's growing nuclear strength, and the 'rest of Asia' will seek salvation in some kind of collective self-neutralization.[5] In this scenario the Russians and the Americans would both eventually come to terms with Peking, and we would all live under a three-power directorate, to borrow a Gaullism. But this assumes a great deal about the persistence of centripetal forces in China, which will astound the world if it can remain united after it becomes modern.

Whatever happens, Asia will from now on contribute more to the world stock of art, thought and invention than the desert of the past century or two might suggest. The Japanese philosopher Ienaga Saburo describes the place of Asia in world culture as follows:

> Western culture is not the only human culture. Besides Europe and America there are various different societies and cultures ... But, since the West's modern culture having a world universality and power of diffusion has swept the globe, it has come to be thought that the Western culture which is the womb of that culture is a model form for world history ... Modern culture which had its source in Europe and America does not simply belong to Westerners only, now it is the world's culture ... However, if you say that modern culture is complete and has no lacks that is not all so ... it contains not a few contradictions and lacks deriving from its womb ... It cannot be that Japan can fail to feel the suffering coming from the contradictions and lacks mentioned above. Now the Japanese together with the other peoples of the world are facing the great task of overcoming the contradictions and lacks of modern culture. Today may be said to be the age of the labour pains of giving birth to a new future.[6]

A Chinese scholar tells his Western colleagues that in political matters, 'If we are to be original in Asia, I think we will still be taking over, as it were, from where you left off ...'[7]

There is, of course, a possibility that Asia – or some Asian power – might in the future pay Europe back in its own coin. Ananda Coomaraswamy had an intuition that the post-industrial social idealism of Europe might be threatened 'by an Industrialism or Imperialism of European origin established in the East'.[8] But Japan will not repeat her mistake of swimming against the world current, and China is surely too large and inward-looking to march along this road. We will be unlucky indeed if we have to face total struggle with any of the Asian powers.

They will become, however, at certain levels, more difficult for the West to understand, and some of the superficial veneer of Westernization will fall away as the serious internal transformation begins. The glass curtain of Raghavan Iyer,[9] the silken curtain of Nirad Chaudhuri,[10] the barriers of ignorance and cultural misunderstanding are not going to be raised in our lifetimes. Our universities and even some of our schools are beginning to make a new start on modern Asian studies and languages, but we have a long way to go before we acquire a minimally realistic assessment of Asia. A survey of British opinion recently showed that one Briton in four believed Japan to be under some form of communist or other dictatorship, while only 30 per cent knew that Japan enjoys a democratic political system.[11] Yet Japan is better publicized abroad than any other Asian country precisely because it has come out of the other end of the modernization tunnel. The old prejudices live on, and Tennyson's 'Better fifty years of Europe than a cycle of Cathay' still lingers with Kipling in the European subconscious. The Asia that has lodged in most European minds has been dead for many decades. We will make the future easier if we can search out the Asia that is alive.

Many Europeans have gone to look for it. Marco Polo was lured by gold, later generations of Westerners by the exoticism of the East, by the opportunities it afforded of pleasures which modernization had made illicit or expensive in Europe (notably power over inferiors, ostentatious living and sexual adventurousness).* Svetlana Alliluyeva, the daughter of Stalin, was willing to abandon the paradise of Soviet society for a marriage with an Indian princeling, and Professor J. B. S. Haldane left the sophistication of scientific London for the chance to bare his feet: 'One of my reasons for settling in India was to avoid wearing socks. Sixty years in socks is enough.'[12] But Nora Waln[13] and Lafcadio Hearn[14] are almost the only Westerners ever to have penetrated

---

*The absence of puritanism about sexual promiscuity and homosexuality in most of Asia may have provided an important fascination for many Western sojourners there.

into the life of the Confucian or Sinic world. Only now are we on the verge of an era when young Westerners will go to Asia, as is already happening on a tiny scale in the Peace Corps, in Voluntary Service Overseas, among the hippies and through one or two other exclusive channels, simply to experience a different way of life and to admire the diversity of culture within the human family.

Notes

For full bibliographical details of items given in the Notes and Recommended Further Reading lists, see the Bibliography, p. 424.

INTRODUCTION

1 *The Asia Magazine* 24 March 1963, p. 4; see also Mulk Raj Anand, 'The Concept of an Asian Mind', *Contemporary Indian Literature* October and November 1964, pp. 6, 8.
2 J. O. Thompson, *History of Ancient Geography* (Cambridge Univ. Press, London, 1948), p. 21. I am indebted to Eric C. Dann for the references in this paragraph.
3 *Breakthrough in Burma*, p. 343.
4 *Identity and Change: Towards a National Definition*, p. 80.

CHAPTER 1: BUILDING NEW NATIONS

1 Vittachi, *The Brown Sahib*.
2 *Discovery of India*, p. 43.
3 Dr Subandrio interviewed in *The Times* 18 February 1966.
4 'Pakistan Perspective', *Foreign Affairs* Vol. 38 (July 1960), p. 549.
5 *Bangkok Post*, 20 October 1968.
6 Irfan Habib, 'India Looks At Herself', *The Times Literary Supplement* 28 July 1966. This essay on historiographical nationalism describes the attempts to present India as the original home of the Aryans.
7 *From Empire to Nations* (Cambridge, Mass., 1960), p. 94.
8 Speech of 3 May 1964. Cf. Sjahrir's remark, that 'we Indonesians are the most nationally characterless people in the world.' (*Out of Exile*, p. 125). A Thai politician has observed that 'no people which tolerated three centuries of Dutch rule can really pose a threat to this region' (cited in Gordon, *Dimensions of Conflict in Southeast Asia*, p. 190).
9 Fukutaka Tadashi, 'The Communal Character and Democratic

Development of Farming Villages', *Journal of Social and Political Ideas in Japan* Vol. II, No. 3 (December 1964), p. 87.

10 *Discovery of India*, p. 48. The incident is also described in Moraes, *Jawaharlal Nehru*, pp. 262–3.

11 See Myrdal, *Asian Drama* Vol. I, pp. 119–20.

12 Weatherbee, *Ideology in Indonesia: Sukarno's Indonesian Revolution.*

13 Feith, *Decline of Constitutional Democracy in Indonesia.*

14 Blacker, *The Japanese Enlightenment*, p. 34.

15 *BBC Summary of World Broadcasts* Part III, 2587/A3/2 of 6 October 1967.

16 K. R. Sundar Rajan, *New Statesman* 17 March 1967.

17 *China News Analysis* No. 408, 16 February 1962.

18 *Fukien Daily* editorial of 11 January 1967, translated in *BBC Summary of World Broadcasts*, Part III, 2364/B/14 13 January 1967.

19 Yang Ying-chieh, *Planned Economy* (November 1958) (cited in Donnithorne, *China's Economic System*, p. 460).

20 *People's Daily* Peking 7 February 1958 (see *China News Analysis* No. 217, 21 February 1958).

21 Pan Fu-sheng: see Adams (ed.), *Contemporary China*, p. 161.

22 Donnithorne, op. cit., p. 507.

23 Kweiyang Radio broadcast, 4 June 1967; translated in *BBC Summary of World Broadcasts* Part III, 2485/B/12 of 8 June 1967.

24 Donnithorne, op. cit., p. 504.

25 Schurmann, *Ideology and Organization in Communist China*, Chapter 3.

26 George Moseley (ed.), *The Party and the National Question in China.*

27 Richardson, *Tibet and Its History.*

28 *People's Daily* Peking II January 1958, quoted in MacFarquhar, *The Hundred Flowers Campaign and the Chinese Intellectual*, p. 257.

29 Sir John Strachey, *India* (London 1888), p. 2.

30 *The Times* 2 June, 1956.

31 *The World and the West*, p. 34.

32 Nehru, *The Unity of India* (Lindsay Drummond, London 1941).

33 By Dr R. K. Hazari, *Bangkok Post* 17 November 1967.

34 Verghese, *Design for Tomorrow*, pp. 83–6.

35 *New York Times* 4 November 1966.

36 Quoted in Harrison, *India, the Most Dangerous Decades*, p. 326. See also Weiner, *The Politics of Scarcity*, pp. 205–7.

37 *The Times* 26 September 1967.

38 'The Challenge to Indian Nationalism', *Foreign Affairs* Vol. 34, No. 4, July 1956, p. 622.

39 *Government and Politics in Pakistan* (Karachi 1963), p. 286.
40 T. Maniruzzaman, 'National Integration and Political Development in Pakistan', *Asian Survey* Vol. VII, December 1967, p. 876.
41 Interview in the *Observer* 24 April 1966.
42 See Anne Lapping, 'Pakistan: A Divided Land', *New Society* 15 June 1967.
43 Bouman, *The South Moluccas, Rebellious Province or Occupied State*.
44 O. G. Roeder, 'A Storm Is Brewing', *Far Eastern Economic Review* 18 July 1968, p. 153.
45 Quoted in E. D. Blanche, 'Seeds of Revolt Ripen in West Irian' (A P despatch from Sukarnapura), *Bangkok Post* 1 September 1968.
46 See e.g. Douglas S. Paauw, 'From Colonial to Guided Economy', in McVey (ed.) *Indonesia*, p. 169. But the complaints are not fully justified: Legge, *Central Authority and Regional Autonomy in Indonesia*.
47 Stephens, *Pakistan: Old Country, New Nation*, p. 64.
48 Skinner (ed.), *Local, Ethnic and National Loyalties in Village Indonesia*, p. 11.
49 Nguyen Huu Thai, speaking on 25 August 1965 (quoted in David Marr, 'Political Attitudes and Activities of Young Urban Intellectuals in South Vietnam', *Asian Survey* Vol. VI, May 1966, p. 257).
50 'The Path which Led Me to Leninism', *Selected Works* Vol. IV, Hanoi 1962, p. 450.
51 S. H. Natsogdorj, *Unen*, Ulan Bator, 31 May 1962 (quoted in Paul Hyer, 'The Re-evaluation of Chinggis Khan', *Asian Survey* Vol. VI December 1966, p. 698).
52 Reuter dispatch from Amritsar, 20 August 1962.
53 Sutter, *Indonesianisasi: Politics in a Changing Economy, 1940–55;* see also Johnson (ed), *Economic Nationalism in Old and New States*.
54 'The Indian Road to Equality', *Economic Weekly* Vol. XII, Special Number, June 1960, p. 867.
55 *The Emergence of Indian Nationalism*, p. 351. Cf. Herbert Feith's dictum about the need for nationalism 'as a source of intense personal commitment for those whose norms had been shaken by social uprooting', 'Dynamics of Guided Democracy', in McVey (ed.), *Indonesia*, p. 313.

RECOMMENDED FURTHER READING

Kennedy, *Asian Nationalism in the Twentieth Century*.
Seal, *The Emergence of Indian Nationalism*.
Pye, *Politics, Personality and Nation Building*.

Harrison, *India: The Most Dangerous Decades.*
Skinner, *Local, Ethnic and National Loyalties in Village Indonesia.*
Legge, *Central Authority and Regional Autonomy in Indonesia.*
Vittachi, *The Brown Sahib.*
Silcock, *Towards a Malayan Nation.*
Romulo, *Identity and Change: Towards a National Definition.*
Mason (ed.), *India and Ceylon: Unity and Diversity.*
Weiner (ed.), *State Politics in India.*

CHAPTER 2: HOMO RELIGIOSUS

1 Paul Masson-Oursel, *La Pensée en Orient*, Paris 1949.
2 Basabe, *Japanese Youth Confronts Religion*, Tokyo 1967.
3 *Japan Information Bulletin* Vol. XV No. 14, London, 15 July 1968, p. 110.
4 *In My View*, 1967.
5 *New York Times* 25 July 1966; *The Scotsman* 21 April 1967.
6 *Bangkok Post* 5 July 1966.
7 John Naylor, *Your Stars for 1968 Atlas*, London.
8 Mary Holland, the *Observer* 21 April 1968.
9 *Time and Tide* 9 March 1940 (quoted in Bolitho, *Jinnah*, p. 127).
10 Alisjahbana, *Indonesia: Social and Cultural Revolution*, pp. 32–3. Cf. Achdiat Kartanihardja's novel *The Atheist*.
11 Smith (ed.), *South Asian Politics and Religion*, p. 18.
12 *Asian Drama* Vol. I, p. 103.
13 e.g. A. B. Shah *Weekend Review* New Delhi, 23 March 1968.
14 *The Central Institute of Islamic Research*, The Central Institute of Islamic Research (Karachi 1963), p. 3.
15 See Part III of Smith (ed.), *South Asian Politics and Religion.*
16 Wertheim, *Indonesian Society in Transition*, p. 366. See also Allan A. Samson, 'Islam in Indonesian Politics', *Asian Survey* Vol. VIII No. 12, December 1968, p. 1001.
17 S. C. Banerji, 'Divine Discontent', *Far Eastern Economic Review* 10 June 1965, p. 499.
18 Don Smith, 'The Political Monks and the Monastic Reform', in *South Asian Politics and Religion*, pp. 490–509.
19 e.g. in Madras: see J. Anthony Lukas' despatch in the *New York Times* 5 August 1965.
20 See *China News Analysis* No. 717, 19 July 1968.
21 R. J. Miller, 'They Will Not Die Hindus', *Asian Survey* Vol. VII, September 1967, p. 637; Eleanor Zelliot, 'Buddhism and Politics in Maharashtra', in Smith (ed.), *South Asian Politics and Religion*,

p. 191; and Towyn Mason, 'Big Buddhist Revival Sweeps India', *Bangkok Post* 17 April 1968.

22 Dharmavijaya Press, Balagoda 1956.

23 McFarland, *The Rush Hour of the Gods*.

24 Harry K. Nishio, 'Comparative Analysis of the Rissho Koseikai and the Soka Gakkai', *Asian Survey* Vol. VII, November 1967, p. 776.

25 Hall and Beardsley, *Twelve Doors to Japan*, p. 340.

26 Halberstam, *The Making of a Quagmire*, p. 214. But the powerful President of the Ceylon Buddhist Congress recently called on his Government to ban the development of fisheries and the rearing of cattle for slaughter as inimical to Buddhism (*The Times* 1 January 1968).

27 'A Brief Discussion of the Future of Buddhism', *Modern Buddhism*, Peking, April 1952 (quoted in the *China Quarterly* No. 22, April 1965, pp. 145–6).

28 Chao Pu-chu, General Secretary of the Chinese Buddhist Association, *Modern Buddhism*, Peking, August 1955 (quoted in the *China Quarterly* ibid., p. 147).

29 Quoted in Holmes Welch, 'Asian Buddhists and China', *Far Eastern Economic Review* 4 April 1963, p. 15.

30 *World Buddhism*, Ceylon, March 1964.

31 *Neak Cheat Niyum* (Phnompenh, 30 April 1961), cited in *Asian Survey* Vol. VII, June 1967, p. 359. See also Ling, *Buddha, Marx and God;* and Yoneo Ishii, 'Church and State in Thailand', *Asian Survey* Vol. VIII, No. 10, October 1968, p. 864.

32 'Vedanta, the Basic Culture of India', *Hindusthan Times* New Delhi 1946, p. 5.

33 Quoted in Van der Kroef, *Indonesia in the Modern World* Vol. I, p. 104. Hatta, Sukarno's Vice-President, said that for true Muslims socialism was 'a commandment of religious belief' (ibid. p. 128).

34 G. D. Khosla, *Stern Reckoning*, p. 299.

35 *The Times* 18 August 1967. See generally J. G. Beaglehole, 'The Indian Christians – A Study of a Minority', *Modern Asian Studies* Vol. I, Part I (January 1967), p. 59.

36 Rosihan Anwar, 'Moslems, Christians, Seen At Variance', *Japan Times* 22 December 1967; O. G. Roeder, 'Churches Afire', *Far Eastern Economic Review* 19 October 1967, p. 128.

37 Roughly two-thirds Catholic and one-third Protestant, the largest concentrations being in the Philippines (26 million), India (13 million) and Indonesia (6 million). *World Christian Handbook 1968* London 1967.

38 *God's Fool*, Faber & Faber Ltd, London 1956.

39 Fitzgerald, *The Birth of Communist China*, p. 128.
40 See, e.g. the report 'Foreign Missionaries' Activities in N.E. India', *The Hindu Weekly* Madras, 21 August 1967, p. 11, which states that recent information confirms 'that the current unrest in the sensitive hill areas of Assam is mainly, if not wholly, the result of the activities of these foreign missionaries'.
41 See M. Searle Bates, 'Churches and Christians in China, 1950–67: Fragments of Understanding', *Pacific Affairs* Vol. XLI, No. 2, Summer 1968, p. 199.
42 See generally S. M. Ali, 'How Powerful Is Islam?' and Husein Rofe, What Does Islam Mean to Asia?', *Far Eastern Economic Review* 16 December 1965, p. 512 and 3 November 1966, p. 257 respectively.
43 Maximo Soliven, *Manila Times* 17 April 1968.
44 *Bangkok Post* 12 November 1966; *Far Eastern Economic Review* 24 November 1966. A World Buddhist Sangha Council was formed in Colombo in 1966.
45 Reuter's dispatch from Nairobi, *Japan Times* 11 August 1968.
46 *Gorkhapatra Kathmandu*, 15 January 1965 (quoted in Leo E. Rose, 'Nepal in 1965', *Asian Survey* Vol. VI, February 1966, p. 88).

RECOMMENDED FURTHER READING

Rahman, *Islam*.
Smith (ed.), *South Asian Politics and Religion*.
Sarkisyanz, *Buddhist Backgrounds of the Burmese Revolution*.
Ling, *Buddha, Marx and God*.
McFarland, *The Rush Hour of the Gods*.
Yang, *Religion in Chinese Society*.
Levenson, *Confucian China and Its Modern Fate*.

CHAPTER 3: CLASSES AND CASTES

1 *The Prevailing Wind*, p. 282.
2 Chen, *Thought Reform of the Chinese Intellectuals*, p. 48.
3 McGee, *The South-East Asian City*.
4 *Japan Times* 2 May 1968.
5 *Japan Information Bulletin* Vol. XIV, No. 11 (London, 1 June 1967), p. 7.
6 M. N. Srinivas, *Economic Weekly* Vol. XII, Special Number, (Bombay June 1960), p. 867.
7 Gray and Cavendish, *Chinese Communism in Crisis*, p. 51.
8 See the excellent summary in the *Reserve Bank of India Bulletin* Vol. XXI, December 1967, p. 1615.

9 Sobhan, *Basic Democracies, Works Programmes and Rural Development in East Pakistan.*
10 Harold Isaacs, *India's Ex-Untouchables*, p. 147.
11 *The Dance of Shiva*, p. 4.
12 ibid, pp. 13, 17.
13 *The Continent of Circe*, p. 62.
14 Zinkin, *Caste Today*, p. 23.
15 Srinivas, *Social Change in Modern India.*
16 See e.g. Chaudhuri op. cit., p. 61.
17 *Caste in Modern India*, p. 41.
18 Pradeep J. Shah, 'Caste and Political Process,' *Asian Survey* Vol. VI, September 1966, p. 520. See Hanson, 'Factionalism and Democracy in Indian Politics,' *World Today* October 1968, p. 436.
19 Bashiruddin Ahmed, 'Communist and Congress Prospects in Kerala', *Asian Survey* Vol. VI, July 1966, p. 399.
20 Harry Izmirlian Jr, 'Dynamics of Political Support in a Punjab Village', *Asian Survey* Vol. VI, March 1966, p. 125.
21 Ramashray Roy, 'Intra-Party Conflict in the Bihar Congress', *Asian Survey* Vol. VI, December 1966, p. 706.
22 Robert L. Hardgrave Jr, 'Varieties of Political Behaviour among Nadars of Tamilnad', *Asian Survey* Vol. VI, November 1966, p. 614. See also Paul R. Brass, *Factional Politics in an Indian State;* and Beteille, *Caste, Class and Power: Changing Patterns of Stratification in a Tanjore Village.*
23 Sheth, *The Social Framework of an Indian Factory.*
24 *The Modernity of Tradition.*
25 Isaacs, op. cit.; Lelah Dushkin, 'Scheduled Caste Policy in India: History, Problems, Prospects', *Asian Survey* Vol. VII, September 1967, p. 626.
26 Peter Hazelhurst, 'Pride and Prejudice in India's Deep South', *The Times* 17 January 1969.
27 R. J. Miller, '"They Will Not Die Hindus": The Buddhist Conversion of Mahar Ex-Untouchables', *Asian Survey* Vol. VII, September 1967, p. 637.
28 See the Indian Government Reports summarized in *The Times* 16 January 1968.
29 De Vos and Wagatsuma, *Japan's Invisible Race: Caste in Culture and Personality*. See also A. E. Cullison, 'Religious Discrimination Lingers on in Japan', *Daily Telegraph* 6 March 1969.

RECOMMENDED FURTHER READING
Zinkin, *Caste Today.*
Isaacs, *India's Ex-Untouchables.*

Srinivas, *Social Change in Modern India*.
Sheth, *The Social Framework of an Indian Factory*.
Rudolph and Rudolph, *The Modernity of Tradition*.
De Vos and Wagatsuma, *Japan's Invisible Race: Caste in Culture and Personality*.
Anand, *Untouchable*.
Geertz, *The Social History of an Indonesian Town*.
McGee, *The South-East Asian City*.
Strong, *The Rise of the Chinese People's Communes*.
Dore, *City Life in Japan*.
Fukutaka, *Japanese Rural Society*.
Dore, *Land Reform in Japan*.

CHAPTER 4: CONFLICTS OF CULTURE

1 Pye, *Politics, Personality and Nation Building*, pp. 32–42. See also Franke, *China and the West*, pp. 140–51; and Karl A. Wittfogel, 'Results and Problems of the Study of Oriental Despotism', *The Journal of Asian Studies* Vol. XXVIII No. 2, February 1969, p. 357; and Maurice Miesner, 'The Despotism of Concepts: Wittfogel and Marx on China', *The China Quarterly*, No. 16, November 1963, p. 99.

2 Translated by Ineko Kondo, Kenyusha, Tokyo, 1954.

3 Coomaraswamy, *The Dance of Shiva*, p. 156.

4 Sasthi Brata, *My God Died Young*, Hutchinson, London, 1968.

5 *Japan's Decisive Century 1867–1967*, p. 23.

6 Tokiomi, *Japanese Education, Its Past and Present*, Kokusai Bunka Shinkokai, Tokyo 1965.

7 Fujio Ikada, speaking in New York on 6 November 1965 (quoted in *Asian Survey* Vol. VII, 1967, p. 600).

8 *Towards Freedom*, p. 353.

9 *The New York Times*, 10 August 1965.

10 *A Nation in the Making*, p. 286.

11 *The Continent of Circe*, p. 298.

12 The will was dated 21 June 1954. This excerpt is taken from *India 1964 Annual Review* (Information Service of India, London), p. IV.

13 Anand, *Is There a Contemporary Indian Civilisation?* p. 173. Compare Coomaraswamy: 'We must demand of a coming race that men should act with European energy and think with Asiatic calm,' *The Dance of Shiva*, p. 138.

14 Cited in *Far Eastern Economic Review*, 25 February 1965, p. 330.

15 *Daily Telegraph* 8 October 1968; *The Times* 2 July 1965.

16 Viscount Montgomery, *Three Continents* (Collins, London 1962), p. 74.

17 Ba Nyein speaking to Harold Sieve, *Daily Telegraph* 8 November 1968.

18 *BBC Summary of World Broadcasts* Part III, 2587/A3/2 of 6 October 1967.

19 Mende, *Conversations with Mr Nehru*, p. 118.

20 *Out of Exile*, pp. 145–6.

21 *My Country and My People*, p. 172.

22 'The New Society Is a Great School', *Jen-min Wên-hsueh*, October 1951 (quoted in *The China Quarterly*, No. 8, October 1961, p. 56).

23 See e.g. *The Times* 22 June 1967; Snow, *Women in Modern China; China News Analysis* No. 83, 13 May 1955; and Robert Edward Mitchell and Irene Lo, *Asian Survey* Vol. VIII, No. 4, April 1968, p. 309.

24 James H. Buck, 'The Japanese Self-Defense Forces', *Asian Survey* Vol. VII, September 1967, p. 602.

25 Govind Narian Singh of Madyha Pradesh: see *The Times* 6 July 1968.

26 Theodore P. Wright Jr, 'National Integration and Modern Judicial Procedure in India: The Dar-us-Salem Case', *Asian Survey* Vol. VI, December 1966, p. 682.

27 Henderson, *Conciliation and Japanese Law*.

28 'Mao Tse-tung's Thought – Banner of Victory in Scaling the Heights of Science and Technology', 3 November 1967, p. 15.

29 Tsai Yuan-pei in 1918, quoted in Teng and Fairbank, *China's Response to the West*, p. 238.

30 *Cardinal Principles of the National Policy*, Ministry of Education, Tokyo 1937, translated by Gauntlett, Harvard University Press 1949, p. 55.

31 *Three Basic Problems of Free India*, p. 24.

32 Quoted in Kikuzo Ito and Minoru Shibata, 'The Dilemma of Mao Tse-tung', *The China Quarterly* No. 35, July 1968, p. 66.

33 *China, Yellow Peril? Red Hope?* p. 221.

34 Harry Baines, 'Modernism and Milk-maids' *Asian Review* Vol. I No. 3 (April 1968), p. 165.

35 *Financial Times* 27 September 1966.

36 Pye, *Politics, Personality and Nation Building*, p. 11.

37 Quoted in André Travert, 'The Attitude of the Communist Party Towards China's Cultural Legacy', in Szczepanik (ed.), *Economic and Social Problems of the Far East*, p. 365.

38 Eric Rhode, reviewing *Redbeard* in the *Listener* 21 November 1968.

39 'Magic and Dependence', *Daily Telegraph Magazine* 18 August 1967.

40 *The Food Problem of Developing Countries*, p. 49.

41 Dore (ed.), *Aspects of Social Change in Modern Japan*, pp. 24, 411–53.

42 *Kindai Nikon Shoshi* Tokyo 1952, Vol. I, p. 10, quoted in Jansen (ed.), *Changing Japanese Attitudes Toward Modernization*, p. 12.

43 Quoted in Edward Seidensticker, 'In Praise of Shadows, A Prose Elegy by Tanizaki', *Japan Quarterly*, Vol. I, No. 1.

RECOMMENDED FURTHER READING

Sjahrir, *Out of Exile.*
Nehru, *Discovery of India.*
Franke, *China and the West.*
Coomaraswamy, *The Dance of Shiva.*
Selosoemardjan, *Social Changes in Jogjakarta.*
Wang, *Chinese Intellectuals and the West.*
Anand, *Is There a Contemporary Indian Civilisation?*
Alisjahbana, *Indonesia: Social and Cultural Revolution.*
Iyer (ed.), *The Glass Curtain Between Asia and Europe.*
Jansen (ed.), *Changing Japanese Attitudes Toward Modernization.*
Dore (ed.), *Aspects of Social Change in Modern Japan.*
Benedict, *The Chrysanthemum and the Sword.*

CHAPTER 5: THE LANGUAGE BATTLE

1 Weerawardena, *Ceylon and Her Citizens*, p. 15.

2 *Bangkok Post* 18 September 1966.

3 Klochko, *Soviet Scientist in China*, p. 22. English has now replaced Russian as the first foreign language learned in Chinese schools.

4 Government of India, Ministry of Education, *Report of the Secondary Education Commission*, New Delhi, 1953.

5 Renato Constantino, quoted in J. M. van der Kroef, 'The Long, Long Hangover', *Far Eastern Economic Review* 14 July 1966, p. 70. See on the future of English in India, David Morgan, 'Renaissance in India', and Jamal Kidwai, 'Now Repeat After Me ...', both in *The Times Educational Supplement* 25 October 1968.

6 UNESCO, *The Use of Vernacular Languages in Education* 1953, p. 11.

7 Government of India, Ministry of Education, *Report of the Committee on Emotional Integration.*

8 Prabhakar Machwe, 'Writers within the Walls of Language', *Asian Review* Vol. 2, No. 1 (October 1968), p. 15.

9 W. H. Morris-Jones, 'Language and Region within the Indian Union', in Mason (ed.), *India and Ceylon: Unity and Diversity*, p. 53.

10 Neville Maxwell, 'India and Language', *New Society* 21 December 1967; S. J. Tambiah, 'The Politics of Language in India and Ceylon', *Modern Asian Studies* Vol. I Part 3, 1967, p. 215.

11 Alisjahbana, *Indonesia: Social and Cultural Revolution*, Chapter 6.

12 Anthony H. Johns, 'Genesis of a Modern Literature', in McVey (ed.), *Indonesia*, p. 437.

13 Sukarno, *An Autobiography*, p. 309.

14 Margaret Roff, 'The Politics of Language in Malaya', *Asia Survey* Vol. VII, May 1967, p. 316.

15 Independence Day speech at Red Fort, Delhi, 15 August 1967 (*The Times* 16 August 1967).

16 Cited in Le Page, *The National Language Question*, p. 67.

17 *China News Analysis*, Nos. 108, 136 and 366, of 11 November 1955, 15 June 1956 and 7 April 1961.

18 Romesh Thapar, *Economic Weekly*, Bombay, 7 October 1961, p. 1553.

RECOMMENDED FURTHER READING

Le Page, *The National Language Question*.

Government of India, Ministry of Education, *Report of the Committee on Emotional Integration*.

Ramos, *Language Policy in Certain Newly Independent States*.

CHAPTER 6: RACIAL PRIDE AND PREJUDICE

1 In a broadcast over the Cambodian Radio on 12 November 1967, translated in *BBC Summary of World Broadcasts* Part III, 2622/A3/8 of 16 November 1967.

2 Nirad Chaudhuri, *The Continent of Circe*, pp. 307–8.

3 Kramer (ed), *The Last Manchu: The Autobiography of Henry Pu Yi, Last Emperor of China*.

4 *An Autobiography*, p. 45.

5 Tarzie Vittachi, 'We Have Our Own Colour Bar', *The Asia Magazine* 28 June 1964.

6 Robert Trumbull, *Bangkok Post* 4 May 1967.

7 See the *Japan Times* editorial of 9 February 1964.

8 James Reston, *The New York Times* 9 September 1965.

382   *Notes*

9 Thompson, *Ta T'ung Shu, The One-World Philosophy of K'ang Yu-wei* (Allen & Unwin, London 1958), p. 148.

10 Hevi, *An African Student in China*.

11 Jansen, *Afro-Asia and Non-Alignment*, p. 306.

12 Statement in Phnompenh of 5 October 1967, translated in *BBC Summary of World Broadcasts* Part III, 2591/A3/4 of 11 October 1967.

13 *Daily Nation* Nairobi 13 March 1962 (report on the Afro-Asian Writers' Conference in Cairo).

14 See e.g. van der Kroef, *Indonesia in the Modern World* Vol. I, pp. 275–308; and Koop, *The Eurasian Population in Burma*.

15 Aubrey Menen, *Dead Men in the Silver Market*.

16 Purcell, *The Chinese in Southeast Asia*.

17 Douglas P. Murray, 'Chinese Education in Southeast Asia', *The China Quarterly* No. 20 1964, p. 67.

18 Williams, *The Future of the Overseas Chinese in Southeast Asia*.

19 Coughlin, *Double Identity, The Chinese in Modern Thailand*.

20 So C. P. Fitzgerald called them 'The Third China', in his book of that name.

21 Kondapi, *Indians Overseas 1838–1949*.

22 *Bangkok Post* 24 July 1967.

23 Harald Munthe-Kaas, 'The Dragon's Seeds' and O. G. Roeder, 'The Road from Bandung', *Far Eastern Economic Review* 5 November 1967, p. 281, and 2 October 1969, p. 57.

24 Urmila Phadnis, 'The Indo-Ceylon Pact and the "Stateless" Indians in Ceylon', *Asian Survey* Vol. VII (April 1967), p. 226.

25 *Sunday Telegraph* 24 October 1968.

26 Van der Kroef, *Indonesia in the Modern World* Vol. I, pp. 250–74.

27 Peter A. Poole, 'Thailand's Vietnamese Minority', *Asian Survey* Vol. VII, December 1967, p. 886.

28 Silcock, *Towards a Malayan Nation*.

29 *Observer* 16 June 1968. See also Elwin, *Nagaland*; and Christoph von Fürer-Haimendorf, 'The Position of the Tribal Population in Modern India', in Mason (ed.), *India and Ceylon: Unity and Diversity*.

30 Anthony Polsky, 'Mao Takes to the Hills', *Far Eastern Economic Review* 31 October 1968, p. 240.

31 At one time some Chinese communist leaders envisaged the sovereign independence of Tibet, Sinkiang, Yunnan and Kweichow, where non-Han races predominate: see *China News Analysis* No. 232, 13 June 1958.

32 This is never publicized: a rare report was 'Last of the Warlords' (*Week-end Telegraph*, 10 March 1967) by Peter Duval Smith who

died in mysterious circumstances in Saigon before it was published. On the Montagnards see Larry R. Jackson, 'The Vietnamese Revolution and the Montagnards', *Asian Survey* Vol. IX, No. 5, May 1969, p. 313.

33 Robert Dickson Crane, 'Asia's Next War', *Observer* 23 June 1968; see also Gial Vung, 'Frontiers of Freedom', *Far Eastern Economic Review* 15 August 1968, p. 316.

34 *Bangkok Post* 21 April 1967.

35 André Tong, 'La Thailande sera-t-elle un Nouveau Vietnam?', *Est et Ouest* No. 377 Paris February 1967, p. 18.

36 Crane, op. cit. Cf. George N. Patterson, 'A Himalayan Confederation', *Far Eastern Economic Review* 6 May 1965, p. 275.

37 George Moseley, 'Voices in the Minority', *Far Eastern Economic Review* 2 March 1967.

38 See S. M. M. 7. Qureshi, 'Pakhtunistan: The Frontier Dispute between Afghanistan and Pakistan', *Pacific Affairs* Vol. XXXIX, Nos 1–2 (Spring–Summer 1966), p. 99.

39 See H. E. Richardson, *Tibet and its History*, Oxford University Press, London 1962; George Patterson, *Tragic Destiny* Faber & Faber, London 1959; *My Land and My People: The Autobiography of H. H. The Dalai Lama* Wiedenfeld & Nicolson, London 1962; and Stuart and Roma Gelder, *The Timely Rain, Travels in New Tibet*, Hutchinson, London 1964.

RECOMMENDED FURTHER READING

Purcell, *The Chinese in Southeast Asia.*
Williams, *The Future of the Overseas Chinese in Southeast Asia.*
Kondapi, *Indians Overseas, 1838–1949.*
Hevi, *An African Student in China.*
Moseley (ed.), *The Party and the National Question in China.*
Coughlin, *Double Identity, The Chinese in Modern Thailand.*
Fitzgerald, *The Third China.*

CHAPTER 7: AMBIGUOUS BORDERS

1 The maps of the Asians themselves were extremely imprecise: Nakamura, *East Asia in Old Maps.*

2 Coedès, *The Making of South-East Asia*, Hall, A History of South-East Asia, Chapter 1 *et. seq.*

3 Srinivas, *Social Change in Modern India*, p. 7.

4 'No greater achievement can be credited to the British than that they brought about India's enduring political consolidation':

V. P. Menon, *The Story of the Integration of the Indian States*, p. 3.

5 Debate of 13 August 1959.

6 *Asian Frontiers*, p. 64.

7 'Findings on the Rann of Kutch', *World Today* Vol. 24, No. 4 (April 1968), p. 134. For continuing resentments over the India–Pakistan border, see Tinker, *Experiment with Freedom*, pp. 146–8; and the *Economist* 20 August 1966.

8 The views of the Kashmiris themselves have been the least considered factor in the dispute, and since an independently conducted plebiscite is politically out of the question we may never know them. But the nearest that the Kashmir question came to solution in recent years was just before Nehru's death, when discussions were going on about a confederal union of some kind between India, Pakistan and Kashmir as three technically equal members: see Richard Critchfield 'Background to Conflict', *Reporter* 4 November 1965. There is no doubt that Kashmiri nationalism is now an important force in the equation, and one that favours neither India nor Pakistan. See generally Lamb, *Crisis in Kashmir*.

9 Lamb concludes that: 'These unresolved territorial and boundary questions must weigh very heavily on the negative side of the British legacy to India and Pakistan; and in the long run they may well turn out to cancel many of the positive achievements of the colonial era' (*Asian Frontiers*, p. 130).

10 P. H. M. Jones, 'Passes and Impasses', *Far Eastern Economic Review* 28 February 1963, p. 443, gives a good account of the fighting and its background.

11 Lamb, *The China-India Border*.

12 Doolin, *Territorial Claims in the Sino-Soviet Conflict*.

13 Maurice Kelly, 'Law Among the Ruins', *Far Eastern Economic Review* 13 October 1966, p. 60, and subsequent correspondence on 16 February 1967.

14 Leifer, *Cambodia: The Search for Security*.

15 *The Northern Territorial Issue*, Ministry of Foreign Affairs, Tokyo 1968.

16 See *Far Eastern Economic Review* 14 May 1959, p. 675; 4 June 1959, p. 768; and 25 June 1959, p. 876. The Spratley Islands in the South China Sea are also disputed between China, Vietnam and the Philippines.

17 See Justus M. van der Kroef, 'West New Guinea: The Uncertain Future', *Asian Survey* Vol. VIII, No. 8 (August 1968), p. 691.

18 Gordon, *The Dimensions of Conflict in Southeast Asia*, Chapter 1; Michael Leifer, 'The Philippines and Sabah Irredenta', *World Today*, October 1968, p. 421. It should be noted that the Sulu

claim involves some Indonesian territory too. In 1928 Max Huber, the Swiss arbitrator, awarded the island of Palmas (or Miangas), midway between Mindanao and Sulawesi, and then disputed between Holland and the United States, to what is now Indonesia, and this could provide ammunition for Philippine nationalism (*Reports of International Arbitral Awards* Vol. II, United Nations 1949, p. 831).

RECOMMENDED FURTHER READING

Lamb, *Asian Frontiers*.
Lamb, *Crisis in Kashmir*.
Watson, *The Frontiers of China*.
Lamb, *The China-India Border*.
Maxwell, *India's China War*.
Gordon, *The Dimensions of Conflict in Southeast Asia*.
Doolin, *Territorial Claims in the Sino-Soviet Conflict*.
Patterson, *The Unquiet Frontier*.

CHAPTER 8: THE AGRICULTURAL BASE

1 *Problems of the Third Plan: A Critical Miscellany* (Ministry of Information and Broadcasting, Government of India, New Delhi, 1961), p. 46.

2 *Population Growth and Land Use*.

3 Roger Revelle's 'Population and Food Supplies: The Edge of the Knife', in *Prospects of the World Food Supply*, p. 43; and B. Napitupulu, 'Hunger in Indonesia', *Bulletin of Indonesian Economic Studies* No. 9, February 1968, p. 60.

4 See, for example, a report from Kerala by J. Anthony Lukas in the *New York Times* of 13 February 1966.

5 In an address delivered to the thirty-eighth Eucharistic Congress in Bombay on 29 November 1964, page 9 of the published text.

6 Donnithorne, *China's Economic System*, pp. 128–9. See also *China News Analysis* No. 478, 26 July 1963.

7 *Economic Bulletin for Asia and the Far East* Vol. XVII No. 3 (December 1966), p. 90.

8 9 August speech in Manila: *Japan Times* 10 August 1967.

9 See Prime Minister Chou En-lai's report to the National People's Congress in Peking in December 1964 (*Peking Review* 1 January 1965, p. 10).

10 Jack Gray of Glasgow University is pursuing this correlation, and I am indebted to him in mentioning it here.

11 Up to 60 per cent of the gross product in China on the eve of the communist take-over, according to Werner Klatt in *The Chinese Model*, p. 96.

12 Dore, *Land Reform in Japan*.

13 See Karl Brandt, 'Economic Development: Lessons of Statecraft in Taiwan', *Orbis* Vol. XI, No. 4 (Winter 1968), p. 1067.

14 Gilbert Etienne, 'Peasants' Progress', *Far Eastern Economic Review* 26 January 1967.

15 *Ibid*.

16 See Donnithorne, *China's Economic System* pp. 43–64.

17 W. R. Geddes, *Peasant Life in Communist China* (Society for Applied Anthropology, New York 1963), p. 55.

18 See Gray and Cavendish, *Chinese Communism in Crisis*, Chapter 5, especially p. 145.

19 *People's Daily* Peking, 22 August 1967 and 7 January 1968 (translated in *BBC Summary of World Broadcasts* Part III, 2550/B/18 and 2664/B/4).

20 A Shanghai poster entitled 'An Appeal to all Revolutionary Commune Members and Poor, Middle and Lower Peasants', signed by Nan Hui Hsien 'Make Revolution' groups and dated 14 January 1967, seen and made available to me by private sources.

21 *New Statesman* 19 July 1968.

22 *China in the Year 2001*, p. 46.

23 See the *Guardian* 11 February 1967; and, for a less pessimistic view, John Rosselli, 'Calcutta: City of Man', *New Society* 24 August 1967.

24 11 September 1958 editorial.

25 Quoted in *China in the Year 2001*, p. 48.

26 *Observer* 29 August 1965. A good case-study of the artificiality and tensions of urbanization is Geertz, *The Social History of an Indonesian Town*.

27 *Economic Survey of Asia and the Far East*, 1967.

28 *Ibid*. See also A. Hariharan, 'Fertilizer to the Fore', *Far Eastern Economic Review*, 9 October 1969, p. 104.

29 See, for example, Werner Klatt's article in the *Guardian* on 20 March 1967.

30 See the despatch by Godfrey Hodgson in the *Sunday Times* on 1 May 1966. For an optimistic analysis of the effect of the new hybrid strains see Harish Agrawal, 'Revolution in the Fields', in *New Scientist* 29 August 1968.

31 Klatt, *op. cit*.

32 See *Food Losses, The Tragedy ... And Some Solutions* (FAO, Rome, 1969).

33 Theodore W. Schulz, in *Prospects of the World Food Supply*, p. 22. See also Dilip Mukerjee's 'First Priority: Food', in *Far Eastern Economic Review* of 10 March 1966, p. 448. J. S. Mann, 'The Impact of P. L. 480 Imports', *Journal of Farm Economics* Vol. XLIX, No. 1, February 1967, calculates that the import of 10 tons of P.L.480 cereals causes a loss of 3 tons of potential Indian-grown cereal.

34 12 November 1965.

35 Roger Revelle in *Prospects of the World Food Supply*, pp. 36–7.

36 *Economic Bulletin for Asia and the Far East* Vol. XVII No. 2 (September 1966), p. 63.

RECOMMENDED FURTHER READING

The Food Problem of Developing Countries (OECD).
Prospects of the World Food Supply (National Academy of Sciences).
Economic Survey of Asia and the Far East, 1969 (UN).
Nair, *Blossoms in the Dust*.
Crooks, *The First Years of Yangyi Commune*.
Dore, *Land Reform in Japan*.
Fukutake, *Japanese Rural Society*.
Hinton, *Fanshen*.
Etienne, *Studies in Indian Agriculture*.
Southworth and Johnston (ed.), *Agricultural Development and Economic Growth*.
The World Food Problem, A Report of the President's Science Advisory Committee.

CHAPTER 9: INDUSTRIALIZATION

1 Editorial of 1 January 1953.

2 See Harris, *Tata*, Chapter 2.

3 *Monthly Bulletin of Statistics*, United Nations (May 1968), p. xvi.

4 *Economic Bulletin for Asia and the Far East*, United Nations (December 1966), p. 90.

5 J. B. Sperling, *Die Rourkela-Deutschen* (Deutsche-Veragsanstalt, Stuttgart, 1965).

6 *Soviet Scientist in China*, p. 187.

7 Lockwood, *The Economic Development of Japan*, pp. 328–9.

8 New China News Agency dispatch, 17 October 1966.

9 New China News Agency, 11 November 1966.

10 Lockwood, op. cit., p. 575.

11 Chiang Kai-shek, *China's Destiny*, p. 277.

12 According to an article broadcast over Chengtu Radio on 3 October 1967 (translated in *BBC Summary of World Broadcasts*, Part 3, 2586/B/19).

13 See the author's 'The Capitalists of Mao Tse-tung', in *Management Today* (April 1968), p. 85.

14 See 'India's Great White Elephant', in *The Economist* 17 August 1968.

15 Rosen, *Democracy and Economic Change in India*, p. 229.

16 Speech to the Ahmedabad Management Association (27 January 1967): p. 17 of the text as published by the Tata Press, Bombay.

17 G. C. Allen, *A Short Economic History of Modern Japan*, pp. 33–5, 52, and 127, also Chapter 5. 'It can be said with truth that there was scarcely any important Japanese industry of the Western type during the later decades of the nineteenth century which did not owe its establishment to State initiative' (p. 34).

18 P. H. M. Jones, 'Cambodia's New Factories', *Far Eastern Economic Review* 9 May 1963, p. 319.

19 *The Sunday Times* 26 February 1967, and *Far Eastern Economic Review* 30 March 1967.

20 Keith Richardson in the *Sunday Times* 19 March 1967.

21 Verghese, *Design for Tomorrow*, p. 94.

22 Op. cit., p. 320.

23 See the *Economist* 28 January 1967.

24 See citations in *China News Analysis* No. 387, 1 September 1961.

25 B. C. Roberts, *Sunday Times* 9 May 1965; see also Kang Chao, 'Labour Institutions in Japan and Her Economic Growth', *Journal of Asian Studies* Vol. XXVIII, No. 1 (November 1968), p. 5.

26 Hong Kong with a population of under 4 million exported manufactured goods made in local factories to the value of £1,000 million in 1971, and the United Nations calculates that it is the biggest single exporter of manufactures from the developing to the developed countries, responsible for a quarter of the entire South's total (*UNCTAD Review of International Trade & Development 1966* (TB/D/82/Add 2, Table 111–13).

27 Wheelwright, *Industrialisation in Malaya*.

28 Tariff protection is necessary initially to get a new industry started, although the Japanese had to industrialize in the late nineteenth century without the benefit of protectionism, and they did not do too badly: see Lockwood, *The Economic Development of Japan*, p. 539. But if prolonged it can prevent an industry from becoming internationally competitive. The Philippine radio industry was virtually wiped out when the Philippines Government liberalized imports in 1967. See A. G. Menon, 'Developing Dilemma', *Far*

Eastern Economic Review 10 November 1966, p. 309 for a discussion of the need for regional cooperation in industry.
29 See Joseph Peterson, *The Great Leap – China*, Chapter 3.
30 See George McRobie, 'New Prospects for India's Villages', in *Asian Review* January 1968, p. 95.

RECOMMENDED FURTHER READING

Harris, *Jamseji Nusserwanji Tata*.
Verghese, *Design for Tomorrow*.
Peterson, *The Great Leap – China*.
Klochko, *Soviet Scientist in China*.
Proceedings of the Asian Conference on Industrialisation (UN).
Wheelwright, *Industrialisation in Malaya*.
Johnson, *The Steel Industry of India*.

CHAPTER 10: THE POPULATION PROBLEM

1 Quoted in *The Times* 21 January 1965.
2 S. Radhakrishnan, in *Third International Conference on Planned Parenthood* (Family Planning Assoication of India, Bombay 1952), p. 12.
3 Ohlin, *Population Control and Economic Development*, p. 28.
4 'Asian Populations: The Critical Decades', in Ng and Mudd (ed.), *The Population Crisis*, p. 85.
5 *The Economic History of World Population*, p. 105.
6 *Ibid.*, p. 88.
7 Dr Jack Lippes, reported in *The Hindu Weekly* Madras, 18 July 1966.
8 Ohlin, op. cit., p. 100.
9 *Wen Hui Pao*, 12 February 1957 (cited in *China News Analysis* Hong Kong 15 March 1957).
10 Frederick Nossall, *Far Eastern Economic Review*, 21 February 1963, p. 353.
11 Thakin Tin, quoted in the *Guardian* 28 June 1961.
12 Quoted by Masri Singarimbun, 'Family Planning in Indonesia', *Bulletin of Indonesian Economic Studies* No. 10 (June 1968), p. 54.
13 Fischer, *The Story of Indonesia*, p. 165. But Indonesian opinion would seem to favour family planning: see R. Murray Thomas, 'Attitudes Toward Birth Control in Bandung', *Indonesia* No. 4 (October 1967), p. 74.
14 *The Asian Population Conference, 1963*, p. 48.
15 *New York Times* 3 December 1959.

16 Christopher Bartlett, 'Planning Japan's Families', *Far Eastern Economic Review*, 15 December 1966, p. 555.

17 *Times of India* 20 July 1967.

18 See e.g. Joseph Lelyfeld's report on the package of disincentives recently adopted by the State of Maharashtra, *New York Times* 14 September 1968; and the report on China in the same newspaper, 27 April 1966.

19 In Haryana: *The Times* 22 June 1967.

20 'Towards A World Population Program', *International Organization* Vol. XXII No. 1 (Winter 1968), p. 332.

21 Dr S. Chandrasekhar, 'Population Policy', the *Guardian* 15 August 1968.

22 'Policies, Programmes and the Decline of Birth Rates: China and the Chinese Populations of East Asia', in *Population Dynamics* (ed. M. Muramatsu and P. A. Harper, Baltimore, 1965), p. 102.

23 *Selected Works of Mao Tse-tung* Vol. 4, Peking, 1961, pp. 453–4.

24 *Proceedings of the Asian Conference on Industrialisation*, pp. 7–8.

25 op. cit., p. 51.

26 Stephen Enke and Richard G. Zind, *Journal of Biosocial Science* Vol. I, p. 41, 1969.

27 Speech of 20 June 1968.

28 Final report of the Asian Conference on Children and Youth in National Development, Bangkok, 8–15 March, 1966.

29 Malcolm Subhan, 'The Population of Asia', *Courrier de L'Extrème-Orient* Brussels 1968, p. 178.

30 *The Guardian* (Rangoon), cited in the *Guardian* (Manchester), 28 June 1961.

31 The Oxford Union resolved on 19 January 1967 that 'This House Fears the Yellow Peril', by 197 votes to 191, in spite of the author's pleas to the contrary.

32 Notably Thompson, *Population and Progress in the Far East*.

RECOMMENDED FURTHER READING

Ohlin, *Population Control and Economic Development*.

Ng and Mudd (ed.), *The Population Crisis*.

The Asian Population Conference 1963 (U N).

Cipolla, *The Economic History of World Population*.

Chandrasekhar (ed.), *Asia's Population Problems*.

Bourgeois-Pichat, *Population Growth and Development*.

Taeuber, *The Population of Japan*.

National Academy of Sciences, *The Growth of World Population*.

Aird, *The Size, Composition and Growth of the Population of Mainland China*.

CHAPTER 11: ECONOMIC DEVELOPMENT

1 *The Red Book and the Great Wall.*

2 Quoted in Chiang Kai-shek, *China's Destiny*, p. 329.

3 Lockwood, *The Economic Development of Japan.*

4 e.g. Nakamura, *Agricultural Production and the Economic Development of Japan 1873–1922*; see also Jacobs, *The Origins of Modern Capitalism in Eastern Asia*; and Dore, *Education in Tokugawa Japan.*

5 Figures for 1963, in *United Nations Statistical Year Book, 1967*, Table 185. It is now increasingly recognized that the comparison of national income figures is extremely misleading because of the arbitrariness of exchange rates, discrepancies in the extent of monetization of different national economies, inflation, and cultural and climatic differences affecting human needs. The difference in price levels alone distorts the figures by 100 per cent or more: *Economic Bulletin for Asia and the Far East* Vol. XVI, No. 1, June 1965, pp. 5–6. It is also possible to have a very low income per head while building up an impressive infra-structure for future development, so that differences in income per head can exaggerate the development gap. Thus two Indian economists calculate, on the basis of other indicators than income per head (including production, irrigation, numbers of factories, radio licences, banking, education, patents, fertilizer consumption, factory employment etc.) that in the last decade the Indian economy has been growing at about $7\frac{1}{2}$ per cent a year – or more than double the $3\frac{1}{2}$ per cent annual rise in *per capita* income: V. V. Divatia and V. V. Bhatt, 'On Measuring the Pace of Development', *Reserve Bank of India Bulletin* Vol. XXII, April 1968, p. 467. See also M. K. Bennett, 'International Disparities in Consumption levels', *American Economic Review* Vol. LXI, No. 4, September 1951. But for the moment the statistics for income per head are the only ones available for the purpose of comparison, and I quote them here with these reservations.

6 i.e. an estimated 1,800 million population out of some 3,600 million as at end-1969; 7.8 million square miles out of 52.4 million; and £58,000 million gross domestic product in 1963 out of the world's £680,000 million.

7 See the address by Paul Streeten at the Inaugural Conference of the Institute of Development Studies at the University of Sussex on 18 September 1966 (the *Guardian* 19 September 1966).

8 op. cit., p. 303.

9 'Tax Potential and Economic Growth in the Countries of the

ECAFE Region' *Economic Bulletin for Asia and the Far East* Vol. XVII, No. 2, September 1966, p. 44.

10 *Annual Plan 1967–1968* Government of India Planning Commission, p. 16.

11 See generally Part One of *Economic Survey of Asia and the Far East, 1967*, 'Policies and Planning for Exports'.

12 Western commentators are often too unkind when they condemn a Sukarno or a Nehru for his innocence in economics. Many a Western leader has been equally ignorant. It is recorded that a British prime minister, Lord Melbourne, after a cabinet meeting in 1841, called down the stairs to the departing Ministers, 'What did we decide? Is it to lower the price of bread or isn't it? It doesn't matter which, but we must all say the same thing'.

13 'Children and Youth in National Planning and Development', *Economic Bulletin for Asia and the Far East* Vol. XVII No. 1 June 1966, p. 40.

14 India, China and Japan have won between them five Nobel Prizes for Physics.

15 Johan Hareide, speaking in a BBC interview on 5 May 1965 (Moncrieff, *Second Thoughts on Aid*, p. 113). Many recent studies underline the potential response of peasants to new incentives: see e.g. Koentjaraningrat (ed.), *Villages in Indonesia*, pp. 393–4.

16 Peterson, *The Great Leap – China*.

17 Hanson, *The Process of Planning: A Study of India's Five Year Plans, 1950–64*.

18 See e.g. the Introduction to the *Economic Survey of Asia and the Far East 1967*: 'What remains in question will be whether a sufficiently rapid rate of economic growth commensurate with popular aspirations can be achieved without long-term and bold planning of the sort that India exemplified in the past.'

19 Thus Professor P. T. Bauer has said: 'Comprehensive planning neither augments resources nor modernizes the minds of people, but merely enlarges or centralizes power....' (*Spectator*, 4 November 1966). George Rosen has commented that 'the present system gives India the hoped-for benefits of neither socialism nor capitalism'. (*Democracy and Economic Change in India*, p. 241).

20 In the 1950s Chinese growth probably averaged at about 5 per cent a year. Several years of disaster followed, but in the mid-1960s the rate of growth was probably about 4 per cent to 5 per cent a year. The Cultural Revolution of 1966–8 slowed down the tempo again. These can only be intelligent guesses in the absence of full information from the Chinese authorities, but if one had to put a single figure to China's average annual growth since 1949 it would, I

suppose, be 4 per cent. Professor Alexander Eckstein would say 3 per cent (*Current Scene* Vol. IV No. 21, 25 November 1966, p. 1).

21 *Economic Survey of Asia and the Far East 1965*, p. 7 (adjusted for growth rates 1965–7). When this report was first presented to the annual conference of ECAFE in New Delhi in 1966, the Indian Government persuaded UN officials to delete the calculation that it would take India, at present rates of growth, 171 years to attain the 1966 income levels of the Japanese (see *Far Eastern Economic Review* 22 December 1966, p. 597).

22 p. 21.

23 See footnote 5 above. For the same reason, simple comparisons of wage rates are misleading. The average factory wage in Hong Kong is about £3 a week, only a quarter of British levels, and yet it is claimed that a textile worker there has to work fewer minutes to earn enough to buy one cigarette than his British counterpart does – because the production cost, distribution margin and sales tax are all much lower than in Britain.

24 *Economist* 29 October 1966, p. 495.

RECOMMENDED FURTHER READING

Myrdal, *Asian Drama.*
Fourth Five Year Plan, A Draft Outline, Government of India.
Kirby, *Economic Development in East Asia.*
Berrill (ed.), *Economic Development with Special Reference to East Asia.*
Zinkin, *Development for Free Asia.*
Lockwood, *The Economic Development of Japan.*
Streeten and Lipton (ed.), *The Crisis of Indian Planning.*
Hanson, *The Process of Planning: A Study of India's Five Year Plans, 1950–64.*
Lewis, *Development Planning.*
Bhagwati, *The Economics of Underdeveloped Countries.*
Ward, *It Can be Done.*
Cutajar and Franks, *The Less Developed Countries in World Trade.*
Eckstein (ed.), *Economic Trends in Communist China.*
The Structure and Development of Asian Economics.

CHAPTER 12: THE APPEAL OF COMMUNISM

1 Lee Kuan Yew of Singapore.

2 John Whitney Hall, 'Changing Conceptions of the Modernization of Japan', in Jansen (ed.), *Changing Japanese Attitudes Toward Modernization*, p. 13.

3 Richard Harris, *The Times* 14 February 1968.

4 Joan V. Bondurant and Margaret W. Fisher, 'The Concept of Change in Hindu, Socialist and Neo-Gandhian Thought', in Smith (ed.), *South Asian Politics and Religion*, p. 247.

5 *Poems from Iqbal*, translated by V. G. Kiernan (Kutub, Bombay 1947), p. 103.

6 See John Coast, 'The Sacrificial Communists of Bali', the *Guardian* 30 August 1966; and Donald Kirk, 'Bali Exorcises an Evil Spirit', *The Reporter* 15 December 1966, p. 42.

7 'Collectivism and the Social Order', in van der Kroef, *Indonesia in the Modern World* Vol. 1, p. 94.

8 Western economics, said Chiang, stress 'selfish individualism and materialism', so China should 'prevent the capitalistic control of the people's livelihood'. Chiang Kai-shek: *China's Destiny and Chinese Economic Theory*, pp. 263 and 277.

9 *BBC Summary of World Broadcasts* Part III, 2684/A2/2 of 1 February 1968.

10 'The Path which Led me to Leninism', *Selected Works* (Hanoi 1962), Vol. 4, p. 449.

11 David Marr, 'Political Attitudes and Activities of Young Urban Intellectuals in South Vietnam', *Asian Survey* Vol. VI May 1966, p. 254.

12 *The Aftermath of Non-Cooperation*, The Communist Party of Great Britain, London 1926, p. 63.

13 *The Burmese Revolution*, Union of Burma Information Department, Rangoon 1952, p. 7.

14 *Speeches and Statements of Iqbal*, Al Mañar Academy, Lahore 1944, p. 151.

15 Scalapino (ed.), *The Communist Revolution in Asia*, pp. 29–32.

16 Floyd, *Mao Against Khrushchev;* Zagoria, *The Sino-Soviet Conflict; The Polemic on the General Line of the International Communist Movement*.

17 Quoted in *Nodong Sinmun* editorial of 28 December 1967, translated in *BBC Summary of World Broadcasts* Part III, 2656/B/11 of 30 December 1967.

18 M. P. Narayana Pillai, 'Building the Tower of Babel', *Far Eastern Economic Review* 6 June 1968, p. 514.

19 Schram, *Mao Tse-tung*, p. 312.

20 An editorial in the Bucharest organ of the Cominform of 6 January 1950 cited in Swearingen and Langer, *Red Flag in Japan*, p. 202.

21 *Tribune* Ambala 13 October 1963, p. 5, as quoted in Scalapino (ed.), *The Communist Revolution in Asia*, p. 336.

22 Pye, *Guerrilla Communism in Malaya*.

23 See e.g. Ithiel de Sola Pool, 'Political Alternatives to the Viet Cong', *Asian Survey* Vol. VII, August 1967, p. 555.

24 *Straits Times* Kuala Lumpur, 2 June 1965.

25 op. cit., p. 111.

26 Quoted in Chiang Kai-shek, *China's Destiny*, p. 329.

27 Frances L. Starner, 'Report from Arayat', *Far Eastern Economic Review* 19 October 1967, p. 144.

RECOMMENDED FURTHER READING

Scalapino (ed.), *The Communist Revolution in Asia*.

Brimmell, *Communism in South East Asia*.

Australian Institute of Political Science, *Communism in Asia: A Threat to Australia?*

Barnett (ed.), *Communist Strategies in Asia*.

Floyd, *Mao Against Khrushchev*.

Schram, *The Political Thought of Mao Tse-tung*.

Schram, *Mao Tse-tung*.

Schurmann, *Ideology and Organisation in Communist China*.

Zagoria, *The Sino-Soviet Conflict*.

The Great Polemic on the General Line of the International Communist Movement.

Liu, *How to be a Good Communist*.

Swearingen and Langer, *Red Flag in Japan*.

Hindley, *The Communist Party of Indonesia*.

Overstreet and Windmiller, *Communism in India*.

Cole, Totten and Uyehara, *Socialist Parties in Postwar Japan*.

Han, *China in the Year 2001*.

Karol, *China, The Other Communism*.

CHAPTER 13: THE NEW POLITICS OF ASIA

1 *The Times* 31 July 1956.

2 *An Autobiography*, pp. 42 and 46.

3 Schram, *Mao Tse-tung*, p. 73; Schram, *The Political Thought of Mao Tse-tung*, p. 143.

4 Werner Levi, 'The Elitist Nature of New Asia's Foreign Policy', *Asian Survey* Vol. VII, November 1967, p. 767.

5 David Wurfel, 'The Saigon Political Elite: Focus on Four Cabinets', *Asian Survey* Vol. VII, August 1967, p. 534–5.

6 *Far Eastern Economic Review* 25 November 1965, p. 368.

7 Letter from William Lim Siew Wai to the editor of the *Far Eastern Economic Review* 16 March 1967, p. 489.

8 Mohammed Ayub Khan, 'Pakistan Perspective', *Foreign Affairs* Vol 38, No. 4 July 1960, p. 547.

9 Ikeda Daisaku, 'For a New Society of Peace and Prosperity – The Vision of the Komeito', *Komei Shimbum* 8 January 1967, as translated in Bursch and Cole (ed.), *Asian Political Systems*, p. 186.

10 Riggs, *Thailand, The Modernization of a Bureaucratic Polity*. For an account of Thai village politics, see Stephen B. Young, 'The Northeastern Thai Village: A noN-Participatory Democracy', *Asian Survey* Vol. VIII No. 11, November 1968, p. 873.

11 *The Times* 27 January 1967.

12 Rajni Kothari, *Economic Weekly* 20 May 1961, p. 783.

13 Robert W. Ward, 'Recent Electoral Developments in Japan', *Asian Survey* Vol. VI, October 1966, p. 547.

14 Lee W. Farnsworth, 'Challenges to Factionalism in Japan's Liberal Democratic Party', *Asian Survey* Vol. VI September 1966, p. 501.

15 *Straits Times* 22 December 1966 and 10 April 1969.

16 *Far Eastern Economic Review* 17 November 1966, p. 379.

17 *The Politics of Succession in India*.

18 O. P. Goyal and Harlan Hahn, 'The Nature of Party Competition in Five Indian States', *Asian Survey* Vol. VI, October 1966, p. 580.

19 Scalapino and Masumi, *Parties and Politics in Contemporary Japan*, p. 53.

20 'The Bureaucracy Preserved and Strengthened', *Journal of Social and Political Ideas in Japan* Vol II No. 3, December 1964, p. 90.

21 Speech to the Indian Merchants' Chamber in Bombay, 20 February 1968 (pp. 21–2 of the text published by the Tata Press). Frank Moraes of the *Times of India* made similar criticisms at that time.

22 B. Taper, *New Yorker* 6 March 1965.

23 Norman D. Palmer, 'India's Fourth General Election', *Asian Survey* Vol. VII May 1967, p. 276.

24 See the discussion in Chapter 1, pp. 11–18 above, and Chapter 2, pp. 28–9.

25 Lucien M. Hanks Jr and Herbert P. Phillips, 'A Young Thai from the Countryside', in B. Kaplan (ed.), *Studying Personality Cross-Culturally* (Dow Peterson, Evanston, Illinois, 1961) p. 642.

26 I. Milton Sacks, 'Restructuring Government in South Vietnam', *Asian Survey* Vol. VII August 1967, p. 524.

27 Joseph W. Elder, 'Religion and Political Attitudes', in Smith (ed.), *South Asian Religion and Politics*, p. 275.

28 Weatherbee, *Ideology in Indonesia*.

29 Michael Leifer, 'The Failure of Political Institutionalisation in Cambodia', *Modern Asian Studies* Vol. 2, Part 2, April 1968, p. 125; and Roger M. Smith, 'Prince Norodom Sihanouk of Cambodia', *Asian Survey* Vol. VII June 1967, p. 353.

30 Mosley, *Hirohito, Emperor of Japan*.

31 Kato Kanju, *Nippon Times* 2 December 1945 (quoted in Evelyn S. Colbert, *The Left Wing in Japanese Politics*, Institute of Pacific Relations, New York 1952, p. 82).

32 Colbert, op. cit., p. 112.

33 Kramer (ed.), *The Last Manchu: The Autobiography of Henry Pu Yi, Last Emperor of China*.

34 Selosoemardjan, *Social Change in Jogjakarta*.

35 See the symposium on Charismatic Leadership in Asia, *Asian Survey* Vol. VII, June 1967, pp. 341–88.

36 Speech in Kampot province of 9 October 1963, quoted in Gordon, *The Dimensions of Conflict in Southeast Asia*, p. 121.

37 Sacks, op. cit., p. 517.

38 Gittings, *The Role of the Chinese Army*. See generally John P. Lovell and C. I. Eugene Kim, 'The Military and Political Change in Asia', *Pacific Affairs* Vol. XL, Nos. 1 and 2, Spring-Summer 1967, p. 113.

39 *Politics in Thailand*, p. 181.

40 Neville Maxwell, 'Must the Military Intervene in India?', *The Times* 28 February 1968.

41 From figures in Table 194 of *United Nations Statistical Yearbook 1967*.

42 *The Military Balance 1969–70* Institute for Strategic Studies, p. 58.

ESTIMATED DEFENCE EXPENDITURE IN US DOLLARS

	Total 1968 (millions)	Total 1969 (millions)	Per Capita 1968	% of GNP 1968
China	7,000	7,250	9	9
India	1,452	1,491	3	4
Japan	1,172	1,344	11	1
North Korea	629	629	37	21
Pakistan	514	542	4	4
North Vietnam	500	500	27	23
South Vietnam	312	444	11	12
Taiwan	300	302	21	8
South Korea	234	290	6	4
Malaysia	130	132	13	4
Thailand	125	154	4	2
Philippines	115	123	3	2
Indonesia	187	229	1	2
Burma	112	111	5	5
Cambodia	63	64	9	6
Laos	19	20	6	9

43 *Parties and Politics in Contemporary Japan*, p. 145.
44 'Preparing for 1970', *Chuo Koron*, November 1965, as translated in Burch and Cole, *Asian Political Systems*, p. 207.
45 Koentjaraningrat (ed.), *Villages in Indonesia*, pp. 394–8.
46 'Panchayati Raj – a General Review', *Reserve Bank of India Bulletin* Vol. XXI December 1967, p. 1615.
47 p. 213.
48 Joshi and Rose, *Democratic Innovations in Nepal* p. 506.
49 Rehman Sobhan, 'Social Forces in the Basic Democracies', *Asian Review* Vol. 1, No. 3, April 1968, p. 166; Khalid Bin Sayeed, 'Pakistan's Basic Democracy', *Middle East Journal* Vol. 15, No. 3, Summer 1961, p. 249. See generally A. T. R. Rahman, 'Rural Institutions in India and Pakistan', *Asian Survey* Vol. VIII, No. 9, September 1968, p. 792.
50 For an example of the role of consensus in a village election, see Geertz, *The Social History of an Indonesian Town*.
51 'In most Western democracies elections from amongst candidates nominated by political parties by majority vote is the accepted way of selecting representives of the people. Fear of loss of face by failure at the polls does not normally deter a candidate from standing. ... In Hong Kong the position is entirely different and it is doubtful whether popular representation at the present time will be successful in bringing forward the best qualified and most widely accepted citizens to participate in local administration. ... The small turn out of voters at Urban Council elections ... indicates either lack of understanding or distrust.... It must also be borne in mind when considering the reactions of a Chinese community to matters relating to government and administration that the familiar pattern is that of strong bureaucratic control by scholars disciplined by strict moral principles.' From the 'Note of Reservation'' by Paul K. C. Tsui, J. C. C. Walden and S. A. Webb-Johnson, *Report of the Working Party on Local Administration*, Hong Kong Government Press, 1966, pp. 82–3.
52 Francis Carnell, 'Political Ideas and Ideologies in South and Southeast Asia', in Rose (ed.), *Politics in Southern Asia*, p. 293.

RECOMMENDED FURTHER READING

Rose (ed.), *Politics in Southern Asia*.
Kahin (ed.), *Government and Politics of Southeast Asia*.
Weatherbee, *Ideology in Indonesia*.
Scalapino and Masumi, *Parties and Politics in Contemporary Japan*.
Burch and Cole (ed.), *Asian Political Systems*.

Gray (ed.), *China's Search for a Political Form*.

Halappa (ed.), *Dilemmas of Democratic Politics in India*.

Landé, *Leaders, Factions and Parties: The Structure of Philippine Politics*.

Smith (ed.), *South Asian Politics and Religion*.

Tinker, *Ballot Box and Bayonet*.

CHAPTER 14: THE CHINESE DRAGON

1 Hudson, *Europe and China*.

2 Hudson (op. cit., p. 10) comments: 'Europe and China are nations of the first division of mankind; they are great continuities of historical development which may embrace many distinct languages and political units. Civilized Europe was one country under the Roman empire, while China has been divided between separate states through a great part of its history; China no less than Europe has had its diversities of spoken language, and the unity bestowed by its common learned language has hardly been greater than that afforded by Latin in mediaeval Europe. The real unity in each case has been one of cultural tradition. Europeans are all peoples and states deriving their dominant cultural form directly or indirectly from Hellenism, Chinese those deriving it from the 'Chinese' empire of the Huang-ho basin in the first millennium B.C. Each of these root cultures was entirely independent of the other; they had no common heritage of literature or of institutions and ideas above the level of barbarism.'

3 The tradition of centrality dies hard. In 1967, in a confidential talk to senior officials, the head of the *People's Daily* Information Department is said to have remarked: 'The focus of history as a whole formerly lay in the West but has now shifted to China. China has become not only the political and economic centre but also the cultural centre. It is unique in the whole world. In the future the centre of science and technology will also shift to China.' *Red Seamen* (*Hungse Hai-yuan*) Canton 24 January 1968, as translated in *Current Background* (US Consulate-General, Hong Kong) No. 850, 3 April 1968.

4 John H. Weakland, 'The Organisation of Action in Chinese Society', *Psychiatry* Vol. XII, 1950, p. 361.

5 Geoffroy-Dechaume, *China Looks at the World*, p. 112.

6 Fairbank, Reischauer and Craig, *East Asia, The Modern Transformation*, p. 884.

7 *Chinese Looking Glass*.

8 Quoted by Richard H. Solomon, 'Communications Patterns and the Chinese Revolution', *China Quarterly* No. 32, October 1967 p. 97.

9 p. 172.

10 Cited in *Chekiang Jihpao* editorial of 21 January 1968 (as translated in *BBC Summary of World Broadcasts* Part III, FE/2679/B/4 of 26 January 1968).

11 Levenson, *Liang Ch'i-ch'ao and the Mind of Modern China*, p. 219. See also Levenson, *Confucian China and its Modern Fate*.

12 *China Youth Daily*, 20 January 1962.

13 Pye, *The Spirit of Chinese Politics*. Richard Harris writes: 'The free, lone, self-reliant, creative individual is not a product of Chinese culture. His upbringing drives him into the group and cultivates his sense of obligation to it. Freedom of choice has hardly existed. This has made for a natural reserve in the expression of opinion; the normal process of argument and debate natural to a democracy is under-developed. Distinctiveness is inhibited; outward conformity is encouraged; unity and harmony are the keystones of the Chinese outlook'. 'The Chinese Personality', in Wint (ed.), *Asia, A Handbook*, p. 488.

14 Matteo Ricci, quoted in Hudson, op. cit., p. 249.

15 See e.g. Donnithorne, *China's Economic System*, pp. 505–8; and Schurmann, *Ideology and Organisation in Communist China*, pp. 213–19; and the discussion in Chapter 1, pp. 12–13 above.

16 See further p. 217 below.

17 Schurmann, *op. cit*.

18 *Mao Tse-tung*, p. 269.

19 W. A. C. Adie, 'China's "Second Liberation" in Perspective', *Bulletin of the Atomic Scientists* Chicago, February 1969, p. 14. The first serious analysis of the internal rivalries of the Chinese Politburo was Roderick McFarquhar, 'Communist China's Intra-Party Dispute', *Pacific Affairs* Vol. XXXI, No. 4, December 1958, p. 323.

20 Mao left China only twice, to visit Moscow in 1949–50 and again in 1957. None of the Chinese Politburo has seen one of the big post-war cities of the capitalist world. See Donald W. Klein, 'Peking's Leaders: A Study in Isolation', *The China Quarterly*, No. 7, July-September 1961, p. 35; and also his 'The "Next Generation" of Chinese Communist Leaders', *China Quarterly*, No. 12, October-December 1962, p. 57.

21 Most easily accessible in *Peking Review* 3 September 1965, p. 9.

22 Whiting, *China Crosses the Yalu*.

23 op. cit., p. 22. See also Fitzgerald, *The Chinese View of their Place*

in the World, and D. P. Mozingo, and T. W. Robinson, 'Lin Piao on "People's War",' Rand Corporation Memorandum, November 1965.

24 21 July 1958 editorial.

25 See pp. 78–84 of Chapter 7 above.

26 Hinton, *Communist China in World Politics*, Chapter 15.

27 Halperin, *China and the Bomb*.

28 *China in the Year 2001*, p. 9.

29 Report on the Afro-Asian Writers' Conference in Cairo, *Daily Nation*, Nairobi, 13 March 1962.

30 *Réalités* Paris 11 September 1965.

31 'China believes that it is the repository of unique values that ought to be accepted by all mankind and that this acceptance should create a willingness to acknowledge Chinese political leadership even in remote areas where China's power cannot reach ...' (Hinton, op. cit., p. 5).

32 W. A. C. Adie, 'Vagaries of Chinese Policy', *Mizan* Vol. 9, No. 6, November-December 1967, p. 231.

33 *History of Western Philosophy*, p. 420.

34 op. cit., p. 222.

35 Kerr, *Formosa Betrayed*.

36 Chen and Lasswell, *Formosa, China and the United States*.

37 Dennis Bloodworth in the *Observer*, 12 August 1962. See also Snow, *The Other Side of the River*, pp. 327 and 765–6.

38 Sandars, *The People's Republic of Mongolia*.

39 See Dennis Bloodworth, 'Mao Skims Cream off Macao', *Observer* 8 October 1967; and 'Gold: A Tale of Two Cities', *Economist* 16 November 1968.

40 Hughes, *Hong Kong: Borrowed Place – Borrowed Time*; Jarvie (ed.), *Hong Kong: A Society in Transition*.

RECOMMENDED FURTHER READING

Reischauer and Fairbank, *East Asia, The Great Tradition*.

Fairbank, Reischauer and Craig, *East Asia, The Modern Transformation*.

Fitzgerald, *China: A Short Cultural History*.

Creel, *Chinese Thought*.

Hudson, *Europe and China*.

McAleavy, *The Modern History of China*.

Schram, *Mao Tse-tung*.

Wilson, *A Quarter of Mankind*.

Snow, *The Other Side of the River*.

Hinton, *Communist China in World Politics*.

Fitzgerald, *The Chinese View of Their Place in the World.*
Schurmann, *Ideology and Organization in Communist China.*
Bloodworth, *Chinese Looking Glass.*
Pye, *The Spirit of Chinese Politics.*
Chen, *Mao and the Chinese Revolution.*
Hughes, *Hong Kong: Borrowed Place – Borrowed Time.*
Kerr, *Formosa Betrayed.*

CHAPTER 15: JAPANESE BALANCING ACT

1 *From Sea to Sea* Vol. 1, 1900, p. 332.
2 With a gross national product in 1971 of £90,000 million.
3 3 September 1967.
4 *Business Week.* 11 March 1967. But see for reservations about the 'miracle', Kozo Yamamura, 'Growth *vs.* Economic Democracy in Japan – 1945–1965', *Journal of Asian Studies*, Vol. XXV, No. 4, August 1966, p. 713.
5 'The Risen Sun', *Economist* 27 May 1967.
6 Ibid.
7 See the author's 'Fat, But Fighting Fit,' *Far Eastern Economic Review* 18 July 1968, p. 151.
8 From an article in *Chuo Koron*, December 1967 (translation supplied by the author).
9 *Glimpses of World History*, p. 454.
10 *The Economic Development of Japan*, p. 11.
11 Komatsu, *The Japanese People;* Hall and Beardsley (ed.), *Twelve Doors to Japan*, Chapter 2; and Robert N. Bellah, 'Japan's Cultural Identity', *The Journal of Asian Studies* Vol. XXIV, No. 4, August 1965, p. 573.
12 *Japan Times* 30 August 1968. The communists came second with over £1.8 million.
13 Robert E. Ward, 'Recent Electoral Development in Japan', *Asian Survey* Vol. VI, October 1966, p. 547.
14 'The Leadership of the Conservative Party': *Journal of Social and Political Ideas in Japan* Vol. II, No. 3, December 1964, p. 4. See also Nathaniel B. Thayer, *How The Conservatives Rule Japan* (Princeton University Press, 1969).
15 Lee W. Farnsworth, 'Challenges to Factionalism on Japan's Liberal Democratic Party', *Asian Survey* Vol. VI September 1966, p. 501 (especially p. 508).
16 *The Communist Revolution in Asia*, p. 45. But see J. A. A. Stockwin,

'Is Japan a Post-Marxist Society?', *Pacific Affairs* Vol. XLI, No. 2, Summer 1968, p. 184.

17 Interview with John Horder, the *Guardian* 26 March 1965.

18 James H. Buck, 'The Japanese Self-Defence Forces', *Asian Survey* Vol. VII, September 1967, p. 597.

19 Summarized in Saul Rose, 'Strange Bedfellows', *Far Eastern Economic Review* 28 March 1968.

20 *Jiyu*, February 1960 (quoted in Burks, *The Government of Japan*, p. 263). See also Kiyoaki Murata, 'The Takayanagi Theory', *Japan Times* 18 June 1967.

21 *Japan Times* 1 May 1968.

22 ibid., 26 July 1968. See the useful summary of arguments in this debate in Nishijima Yoshiji, 'The Peace Constitution Controversy', *Japan Quarterly* Vol. X, No. 1, January 1963, p. 18.

23 See Tsukasa Matsueda and George E. Moore, 'Japan's Shifting Attitudes Towards the Military', *Asian Survey* Vol. VII September 1967, p. 614.

24 *Japan's American Interlude*, p. 243.

25 *Journal of Social and Political Ideas in Japan* Vol. II, No. 2, August 1964, p. 2.

26 *City Life in Japan*. See also the final Chapter of Basabe, *Japanese Youth Confronts Religion*.

27 *Japan, An Attempt at Interpretation*, p. 71.

28 *The Chrysanthemum and the Sword*, p. 98.

29 Iizuka Kooji, *Nihon no Seishinteki Fundo*, 1952, p. 69 (quoted in Dore, *City Life in Japan*, p. 393).

30 See Douglas Gilbert Haring, 'Japanese Character in the 20th Century', *Annals of the American Academy of Political and Social Sciences* Vol. 370, March 1967, p. 139.

31 *The Times* 14 November 1968.

32 Vogel, *Japan's New Middle Class*.

33 John W. Bennett, 'Japanese Economic Growth: Background for Social Change', in Dore (ed.), *Aspects of Social Change in Modern Japan*, p. 411.

34 Stoetzel, *Without the Chrysanthemum and the Sword*. See also Kiyoaki Murata, 'Depoliticalisation of Youth – Decreasing Interest in Leftism', *Japan Times* 31 July 1969.

35 See *The Times* of 26 July 1968, summarizing Mishima Yukio's article in *Chuo Koron* of that summer.

36 McFarland, *The Rush Hour of the Gods*, p. 236. See also Harry K. Nishio, 'Comparative Analysis of the Rissho Koseikai and the Soka Gakkai', *Asian Survey* Vol. VII November 1967, p. 776.

37 *Parties and Politics in Contemporary Japan*, p. 145.

38 *The Second World War. The Gathering Storm* Vol. I, p. 11.

39 16 April 1966.

40 Nobutaka Ike, 'Japan, Twenty Years After Surrender', *Asian Survey* Vol. VI, January 1966, p. 18.

41 Abe Genki, writing in *Sekai to Nihon* (quoted in Robert Trumbull, 'Japan: The Intellectuals and Rearmament', *New York Times* 22 June 1965).

42 *Seikai Orai*, August 1966: see *The Times* 26 July 1966.

43 See Douglas H. Mendel Jr's articles on Japanese public opinion on foreign policy issues in *Asian Survey* Vol. IX August 1969, p. 625; and *Far Eastern Economic Review*, 26 March 1970, p. 35.

44 Quoted in *Japan Times* 23 January 1964.

45 Chapter 19 below.

46 See Jay B. Sorensen, 'Siberia: Another Try', *Far Eastern Economic Review* 10 October 1968, p. 112; and Kazuo Takita, 'Too Big a Bite', ibid., 27 July 1967, p. 199.

47 *Japanese People and Politics*, p. 380.

48 See Chapter 19 below, pp. 288-90.

49 N. J. Nanporia, 'The Psychological Gap: As Wide As Ever', *Bangkok Post* 26 April 1968. See also Ichiso Kawasaki, *Japan Unmasked* (Tuttle, Tokyo 1969).

50 *Thought and Behaviour in Modern Japanese Politics*, p. 153.

51 Op. cit., footnote 25 above.

52 Cited in *Japan Times* 24 October 1968.

53 Chong-Sik Lee and Kiwan Oh, 'The Russian Faction in North Korea', *Asian Survey* Vol. VIII April 1968, p. 270; and Roy V. T. Kim, 'Sino-North Korean Relations', ibid., August 1968.

54 See S. M. Ali, 'Mandate Confirmed', and Hwang Don, 'The Bull and the Bulldozer', *Far Eastern Economic Review* 11 May 1967, p. 293 and 25 May 1967, p. 452.

55 See Robert Elegant, 'Political Crisis for R O K?', *Bangkok Post* 13 November 1968.

56 Derek Davies, 'Seoul Searching', *Far Eastern Economic Review* 9 January 1969, p. 51.

RECOMMENDED FURTHER READING

Reischauer and Fairbank, *East Asia, The Great Tradition.*

Fairbank, Reischauer and Craig, *East Asia, The Modern Transformation.*

Sansom, *Japan, A Short Cultural History.*

Storry, *A History of Modern Japan.*

Hall and Beardsley, *Twelve Doors to Japan.*

Burks, *The Government of Japan.*

Hasegawa, *The Japanese Character*.
Maruyama, *Thought and Behaviour in Modern Japanese Politics*.
Yoshida, *Japan's Decisive Century 1867–1967*.
Benedict, *The Chrysanthemum and the Sword*.
Vogel, *Japan's New Middle Class*.
Dore, *City Life in Japan*.
Yanaga, *Japanese People and Politics*.
Arima, *The Failure of Freedom*.
Scalapino and Masumi, *Parties and Politics in Contemporary Japan*.
Kawabata, *Snow Country*.
De Bary (ed.), *Sources of Japanese Tradition* (2 vols).
Allen, *A Short Economic History of Modern Japan*.
Oh, *Korea, Democracy on Trial*.

CHAPTER 16: THE INDIAN SUB-CONTINENT

1 Dom Moraes, in a BBC Television programme in December 1968.
2 *The Discovery of India*, p. 91.
3 Jonathan Cape, London 1927. Miss Mayo argued that: 'The whole pyramid of the Indian's woes, material and spiritual – poverty, sickness, ignorance, political minority, melancholy, ineffectiveness, not forgetting that subconscious conviction of inferiority which he forever bares and advertises by his gnawing and imaginative alertness for social affronts – rests upon a rock-bottom physical base. This base is, simply, his manner of getting into the world and his sex-life thenceforward' (p. 29). Gandhi called the book 'a drain-inspector's report', and it provoked numerous books in rebuttal.
4 Leonard Beaton, 'Anglo-Indian Relations: Are They Immature?', *The Times* 19 December 1968.
5 See Chapter 3, pp. 36–40 above.
6 Srinivas, *Social Change in Modern India;* Rudolph, *The Modernity of Tradition*.
7 Discussed in more detail in Chapter 5, pp. 60–61 above.
8 Morris-Jones, 'Language and Region within the Indian Union', in Mason (ed.), *India and Ceylon: Unity and Diversity*. Neville Maxwell, 'India and Language', *New Society* 21 December 1967.
9 *Caste in Modern India*, p. 110; see also Weiner (ed.), *State Politics in India*.
10 Elwin, *Nagaland*.
11 See Michael Scott's statement and the official Indian reply in *The Times* 31 May and 1 June 1966.

12 George N. Patterson, 'Delhi and the Nagas', *Far Eastern Economic Review* 19 May 1966.

13 Anthony Polsky, 'Mao Takes to the Hills', *Far Eastern Economic Review* 31 October 1968, p. 240.

14 Norman D. Palmer, 'India's Fourth General Election', *Asian Survey* Vol. VII, May 1967, p. 275; see also Chandidas, etc., (ed.), *India Votes*, for full details of all four elections.

15 Michael Brecher, 'Succession in India 1967', *Asian Survey* Vol. VII, July 1967, p. 429.

16 Atulya Ghosh, quoted in Marcus F. Franda, 'The Political Idioms of Atulya Ghosh', *Asian Survey* Vol. VI, August 1966, p. 428·

17 Erdman, *The Swatantra Party and Indian Conservatism*.

18 See *The Times* 8 February 1967.

19 Robert L. Hardgrave, 'Religion, Politics and the DMK', in Smith (ed.), *South Asian Politics and Religion*, p. 213.

20 P. S. Goswami, 'Spectre of Fascism Looms over India', *The Scotsman* 5 April 1968. It is noteworthy that of the three independence heroes whose worship survives on an all-India basis, Gandhi and Nehru are the saint and the statesman respectively, while 'Netaji' Subhas Chandra Bose is the soldier.

21 26 and 27 January 1967.

22 Neville Maxwell, *The Times* 10 February 1967.

23 *Guardian* 9 May 1967.

24 See Hugh Tinker, in Mason (ed.), *India and Ceylon: Unity and Diversity*, p. 292; also Kaul, *The Untold Story*, and Neville Maxwell, 'Must the Military Intervene in India?', *The Times* 28 February 1968.

25 Nair, *Blossoms in the Dust*, p. 196.

26 Carstairs, *The Twice-Born*, is a valuable study of Hindu personality-formation.

27 Dhipendra Narain, 'Indian National Character in the Twentieth Century', *Annals of the American Academy of Political and Social Science* Vol. 370, March 1967, p. 124. Narain's comment is confirmed by the findings of Joseph E. Elder, 'Religious Beliefs and Traditional Attitudes', in Smith (ed.), *South Asian Politics and Religion*, p. 249.

28 'The Indian Personality', in Wint (ed.), *Asia: A Handbook*, p. 486.

29 See generally Rudolph and Rudolph, *The Modernity of Tradition*.

30 Rosen, *Democracy and Economic Change in India*.

31 Streeten and Lipton (ed.), *The Crisis of Indian Planning*.

32 Lamb, *Crisis in Kashmir*.

33 K. R. Sundar Rajan, *New Statesman* 7 July 1967.

34 Richard Critchfield, 'Background to Conflict', *Reporter* 4 November 1965.

35 Brines, *The Indo-Pakistan Conflict*.

36 e.g. Kingsley Martin, 'Reflections on Kashmir', *New Statesman* 17 September 1965; also Taya Zinkin, 'How Not to Solve the Kashmir Problem', *Asian Review* Vol. 2, October 1968, p. 41.

37 But another conflict looms over the Farakka barrage which India is building and which will divert River Ganges water away from East Bengal.

38 See Arthur Lall's proposals for reconciliation in the *Observer* 13 June 1965.

39 Karan and Jenkins, *The Himalayan Kingdoms*.

40 Anthony Polsky, 'Brave New World', and 'All the King's Men', *Far Eastern Economic Review* 19 and 26 September 1968, pp. 583 and 623.

41 George N. Patterson, 'A Himalayan Confederation', *Far Eastern Economic Review* 6 May 1965, p. 275.

42 Paul F. Power, 'India and Vietnam', *Asian Survey* Vol. VII, October 1967, p. 740.

43 *Guardian* 23 March 1965.

44 V. P. Dutt, Sisir Gupta and others, in a statement of 28 February 1967.

45 According to the poll taken by the *Los Angeles Times*, reported by Arthur Dommen in *International Herald Tribune* Paris, 20 May 1967.

46 In 1965 the *New Statesman* and *Hindusthan Times* opted for the former, *Times of India* for the latter approach.

47 This is the 'hawkish' policy exemplified in Patwant Singh's *India and the Future of Asia* Faber & Faber, London 1967.

48 Feldman, *Revolution in Pakistan*.

49 See Freeland Abbott, 'Pakistan and the Secular State', in Smith (ed.), *South Asian Politics and Religion*, p. 352.

50 Von Vorys, *Political Development in Pakistan*.

51 Sharif Al-Mujahid, 'Pakistan's First Presidential Elections', and 'The Assembly Elections in Pakistan', *Asian Survey* Vol. V June and November 1965, pp. 280 and 538.

52 W. M. Dobell, 'Ayub Khan as President of Pakistan' *Pacific Affairs* Vol. XLII No. 3, Fall 1969, p. 294.

53 See especially Barbara Ward, 'Pakistan's Ambitious Planners', *Economist* 5 June 1965. Harvard University advisers played an important role in this.

54 'Pakistan Perspective', *Foreign Affairs* Vol. 38, July 1960, p. 547.

55 S. U. Durrani of the Investment Corporation of Pakistan, quoted in *Far Eastern Economic Review* 20 June 1968.

56 Bhutto, The Quest for Peace, Karachi, 1966.
57 Farmer, *Ceylon, A Divided Nation*. S. Arasaratnam, 'Nationalism,
   Communalism and National Unity in Ceylon', in Mason (ed.),
   India and Ceylon: Unity and Diversity, p. 260.
58 James Jupp, 'Constitutional Developments in Ceylon since Independence', *Pacific Affairs* Vol. XLI, No. 2, Summer 1968, p. 169.
59 G. Uswatte Aratchi, 'Why Ceylon Needs Foreign Aid', *Asian
   Review* Vol. 1, January 1968.

RECOMMENDED FURTHER READING

Tinker, *India and Pakistan: A Political Analysis*.
Park, *India's Political System*.
Morris-Jones, *The Government and Politics of India*.
Spear, *A History of India*, Vol. 2.
Gandhi, *An Autobiography*.
Nehru, *Toward Freedom*.
Nehru, *The Discovery of India*.
Harrison, *India, The Most Dangerous Decade*.
Rosen, *Democracy and Economic Change in India*.
Srinivas, *Social Change in Modern India*.
Nair, *Blossoms in the Dust*.
Weiner, *The Politics of Scarcity*.
Segal, *The Crisis of India*.
Carstairs, *The Twice-Born*.
Sayeed, *The Political System of Pakistan*.
Stephens, *Pakistan*.
Von Vorys, *Political Development in Pakistan*.
Mason, *Economic Development in India and Pakistan*.
Smith (ed.), *South Asian Politics and Religion*.
Pakeman, *Ceylon*.

CHAPTER 17: SOUTH-EAST ASIA

1 'A Legal and Historical Review of Indonesia's Sovereignty Over the
  Ages' *Dewan Nasional*, Djakarta, September 1958 (quoted in
  Gordon, *The Dimensions of Conflict in Southeast Asia*, p. 81). Even
  the southern Philippines feels threatened: see the despatch from
  Bernardino Ronquillo, *Far Eastern Economic Review* 1 April 1965,
  p. 10. But Yamin is not in the main stream of Indonesian thought
  and his influence should not be exaggerated.
2 Kahin, *Nationalism and Revolution in Indonesia*.
3 Feith, *The Decline of Constitutional Democracy in Indonesia*.

4 Hindley, *The Communist Party of Indonesia, 1951–1961*.

5 See the four vivid articles by Jean Contenay, 'Another Bloodbath', 'Heritage of Blood', 'Smoking Volcano', and 'Menacing Shadows', *Far Eastern Economic Review* 23 November 1967 (p. 357), 14 December 1967 (p. 509), and 11 and 25 January 1968 (pp. 70, 156).

6 Hughes, *The End of Sukarno*.

7 Estimates of deaths in the winter of 1965–6 range from the Government's 200,000 to some observers' 1 million: see Seymour Topping's despatch in the *New York Times* 24 August 1966, and the *Economist* 26 August 1966.

8 From a 1946 pamphlet quoted in van der Kroef, *Indonesia in the Modern World* Vol. 1, p. 115. This phenomenon is surprising in view of the rise in the literacy rate from a mere 7 per cent at independence to a probable 70 per cent today.

9 Legge, *Central Authority and Regional Autonomy in Indonesia*.

10 Willmott, *The National Status of the Chinese in Indonesia, 1900–1958*.

11 See P. J. Zoetmulder's lucid pamphlet, *The Cultural Background to Indonesian Politics*, University of South Carolina, Columbia SC, 1967.

12 The army would have preferred US military aid, but Eisenhower refused this in 1960.

13 Frederick P. Bannell, 'Guided Democracy Foreign Policy: 1960–1965', *Indonesia* No. 2, October 1966, p. 37.

14 'Lost: One Budget', *Far Eastern Economic Review* 1 December 1966, p. 482.

15 See K. D. Thomas and J. Panglaykim, 'Indonesian Exports: Performance and Prospects 1950–1970', *Bulletin of Indonesian Economic Studies* No. 5, October 1966, p. 71, and No. 6, February 1967, p. 66.

16 For a recent survey of agricultural problems see D. H. Penny, 'The Economics of Peasant Agriculture: The Indonesian Case', *Bulletin of Indonesian Economic Studies* No. 5, October 1966, p. 22.

17 A. R. Soehoed, 'Manufacturing in Indonesia', *Bulletin of Indonesian Economic Studies* No. 8, October 1967, p. 80.

18 Ingrid Palmer and Lance Castles, 'The Textile Industry', *Bulletin of Indonesian Economic Studies* No. 2, September 1965, p. 34.

19 M. Sadli, 'New Policy to Attract Foreign Investment', *Financial Times* 24 October 1968.

20 J. Panglaykim and K. D. Thomas, 'The New Order and the Economy', *Indonesia* No. 3, April 1967, p. 73.

21 Weatherbee, *Ideology in Indonesia*. For a reasoned critical Indonesian assessment of Sukarno, see Alisjahbana, *Indonesia: Social and Cultural Revolution*, Chapter 12.

22 Golay (ed.), *The Philippines and the United States.*

23 In an interview in the *Asia Magazine* 6 March 1966.

24 Frances L. Starner, 'Which Way from Here', *Far Eastern Economic Review* 22 August 1968, p. 355.

25 Hector R. R. Villanueva (a London School of Economics graduate), writing in the *Manila Bulletin* in 1964 (quoted in the author's 'Philippine Fanfares', *Far Eastern Economic Review* 24 September 1964, p. 553).

26 Landé, *Leaders, Factions and Parties: The Structure of Phillippine Politics;* and Carl H. Landé, 'Parties and Politics in the Philippines', *Asian Survey* Vol. VIII, No. 9, September 1968, p. 725.

27 Peter Forzman, 'Father Knows Best', *Far Eastern Economic Review* 24 October 1968, p. 192.

28 Romulo, *The Magsaysay Story.*

29 Bernardino Ronquillo, 'Reformers or Revolutionaries?', *Far Eastern Economic Review* 1 September 1966, p. 405.

30 See e.g. Frances L. Starner, 'Report from Arayat', *Far Eastern Economic Review* 19 October 1967, p. 144.

31 Silcock, *Towards a Malayan Nation*, p. 2.

32 Lee noted that some politicians in Kuala Lumpur had been born in Indonesia and emigrated as young men. But these remarks were received as an 'insult to the Malay race' and prehistoric origins were found for a peninsular Malay State. See *The Times* 10 May 1965.

33 *Opinion* Kuala Lumpur, August 1976.

34 Malays are guaranteed an overwhelming majority of Government jobs despite their relative educational weakness. Rahman has several adopted Chinese children.

35 Harvey Stockwin, 'A Matter of Degree', *Far Eastern Economic Review* 28 July 1966, p. 138. Only one in ten of Malaysian students abroad is Malay!

36 One state – Kelantan – is ruled by the opposition Pan-Malayan Islamic Party, which is ardently pro-Malay, won a seventh of the votes in the 1964 elections and opposed the creation of the Federation.

37 Bob Reece, 'The Parting of the Ways' and 'Deepavali Blues', *Far Eastern Economic Review* 19 June 1969, p. 662 and 30 October 1969, p. 266.

38 Chapter 7 above, pp. 89–91. See Brackman, *South-east Asia's Second Front.*

39 Harvey Stockwin, 'Look Back in Sorrow' and 'Look Forward with Hope', *Far Eastern Economic Review* 11 and 18 August 1966, pp. 271, 312.

40 *Bangkok Post* 16 October 1967.

41 Interview in the *New York Times* 17 September 1965.

42 Half the parents of the Singaporean Cabinet live in Malaysia, and three-quarters of the island's water supplies derive from Malaysia. See generally David W. Chang, 'Nation-Building in Singapore', *Asian Survey* Vol. VIII, No. 9, September 1968, p. 761.

43 Riggs, *Thailand: The Modernisation of a Bureaucratic Polity.*

44 Wilson, *Politics in Thailand*, p. vii.

45 'Constitutional Concern', *Far Eastern Economic Review* 11 July 1968; 'A Leader on Trial', ibid., 13 March 1969, p. 452; and Donald Hindley, 'Thailand: The Politics of Passivity', *Pacific Affairs* Vol. XLI, No. 3, Autumn 1968, p. 355.

46 André Tong, 'La Thailande sera-t-elle un Nouveau Vietnam?', *Est et Ouest* (Paris) No. 377, February 1967, p. 18; and 'Symposium on Northeast Thailand', *Asian Survey* Vol. VI, No. 7, July 1966, p. 349.

47 Stanley Karnow, 'The Looking-Glass War', *Far Eastern Economic Review* 21 December 1967, p. 539.

48 W. A. Standish, 'Malay Moslem Mixtures', *Far Eastern Economic Review* 6 July 1967, p. 19.

49 For a good review of the agricultural disappointments, see L. F. Goodstadt, 'Peasants' Parliament', *Far Eastern Economic Review* 23 March 1967, p. 573.

50 MacDonald, *Angkor.*

51 See Willmott, *The Chinese in Cambodia;* and 'Friendship with Frictions', *Far Eastern Economic Review* 15 June 1967, p. 623.

52 Letter to the editor, *The Asia Magazine* 10 July 1966; F. T. Mits, 'Cambodia's Neutralist Flair', *Far Eastern Economic Review* 13 May 1965, p. 321.

53 Leifer, *Cambodia: The Search for Security.*

54 *Independence and After*, p. 19.

55 Simon Head, 'Balance of Powers' and 'Common Denominator', *Far Eastern Economic Review* 30 March and 6 April 1967, pp. 27, 606.

56 *Far Eastern Economic Review* 1 April 1965, p. 13; Leifer, *op. cit.*

57 Interview in *Secolo d'Italia* October 1966, reported in *Bangkok Post* 12 October 1966.

58 *The Making of South East Asia*, p. 230.

59 Dennis J. Duncanson, '"Unrecognized Frontier" in South-East Asia', *Royal Central Asian Journal* Vol. LV, Part 2, June 1968, p. 150.

60 Op. cit., p. 9. The idea of this division was further elaborated in 'The Unrecognised Frontier', *The Listener* 6 September 1962. For a

dissent to the placing of the dividing line on the Vietnamese border, see Duncanson, op. cit.

61 Chapter 6, pp. 68–70 above. See Purcell, *The Chinese in Southeast Asia*.
62 Wiens, *China's March Into the Tropics*, p. 109.
63 Muscat, *Development Strategy in Thailand*.

RECOMMENDED FURTHER READING

Kahin (ed.), *Governments and Politics of Southeast Asia*.
Hall, *A History of Southeast Asia*.
Mintz, *Indonesia, A Profile*.
Palmier, *Indonesia*.
Sukarno, *An Autobiography*.
McVey (ed.), *Indonesia*.
Wertheim, *Indonesian Society in Transition*.
Geertz, *The Social History of an Indonesian Town*.
Selosoemardjan, *Social Changes in Jogjakarta*.
Lubis, *Twilight in Djakarta*.
Grant, *Indonesia*.
Alisjahbana, *Indonesia: Social and Cultural Revolution*.
Landé, *Leaders, Factions and Parties: The Structure of Philippine Politics*.
Gullick, *Malaya*.
Wilson, *Politics in Thailand*.
Blanchard (ed.), *Thailand, Its People, Its Society, Its Culture*.
Tinker, *The Union of Burma*.
Cady, *A History of Modern Burma*.
Duncanson, *Government and Revolution in Vietnam*.
Fall, *The Two Vietnams*.
Leifer, *Cambodia: The Search for Security*.
Toye, *Laos, Buffer State or Battleground?*
Purcell, *The Chinese in Southeast Asia*.

CHAPTER 18: POLITICAL COOPERATION

1 At a Press conference in March 1964, cited in Gordon, *The Dimensions of Conflict in Southeast Asia*, p. 62.
2 New China News Agency report of a National People's Congress meeting, cited in *Keesing's Contemporary Archives*, p. 16801.
3 23 March 1947, as published in Nehru, *India's Foreign Policy*, p. 250.
4 See Jansen, *Afro-Asia and Non-Alignment*, Chapter 9.
5 In a statement issued in New Delhi on 28 June 1954.

6 See the author's 'The Algiers Fiasco', *Far Eastern Economic Review* 18 November 1965, p. 327.

7 Jansen, op. cit., p. 73.

8 'South East Asia at "Threes and Fives"', *Far Eastern Economic Review* 14 July 1960, p. 50.

9 M. P. Gopalan, 'The Launching of ASA', *Far Eastern Economic Review* 21 September 1961, p. 548.

10 Brackman, *Southeast Asia's Second Front*, Chapter 15, also pp. 122–4.

11 Message of 1 January 1966.

12 New China News Agency 9 August 1967.

13 'An Asian Balance of Power?', *Australian Journal of Politics and History* Vol. XII, No. 2, August 1966, p. 278.

14 Miller (ed.), *India, Japan, Australia – Partners in Asia?*

15 Coral Bell, 'The Asian Balance of Power; A Comparison with European Precedents', *Adelphi Papers* No. 44, February 1968 (Institute for Strategic Studies, London), p. 12.

16 See Matsumoto Shigeharu, 'Japan and China', in Halpern (ed.), *Policies Toward China*.

17 Royama Michio, 'The Asian Balance of Power: A Japanese View', *Adelphi Papers* No. 42, November 1967 (Institute for Strategic Studies, London).

18 Russell Braddon and Dennis Warner belong to this school.

19 See for a good summary, Lawrence W. Beer, 'Some Dimensions of Japan's Present and Potential Relations with Communist China', *Asian Survey* Vol. IX, No. 3, March 1969, p. 163.

20 See Foreign Minister Miki's speech in Tokyo on 22 May 1967 (*Asahi Shimbun*, 23 May 1967).

21 In a speech at Middlebury College, Vermont, on 12 June 1967.

22 'Asian Regionalism', *Japan Quarterly* Vol. XIV, No. 1, January 1968, p. 60. One South-East Asian prime minister privately describes ASEAN and ASPAC as 'exercises in collective soliciting', but this is unfair.

RECOMMENDED FURTHER READING

Jansen, *Afro-Asia and Non-Alignment*.

Gordon, *The Dimensions of Conflict in Southeast Asia*.

Kahin, *The Asian-African Conference*.

Kennedy, *The Security of Southern Asia*.

Buchan (ed.), *China and the Peace of Asia*.

Brackman, *Southeast Asia's Second Front*.

Miller (ed.), *India, Japan, Australia – Partners in Asia?*

CHAPTER 19: ECONOMIC COOPERATION

1 Quoted in Gordon, *The Dimensions of Conflict in Southeast Asia*, p. 32.

2 'Approaches to Regional Harmonisation of National Development Plans in Asia and the Far East', an ECAFE report dated 25 September 1964.

3 *Far Eastern Economic Review* 5 September 1968, p. 463.

4 *Bangkok Post* 2 June 1967. As Adam Malik, the Indonesian foreign minister, has ruefully remarked: 'Indonesia itself is not yet a Common Market' (*Economist* 23 March 1968).

5 Palns for a £80 million petrochemical complex to serve the entire ASEAN market, to be followed by an integrated steel complex, were revealed in the *Bangkok Post* on 24 October 1968.

6 Daniel Wolfstone, 'The Colombo Plan After Ten Years', *Far Eastern Economic Review* 3 August 1961, p. 222.

7 Wightman, *Toward Economic Cooperation in Asia*.

8 L. F. Goodstadt, 'What's Wrong with ECAFE', *Far Eastern Economic Review* 22 December 1966, p. 597.

9 *Far Eastern Economic Review* 24 March 1966.

10 See W. R. Derrick Sewell, 'The Mekong Scheme', and David Jenkins, 'The Lower Mekong Scheme', *Asian Survey* Vol. VIII, June 1968, pp. 448, 456.

11 P. H. M. Jones, 'Everybody's Bank', *Far Eastern Economic Review* 14 April 1966, p. 59; and 'Whose Child', ibid., 26 November 1968.

12 *Japan Times* 20 March 1967.

13 See John White, 'The Asian Development Bank: A Question of Style', *International Affairs* Vol. 44, No. 4, October 1968, p. 687.

14 See e.g. Dennis Warner in the *Reporter* 18 May 1967, p. 30.

15 i.e. Burma, Philippines, Indonesia and South Vietnam, plus (under slightly different labels) Laos, Cambodia, Thailand and South Korea. Britain and Nationalist China waived their claims to war reparations after the Peace Treaty, and so Taiwan, Malaysia and Singapore have not received any. The latter two have recently accepted special aid from Japan in payment of 'blood debt', however, and there are fears in Tokyo lest Peking open the question of reparations once diplomatic recognition is extended. See generally Daniel Wolfstone, 'Japan's Helping Hand', *Far Eastern Economic Review* 31 October 1963, p. 237.

16 Charles Smith, *The Financial Times* 22 September 1969.

17 Quoted in Wolfstone, op. cit. (footnote 15 *supra*), p. 239.

18 Kiyoshi Kojima, 'Japan's Role in Asian Agricultural Development', *Japan Quarterly* Vol. XIV, No. 2, April 1967, p. 158.

19 Kojima (ed.), *Pacific Trade and Development*. Latin America might also become eligible at a later stage.

20 See especially Miki's address to the Foreign Correspondents' Club in Tokyo on 16 June 1967 (*Japan Information Bulletin* London, 1 August 1967); and Professor G. C. Allen's pamphlet, *Japan's Place in Trade Strategy* (Atlantic Trade Study, 1968).

21 See the author's 'New Trade Winds Over the Pacific', *Sunday Times*, 11 September 1966, and 'PAFTA and NAFTA', *Far Eastern Economic Review*, 12 January 1967. An Australian dissent may be read in H. W. Arndt, 'Pacific Free Trade Area: An Australian Assessment', *Intereconomics* No. 10, October 1967, p. 271; countered by Kiyoshi Kojima, 'A Pacific Free Trade Area', ibid., No. 3, March 1968, p. 75.

22 *The Asia Magazine* Hong Kong, 25 September 1966.

23 Cutajar and Franks, *The Less Developed Countries in World Trade*.

24 i.e. the average prices fetched by the South's exports, in relation to the average prices it pays for its imports.

25 See the author's 'Strategy for the South', *Far Eastern Economic Review* 20 October 1966, p. 129.

26 See the author's 'The Preference Game', *Far Eastern Economic Review* 18 April 1968.

27 See Table 15, p. 50, in *UNCTAD Review of Recent Trends in Trade in Manufactures*, 1 October 1968, set out in *Far Eastern Economic Review* 28 August 1969, p. 579.

28 To take one situation of interest to Asia: in 1961 Africa bought 60 per cent of its textiles and garment imports from Western Europe, only 10 per cent from developing Asia. See the author's 'Deeds not Words', *Far Eastern Economic Review* 28 December 1967, p. 588.

RECOMMENDED FURTHER READING

Wightman, *Towards Economic Cooperation in Asia*.
Singh, *The Politics of Economic Cooperation in Asia*.
Gordon, *The Dimensions of Conflict in Southeast Asia*.
Cutajar and Franks, *The Less Developed Countries in World Trade*.
Kojima (ed.), *Pacific Trade and Development*.
Jalée, *The Pillage of the Third World*.
UNCTAD Basic Documents. The Colombo Plan Story.
Johnson, *Economic Policies Towards Less Developed Countries*.
Asia's Economic Growth and Intra-Regional Cooperation.

CHAPTER 20: THE VIETNAM WAR

1 Duncanson, *Government and Revolution in Vietnam*, p. 2.
2 Eden, *Towards Peace in Indo-China*.
3 'The Struggle for the Unification of Vietnam', *The China Quarterly*, No. 9, January 1962, p. 16.
4 *The Making of a Quagmire*, p. 206.
5 18 August 1967.
6 See Dennis J. Duncanson, 'Vietnam as a Nation-State', *Modern Asian Studies* Vol. 3, Part 2, April 1969, p. 117. The two quotations from President Johnson are from his speech at Johns Hopkins University, 7 April 1965.
7 Devillers, ibid., p. 21.
8 See Richard Harris, 'The Rivalry Between China and North Vietnam', *The Times* 1 January 1969; also Pike, *Viet Cong*.
9 See Rhoads Murphey, 'China and the Dominoes', *Asian Survey* Vol. VI, September 1966, p. 510.
10 'Long Live the Victory of People's War', *Peking Review* 3 September 1965, p. 9.
11 D. P. Mozingo and T. W. Robinson, *Lin Piao on 'People's War': China Takes a Second Look at Vietnam*, Rand Corporation Memorandum, November 1965.
12 Testimony of 31 January 1967, p. 13.
13 Speech of 25 September 1967 (*Japan Times* 26 September 1967).
14 See e.g. Michio Royama, *The Asian Balance of Power: A Japanese View* Adelphi Paper 42, Institute for Strategic Studies, November 1967, p. 10.
15 Miller (ed) *India, Japan, Australia* p. 120

RECOMMENDED FURTHER READING

Gettleman (ed.), *Vietnam*.
Duncanson, *Government and Revolution in Vietnam*.
Fall, *The Two Vietnams*.
Honey, *Genesis of a Tragedy: The Historical Background to the Vietnam War*.
Halberstam, *The Making of a Quagmire*.
Eden, *Towards Peace in Indo-China*.
Pike, *Viet Cong*.
Smith, *Vietnam and the West*.
Lacouture, *Ho Chi Minh*.

CHAPTER 21: THE WESTERN BURDEN

1 Speech by Rogaciano M. Mercado in Manila on 2 December 1968 (*Bangkok Post* 3 December 1968).
2 Address at the Bangkok Seminar on 'Beyond Nationalism', *Bangkok Post* 20 October 1968.
3 *The Present-Day Experiment in Western Civilisation*, p. 29. For a dignified dissent see Silcock, *Towards a Malayan Nation*, pp. 4–5.
4 *Breakthrough in Burma*, pp. xxi-xxii.
5 Donald E. Weatherbee, 'Portuguese Timor: An Indonesian Dilemma', *Asian Survey* Vol. VI December 1966, p. 683.
6 See the author's 'Britain's Bargain Bases', *Far Eastern Economic Review* 28 July 1966, p. 151.
7 *Guardian* 20 September 1965.
8 Interview with Sihanouk, *Far Eastern Economic Review* 9 December 1965, p. 456.
9 15 April 1968.
10 Kojima (ed.), *Pacific Trade and Development*.
11 Professor Manning Clark, 'Price of Survival Could Be End of Europeanism', *The Times* 23 January 1968.
12 Huck, *The Chinese in Australia*.
13 Peter Grey, 'Trouble in Keeping "White"', *Far Eastern Economic Review* 15 September 1966, p. 512.
14 Starke, *The Anzus Treaty Alliance*: Millar, *Australia's Foreign Policy*.
15 *Siam Rath*, Bangkok, December 1967 (quoted in *International Herald-Tribune* 30 December 1967).
16 *The New York Times* 1 September 1965.
17 Quoted in *Far Eastern Economic Review* 14 July 1966, p. 73.
18 *The Continent of Circe*, p. 84.
19 'Pakistan Perspective', *Foreign Affairs* Vol. 38 No. 4 July 1960, p. 556.
20 House of Commons, 14 October 1965.
21 Richard H. Solomon, 'Parochialism and Paradox in Sino-American Relations', *Asian Survey* Vol. VII December 1967, p. 835.
22 *The Times* 9 December 1965.
23 *China, Yellow Peril? Red Hope?* pp. 220–1.
24 *The Asian Balance of Power*, Adelphi Paper No. 44, Institute for Strategic Studies, February 1968, p. 13.
25 *Asia, The Pacific and the U.S.* Hearing before the Committee on Foreign Relations, U.S. Senate, first session with Edwin O. Reischauer, 31 January 1967, p. 11.

26 12 August 1968.
27 Stanley Karnow, *Far Eastern Economic Review* 21 December 1967, p. 547.
28 See Solomon, op. cit., and Richard Harris' three articles in *The Times* of 12, 13, and 14 February 1968.
29 Cf. Edgar Snow's verdict: 'The fact that the United States has for a decade followed a policy of armed intervention in China's affairs, that this policy has served to discredit influential Chinese in the mainland once friendly to America and has added great force to Peking's ideological attacks on imperialism – which might otherwise seem as obsolete to Chinese intellectuals as they do to Mr Nehru – is little understood by those Americans most anxious to bring about the downfall of the Communists.' (*The Other Side of the River*, pp. 86–7).
30 *The Times* 20 September 1965. The Indian Government will not confirm that these requests were made.
31 Speech in the US Senate, 22 July 1966.
32 *International Herald-Tribune*, 19 November 1966.
33 Australian Institute of Political Science, *Communism in Asia: A Threat to Australia?*, p. 17.
34 Pike, *Viet Cong*.
35 Speech at University of North Carolina, 9 May 1967.
36 Speech of 13 March 1965.
37 Bell, op. cit., p. 11.

RECOMMENDED FURTHER READING
Smith, *Vietnam and the West*.
Pannikar, *Asia and Western Dominance*.
Millar, *Australia's Foreign Policy*.
Starke, *The Anzus Treaty Alliance*.
Buchan (ed.), *China and the Peace of Asia*.
Blum, *The United States and China in World Affairs*.
China, Vietnam and the United States: Highlights of the Hearings of the Senate Foreign Relations Committee.

CHAPTER 22: THE SOVIET IMAGE

1 *Pravda* 17 August 1964 (quoted in Conolly, *Beyond The Urals*, pp. 361–2).
2 See Nove and Newth, *The Soviet Middle East*, p. 43.
3 Charles K. Wilbur, *Soviet Studies* Vol. XVII, April 1966, p. 408.
4 Vaidyanath, *The Formation of the Soviet Central Asian Republics*.

5 *The Soviet Economy*, Allen & Unwin, London 1965, p. 321. Soviet failures in agriculture are well known.

6 Conolly, *Beyond the Urals*, p. 361.

7 Wheeler, *The Peoples of Soviet Central Asia;* Bacon, *Central Asians Under Russian Rule*. Similar comments could be made on the role of the minorities in China, too.

8 Nove and Newth, op. cit., p. 122.

9 Floyd, *Mao against Krushchev*, pp. 10–12.

10 *The Great Polemic on the General Line of the International Communist Movement*.

11 19 November 1963.

12 Zagoria, *The Sino-Soviet Conflict, 1956–61*. See John Gittings' 'How They Lost China' *Far Eastern Economic Review* 13 November 1969, p. 371.

13 Daniel Tretiak, 'Marxist Merryground', *Far Eastern Economic Review* 8 February 1968, p. 229.

14 Arthur Stein, 'India and the USSR: The Post-Nehru Period', *Asian Survey* Vol. VII, March 1967, p. 165.

15 Sheldon W. Simon, 'The Kashmir Dispute in Sino-Soviet Perspective', *Asian Survey* Vol. VII, March 1967, p. 176.

16 'The Bottomless Well of Russian Assistance', *Financial Times* 9 May 1968.

17 See the United Nations ECOSOC Document E/4495 of 20 May 1968, *UN Secretary-General's Review of Recent Trends of International Flow of Capital and Assistance, External Financing of Economic Development of the Developing Countries*, Table 4, p. 19. The 1954–67 commitments are there given at $3,290 million, but Chinese aid is included in that, and a discount should be made for disbursements failing to match commitments. See also Goldman, *Soviet Foreign Aid*, and Vassil Vassilev, *Policy in the Soviet Bloc on Aid to Developing Countries* (OECD, Paris, 1969).

18 *Economist* 28 October 1967.

19 David Morison, 'Recent Soviet Interest in Population Problems of the Developing Countries', *Mizan* Vol. 9, No. 5, September 1967, p. 181.

20 'Soviet Relations with Malaysia and Singapore', and 'The Soviet Union and the Philippines: Prospects for Improved Relations', *Mizan*. Vol 10, Nos. 1 and 3, January and May 1968, pp. 29, 96.

21 'Russia, China and South-East Asia', *Mizan* Vol. 10, No. 4, July 1968, p. 156.

22 *Pravda* 3 January 1968 (summarizing Prof. R. Ulyanovsky's longer exposition in *Peoples of Asia and Africa* No. 5, 1967).

RECOMMENDED FURTHER READING

Nove and Newth, *The Soviet Middle East*.

Conolly, *Beyond the Urals*.

Bacon, *Central Asians Under Russian Rule*.

Wheeler, *The Peoples of Soviet Central Asia*.

Goldhagen (ed.), *Ethnic Minorities in the Soviet Union*.

Goldman, *Soviet Foreign Aid*.

Sawyer, *Communist Trade with Developing Countries: 1955–65*.

Floyd, *Mao Against Khrushchev*.

Zagoria, *The Sino-Soviet Conflict, 1956–61*.

The Great Polemic on the General Line of the International Communist Movement.

Patterson, *The Unquiet Frontier*.

CHAPTER 23: FOREIGN AID

1 *Geographical Distribution of Financial Flows to Less Developed Countries 1960–1964* (OECD), Paris, 1966), and *The Flow of Financial Resources to Less Developed Countries 1961–1965* (OECD, Paris, 1967), p. 155.

2 White, *Pledged to Development*.

3 OECD, *Development Assistance, 1968 Review*, p. 271.

4 Quoted in *The Times* 22 February 1966.

5 One scholar has calculated that the tying of aid in the case of Pakistan has raised the average price of all commodities imported under aid arrangements by 15 per cent: Mahbub ul Haq, 'Tied Credits – A Quantitative Analysis', in Adler, *Capital Movements and Economic Development*.

6 R. B. Sutcliffe, *New Society* 5 September 1968, p. 346.

7 Nan Han-chen, speaking at the Second Asian Economic Seminar at Pyongyang in June 1964 (cited in *Far Eastern Economic Review* 9 July 1964, p. 42).

8 See *The Times* editorial of 25 June 1966.

9 e.g. in the *Sunday Telegraph* 30 October 1966.

10 See e.g. the *Spectator* 4 November 1966.

11 24 September 1966.

12 Lu Hsun, 'On China's Guideline for Self-Reliance in Socialist Construction', *Ching-chi Yenchiu* 20 July 1965 (as translated in *Survey of Chinese Mainland Magazines*, Hong Kong, No. 488).

13 *Development for Free Asia* p. 46.

14 *The Continent of Circe*, p. 22.

15 Cited by Albert Axelbank. 'Peking is on the Outside', *Far Eastern Economic Review* 8 August 1968.

16 Address to Indonesian diplomats on 5 October 1967 (as translated in *BBC Summary of World Broadcasts*, Part III, FE/2593/B/16).

17 12 June 1952, as published in *India's Foreign Policy*, p. 63.

18 Abdur Razzaq, in an unpublished paper delivered at Harvard. Michael Kidron has remarked: 'If the ruling elites in backward countries can substitute imported for extracted resources, can use aid and foreign investments instead of structural reform, they will do so – and hobble development planning in the process' (*New Society* 3 October 1968, p. 498). But Warren F. Ilchman has argued (in 'A Political Economy of Foreign Aid: The Case of India', *Asian Survey* Vol. VII, October 1967, p. 667) that aid does not yield the donor direct political results in terms of changing attitudes, showing that the Congress Party has not gained politically in constituencies benefiting from foreign aid.

19 'India's Lack of Metal', *Far Eastern Economic Review* 2 December 1965, p. 433.

20 Nairn, *International Aid to Thailand*.

21 George Woods, quoted in the *Economist* 30 September 1967.

22 *UN Secretary-General's Review of Recent Trends of International Flow of Capital and Assistance, External Financing of the Economic Development of the Developing Countries*, ECOSOC Document E/4495 of 20 May 1968, Table 4, p. 19.

23 Bernier, *Travels in the Mogul Empire*, p. 200–1.

24 See the excellent article by J. H. Plumb in the *Spectator*, 17 March 1967, p. 307.

25 See e.g. O. P. Dwivedi, 'Bureaucratic Corruption in Developing Countries', *Asian Survey* Vol. VII, April 1967, p. 245; and James N. Anderson in *Asian Survey* Vol. IX, September 1969, p. 662.

26 Moncrieff (ed.), *Second Thoughts on Aid*, p. 53.

27 Address to the Board of Governors of the World Bank, Washington, 30 September 1968 (p. 7 of the Bank's published text).

28 *The Attack on World Poverty*, p. 6.

29 Jacoby, *U.S. Aid to Taiwan*.

30 *Reserve Bank of India Bulletin*, Vol. XXII, April 1968, p. 435.

31 John Davies (now a Government Minister), quoted by Lombard in the *Financial Times* of 23 September 1968.

32 Kidron, *Foreign Investments in India*, p. 186.

33 ibid., p. 310.

34 See Joyce Gibson, 'Production-Sharing', *Bulletin of Indonesian*

Economic Studies No. 3 (February 1966), p. 52, and No. 4 (June 1966), p. 75; and also Gregory Clark, 'Japanese Production-Sharing Projects, 1966–68', *Bulletin of Indonesian Studies*, No. 10 (June 1968), p. 68.

35 Derek Davies, 'Refining With Thais', *Far Eastern Economic Review*, 7 January 1965, p. 21.

36 ibid. (footnote 26 above), p. 2.

RECOMMENDED FURTHER READING

Little and Clifford, *International Aid.*
Mikesell, *The Economics of Foreign Aid.*
Shonfield, *The Attack on World Poverty.*
White, *Pledged to Development.*
Kidron, *Foreign Investments in India.*
Moncrieff (ed.), *Second Thoughts on Aid.*
Goldman, *Soviet Foreign Aid.*
Pearson, *Partners in Development.*

CONCLUSION

1 *The Ideals of the East*, p. 1. This was written after visiting for the first time the India of Tagore and Lord Curzon.

2 Speech at Lucknow, 3 October 1950. Nehru, *India's Foreign Policy*, p. 265.

3 31 July 1968.

4 p. 239.

5 See e.g. the Korean views reported in *Asian Survey* Vol. VII, January 1967, p. 27; and Dr Ismail's proposals in the Malaysian Parliament on 23 January 1968.

6 *Shin Nihonshi*, pp. 306–7, as quoted in translation in Jansen (ed.), *Changing Japanese Attitudes Toward Modernization*, p. 415.

7 Wang Gung-wu, in Rose (ed.), *Politics in Southern Asia*, p. 300.

8 *The Dance of Shiva*, p. 166.

9 *The Glass Curtain Between Asia and Europe.*

10 *The Continent of Circe*, p. 30.

11 *Japan Information Bulletin* London, Vol. XIV, No. 19, 1 October 1967, p. 3.

12 Ronald Clark, *J.B.S. The Life and Works of J.B.S. Haldane* (Hodder and Stoughton, London 1968).

13 Nora Waln, *The House of Exile* (The Cresset Press, London 1933). The authoress was adopted by a Chinese family during the 1920s.

14 Elizabeth Stevenson, *Lafcadio Hearn* (Collier Macmillan, London

1963). Hearn settled in Japan in middle age, married a Japanese, took a Japanese name and lived in Japanese style, writing many books (in English) on his observations. See also 'Gaijin Living in Zen' *The Asia Magazine* 21 April 1968.

Bibliography

Adler, J. (ed.), *Capital Movements and Economic Development*. International Economics Association, London, 1967.

Ahmad, Mushtaq, *Government and Politics in Pakistan*. Pakistan Publishing House, Karachi, 1963.

Aird, John S. *The Size, Composition and Growth of the Population of Mainland China*. Bureau of the Census, Department of Commerce, Washington, DC, 1961.

Alisjahbana, S. Takdir, *Indonesia: Social and Cultural Revolution*. Oxford University Press, London, 1966.

Allen, G. C., *A Short Economic History of Modern Japan 1867–1937*. Unwin University Books, London, 1950.

Anand, Mulk Raj, *Is There a Contemporary Indian Civilization?* Asia Publishing House, London, New York, 1963.

Anand, Mulk Raj, *Untouchable*. Hutchinson, London, 1953.

An Economic Profile of Mainland China, Studies Prepared for the Joint Economic Committee, Congress of the United States (2 vols.). US Government Printing Office, Washington, DC, 1967.

Apter, David E., *The Politics of Modernization*. University of Chicago Press, Chicago, 1965.

Arima, Tatsuo, *The Failure of Freedom, A Portrait of Modern Japanese Intellectuals*. Harvard University Press, Cambridge, Mass., 1969.

Asia's Economic Growth and Intra-Regional Cooperation. The Institute of Asian Economic Affairs, Tokyo, 1967.

Australian Institute of Political Science, *Communism in Asia: A Threat to Australia?* Angus and Robertson, Sydney, 1967.

Bacon, Elizabeth E., *Central Asians Under Russian Rule: A Study in Culture Change*. Oxford University Press, London, 1966; Cornell University Press, Ithaca, NY, 1966.

Ba Maw, *Breakthrough in Burma, Memoirs of a Revolution, 1939–1946*. Yale University Press, New Haven, 1968.

Banerjea, Sir Surendranath, *A Nation in the Making*. Oxford University Press, London, 1963.

Barnett, A. Doak, *Communist Strategies in Asia: A comparative Analysis of Governments and Parties*. Praeger, New York, 1963.

Basabe, Fernando M., *Japanese Youth Confronts Religion*. Sophia University, Tokyo, 1967.

Benedict, Ruth, *The Chrysanthemum and the Sword, Patterns of Japanese Culture*. Houghton Mifflin, Boston, 1946.

Berrill, Kenneth (ed.), *Economic Development with Special Reference to East Asia*. Macmillan, London, 1965.

Beteille, André, *Caste, Class and Power, Changing Pattern of Stratification in a Tanjore Village*. University of California Press, Berkeley, 1966.

Bhagwati, Jagdish, *The Economics of Underdeveloped Countries*. Weidenfeld and Nicolson, London, 1966; McGraw-Hill, New York, 1966.

Blacker, Carmen, *The Japanese Enlightenment: A Study of the Writings of Fukuzawa Yukichi*. Cambridge University Press, London, 1964.

Blanchard, Wendell, *Thailand, Its People, Its Society, Its Culture*. HRAF Press, New Haven, 1958.

Bloodworth, Dennis, *Chinese Looking Glass*. Secker and Warburg, London, 1967.

Blum, Robert, *The United States and China in World Affairs*. McGraw-Hill, New York, 1966.

Bolitho, Hector, *Jinnah*. Murray, London, 1954.

Bondurant, Joan, *Conquest of Violence*. University of California Press, Berkeley, 1965.

Bose, Buddhaveda: *An Acre of Green Grass, A Review of Modern Bengali Literature*. Longmans, Calcutta, 1948.

Bose, S. C., *The Indian Struggle 1920–1934*. Wishart, London, 1935.

Bouman, J. C. et al., *The South Moluccas, Rebellious Province or Occupied State*. Sythoff, Leyden, 1960.

Bougeois-Pichat, Jean, *Population Growth and Development*. Carnegie Endowment for International Peace, New York, 1966.

Brackman, Arnold C., *Southeast Asia's Second Front, The Power Struggle in the Malay Archipelago*. Pall Mall, London, 1966; Praeger, New York, 1966.

Brass, Paul R., *Factional Politics in an Indian State*. University of California Press, Berkeley, 1965.

Brecher, Michael, *Nehru's Mantle: The Politics of Succession in India*. Praeger, New York, 1966.

Brimmell, J. H. *Communism in South East Asia: A Political Analysis*. Oxford University Press, London, New York, 1959.

Brines, Russell, *The Indo-Pakistani Conflict*. Pall Mall, London, 1968.

Buchan, Alastair (ed.), *China and the Peace of Asia*. Chatto and Windus, London, 1965.

Burch, Betty B., and Allan B. Cole (ed.), *Asian Political Systems*,

Readings on China, Japan, India, Pakistan. Van Nostrand, Princeton, NJ, 1968.

Burks, Ardath W., *The Government of Japan.* Crowell, New York, 1961; Methuen, London, 1966.

Cady, John F., *A History of Modern Burma.* Cornell University Press, Ithaca, 1958.

Carstairs, G. Morris, *The Twice-Born, A Study of a Community of High-Caste Hindus.* Hogarth Press, London, 1957; Indiana University Press, Bloomington, 1961.

Chandidas, R., et al. (ed.), *India Votes, A Source Book on Indian Elections.* Popular Prakashan, Bombay, 1968.

Chandrasekhar, S. (ed.), *Asia's Population Problems.* Allen & Unwin, London, 1967; Praeger, New York, 1967.

Chaudhuri, Nirad C., *The Continent of Circe, Being an Essay on the Peoples of India.* Chatto and Windus, London, 1965.

Ch'en, Jerome, *Mao and the Chinese Revolution.* Oxford University Press, London, New York, 1967.

Chen, Lung-chu, and Harold D. Lasswell, *Formosa, China and the United Nations.* St. Martin's Press, New York, 1967.

Chen, Theodore E. H., *Thought Reform of the Chinese Intellectuals.* Hong Kong University Press, 1960.

Chiang Kai-shek, *China's Destiny and Chinese Economic Theory.* Dobson, London, 1947; Roy, New York, 1947.

China, Vietnam and the United States: Highlights of the Hearings of the Senate Foreign Relations Committee. Public Affairs Press, Washington, D C, 1966.

Cipolla, Carlo M., *The Economic History of World Population.* Penguin, Harmondsworth, Baltimore, 1964.

Clark, Colin, *Population Growth and Land Use,* Macmillan, London, 1967; St. Martin's Press, New York, 1967.

Coedès, G., *The Making of Southeast Asia.* University of California Press, Berkeley, 1966; Routledge & Kegan Paul, London, 1967.

Cole, Allan B., et al., *Socialist Parties in Postwar Japan.* Yale University Press, New Haven, 1966.

Conolly, Violet, *Beyond the Urals, Economic Developments in Soviet Asia.* Oxford University Press, London, 1967.

Coomaraswamy, Ananda K., *The Dance of Shiva.* Noonday Press, New York, 1957; Peter Owen, London, 1958.

Coughlin, Richard J., *Double Identity, The Chinese in Modern Thailand.* Hong Kong University Press, 1960.

Creel, H. G., *Chinese Thought, From Confucius to Mao Tse-tung.* University of Chicago Press, 1953; Methuen, London, 1962.

Crook, Isabel and David, *The First Years of Yangyi Commune*. Routledge & Kegan Paul, London, 1966.

Cutajar, Michael Zammit, and Alison Franks, *The Less Developed Countries in World Trade, A Reference Handbook*. Overseas Development Institute, London, 1967.

De Bary, William Theodore (ed.), *Sources of Japanese Tradition* (2 vols.). Columbia University Press, New York, 1964.

De Vos, George, and Hiroshi Wagatsuma, *Japan's Invisible Race: Caste in Culture and Personality*. Cambridge University Press, London, 1966; University of California Press, Berkeley, 1966.

Donnithorne, Audrey, *China's Economic System*. Allen & Unwin, London, 1967.

Doolin, D. J., *Territorial Claims in the Sino-Soviet Conflict*. Stanford University Press, California, 1965.

Dore, R. P. (ed.), *Aspects of Social Change in Modern Japan*. Princeton University Press, NJ, 1967.

Dore, R. P., *City Life in Japan, A Study of a Tokyo Ward*. Routledge & Kegal Paul, London, 1958; University of California Press, Berkeley, 1963.

Dore, R. P., *Education in Tokugawa Japan*. Routledge & Kegan Paul, London, 1965.

Dore, R. P., *Land Reform in Japan*. Oxford University Press, London, New York, 1959.

Dumont, Louis, *Homo Hierarchicus*. Gallimard, Paris, 1967.

Duncanson, Dennis J., *Government and Revolution in Vietnam*. Oxford University Press, London, New York, 1968.

Eckstein, Alexander, Walter Galenson and Ta-Chung Liu, *Economic Trends in Communist China*. Edinburgh University Press, 1968.

Economic Survey of Asia and the Far East 1968. United Nations, New York, 1969.

Eden, Anthony, *Towards Peace in Indo-China*. Oxford University Press, London, 1966; Houghton Mifflin, Boston, 1966.

Elwin, Verrier, *Nagaland*. Dutta, Shillong, 1961.

Erdman, Howard L., *The Swatantra Party and Indian Conservatism*. Cambridge University Press, London, 1968.

Etienne, Gilbert, *Studies in Indian Agriculture: The Art of the Possible*. University of California Press, Berkeley, 1968.

Fairbank, John K., Edwin O. Reischauer and Albert M. Craig, *East Asia, The Modern Transformation*. Allen & Unwin, London, 1965.

Fall, Bernard B., *The Two Vietnams, A Political and Military Analysis*. Praeger, New York, 1967.

Farmer, B. H., *Ceylon, A Divided Nation*. Oxford University Press, London, New York, 1963.

Fauconnier, Henri, *The Soul of Malaya*. Macmillan, New York, 1931; Oxford University Press, Kuala Lumpur, 1966 (reprint).

Feith, Herbert, *The Decline of Constitutional Democracy in Indonesia*. Cornell University Press, Ithaca, NY, 1962.

Feldman, Herbert, *Revolution in Pakistan, A Study of the Martial Law Administration*. Oxford University Press, London, 1967.

Field, Michael, *The Prevailing Wind, Witness in Indo-China*. Methuen, London, 1965.

First Malaysia Plan 1966–1970. Government Printer, Kuala Lumpur, 1965.

Fischer, Louis, *The Story of Indonesia*. Harper, New York, 1959.

Fitzgerald, C. P., *The Birth of Communist China*. Penguin, Harmondsworth, 1964; Praeger, New York, 1966.

Fitzgerald, C. P., *The Chinese View of Their Place in the World*. Oxford University Press, London, New York, 1966.

Fitzgerald, C. P., *The Third China*. Cheshire, Melbourne, 1965.

Fitzgerald, C. P., *China – A Short Cultural History*. Cresset Press, London, 1950.

Floyd, David, *Mao Against Khrushchev, A Short History of the Sino-Soviet Conflict*. Praeger, New York, 1964.

Franda, Marcus F., *West Bengal and the Federalising Process in India*. Oxford University Press, London, 1968; Princeton University Press, NJ, 1968.

Franke, Wolfgang, *China and the West*. Basil Blackwell, Oxford, 1967.

Fukutake, Tadashi, *Japanese Rural Society*. Oxford University Press, London, 1967.

Gandhi, *An Autobiography, The Story of My Experiments with Truth*. Phoenix, London, 1949; Beacon Press, Boston, 1957.

Geertz, Clifford, *The Social History of an Indonesian Town*. M.I.T. Press, Cambridge, Mass., 1965.

Geoffroy-Dechaume, François, *China Looks at the World, Reflections for a Dialogue: Eight Letters to T'ang-lin*. Faber & Faber, London, 1967.

Gettleman, Marvin E. (ed.), *Vietnam, History, Documents, and Opinions on a Major World Crisis*. Penguin, Harmondsworth, 1966.

Gittings, John, *The Role of the Chinese Army*. Oxford University Press, London, New York, 1967.

Golay, Frank H. (ed.), *The Philippines and the United States*. Prentice-Hall, Englewood Cliffs, N J, 1966.

Goldhagen, E. (ed.), *Ethnic Minorities in the Soviet Union*. Praeger, New York, 1968.

Goldman, Marshall I., *Soviet Foreign Aid*. Praeger, New York, 1967.

Gordon, Bernard K., *The Dimensions of Conflict in Southeast Asia*. Prentice-Hall, Englewood Cliffs, N J, 1966.

Government of India, Ministry of Education, *Report of the Committee on Emotional Integration*. New Delhi, 1962.

Government of India, Planning Commission, *First Five-Year Plan*. New Delhi, 1953.

Government of India, Planning Commission, *Fourth Five-Year Plan. A Draft Outline*. New Delhi, 1966.

Grant, Bruce, *Indonesia*. Penguin, Harmondsworth, 1967.

Gray, Jack (ed.), *China's Search for a Political Form*. Oxford University Press, London, 1968.

Gray, Jack, and Patrick Cavendish, *Chinese Communism in Crisis, Maoism and the Cultural Revolution*. Pall Mall Press, London, 1968.

Greene, Felix, *The Wall Has Two Sides*. Cape, London, 1962.

Gullick, J. M., *Malaya*. Ernest Benn, London, 1964; Praeger, New York, 1964.

Halappa, G. S. (ed.), *Dilemmas of Democratic Politics in India*. Manaktalas, Bombay, 1966.

Halberstam, David, *The Making of a Quagmire*. Random House, New York, 1965; Bodley Head Press, London, 1965.

Hall, D. G. E., *A History of South-east Asia*. St Martin's Press, New York, 1964; Macmillan, London, 1964.

Hall, John Whitney, and Richard K. Beardsley (ed.), *Twelve Doors to Japan*. McGraw-Hill, New York, 1965.

Halperin, Morton H., *China and the Bomb*. Pall Mall Press, London, 1965; Praeger, New York, 1965.

Halpern, A. M. (ed.), *Policies Toward China: Views from Six Continents*. McGraw-Hill, New York, London, 1965.

Hanson, A. H., *The Process of Planning: A Study of India's Five Year Plans 1950–1964*. Oxford University Press, London, 1966.

Han Suyin, *A Mortal Flower*. Cape, London, 1966; Putman, New York, 1966.

Han Suyin, *Birdless Summer*. Cape, London, 1968.

Han Suyin, *Cast But One Shadow and Winter Love*. Cape, London, 1962.

Han Suyin, *China in the Year 2001*. G. A. Watts, London, 1967; Basic Books, New York, 1967.

Han Suyin, *The Crippled Tree*. Cape, London, 1965; Putnam, New York, 1965.

Harris, F. R., *Jamsetji Nusserwanji Tata, A Chronicle of His Life*. Blackie & Son, Bombay, 1958.

Harris, Richard, *Independence and After, Revolution in Underdeveloped Countries*. Oxford University Press, London, New York, 1962.

Harrison, Selig, *India, The Most Dangerous Decades*. Oxford University Press, London, 1960; Princeton University Press, NJ, 1960.

Hasegawa, Nyozekan, *The Japanese Character, A Cultural Profile*. Kodansha International, Tokyo and Palo Alto, Calif., 1966.

Hearn, Lafcadio, *Japan, An Attempt at Interpretation*. Macmillan, New York, 1910; Charles E. Tuttle, Rutland, 1967.

Henderson, Dan Fenno, *Conciliation and Japanese Law*. University of Washington Press, Seattle, 1965.

Hensman, C. R., *China, Yellow Peril? Red Hope?* SCM Press, London, 1968.

Herbert, Jean, *An Introduction to Asia*. Allen & Unwin, London, 1965; Oxford University Press, New York, 1965.

Hevi, Emmanuel John, *An African Student in China*. Pall Mall Press, London, 1963.

Hindley, Donald, *The Communist Part of Indonesia 1951–1961*. University of California Press, Berkeley, 1966.

Hinton, Harold C., *Communist China in World Politics*. Macmillan, London, 1966.

Hinton, William, *Fanshen, A Documentary of Revolution in a Chinese Village*. Monthly Review Press, New York, 1966.

Honey, P. J., *Genesis of a Tragedy: The Historical Background to the Vietnam War*. Ernest Benn, London, 1968.

Huck, Arthur S., *The Chinese in Australia*. Longmans, Melbourne, 1968.

Hudson, G. F., *Europe and China, A Survey of Their Relations from the Earliest Times to 1800*. Beacon Press, Boston, 1961.

Hughes, John, *The End of Sukarno*. Angus & Robertson, London, 1968.

Hughes, Richard, *Hong Kong, Borrowed Place – Borrowed Time*. André Deutsch, London, 1968; Praeger, New York, 1968.

Isaacs, Harold R., *India's Ex-Untouchables*. Day, New York, 1964.

Iyer, Raghavan (ed.), *The Glass Curtain Between Asia and Europe*. Oxford University Press, London, New York, 1965.

Jacobs, Norman, *The Origin of Modern Capitalism in Eastern Asia*. Hong Kong University Press, 1958.

Jacoby, Neil H., *U.S. Aid to Taiwan*. Praeger, New York, 1966.

Jalée, Pierre, *The Pillage of the Third World*. Monthly Review Press, New York, 1968.

Jansen, G. H., *Afro-Asia and Non-Alignment*. Faber & Faber, London, 1966. Published in United States as *Non-alignment and the Afro-Asian States*. Praeger, New York, 1966.

Jansen, Marius B. (ed.), *Changing Japanese Attitudes Toward Modernization*. Princeton University Press, NJ, 1965.

Jarvie, I. C. (ed.), *Hong Kong: A Society in Transition, Contributions to the Study of Hong Kong Society*. Routledge & Kegan Paul, London, 1969.

Johnson, Harry G. (ed.), *Economic Nationalism in Old and New States*. Allen & Unwin, London, 1968.

Johnson, Harry G., *Economic Policies Towards Less Developed Countries*. Allen & Unwin, London, 1967; Brookings Institution, Washington, DC, 1967.

Johnson, William A., *The Steel Industry of India*. Harvard University Press, Cambridge, Mass., 1966.

Joshi, Bhuwantal, and Leo E. Rose, *Democratic Innovations in Nepal*. University of California Press, Berkeley, 1966.

Kahin, George McT. (ed.), *Governments and Politics of Southeast Asia*. Cornell University Press, Ithaca, NY, 1964.

Kahin, George McT., *Nationalism and Revolution in Indonesia*. Cornell University Press, Ithica, NY, 1952.

Kahin, George McT., *The Asian-African Conference*. Cornell University Press, Ithica, NY, 1956.

Karan, Pradyumna P., and William M. Jenkins, Jr, *The Himalayan Kingdoms, Bhutan, Sikkim and Nepal*. Van Nostrand, Princeton, NJ, 1963.

Karol, K. S., *China, The Other Communism*. Heinemann, London, 1967; Hill & Wang, New York, 1967.

Kaul, Lt.-Gen. B. M., *The Untold Story*. Allied Publishers, New Delhi, 1967.

Kawabata, Yasunari, *Snow Country*. Knopf, New York, 1956.

Kawai, Kazuo, *Japan's American Interlude*. University of Chicago Press, 1960.

Kennedy, D. E., *The Security of Southern Asia*. Chatto & Windus, London, 1965; Praeger, New York, 1965.

Kennedy, J., *Asian Nationalism in the Twentieth Century*. Macmillan, London, 1968.

Kerr, George H., *Formosa Betrayed*. Houghton Mifflin, Boston, 1965; Eyre & Spottiswoode, London, 1966.

Kidron, Michael, *Foreign Investments in India*. Oxford University Press, London, New York, 1965.

Kirby, E. Stuart, *Economic Development in East Asia*. Allen & Unwin, London, 1967.

Klatt, Werner (ed.), *The Chinese Model, A Political, Economic and Social Survey*. Hong Kong University Press, 1965.

Klochko, Mikhail T., *Soviet Scientist in China*. Hollis & Carter, London, 1964.

Kochanek, Stanley A., *The Congress Party of India: The Dynamics of One-Party Democracy*. Oxford University Press, London, 1968; Princeton University Press, NJ, 1968.

Koentjaraningrat, *Villages in Indonesia*. Cornell University Press, Ithaca, NY, 1967.

Kojima, Kiyoshi (ed.), *Pacific Trade and Development*. Japan Economic Research Center, Tokyo, 1968.

Komatsu, Isao, *The Japanese People, Origins of the People and the Language*. Kokusai Bunka Shinkokai, Tokyo, 1962.

Kondapi, C., *Indians Overseas, 1838–1949*. Oxford University Press, London, 1951.

Koop, John C., *The Eurasian Population in Burma*. Yale University Press, New Haven, 1961.

Kramer, Paul (ed.), *The Last Manchu: The Autobiography of Henry Pu Yi, Last Emperor of China*. Putnam, New York, 1966.

Lacouture, Jean, *Ho Chi Minh, A Political Biography*. Vintage Books, New York, 1968.

Lamb, Alastair, *Asian Frontiers, Studies in a Continuing Problem*. Pall Mall Press, London, 1968.

Lamb, Alastair, *Crisis in Kashmir, 1947–1966*. Routledge & Kegan Paul, London, 1966.

Lamb, Alastair, *The China-India Border, The Origins of the Disputed Boundaries*. Oxford University Press, London, New York, 1964.

Landé, Carl H., *Leaders, Factions and Parties: The Structure of Philippine Politics*. Yale University Press, New Haven, 1965.

Le Page, R. B., *The National Language Question, Linguistic Problems of New Independent States*. Oxford University Press, London, 1964.

Lee Kuan Yew, *The Battle for a Malaysian Malaysia*. Ministry of Culture, Singapore, 1965.

Legge, J. D., *Central Authority and Regional Autonomy in Indonesia: A Study in Local Administration 1950–1960*. Cornell University Press, Ithaca, NY, 1961.

Leifer, M., *Cambodia: The Search for Security*. Pall Mall Press, London, 1968.

Levenson, Joseph R., *Confucian China and Its Modern Fate* (3 vols.) Routledge and Kegan Paul, London, 1958.

Levenson, Joseph R., *Liang Ch'i-ch'ao and the Mind of Modern China*. University of California Press, Berkeley, 1967.

Lewis, W. Arthur, *Development Planning*. Allen & Unwin, London, 1967.

Lin Yutang, *My Country and My People*. Heinemann, London, 1937; rev. ed., Reynal & Hitchcock, New York, 1938.

Ling, Trevor, *Buddha, Marx and God*. Macmillan, London, 1966.

Little, I. M. D. and J. M. Gifford, *International Aid*. Allen & Unwin, London, 1965.

Liu Shao-chi, *How to be a Good Communist*. Foreign Language Press, Peking, 1964.

Lockwood, William W., *The Economic Development of Japan, Growth and Structural Change 1868–1938*. Princeton University Press, NJ, 1954.

Lubis, Mochtar, *Twilight in Djakarta*. Hutchinson, London, 1963; Vanguard Press, New York, 1964.

MacDonald, Rt Hon. Malcolm, *Angkor*. Cape, London, 1958.

Maruyama, Masao, *Thought and Behaviour in Modern Japanese Politics*. Oxford University Press, London, New York, 1963.

Mason, E. S., *Economic Development in India and Pakistan*. Harvard University Press, Cambridge, 1966.

Mason, Philip (ed.), *India and Ceylon: Unity and Diversity*. Oxford University Press, London, 1967.

Maxwell, Neville, *India's China War*. London, Cape, 1970.

McAleavy, Henry, *The Modern History of China*. Weidenfeld & Nicolson, London, 1967; Praeger, New York, 1967.

McFarland, H. Neill, *The Rush Hour of the Gods, A Study of New Religious Movements in Japan*. Macmillan, New York, 1967.

McFarquhar, Roderick (ed.), *The Hundred Flowers Campaign and the Chinese Intellectual*. Praeger, New York, 1960.

McGee, T. G., *The South-East Asian City*. Bell, London, 1967; Praeger, New York, 1967.

McVey, Ruth R. (ed.), *Indonesia*. Human Relations Area Files, New Haven, 1963.

Mende, Tibor, *Conversations with Mr Nehru*. Secker & Warburg, London, 1956. Published in United States as *Nehru: Conversations on India and World Affairs*. Braziller, New York, 1956.

Menon, V. P., *The Story of the Integration of the Indian States*. Longmans, Green, London, 1956.

Mikesell, Raymond F., *The Economics of Foreign Aid*. Weidenfeld &

Nicolson, London, 1968; Aldine Publishing Co., Chicago, 1968.

Millar, T. B., *Australia's Foreign Policy*. Angus & Robertson London, 1968.

Miller, J. D. B. (ed.), *India, Japan, Australia – Partners in Asia?* Australian National University Press, Canberra, 1968.

Mintz, Jeanne S., *Indonesia, A Profile*. Van Nostrand, Princeton, NJ, 1961.

Moncrieff, Anthony (ed.), *Second Thoughts on Aid, A Series of Broadcasts in the BBC Third Programme*. The British Broadcasting Corporation, London, 1965.

Moraes, Frank, *Jawaharlal Nehru, A Biography*. Macmillan, New York, 1956.

Moravia, Alberto, *The Red Book and the Great Wall*. Secker & Warburg, London, 1968.

Morris-Jones, W. H., *The Government and Politics of India*. Hutchinson, London.

Moseley, George (ed.), *The Party and the National Question in China*. MIT Press, Cambridge, Mass., 1966.

Moseley, Leonard, *Hirohito, Emperor of Japan*. Weidenfeld & Nicolson, London, 1966; Prentice-Hall, Englewood Cliffs, NJ, 1966.

Muscat, Robert J., *Development Strategy in Thailand*. Praeger, New York, 1966.

Myrdal, Gunnar, *Asian Drama, An Inquiry into the Poverty of Nations* (3 vols.). Allen Lane, The Penguin Press, London, 1968; The Twentieth Century Fund, New York, 1968.

Naipaul, V. S., *An Area of Darkness*. André Deutsch, London, 1964.

Nair, Kusum, *Blossoms in the Dust, The Human Element in Indian Development*. Gerald Duckworth, London, 1964.

Nairn, Robert C., *International Aid to Thailand: The New Colonialism?* Yale University Press, New Haven, 1967.

Nakamura, Hiroshi, *East Asia in Old Maps*. East-West Center Press, Honolulu, 1964.

Nakamura, James I., *Agricultural Production and the Economic Development of Japan 1873–1922*. Princeton University Press, NJ, 1966.

Narayan, Jayaprakash, *Three Basic Problems of Free India*. Asia Publishing House, London, 1964.

National Academy of Sciences, *The Growth of World Population*. Washington, DC, 1960.

Needham, Joseph, *Science and Civilization in China* (4 vols.). Cambridge University Press, London, 1954–1962.

Nehru, Jawaharlal, *Glimpses of World History*. Day, New York, 1948.

Nehru, Jawaharlal, *India's Foreign Policy, Selected Speeches, September 1946–April 1961*. Publications Division, Government of India, 1961.

Nehru, Jawaharlal, *The Discovery of India*. Day, New York, 1946; Meridian Books, London, 1960.

Nehru, Jawaharlal, *Toward Freedom, The Autobiography of Jawaharlal Nehru*. Day, New York, 1941.

Ng, Larry K. Y. and Stuart Mudd (ed.), *The Population Crisis*. Indiana University Press, Bloomington, 1965.

Nove, Alec and J. A. Newth, *The Soviet Middle East, A Model for Development?* Allen & Unwin, London, 1967.

Oh, John Kie-Chiang, *Korea, Democracy on Trial*. Cornell University Press, Ithaca, NY, 1968.

Ohlin, Goran, *Population Control and Economic Development*. Organization for Economic Cooperation and Development, Paris, 1969.

Overstreet, Gene D., and Marshall Windmiller, *Communism in India*. University of California Press, Berkeley, 1959.

Pakeman, S. A., *Ceylon*. Ernest Benn, London, 1964.

Palmier, Leslie, *Indonesia*. Thames & Hudson, London, 1965; Walker, New York, 1966.

Panikkar, K. M., *Asia and Western Dominance*. Allen & Unwin, London, 1959.

Park, Richard L., *India's Political System*. Prentice-Hall, Englewood Cliffs, NJ, 1967.

Patterson, George N., *The Unquiet Frontier, Border Tensions in the Sino-Soviet Conflict*. International Studies Group, Hong Kong, 1966.

Pearson, Lester B. et al., *Partners in Development*. Praeger, New York, 1969; Pall Mall, London, 1969.

Peterson, Joseph, *The Great Leap – China*. B. I. Publications, Bombay, 1966.

Pike, Douglas, *Viet Cong: The Organization and Techniques of the National Liberation Front of South Vietnam*. Cambridge, Mass., 1966.

Proceedings of the Asian Conference on Industrialisation. Manila, 1965, UNECAFE Document E/CN.11/719 of 10 January 1966.

Prospects of the World Food Supply. National Academy of Sciences, Washington, DC, 1966.

Purcell, Victor, *The Chinese in Southeast Asia*. Oxford University Press, London, New York, 1965.

Pye, Lucian W., *Guerrilla Communism in Malaya: Its Social and Political Meaning*. Princeton University Press, NJ, 1956.

Pye, Lucian W., *Politics, Personality and Nation Building: Burma's*

Search for Identity. Yale University Press, New Haven, London, 1962.

Pye, Lucian W., *The Spirit of Chinese Politics, A Psychocultural Study of the Authority Crisis in Political Development.* M.I.T. Press, Cambridge, Mass., 1968.

Rahman, Fazlur, *Islam.* Weidenfeld & Nicolson, London, 1967.

Ramos, Maximo, *Language Policy in Certain Newly Independent States.* Philippine Center for Language Study, Pasay City, 1961.

Reischauer, Edwin O., and John K. Fairbank, *East Asia, The Great Tradition.* Houghton Mifflin, Boston, 1960.

Riggs, Fred W., *Thailand: The Modernization of a Bureaucratic Polity.* East-West Center Press, Honolulu, 1966.

Romulo, Carlos P., *Identity and Change: Towards a National Definition.* Solidaridad, Manila, New York, 1965.

Romulo, Carlos P., *The Magsaysay Story.* Day, New York, 1956.

Rose, Saul (ed.), *Politics in Southern Asia.* Macmillan, London, 1963.

Rosen, George, *Democracy and Economic Change in India.* University of California Press, Berkeley, 1967.

Rudolph, Lloyd and Susanne, *The Modernity of Tradition: Political Development in India.* University of Chicago Press, 1968.

Sanders, A. J. K., *The People's Republic of Mongolia, A General Reference Guide.* Oxford University Press, London, New York, 1968.

Sansom, Sir George, *The Western World and Japan: A Study in the Interaction of European and Asiatic Cultures.* Knopf, New York, 1950.

Sansom, Sir George, *Japan, A Short Cultural History.*

Sarkisyanz, E., *Buddhist Backgrounds of the Burmese Revolution.* Martimus Nijhoff, The Hague, 1965.

Sawyer, C. A., *Communist Trade with Developing Countries 1955–65.* Praeger, New York, 1967.

Sayeed, Khalid B., *The Political System of Pakistan.* Houghton Mifflin, Boston, 1967; Allen & Unwin, London, 1968.

Scalapino, Robert A. (ed.), *The Communist Revolution in Asia, Tactics, Goals and Achievements.* Prentice-Hall, Englewood Cliffs, NJ, 1965.

Scalapino, Robert A., *The Japanese Communist Movement, 1920–1966.* University of California Press, Berkeley, 1967; Cambridge University Press, London, 1967.

Scalapino, Robert A., and Junnosuke Masumi, *Parties and Politics in Contemporary Japan.* University of California Press, Berkeley, 1962.

Schram, Stuart, *Mao Tse-tung.* Allen Lane The Penguin Press, London, 1967.

Schram, Stuart, *The Political Thought of Mao Tse-tung*. Pall Mall Press, London, 1963; Praeger, New York, 1963.

Schurmann, Franz, *Ideology and Organization in Communist China*. University of California Press, Berkeley, 1966.

Seal, Anil, *The Emergence of Indian Nationalism, Competition and Collaboration in the Later Nineteenth Century*. Cambridge University Press, London, 1968.

Segal, Ronald, *The Crisis of India*. Allen Lane The Penguin Press, London, 1965.

Selosoemardjan, *Social Changes in Jogjakarta*. Cornell University Press, Ithaca, N Y, 1962,

Sheth, N. R., *The Social Framework of an Indian Factory*. Manchester University Press, 1968.

Shonfield, Andrew, *The Attack on World Poverty*. Chatto & Windus, London, 1960; Random House, New York, 1960.

Silcock, T. H., *Towards a Malayan Nation*. Eastern Universities Press, Singapore, 1961.

Singh, Lalita Prasad, *The Politics of Economic Cooperation in Asia: A Study of Asian International Organizations*. University of Missouri Press, Columbia, 1966.

Sjahrir, Soetan, *Out of Exile*, Day, New York, 1949.

Skinner, G. William (ed.), *Local, Ethnic, and National Loyalties in Village Indonesia: A Symposium*. Yale University, Southeast Asia Studies, New York, 1959.

Smith, Donald Eugene (ed.), *South Asian Politics and Religion*. Princeton University Press, N J, 1966.

Smith, Ralph, *Vietnam and the West*. Heinemann, London, 1968.

Snow, Edgar, *Red Star over China*. Victor Gollancz, London, 1937; Garden City Publishing Co., New York, 1939.

Snow, Edgar, *The Other Side of the River, Red China Today*. Random House, New York, 1962; Victor Gollancz, London, 1963.

Snow, Helen Foster, *Women in Modern China*. Mouton, The Hague, 1967.

Sobhan, Rehman, *Basic Democracies, Works Programmes and Rural Development in East Pakistan*. Dacca University Bureau of Economic Research, 1968.

Southworth, Herman M., and Bruce F. Johnston (ed.), *Agricultural Development and Economic Growth*. Cornell University Press, Ithaca, N Y, 1967.

Spear, Percival, *A History of India*, Vol. 2. Penguin, Harmondsworth, 1965.

Srinivas, M. N., *Caste in Modern India, and Other Essays*. Asia Publishing House, Bombay, 1962.

Srinivas, M. N., *Social Change in Modern India*. University of California Press, Berkeley, 1967.

Stamp, L. Dudley, *Our Developing World*. Faber & Faber, London, 1960.

Starke, J. G., *The Anzus Treaty Alliance*. Cambridge University Press, London, New York, 1966.

Stephens, Ian, *Pakistan: Old Country, New Nation*. Penguin, Harmondsworth, 1964.

Stoetzel, Jean, *Without the Chrysanthemum and the Sword, A Study of the Attitudes of Youth in Post-War Japan*. Heinemann, London, 1955; Columbia University Press, New York, 1955.

Storry, Richard, *A History of Modern Japan*. Penguin, Harmondsworth, Baltimore, 1960.

Streeten, Paul, and Michael Lipton (eds.), *The Crisis of Indian Planning, Economic Planning in the 1960's*. Oxford University Press, London, 1968.

Strong, Anna Louise, *The Rise of the Chinese People's Communes*. New World, Peking, 1959.

Sutter, John O., *Indonesianisasi: Politics in a Changing Economy, 1940–1955*. Cornell University Press, Ithaca, NY, 1959.

Sukarno, *An Autobiography, as told to Cindy Adams*. Bobbs-Merrill, New York, 1965.

Swearingen, Rodger, and Paul Langer, *Red Flag in Japan, International Communism in Action, 1919–1951*. Harvard University Press, Cambridge, 1952.

Szczepanik, Edward (ed.), *Economic and Social Problems of the Far East*. Hong Kong University Press, 1962.

Taeuber, Irene B., *The Population of Japan*. Princeton University Press, NJ, 1958.

Tanizaki, Junichiro, *Some Prefer Nettles*. Knopf, New York, 1955.

Tanizaki, Junichiro, *The Makioka Sisters*. Knopf, New York, 1957.

Teng, Ssu-yü, and John K. Fairbank, *China's Response to the West, A Documentary Survey 1839–1923*. Harvard University Press, Cambridge, 1954.

The Asian Population Conference 1963. United Nations, New York, 1964.

The Colombo Plan Story. Colombo Plan Bureau, Colombo, 1961.

The Far East and Australasia 1969, A Survey and Directory of Asia and the Pacific. Europa Publications, London, 1969.

The Food Problem of Developing Countries. Organization for Economic Cooperation and Development, Paris, 1968.

The Polemic on the General Line of the International Communist Movement. Foreign Language Press, Peking, 1965.

The Structure and Development of Asian Economies. The Japan Economic Research Center, Tokyo, 1968.

The World Food Problem. A Report of the President's Science Advisory Committee (2 vols.). The White House, Washington, D C, 1967.

Thompson, W. S., *Population and Progress in the Far East.* Chicago University Press, 1959.

Tinker, Hugh, *Ballot Box and Bayonet, People and Government in Emergent Asian Countries.* Oxford University Press, London, New York, 1964.

Tinker, Hugh, *Experiment with Freedom, India and Pakistan, 1947.* Oxford University Press, London, 1967.

Tinker, Hugh, *India and Pakistan: A Political Analysis.* Pall Mall Press, 1962.

Tinker, Hugh, *The Union of Burma.* Oxford University Press, London, New York, 1967.

Toye, Hugh, *Laos, Buffer State or Battleground?* Oxford University Press, London, 1968.

Toynbee, Arnold J., *The World and the West.* Oxford University Press, London, New York, 1953.

Vaidyanath, R., *The Formation of the Soviet Central Asian Republics.* People's Publishing House, New Delhi, 1967.

Van der Kroef, J. M., *Indonesia in the Modern World* (2 vols.). Masa Buru, Bandung, 1954 and 1956.

Verghese, B. G., *Design for Tomorrow, Emerging Contours of India's Development.* The Times of India Press, Bombay, 1965.

Vittachi, Tarzie, *The Brown Sahib.* André Deutsch, London, 1962.

Vogel, Ezra F., *Japan's New Middle Class. The Salary Man and His Family in a Tokyo Suburb.* University of California Press, Berkeley, 1967.

Von Vorys, Karl, *Political Development in Pakistan.* Oxford University Press, London, 1965; Princeton University Press, N J, 1965.

Wang, Y. C., *Chinese Intellectuals and the West 1872–1949.* University of North Carolina Press, Chapel Hill, 1966.

Ward, Barbara, *It Can Be Done, An Approach to the Problem of World Poverty.* Geoffrey Chapman, London, 1965.

Watson, Francis, *The Frontiers of China.* Chatto & Windus, London, 1966.

Weatherbee, Donald E., *Ideology in Indonesia*. Yale University, Southeast Asian Studies, Monograph No. 8, New Haven, 1966.

Weerawardena, I. D. S. and M. I., *Ceylon and Her Citizens*. Oxford University Press, London, 1956.

Weiner, Myron, *Party Building in a New Nation: The Indian National Congress*. University of Chicago Press, 1968.

Weiner, Myron (ed.), *State Politics in India*. Oxford University Press, London, 1968.

Weiner, Myron, *The Politics of Scarcity: Public Pressure and Political Response in India*. University of Chicago Press, 1962.

Wertheim, W. F., *Indonesian Society in Transition, A Study of Social Change*. W. Van Hoeve, The Hague, 1965.

Wheeler, Geoffrey, *The Peoples of Soviet Central Asia*. Bodley Head, London, 1966; Dufour, Chester Springs, Penn., 1966.

Wheelwright, E. L., *Industrialisation in Malaya*. Melbourne University Press, 1965; Cambridge University Press, London, New York 1965.

White, John, *Pledged to Development: A Study of International Consortia and the Strategy of Aid*. Overseas Development Institute, London, 1967.

Whiting, Allen S., *China Crosses the Yalu*. Macmillan, New York, 1960.

Wiens, Harold J., *China's March into the Tropics*. Office of Naval Research, Washington, DC, 1952.

Wightman, David, *Toward Economic Cooperation in Asia, The United Nations Economic Commission for Asia and the Far East*. Yale University Press, New Haven, 1964.

Williams, Lea E., *The Future of the Overseas Chinese in Southeast Asia*. McGraw-Hill, New York, London, 1966.

Willmott, Donald E., *The National Status of the Chinese in Indonesia, 1900–1958*. Cornell University Press, Ithaca, MY, 1961.

Willmott, William E., *The Chinese in Cambodia*. University of British Columbia, Vancouver, 1967.

Wilson, David A., *Politics in Thailand*. Cornell University Press, Ithaca, NY, 1966.

Wilson, Dick, *A Quarter of Mankind, An Anatomy of China Today*. Allen Lane, The Penguin Press, London, 1968. Published in USA as *Anatomy of China*, New American Library Mentor Books, 1969.

Wint, Guy (ed.), *Asia, A Handbook*. Penguin, London, 1969; Praeger, New York, 1966.

Wittfogel, Karl A., *Oriental Despotism*. Yale University Press, New Haven, 1957.

World Population Prospects as Assessed in 1963. United Nations, New York, 1964.

Wu, Yuan-li, *The Economy of Communist China*. Pall Mall Press, London, 1965; Praeger, New York, 1965.

Yanaga, Chitoshi, *Japanese People and Politics*. John Wiley, New York, 1856.

Yang, C. K., *Religion in Chinese Society*. University of California Press, Berkeley, 1961.

Yoshida, Shigeru, *Japan's Decisive Century 1867–1967*. Praeger, New York, 1967.

Zagoria, Donald S., *The Sino-Soviet Conflict 1956–61*. Oxford University Press, London, 1962; Princeton University Press, NJ, 1962.

Zinkin, Maurice, *Development for Free Asia*. Essential Books, Fair Lawn, NJ, 1956; Chatto & Windus, London, 1963.

Zinkin, Taya, *Caste Today*. Oxford University Press, London, New York, 1962.

PERIODICALS

The most useful periodicals for current Asian affairs are:

Far Eastern Economic Review, weekly, Hong Kong.
Asian Survey, monthly, Berkeley, California.
Pacific Affairs, quarterly, Vancouver, BC.
Asian Review, monthly, London.
Asia Research Bulletin, monthly, Singapore.
The Journal of Asian Studies, quarterly, Ann Arbor, Mich.
Modern Asian Studies, quarterly, London.
BBC Summary of World Broadcasts, Part 3, Far East, daily, Reading, Berks., England.

REFERENCE BOOKS

The Far East & Australasia 1971, A Survey and Directory of Asia and the Pacific, Europa Publications, London, 1971.

Guy Wint (ed.): *Asia, A Handbook*, Penguin Books, London, 1969.

P. H. M. Jones (ed.): *Golden Guide to South and East Asia*, Far Eastern Economic Review, Hong Kong, 1971.

Far Eastern Economic Review 1972 Yearbook,

Index